A Taste of War

Alfred de Grazia

A Taste of War

Soldiering in World War Two

Memoirs

metron

ISBN 978-1-60377-079-8
© Metron Publications, April 2011
All rights reserved

"A Taste of War" is a new edition of "The Taste of War," by Alfred de Grazia, first published in 1992 by Quiddity Press, Princeton, N.J.
Entirely revised and rewritten by the author
Metron Publications, P.O. Box 1213, Princeton, N.J. USA
www. metron-publications.com

"Xerxes had been reviewing the immeasurable greatness of his armies as they were crossing the Hellespont for the invasion of Greece. At first he thrilled with pleasure at the sight of the myriads of men in his service, and his face lit up with delight. But suddenly, at that very moment, the thought crossed his mind, how all these lives would be extinguished in the same century at most, his brows knitted in anguish, and he was reduced to tears."

Montaigne, *Essays*, 38

*To Miles Vanderpool,
Jill's great-grandson
and mine*

Cover picture: A party of the 1st MRBC, celebrating the surrender of Axis Forces in Tunis in 1943, groups for a photo which appears here as it did in the trade journal *Printer's Ink* in America. (I am sitting front row center, with "dress cap" and a moustache.)
Cover design by synergie-bg.com.

Foreword

World War II was too vast and enveloping to allow us only portraits of generals and politicians making "command decisions," or Hollywood images of "our boys in uniform" clashing terrifically with enemy counterparts in battles neatly named. It was as total as mankind could make it, up to that time.

I observed it from its sinister origins, years before, indeed going back to childhood, for I was born the very year, 1919, in which the United States government abjured its creation, the League of Nations. Ultimately I saw the full War, first as a civilian with the rest of America, and then as a soldier acting in a number of roles. Few men had so varied an experience in the War as I, which is one reason to write about it at fifty, and seventy years later. Also, I've spent a lifetime studying world politics and psychology, and catastrophes, a second license for the job.

There was this awful contrariness about America at War: a very small proportion of its people - roughly one in a hundred - encountered once or repeatedly high risk of life and limb. Half of these were disabled or killed. A vast number of others underwent disjointed and dismal years as military or civilians to enable these men to suffer and die "victoriously." A similarly vast number were too young or old to do but carry on and lend a cheer. Besides, there was also a large number who prospered during the War and in consequence of it.

"They never had it so good," even when in uniform and in a theater of operations.

I was enabled to taste something of all this, which adds up to a lot, and will lead many to conclude that so rich and rare an experience must be envied. I find even myself believing so on occasion, perhaps because I survived and have lived to a vigorous old age. Actually I've never been so thankful as I was when the war experience ended. Furthermore, let no one imagine that, when in my right mind, I fail to recall the War as a misery and horror for hundreds of millions of people and a curse upon the human record.

Alfred de Grazia

Table of Contents

Foreword: 11
CHAPTER ONE:
    Called Up in Chicago 17
CHAPTER TWO:
    A Private at Paris, Tennessee 31
CHAPTER THREE:
    A Cadet in North Carolina 68
CHAPTER FOUR:
    Texas and the Mohave Desert ... 102
CHAPTER FIVE:
    A Spy Camp near Washington ... 128
CHAPTER SIX:
    Africa, from Oran to Tunis 151
CHAPTER SEVEN:
    The Invasion of Sicily 173
CHAPTER EIGHT:
    Italy Toe and Heel 199
CHAPTER NINE:
    Algiers and Palermo 215
CHAPTER TEN:
    The Battle of Monte Cassino 231
CHAPTER ELEVEN:
    Naples, Sardinia, Anzio 274
CHAPTER TWELVE:
    The Liberation of Rome 302
CHAPTER THIRTEEN:
    The Provence Campaign 317
CHAPTER FOURTEEN:
    Alsace and Lorraine 354

CHAPTER FIFTEEN:
   The Battle of Germany 390
CHAPTER SIXTEEN:
   The Dissolving Reich 418
CHAPTER SEVENTEEN:
   Schloss De Grazia 445
CHAPTER EIGHTEEN:
   At the Victors' Table 482
CHAPTER NINETEEN:
   The Slow Boat Home 492

ABOUT THE AUTHOR 508

BOOKS BY ALFRED DE GRAZIA 509

CHAPTER ONE

CALLED UP IN CHICAGO

I HAD just turned into my twenty-second year, and I was healthy, fast food for the slavering Army. Seventy-three days after Japanese airplanes had dismembered the American Pacific fleet at Pearl Harbor, Draft Board Number 9 of Chicago, Cook County, Illinois, USA, called upon me to go redeem the National Honor. It was a simple procedure: send this specimen a piece of paper in curt summons; the postman enjoys delivering it: 1235 Addison Street, the two-story grey stone house, the one with the not always amiable black dog.

The day was February 19, 1942, downcast skies, the temperature freezing. On the same day, a tentacle of the giant Japanese octopus was reaching in to partially destroy Darwin, Australia; another tentacle even touched India. I arose before dawn, leaving the warm body of my girl Jill slumbering upon our jouncy bed in the little room in back. (It was a sign of the times that unmarried young lovers might sleep together in a respectable family setting.) All dressed, I bent down to kiss her one last time. The black dog by the bed wagged his tail limply; no low whistle to get him up today. My two young brothers were sleeping in the front bedroom; their call to arms would come one day, unlikely as it appeared just now.

My mother, more dutiful than my consort, was up frying bacon and eggs for me, made toast, poured juice and coffee; we had agreed that she would not provide anything so special as waffles or hash. My father had preceded me to the washroom, where I, soon to become EM #3631-9558, now shaved. It was considered that seeing the soldier off to war was a man's job - said with a smile; the Dad wouldn't have it otherwise. Little else was said.

The draftee was in a decent mood. Maybe no time was a good time to join the Army, but for me it was high time. I felt that I had been procrastinating, considering how strongly I supported the President's provocations of the Axis. Myself, I had been inclined toward a Holy War against Fascism since 1936, even as a boy.

A private in the Army? I didn't mind that either, though people with lots of education were supposed to be officers, somehow. Leaving Jill did give me pain. We had been spit-fire lovers for nearly two years, splitting sometimes, then clanking together like hitching freight cars. I had lots of ideas about winning the war and could imagine that I should have been put in charge, directly under Franklin Delano Roosevelt, the Commander-in-Chief, say. Next best thing was to be a private, and rise from the ranks, for promotions came fast and there seemed to be little enough to be done to win the war at any rank below General. He was a dreamer, our lad.

My father walked alongside me up the cold pavements, north on Herndon, then over toward Clark Street. The ragged City was looming up, shaping itself out of the dark, about to lurch heavily into the War Effort. A clutch of types slouched disconsolately about the premises of the Draft Board. Soon we were all made to pile into a trolley car. Then off we went, with an electric hiss and metallic clatter, past Wrigley Field: "Home of the Chicago Cubs." Dad was left standing.

The Dad felt things strongly, didn't say them, especially not now, but practically never anyhow. (I hadn't wanted him to come: it would be a lonely walk back for him.) A son is a son, each was as the Only One - so he would say when he erred, and called me by one of the others' names - Bussie, Ed, Vic. He wouldn't have liked to lose one and I knew that he felt that I was the kind of son who would get to shouting "Banzai!" or "Geronimo!" or whatever the guys are supposed to shout who are up ahead and get shot first. So the Dad didn't feel too good about it all, and would not have sensed his usual elation at going out in the morning, first in the neighborhood, never because he had to leave the house, but because he wished to greet life at dawn.

Whereas I, the Recruit, now riding the streetcar, was pulling myself together as a soldier, getting into the mood, the role, the act. How do you behave - unsurprised, uneager, unashamed, not too sympathetic, unaggressive, not too much of a groupie, not snappishly for or against orders, not ideological, not up-front, not a laggard - exhibiting little of your education, loves, travels, workaday life, or any military experience.

Military experience! My 106th Cavalry Regiment had gone South, someone told me - our old friends, our horses, the large, black, big-bellied steeds, had been taken away from their riders, from Johnny Dearham, Jim Cowhey, Frenchy Duvall, Bassdrum Beck - hey, guys, how're the shit-kickers doing now in the hot swamps? I hadn't learned much, ridden some, gentleman's outfit, but no gentlemen, just nice guys with a plain spacious club at the Armory off Chicago Avenue near the Lake. I had been too busy with my rag-bag of jobs and making love to my beloved to spend much time drinking and card-playing, or even riding with the gang.

There had been the days of fooling around with a machine-gun, and ammunition belts, loading my horse with the antiquated military gear of cavalry - I loved horses, but believed in the superiority of infantry. The Romans won on foot. Discipline did it. Even more, the machine-gun - it was amazing how fast and hard it exploded death - and, of course, the tank, as an iron horse: these finished off the battle-horse. And now the infantry rode to battle in trucks, quarter-ton, half-ton, one and a half tons, two-tons - some armored - that's about all I knew. Ridiculous that I knew more about horses than about trucks. What explained the Black Horse Troop? - mossback generals, romance, politicians, playboys, fun, parades. Why did the Battleship persist, the Dreadnaught, a sitting duck for warplanes, hadn't the Japanese just knocked out two British capital ships?

Then I had gone off to Columbia University Law School and had to quit, and while I was there, the Black Horse Troop had gone South without me.

I had closeted my trumpet for "the Duration" (a good word, that, it meant for so long as the War might last). The day before, I had packed it in with a few final tunes. O, to blast your trumpet over the laid-back ears of one of these mean black steeds: damn, how it hurt when the animal's skull tossed back and bumped the horn and drove the brass mouthpiece against your lips, leaving them bleeding and swollen.

By the time the trolley car was rattling across the Chicago River bridge, I had regressed in thoughts to marching bands, at high school and in college, drill, uniforms, khaki, olive drab (I had worn it), the bugle calls - "Come to think of it, I can play them all." I would have scorned to recall my longest military experience, the years on the parlor floor with the lead soldiers. Our parlor held no place for the braggadocio of militarists of Bolivia and China and Germany, captured by the newsreel cameras and the chocolate-colored rotogravure section of the newspapers, but I distilled and acted out their fury of riot and battle. Our dear old friend, Mrs. Villiers, conducted for me a tiny tot's tour of the Civil War battlefields via her great heavy picture book and her father's memories transmitted over sixty years. And "Give a Big H for Hollywood:" *Over the Top, All's Quiet on the Western Front.* Harken, also, to the jeering child singing:

> *You're in the Army now,*
> *you're not behind a plow,*
> *you'll never get rich,*
> *you son of a bitch..."*

I knew all about it.

What of the drunken soldiers quarreling with me and Bob King when we, the students, were sauntering along the whorehouse strip of Madison Street one night? I knew the low prestige of the peacetime army.

The theory of warfare, yes, even that I had touched upon - in my writing an honors paper on the Italian aggression in Ethiopia, in arguing over the Spanish civil war, sorting out the ideas of war and peace conveyed by the lower schools and at University, in playing the cold Machiavellian, who portrayed violence conquering virtue, and admiring the Clausewitz dictum that war is "the conduct of politics by other means."

Surprisingly, a pacifist current was still running strong beneath

Called Up in Chicago 21

all this: war is hell, butchery, un-Christian, stupid, unnecessary; all men are equal and brothers. But there was a time for peace and a time for war, said *Ecclesiastes,* and so argued I. With myself. Seven years of indignation without action were ending. My war against the Axis began in 1931 at the age of eleven when the Japanese invaded Manchuria and in 1933, at thirteen, when Hitler became *Der Führer* of Germany.

THE PATH OF WAR and RESPONSES OF OUR CITIZEN

1. Hitler becomes Full Dictator while He, in High School, debates vs. Fascism. (1934-35)
2. Japan resumes China Aggression, which He denounces. Enters University. (1935)
3. Mussolini invades Ethiopia, against which Aggression He writes Thesis. (1935-36, 1938)
4. Spanish engage in Civil War; He opposes Spanish Falangists. (1936-39)
5. Austrian Anschluss occurs, which He opposes. He visits Europe twice (1938-39).
6. Munich Pact appeases Hitler and He denounces Czech Dissolution. (1938-9; A.B. 1939. Joins 106 Cavalry Reserve.)
7. Nazi-Soviet Treaty signed and makes Him intensely hostile to Stalinism. (August 21, 1939; He is Grad. Res. Asst., 1939-40)
8. World War II begins, whereupon He voices strong Support for Allies. (September 3, 1939)
9. Soviets Invade Finland, and once more He denounces Communists. (November 30, 1939)
10. Destruction of Allied Armies impels Him to join "Help-Britain" Committee. (May-June, 1940; He falls in love; goes to Columbia University in November.)
11. Germans invade Soviet Union and He echoes Churchill on giving Soviets Aid. (June 22, 1941; back in Chicago, researches & teaches at Indiana U.)
12. Japanese bomb Pearl Harbor and He begins personal Steps to War. (December 7, 1941, whereupon He moves and stores Belongings.)
13. Japanese reach Australia & India, on which Date He enters Army.

So, surprisingly, a full mental and physical war-kit had been provided this peaceable citizen - myths, skills, information, and attitudes - and then these thirteen steps had carried him straight into the great conflict. A typical peaceable-bellicose American I was, for actually America was not a peaceful nation; it just pretended to be pacific while it continually carried on warfare, on both a large and a small scale; hardly ever was America truly at peace.

On December 7, 1941, the crisis had finally climaxed while Jill and I were reading newspapers, brunching in the large old kitchen of the first floor at 5479 South University Avenue, listening to a concert of classical music on the radio. The apartment was next to the University of Chicago, two large rooms and bath, premises handed along to us by my brother Sebastian and Miriam, his wife. Bro Bus had entered the Foreign Broadcast Monitoring Service of the Federal Communications Commission in Washington and was working at the analysis of radio broadcasts from Berlin and Rome, along with Fred Schuman, John Gardiner, Goodwin Watson, Ed Shils, Nathan Leites, Hans Speier, and other high-brows.

The attack was still going on when the concert was roughly interrupted. I was incredulous. I felt that I should leap to the roof, swoop off into the blue and counterattack. I put my crazed imagination onto the enemy:"The Japanese are crazy!" I shouted, "I can't believe it!" After hearing another hour of the bad news, we betook ourselves to the apartment of our friends Jay and Ruth Hall, down the street, there to expostulate noisily, and thence to Steinway's Drug Store on 57th Street, where we would be sure to find people like ourselves, disgorging novel expressions, like "The Japanese must be crazy. I can't believe it!" We waited upon fresh newspapers, which, arriving finally upon breathless headlines, added nothing to the instant flow of information and directives emitting from everyone's turned-up radio.

I had been paying attention to Europe, had expected to be drawn in there. Just two days before, the *Chicago Tribune* had exposed a secret top government plan, envisioning an army of five million men to be landed in Europe to fight the Germans - and the Italians, if they were still around. I discounted the isolationist newspaper as a reliable source, but was nonetheless pleased with

Called Up in Chicago 23

the forward thinking of the White House and Pentagon. Then the attack came instead from Japan, what a shock! Nor could we grasp then how serious was the defeat at Pearl Harbor.

Or dream that a Japanese army might cross to Southeast Asia so swiftly, and even take the Philippines, and invest, indeed, the whole of the Chinese and Malayan worlds and venture towards India and Australia, even while I was squaring away to join the Army. The Japanese were plaguing the Dutch East Indies, attacking on the Road to Mandalay, and closing in upon Manila.

Hardly had I left home when President Roosevelt ordered General Douglas MacArthur to escape from the Philippines, where a mostly Filipino Army still vigorously but hopelessly resisted the invaders. The first great credit of one billion dollars had just this moment, finally, been granted the Soviet Union to cover purchases of whatever was needed wherever it could be found. The Red Army had stopped the Germans for the Winter, within sight of the Kremlin's towers, and was counterattacking with amazing success. In North Africa, within the space of several weeks, the British forces had swept the Axis army through Libya and had been just as untidily brushed back.

The Western Front, somnolent after the destruction of the Allied Armies there in 1940, awaited this Hero. The seed of the greatest armada in history was just now being planted: the U.S. War Plans Group was issuing (in secrecy, of course, and absurdly, it happened) a "Plan for Operations in Northwest Europe," foreseeing a small-scale invasion, to be termed "Sledgehammer," by Fall of the year 1942, if the Soviets showed signs of collapse, and a main invasion termed "Roundup" to be launched in the Spring of 1943. If this was far from reality, even farther out was the 1942 "Declaration by the United Nations" that was signed on the first day of the year. Still, I agreed 100% with all of this, as I had with the Four Freedoms, which Roosevelt had proposed to the "Congress for the World" on January 6, 1941, two years earlier.

When, on June 22 of the year just passed, the Soviet Union had been attacked, and Jill and I gaped at the headlines on the newsstand in front of Steinway's, where we had gone to breakfast, I had been heartened, and wondered at the temerity of Hitler in opening up a Second Front, a "No-No!" to all strategists since Napoleon. Yet when I then spoke with that awesome authority on things European, Professor Nathan Leites, I found him most pessimistic: the German armies, Leites predicted, would knock out the Union of Soviet Socialist Republics in the several months before the onset of winter, so weakened were the Soviets by Stalin's mass purges of the nation's leaders, and by the population's general incompetence and backwardness. Leites had been barely wrong.

Fallen in love and distracted by this worldwide conflict, I could hardly have been expected to stay on at the Law School of Columbia University or persist at philosophical researches or count off a day-by-day routine on a civilian job. In the two years just passed, I had done a lot of creative work, but knew that I would not be able to go on. I was teetering; it was only a question of who would make the first move to tip me over.

But why didn't I enlist earlier? Perhaps because it would seem like the act of a farm-boy or hill-billy: these were forever enlisting. Or a romantic; I would not play the hero; it embarrassed me. I asked about direct commissions, not avidly but diffidently; I made a mild attempt at a job under my former Professor, Harold Gosnell, that would fit me into the War Effort at Washington, because that was the way most of the University was going: intellectuals were not soldiers. In sum, I couldn't think what to do, so I shilly-shallyed. Being inextricably in love did not help matters; though I did not speak of it, the thought of breaking up bothered me continuously.

But, hell and ye gods, in fact I was a soldier, a warrior, and it was with relief that I got the Call: I knew what the War was all about and I felt at home in the Army even as we boarded the trolley car. I looked with a maternal sentiment upon the civilian lads around me. Naive, quite unconvinced about the War, except for a simplistic, readily stimulated anger; knowing that their sentiments were shared by all, they might assuredly curse the "treacherous Japs." The media, the government, the elite of the Great Republic generally saw to it that the impression of unanimity over the Yellow Peril had logically to take in the Nazi Germans, the Italian Fascists and all their minor allies, so that, if anybody doubted himself or the unanimity of public opinion, he would think himself to be an odd exception who had better shut up. This despite public opinion polls that showed an isolationist sentiment prevailing among half the citizenry.

There were a dozen or so recruits in the trolley car, and shortly we paused to pick up another gang. We were all ordered off at the southern end of the Loop and led to a dilapidated building. It was an area where small loft businesses and marginal enterprises might hold a losing grip on the Chicago economy. I had actually worked only a few steps away for a couple of months just recently, with Franklin Meine and Harold Hitchens and the rest of the crew that was revising *Nelson's Encyclopedia,* and these characters would in a few minutes be arriving at work, unknowing of my fate. I felt a pang of nostalgia, one of my weaknesses.

As the rookies approached the decrepit elevator shaft, a sign greeted them with: "Civilians only! All others walk up." I tried sarcasm: "Now you guys know what you're in for!" and they laughed; they knew, alright. So up the iron stairs we trudged to where a lot of men congregated, and we turned over our identity slips to some clerks who were continually hollering out names, and I met one of my former students, from East Chicago, where I had been teaching American Government, at Indiana University there, last semester. I had left this guy in the classroom: "Poor chap," I was thinking, "I have left a lot of living behind me, but he feels worse, probably, than I do, because what he left behind him, it took a lot for him to get - you can see it in his Slavic working class features, in his toughened hands, in the tired expression on his face, and he knows he hasn't much on the ball, and he is several years older than I".

I had now left that scene too, but not before the Dean at Indiana had given a little tea party in my honor, sending me off as a hero; the faculty and staff felt just fine at making this sacrifice on behalf of the War Effort. I said ironically to my former student: "Well, now you can see the practical side of American Government."

We rode out to Camp Grant together, a couple of hours from the City, so the man, my former student, came to feel better, but that was the last seen of him. I was used to High Mobility, and would have much more of it - "the last I saw of him was...:" it would match thousands of encounters to come, companies, battalions, boat loads, landing party loads, visiting parties, gangs on leave, detachments, friendlies, allies, enemies, co-belligerents, crowds of faces of all degrees of cognizance, as expendable as ammunition.

And now it was the same day and afternoon, and at Camp Grant the Lake View men were diffused among thousands upon thousands going this way and that among scores of wooden barracks, and eventually we lost sight of one another. Medical examinations, "short arm inspection" included: "drop your shorts and peel back your foreskin," yells the corporal in charge of the group, while the medico comes hurrying past, casting a sharp eye downwards. Meanwhile the recruits glance up into space or down uncomfortably, or compare their own genitals with the run of the mill; this particular recruit estimates himself on the average, whereas he had felt less than average on the swim team at college but larger than Mac the Coach who weighed 300 pounds, moved through the water like a flying saucer, and never saw himself piss. What happens to them when they stand stiff; do they rise all proportionately, equally erect? Grubby thoughts. But what else can men think about, lined up there stupidly?

We spent much of the time with our clothes off and bundled in our arms, and holding an envelope that we were told would be more important than ourselves before long, because it would become "Your Record!" and there would be nothing but the Guardhouse for us without that folder. And the dog-tags that soon came our way: what religion? (I answered "Catholic" because I wasn't told I could say "non-sectarian"); what blood type? "B" the Army told me after drawing my blood - the Army thinks ahead: what are the last two things you will ever need? A blood transfusion and a prayer in your cultic jargon. And then the woolen khaki uniform, complete from the overseas cap to the high-laced thick shoes, none of it fitting well, no stitch of distinction, badge, medal, stripe, unit affiliation, nothing - just quintessential General Issue, the perfect G.I.

The medical examination caused no trouble; the shots were a

pain - smallpox, typhoid, tetanus vaccinations, blood samples for syphilis and blood-types - and a couple of guys got sick and vomited; sore in the arms and feverish, nobody was feeling too well. Many had been the honored guests of sending-off parties, and had drunk themselves sick the night before. And nearly everybody, of course, was smoking cigarettes by the pack. Not to mention that the stuff dumped upon our metal plate at mealtime was no gourmet cooking, or even fast-food.

As I glumly edged through the chow-line, I heard a cheery bellow: "Al de Grazia!" and looked about; it was Tom Stauffer, stalwart and relaxed, a Big Intellectual on Campus now camouflaged in fatigue greens, nestling a huge pot between his long legs and peeling potatoes; we laughed, exchanged a few words, and that was the end of him.

Without regard to the misery and stupor of the newcomers, uncaring of their hangovers and agonized heads, our custodians administered to us beautifully designed and pretested examinations, whose scores would affect our placement in the infinite variety of Army jobs, from rifleman to electronic technician, and determine whether we might apply for Officer Candidates School.

The psychiatrist, like the rest, was handling men fast, a couple of questions and then if the guy seemed to be a nervous wreck or claimed to be a creep or a homosexual or congenital criminal, they put him aside, examined him later and maybe sent him away to annoy the rest of society. The most obvious cases, and some of the subtle ones, had surfaced in pre-induction examinations. Yet some draft boards were so crazily patriotic as to believe everyone was normal when it came to defending his country. In the end, at least two kinds of weirdos made it into Service: those who hoped to get all the financial benefits of honorably discharged veterans after the discovery of their symptoms, and those who wanted to get into the military more than anything in the world; it was as much of a problem to keep them out as it was to evaluate the seemingly larger number of guys who wanted to stay out at the slight cost of being deemed lunatic.

When I was beckoned into one of the dozen cubicles, the psychiatrist within asked, is there anything in the way of medical information you have not yet provided, or have you any other kind of problem - you know, "Problem?" - that is bothering you? I pondered for a moment, and said, well, I don't know what's to be done about it, but I worry a little with this trick shoulder of mine; it slips out of joint easily, I might dislocate it while thrusting a bayonet, or maybe in hand-to-hand combat. The medic looked at me as if he had found the prize nut of the day, but then said it would not matter, and passed me along hurriedly. He probably had a good story to tell at mess.

It wasn't an hour later that, now a Private in the Army of the United States, I found myself standing at a desk before an Assignment Corporal, who put soldiers onto their Army career path - headed for extermination, or for a cushy seat in the Quartermaster Corps, and who would it be but Stanley Beves, a student from the correspondence courses in politics that I had offered through the University of Chicago this last year, who just now could not talk politics but was delighted to see me - he got a good grade, and, with a glance at the long line waiting behind me, told me that he, Stanley, was assigned permanently to Camp Grant, where life wasn't bad, and then, remarking my proficiency as a musician, with experience in the administration of bands, he said: "I can get you into the Camp Grant Band. Would you like to be assigned to Camp Grant?"

Just imagine, I told myself, fast as lightning, you can be at a great place, near home, living with pussycat, doing some of the things you are best at, terrific! but then I said: "Well, I'm in the War now. This wouldn't be much of a war. I wouldn't feel right. How can I get a little closer to the action? How can I get to where I can become an officer after a while?" and Stanley, instead of berating me for a fool and assigning me forthwith to the Camp Grant Station Band for the Good of the Country, looks at me with a slightly envious regard, yet a friendly look, and says that I could probably get into officer's training soon enough from where he will be sending me; he labels me as "Branch Immaterial," and puts me down for shipment with a gang of other guys, saying, wryly: "It's a secret where."

It was the last time that I would see Stanley. I knew little about the army or war, yet thought I might control everything - I had a streak of megalomania. Still, I felt less proud than dismal as I walked away from Stanley's desk and its promise, for I remembered that I was in love, hence, as soon as I could, I called home, there to learn from my kid brother Vic that Jill had gone off on a skiing trip with some friends to La Crosse, Wisconsin, whereupon I felt jealous and neglected. She had spoken of it longingly. Still, she should have stayed with the folks and worn black for a couple of days anyhow, I wanted to tell the world - but I never told anybody of such thoughts anyhow, anytime, ever.

I groused about the barracks grounds, itching and scratching in my new Army uniform; it had been tossed to me piece by piece at the warehouse. My civilian clothes had been sent home; the Army was insistent upon this; the U.S. Mails obliged. Tomorrow, I reflected, they will tell me where I'll be and it will be a real army camp where I'll be enjoying the experience of a new gang of guys, and then afterwards I could arrange to see her somehow. So the day and the night passed, and the germs of tetanus, small pox and typhoid made my arm hurt, while a fever disturbed my sleep.

The next morning I knew that I was heading toward the Southland: my mimeographed Special Order, tucked in my folder, told me so. A railroad took us there, a clumsy troop train hitched onto a freight train, powered by a steam locomotive. There was track all around the USA in those times, up every alley and byway. No longer was so much of it overgrown and rusting. You could still get anywhere and nowhere by train - with most Army camp sites located in Nowhere - and every rusty tank-car, flatcar, boxcar, and battered coach was employed, every rail shining pridefully with use.

I merged now into a roaring obstructive nuisance such as blocked the roads in those war days when an overpass was rare. As our car banged over the crossings, I well remembered waiting inside a bus at one and then another of them, going to and from the classes I taught at Indiana University, those times when I was impatient to get home to the Midway and cursing the hundred-car conglomerates screeching and rattling by. I had changed places, but it was from the frying pan into the fire. Ugly, ugly, too, foul upon all the senses, uglier than battle!

The Nation's self-destruction advanced in stages: there had been the age of the razing of the land in the name of Progressive Agriculture, then the coal and steel holocaust in the name of Industrial Progress, followed, after ten years of catatonic Depression, by the delirious War Effort. Everything that the Hog Butcher of the World could command was bull-horned to out-totalize the totalitarian foe. Myself included. I was a proud piglet of the War Effort of the Republic.

Jill

Chapter Two

A PRIVATE AT PARIS, TENNESSEE

FINE old military stations like the Presidio of San Francisco sufficed to prepare an Army for battle against Sioux Indians. But the many great wartime camps needed to ready onslaughts against the Hordes of World Fascism had to be jerry-built upon ever more drab stretches of land, promoted by local Congressmen: such was Camp Tyson, Tennessee. The troop train from Camp Grant rumbled into a village next to the Camp, named by its deluded pioneers "Paris," now re-designated from behind the train's grimy windows unequivocally: "Asshole of the World."

Futile jerky attempts to chug the train in close to the mud flats of the Camp proper ended amid a disordered collectivity of shacks and houses. The soldiers, for that's what we now were, obeyed various shouts to detrain, under the impassive eyes of lolling blacks and whites, probably unemployed, else hired to camouflage a Hi-tech War Machine, or retained to freeze an image of the Unreconstructed South.

We clambered into buses, colored olive-drab like the total Army down to the soil upon which it dwelt, and were driven to a vast expanse of mud crisscrossed by roads, connecting rows of barracks of raw lumber painted white (so much for over-generalizing about the Army's color scheme), though some were not yet painted and others were windowless and some were still only slabs of concrete. A glum sky glowered, damp, cold - a treasure trove of bronchitis.

We tramped hither and yon, chilly above, muddy below the knees, dropping off contingents randomly. Then suddenly you arrived home: "From here on down the line, this is your barracks.

Take your Bag and go on in and find a bunk." Typical of 100,000 across the Nation, the barracks might be of one or two stories, with entrances front and back, stoops as well, for they were lifted to air their bottoms above the elements, well-windowed; inside two rows of beds were footed upon a center aisle running the length of the building; at the front end you passed a large washroom where everyone might shower, shave and shit together. A man steeled himself each morning against finding his name on the list of latrine orderlies, or, missing this assignment, on the list of kitchen police, the next worst job. A small room housed the sergeant in charge.

We went out again and over to supply sheds where additional items of clothing and equipment were checked out to us. Some rookies had recovered from their trauma of indignities to a point where they actually could complain, but rude laughs would rebut any suggestion of changing a grotesque fit. Every last item on your list, the recruits were warned, possessed such great value that its loss would occasion, if not severe company punishment, then a deduction from your pay check that would keep you penniless into the distant future. As for selling as much as a pair of socks, a Court Martial and bitter lingering death in the guardhouse were foretold. From now on, one must forego even civilian underwear in favor of the General Issue. We were G.I.'s, wouldn't you know?

There was a prescribed place for everything that one owned or was allocated, a shelf on the wall above the head of the bed, a barracks bag below the bed, and a foot locker standing at the foot of one's bed. Civilian clothing was an obscenity and any remaining bits of it, uprooted during the first Inspection, had to be sent home with pleas to preserve them until Johnny came marching home.

"The Duration and Six Months" was the military confinement visited upon us by our elected representatives in Congress; everyone used the phrase. For me, the phrase was to be prophetic. It opened up an awful chasm of time that yawned before me daily, as it would before all separated lovers. No sooner had I a bunk whereupon to sit and write, than I despatched to Her a resentful letter:

My only darling,

You were very inconsiderate to take off on a pleasure trip the day I gave up my rights as a citizen, freeman, and happy lover. It was such a moment for a token gesture of attachment. As matters turned out, it didn't make much of a practical difference, since I couldn't get leave to see you, but the fact of your deliberate action was painful to me. I realize, however, that I am in no position to make demands and hereby renounce any expectations implied in past agreements. If I felt you were splurging your id *because of our engagement, I would be very sorry for you and myself.*

So much for a page as dismal as the weather here. The skies spit on us day after day, splattering red mud on our disconsolate, stooped forms and adding to the nostalgia of everyone in the camp. Camp Tyson is new, with all the evil connotations of the word. No books, no service club, no established routines in many cases, no communication with the outside world. Paris is the nearest town. For the cost of a bus trip one can get the variety a new kind of monotony affords. He can pay twice as much for a theater, gape at women, & pick up a girl at a price. He can walk on cement, see seniles, admire babies and jostle civilians.

For four weeks our battery is confined to post, going through a so-called stiff training period. After that, we can get week-end leaves. Chicago is too far for a one and a half-day leave and I won't be able to come to Chicago except on leave...

This was written on February 25. However, "back at the ranch," as they say, SHE had been writing ME. Hardly had I sent off my letter when HERS caught up with me in my foul circumstances, telling me of her joyful weekend:

Hotel Stoddard

La Crosse, Wisconsin
Saturday nite
My darling –

This is the ski weekend you heard so much about – and it's been so much fun so far that it makes me all the more sad that we can't share these simple (well – they are simple, next to bars, movies and the competitive labor market) joys together.

The weekend is really a lot more elaborate & weekend-ish than I had expected. For one thing, La Crosse is 400 miles from Chicago, compared to the place we went to last weekend, which was only 90. We left at 4 yesterday - Friday afternoon on - joy, oh joy! - the Burlington Zephyr. I take back everything I said about the Western trains - this one was the tops. We got here about 8 last night - ate & went to bed. There are 5 of us, Bets, Swish her sister & 2 boys, Jim McElroy & Doug Carroll. They were really going alone 1st - being wonderful skiers - but we girls kind of homed in on them.

And guess what? The train went through Rockford. I felt like jumping off the train when I saw the barracks. Well, I know where I'll spend the succeeding week-ends.

Today's skiing was swell. The hills are really lovely around here & the one that has the tow on it is just swell.

I hope this letter gets to you - considering I don't know your company or anything.

Darling, I hope you're well and relatively happy. It's sort of stupid for me to say a lot of comforting things - or issue enjoinders to be brave etc. - You don't need them and, in a way, I'm not in a position to say them. After all, I am a girl & unfortunately we still - & probably will have it very easy indeed. And, in a way, I feel guilty having a good time without you - altho I know you wouldn't have it so. I'll write more when I'm surer of your address & am less chilled. Just wanted to say hello.

Your loving Jill

But then the grim truth dawned upon her: life was not to be so controllable, not with the Army in charge. She hastens to write:

THE UNIVERSITY OF CHICAGO
Chicago, Illinois

Wednesday
9:30 nite
Darling -

I'm writing this in an awful hurry because I want it to get out tonite. I just spoke to Vic - been calling them all night - and found out where you are. I've really been awfully worried - well, maybe worried isn't the right word but I can't think of anything else to describe the awful hollow feeling inside me. When I heard you'd left Camp Grant Saturday I felt just awful. I would have never gone skiing had I known you would be taken away in such short notice. You yourself assured me that you'd be around Chicago for just weeks - and I had no reason to believe otherwise. So forgive me for my ill-timed trip (incidentally, I did tell you I would probably go).

I wrote you from La Crosse Saturday to Camp Grant but don't suppose you got it.

Not much new. Job same except they are threatening me with all kinds of reprisals if I'm late again.

Please, darling, write me as soon as you get this letter - well, after the day's maneuvers are done, anyway. I love you and miss you so much. Maybe if & when you're settled on the coast or somewhere, we can be together again.

And please, darling, believe me. I really think you're the only man in the world I'll ever love. No, I haven't been seeing other men - except at a distance. This just arises out of a deep inner conviction.

Hey - my birthday was yesterday. Remember?

All my love,

Jill

and I'm so glad you're here. For a while I actually thought they'd shipped you to Tokyo!

It might as well have been Tokyo to my mind. A reign of terror appeared to be underway, conducted by the Cadre of corporals and sergeants. The work day began in chilly pre-dawn darkness with a flurry of whistles, recorded blare of the bugle, and bright lights flicked on by our buck Sergeant with a cheery shout of: "Awright, men, drop your cocks and grab your socks!" This gem of poesy had been learned by Sergeant Fazio on his first hitch, back in times immemorial. A routine of rush-and-wait ensued until the dusk of evening. The work-week culminated in an tense inspection on Saturday morning, this itself prefaced by scarifying threats from the buck sergeant in charge of the floor, and the confinement of half the soldiers to Camp for the weekend.

Much of the remaining time was spent waiting with muttered complaints for one thing or another - the distribution of an article; assistance rendered the least competent, least willing, or most stupid; movement from one spot to another; hashing names in roll-calls; trivial announcements; and threats of punishment for offenses unimaginably numerous. Probably it was well, if unintended, that every soldier begin military life viewing candidly the human make-up with which the Struggle for the World would have to be won. It forbade illusions.

The Army proceeded on the theory that all needs were uniform and that all could be uniformly met, that all exceptions were violations of the rule of uniformity. The fountainhead of uniformity was close-order drill. Thence flowed a stream of rules for all behavior. Thus: "Men have been smoking in bed. This practice is forbidden at any and all times, under all circumstances. Offenders will be punished. By order of the Commanding Officer.".. "Slippers and sport shoes are not to be exposed under the bed. They may be stored neatly in foot-locker. By order of the Commanding Officer." There were rules for lining up outside the door of the mess hall, for placing yourself at table, for eating, clearing the tables, scraping your dishes, and leaving the dining room.

There was passed along a *pasticcio* of barracks wisdom, which sat atop the formal rules, telling you, for instance, that the buck sergeant (3 stripes) was the most important man in the Army, the First Sergeant the most powerful man. Also: "Don't volunteer for anything."..."Do bunk fatigue (rest on your bunk) whenever you can." The men added their own rules, whether of mealtime or in general, and one doesn't know when and where they originated - in a silly peaceful Army of the remote past, it would seem. And: "when a pitcher of milk or bowl of food is being passed along the table because someone asked for it, don't short-stop it!" And: " whoever takes the last portion of food from a bowl or the last of the liquid from a pitcher must get up and return to the kitchen counter for more (near the end of the meal he can ask if anybody wants any more and, if not, then take it and is not required to go up)..."

I found that I could always eat until my belly was stuffed. The food appeared ample, varied and nourishing. But, in fact, the Army managed at its peak of culinary incompetence to serve thirty million bad meals a day. Most of the vitamins had been killed by excessive watery cooking (after which the water was poured down the drain), by peeling them off (with knives that, in inept hands, cut off the best parts of whatever they sliced into), or by burning (by ultra-hot frying). The lard, greasy fried bacon, fat beef and pork, eggs, ice cream, butter, milk, and thick pastries guaranteed an abundance of harmful cholesterol and a wave of post-war heart disease. Renowned for serving pork and beans since time immemorial, the Army surprised me by offering them only occasionally. (For, it was literally true: "Nothing is too good for our boys," as the Great Guilty Civilian Conscience continuously exclaimed, but, a]. they didn't know what was good for the boys, and b]. the boys contributed to the ruin of the good.) Peas and other standard vegetables came in great cans. It felt strange, as looking through giant lenses at the world, to see the familiar labels from childhood *(Del Monte, Campbell's)* now grown gigantic on monster tins. Fruits came swimming in sugar-water, canned.

A vegetarian meal would have caused mutiny and therefore was impossible; a vegetarian would have been regarded as un-American, like a pacifist or a homosexual. Fish were safe from the U.S. Army. Catholics were assured by their chauvinistic priests that eating meat on Friday could be deemed patriotic, a sacrifice canceling a sacrifice. Kosher food was under similar stricture, with the connivance of bellicose rabbis in khaki. Priests, rabbis, ministers, and pastors - all enjoyed the uniform and privileges of an officer but were supposed to mix with the enlisted men in ways that officers were discouraged from doing; they were voluntary commissars of morale. They ate with the officers and slept God knows where.

To make up for the mineral and vitamin deficiencies of his regular diet, a man could spend his meager pay on more pastries, chewing gum, ice cream, soda pop, and cookies at the Post Exchange and could buy a kind of beer that, despite its 3.2% alcoholic limit, put many a soldier on his way to the guardhouse, drunk. Some of the smarter men wondered how this could be possible; I ascribed it to psychosomatic effects, the beverage being an excuse for venting one's misery. The Chief, largest of the several Indians in my Battery and the most silent, and therefore called "Chief," could get drunk on anything purporting to be alcoholic, down to one part in a hundred. He preferred whiskey, however, and roamed the premises and beyond the gates, melancholy in search of it.

The Mess Sergeant and Cook, also a sergeant, had gone to Army schools that taught them the names of utensils, instructed them how to handle bulky metal equipment, and that had set them free upon companies of men whose own taste was hardly developed enough to complain about any diet that gave them large amounts of beef and potatoes, along with gobs of real butter and lots of fresh milk. Coffee, too, with evaporated canned milk and spoonfuls of pure refined white sugar. There was, if you must know, an ideology behind it all: "Anybody who knows good food is a sissy," and probably un-American.

I was one of the few who complained, my flanks protected by pals and proto-gourmets, so that I could not be set upon as odd or picky; anyhow, it was commonly agreed that the food was tasteless and badly prepared. Whatever my opinion, I was a chow-hound: "It tastes like horse manure, but it's good!" If not usually among the first in, I was ordinarily with the last to go out; I enjoyed sitting around with buddies, talking, and watching the KPs come closer and closer, cleaning up, and then we went out for a smoke.

The cigarette habit afflicted a sizeable majority. Yet butts were rarely to be detected: discarding a butt occasioned a penalty; an unassignable butt might drive the proximate troop of soldiers into a long line to traverse the area, on the command: "Pick up Butts, Forward March!" Where cans were missing, butts could be toted in socks or pockets or carefully picked apart until they disappeared as dust (no one smoked filter cigarettes). I smoked Lucky Strikes, whose "Lucky Strike Green Has Gone to War," according to the ads - there had been a valuable ink on the pack before it turned white. (By now you wouldn't draw a breath without claiming it to be part of the War Effort.) I smoked a cigarette after breakfast, one during the mid-morning break, one after dinner, then one in an afternoon break, one before supper, and a couple after supper, or

A Private in Paris, Tennessee

more if gambling or hanging around the PX; it added up to less than half the typical man's smoking; yet perhaps a fourth of my barracks did not smoke at all. About half drank no alcohol. Marihuana, cocaine, heroin, and other drugs were not seen and hardly discussed.

Within a couple of days of arrival, you could begin to feel, well, these are the men of my company, which you learned quickly to call your "Battery." I was now, it appeared, in the Coast Artillery. It was useless to ask: "Why, then, is Camp Tyson so far from any coast?" This was basic training and basic it was. It consisted of basic hygiene, housekeeping, close order drill, cleaning and polishing shoes and buckles, saluting ("military courtesy" the recipients of the courtesy called it, just more "chicken shit" to the rank and file), handling and firing Enfield single-shot rifles from World War I, gesturing with fixed bayonets (What a lovely silly game: "Fix bayonets! Charge!"), clearing and setting tables and putting out food and washing pots and pans (the KPs were occasionally too liberal with the strong yellow bar-soap that was used for every purpose, so that the latrine would become busy in the middle of the night, with half of Battery A diarrhoeic with "the G.I's").

Only serious cases went to the hospital; I went once with the flu and 104 degrees of fever. At first roll-call, you responded to the command: "Sick Call, Fall Out!" and assembled near the battery Headquarters, leered at suspiciously as a malingerer by the Corporal who was Charge of Quarters, and, after standing out in the cold morning awaiting a truck, while the rest of the battery marched off, you were transported to the complex of long wooden hospital barracks, there assigned a bed and issued the white gown of a patient. Your clothes were put under lock and key against any attempt at escaping the premises improperly discharged.

You were examined once a day by a doctor, with occasional readings of your temperature by a medic, and rarely you would spot a nurse dodging about. Only cough medicines and aspirin were doled out, laxatives and nose drops if needed. Penicillin was somewhere in the future. The main point was to get you out of the way of the Battery and near such therapeutic facilities as might be employed if your illness approached the terminal stage.

In a day I felt well enough to join a poker game laid out on an empty bed and enjoyed passing the time that way, though a kibitzer, a jolly rotund type whose twinkling blue eyes concealed malice and envy, managed, by several sarcastic remarks, none of them intelligible except by inflection and direction, to get under my skin, so I stopped playing the game at one point, leaned toward him with a mean look and told him to shut up or else, which situation let another player, a dark saturnine type, say to me sympathetically: "Let it go," so I let it pass and the snotty fatso shut up. A trivial yet sole hostile confrontation, indicating the low order of personal violence in the Army then, while the films and pulp novels depicted brutal fisticuffs as the order of the day.

There was a chance for a little reading there, too, but the ambiance was not designed to make men happy away from home. I missed my friends and the stupid training games, and was glad to be released and walk back to the barrack, feeling quite like a child with permission to go to school at midmorning when all was quiet on the streets. My barrack: it looked like them all, yet already, after a mere month, embraced my closest friends. And they did seem pleased enough to have me back.

It happened now that a notice was pinned upon the Battery Bulletin Board stating: "Men with any previous military training leave their names with CQ." That would be people like myself, I thought, recalling the Black Horse Troop and the close-order drill and so on, and musing that I might be able to help train some of the more inept stumblebums of the battery. Perhaps that was the idea; if so, though I put down my name, I never heard more of it.

Instead, I found my name repeatedly on the list of KP's for the day. Once every twenty-one days is OK, with perhaps one or two extra days for violating a rule, or returning after taps to the barrack, or arguing an order, or dragging your feet at an exercise, etc. None of this had happened. Still, day after day, I found my name posted on the list. After a couple of days of this, I realized that they wanted to teach a pretentious guy a lesson; theoretically, they might also have had the bright idea of keeping the least experienced men actively at drill, but this would have excessively taxed the brains of these regular army types, I figured, and a couple of friends agreed.

A Private in Paris, Tennessee

I was aroused at 4:30, worked until 13:30, was off for two hours, and worked until 9 PM or 21:00 hours. (All Army documents were couched in the 24-hour idiom, but the soldiers, stubborn mules that they were, never would speak except in terms of the 12-hour rounds of the clock.) Brutal, unjust, fatiguing, stupid, yes: still there is no job in the world from which something constructive cannot be made. I knew what the menus were, ahead of time, and would tell the ever-hungry troops about their next meal; I could help myself to enticing tid-bits - words too delicate for the pound slice of apple pie and double dipper of ice cream taken in mid-afternoon. I became a guide like Virgil in Hell to the incoming Kitchen Police, introducing them to the horrors and warning them of the menaces thereabouts. I learned what was at the bottom of Army cookery, however gruesome the truth.

I watched with awe the process of fabricating the famous Army dish, "Creamed Chip Beef on Toast," so often served for breakfast, or whenever the Mess Sergeant was in a poor mood. You put hundreds of slices of white pre-sliced bread into the ovens until toasted. You meanwhile fill great aluminum pots with water. You pour large sacks of pure refined white flour into a large pot and stir in water until you have a uniform thick paste. You mix batches of paste with the pots of water to a satisfactory consistency, and bring them all up to a boil. You open a huge sack of shavings of dried beef, highly salted and anointed with dubious chemicals. You allocate quotas of this to the several pots and simmer them all. You place the toast on the tables, still slightly warm, with pitchers of the hot sauce. You let in the men. The men pour the treacle over the toast: *voilá*, "Shit on a Shingle!" It is a comforting way to begin the day.

The exercise paraphernalia was impressive: huge pots that one could almost crawl into, great trays of flatware, frying pans large enough for performing a *pas-de-deux*. Exhausting but healthful. Better, actually, than what the other guys were doing, dressed in funny cotton blue fatigue uniforms for hard work, but mostly sitting around bored and dully listening, while a practical illiterate explained, time and time again, the handling of gas cylinders for a balloon or the care of your equipment, the limits to be imposed on your pathetic collection of toiletries and personalia, how to make your uniform last forever, the making up of one's bed. "There is only one way to do a thing: the Army Way!," or "There's the Army way and the Wrong Way!" which became corrupted to "There's the Army Way and the Right Way!" and only finally was something said about guns, the end-all of the game, or so I believed.

After dull hours of throwing oneself into positions from which one was supposed to be able to fire accurately at an enemy approaching in a line like the British troops at the Battle of New Orleans - on the ground and elbows, pointing; on your knees; on your feet. "Imagine you're holding a gun," we were commanded. The great day came when everyone was given a gun without ammunition, trained to carry it this way and that way, and finally marched to the butts where everyone was allowed to fire a few shots and qualify as marksman, which I did because by then I was back under arms, so to speak.

For, one day in the afternoon of my KP stint, aroused by the spring air and the drying of the mud, I walked out and down a lonely path on the outskirts of the camp, not feeling especially morose, and encountered a new First Lieutenant from my Battery. He was a ROTC man it was said, Lt. Lesser, a dark guy about my size, with a decent look about him. After an exchange of salutes, he asked me why I was walking around alone: "You must have a personal problem!" - but the answer came as, no, really, just walking around thinking of this and that (wondering now, maybe it was the other who was lonely, or perhaps homosexual.)

So we walked along and exchanged questions and answers about schools and the war, and it occurred to me that I might mention being on permanent KP and so I did wonder about it out loud. (Enlisted men quickly learned not to carry a complaint or suggestion directly to an officer, indeed, not to speak to an officer, much less strike up a friendship with one; the two of us, standing on the sunlit path far from the others, speaking of the rules, seemed almost *ipso facto* to be breaking rules.)

The Lieutenant thought that something must be wrong and said he would look into it. We went our ways and the Lieutenant was as good as his word. My name disappeared from the KP roster for quite a while. I was on hand, therefore, for the great day of maneuvers about which we shall quote a few words from a letter to Jill:

> *The briars and thorns... They were camouflaged and deceiving. They were tough as nails. And they were as numerous as the sands of time. I dived, time after time, into them and fear and hate them worse than barb-wire. My hands were bleeding in a dozen places and my friend Jester's nose had a vicious cut from one of the monster varieties. He wriggled around and yelled 'De Grazia! I'm beginning to see red,' and I yelled back, 'Stick it in the mouth of your canteen.' And we resumed firing. The attack had just started... To my left was Tommaso, a tough little guy and a boy from N.Y.C. they call 'Junior' for obvious reasons. Well, Jr. wandered into my territory and fell in the gully. So Tomas hollered out, 'Hold Everything! Hold 'er up, someone's bin hurt!' I laughed so hard...*

Some men liked maneuvers; they were a relief from the balloon drills and the sedentary aspects of training. Some were even imaginative and got into the spirit of battle, at least so long as real bullets and shells were not coming their way: such was I.

At night, I did guard duty:

> *A guard post is a personal thing after the first hour. I know when I pass the great rustling tree hereafter I'll think of us playing on the beaches of California, because the noise was that of the sea. In the background of that whole stream of consciousness during the black watch from two to four A.M. was the measured clump of my shoes which persists like a metronome in the recollection. A sentry's night is a funny thing, mostly confused impressions on a dulled mind. A grunt, mumble, and squeaking of springs when the second relief is wakened in the middle of the night. Then a stumbling for the door, a second of attentive bodies, a "right face", and off to relieve the old guard. The new & old meet, a greeting is muttered, cartridges are transferred from one rifle to the other and you are left alone. What did the other sentry*

say? Something like "I've been walking guard with a big, black snake." Pleasant thought!

On my second slow round I see my companion. He is slithering along ahead of me. I have half a mind to let him be, any company being something, when two tippling bucks come along & I challenge them. "Pass," I say, "and watch out for the snake." Their sodden eyes see a huge serpent and after a furious battle of stones and words, crush the demon and walk away, arm in arm.

"Nobody loves a snake," I thought. "A worm, yes, but not a snake."

My shadow seemed like a snake, thirty feet of legs and rifle. With the natural persistence that makes it just to call love an obsession, I think of you and wonder if you're sleeping well. Just as I pass, and greet the neighboring sentry, the relief marches into view. I eject my cartridges. "Nice night" I say to my relief. "There's a dead snake in the road; don't mind him." He stirs and laughs a little and begins to walk. I feel very happy, light a cigarette, and head for my bunk.

She replied in her very next letter that she liked snakes: "I really do," and regretted its passing. Typically, our letters worked hand in glove, hers only several days apart from mine. If she wrote that she was reading *War and Peace* and the short stories of Thomas Mann, I would hasten to reply that I was reading William Saroyan's *My Name is Aram,* and launch into an essay on humor, identifying him with S.J. Perelman. I added a review of René Chambrun's *I Saw France Fall,* dismissing it as a "book of *ex post facto* predictions," by a "bourgeois lawyer of Paris. Ghastly analysis! Blames the Popular Front without any first-hand reason. Repeats capitalist slogan thinking. Account of Battle of France and the Maginot Line interesting and not too grim for the tea room." And I announce: "Coming soon: Review of *Dragon's Teeth,* by Upton Sinclair."

The Chicago *Tribune* and *News, Time* and *Life* magazines, politics on all levels, cats, dogs, little brothers, the strategy of war, jobs at *Esquire* magazine, at Montgomery Ward's Department Store, bicycles and their use and maintenance, all the details of existence in camp and city burgeon from this interminable correspondence

A Private in Paris, Tennessee

of wartime. Her epistolary world is Dickensian, with its multitude of characters of the Home Front candidly portrayed; her style is slash and burn, snap and crackle. Her morale is heartening:

> *I can't say too often how proud I am that you're in the Army. Perhaps it is a smug pride - after all, it's you who have to suffer the discomforts and ennui of Army life. I wish I could, too, just to keep things even. I get awfully mad at all these punks, particularly around the University of Chicago, who are looking for a nice, safe desk job. John* [John Hess, Tanks Corps EM, friend on furlough] *and I ran into Stud* [former object of her affections] *at the U.T. last Thursday night, and he assured us that he was going to be able to stay out of the armed forces. It was pretty disgusting. And the ensigns - most of them - aren't much better.*

And then I asked for and got from the Charge of Quarters, without the usual runaround and sneers, the rules for applying for officer training. Hank Dannenberg was all in favor of my trying for a commission. Such support was important: I wouldn't have wanted the guys to feel that I put myself above them and wished to desert them, nor did I in fact want to leave them. Life was a drag, but it was also a jolly shared mock-demanding pastime. Many a soldier refused officer candidature for just such reasons.

I tried to get Hank and Johnny Chingos to apply with me, but they balked. My application papers did not go swimming through the channels of Camp Tyson. I am reporting to my beloved on May 15:

> *...I enquired about my application & was thoroughly enraged when I heard it was still dormant. I took over personally and, with application in hand, barged in upon office after office, shocking all Army standards of procedural propriety. I saw majors, captain, lieutenants and numerous sergeants with blunt requests for action. Our captain, poor soul, was perplexed no end by the irregularity. He was actually horrified to have my paper in the office and complained time after time that he couldn't understand how the papers were there. I ignored the asides. But lord, how they strained and squirmed to pass*

the buck on any number of details. Now it is completed...

I could not help but urge Hank again and again to apply. Hank had some ear trouble, an open ear drum from a boxing blow; it might block him; it might even cause an examining doctor to issue him a discharge, which would hurt Hank more than anything. I would have waived all such nonsense had I the right and power: Hank was magnificent as a leader of men, an organizer, an enthusiast, a warm guy full of sympathy for human problems, yet as tough as they come, a perfect soldier from the point of view of both non-coms and officers. He had been married and was in the throes of divorce, not bothered by what must have been a lingering separation. He was in his middle thirties, 225 pounds of blonde hairy muscle, a professional boxer early on, a movie house manager for United Artists, one time with several theaters in hand, a dead ringer for movie star Kirk Douglas, had anyone known of Kirk Douglas yet. A bantam Boston Irishman confided in me (a scholar if not a priest) that "He's the hardest working Jew I've ever seen." He meant, putting a compliment into his antisemitism, that Hank could peel potatoes and dig ditches and send a balloon aloft better and faster than anyone in the Battery, always, too, in hearty good temper.

We formed a leading clique, had several guys who were close to us but none were so close as the two of us - Chester Dubois, Dominick Albano, Farley Reston, Johnny Chingos, who was the next strongest man in the company, and showed it one day when he came close to besting Hank in a rough and tumble wrestling match. But nobody would mix it with Chief, the towering Comanche, who was the first man to be in and out of the guardhouse from the battery, for resisting arrest while drunk, and who could shoot a rifle better than anybody.

The village anti-named Paris was a gloomy setting for a Great Love. No lover in her right mind would voyage to these parts. That's why, shortly after arrival at Camp, I grew an obsession that a calloused outside world had enveloped us in a murky time-freezing capsule. Nonetheless, in the numerous letters that we were writing to each other it became increasingly evident that a visit to

A Private in Paris, Tennessee

Paris by her was in order and it had to be timed of a weekend, when I could get a pass to leave the Camp, which would not be allowed until one's first six weeks had come and gone.

Then it did all jell: I managed to call her from the PX, she happened not to be in menstruation and managed to catch a train, and I managed to reserve a room in the tumbledown frame structure called the 'Paris Hotel.' Down she came and we were delighted, I with her presence, she with the exotic barbarity of the setting. I took her to Camp and introduced her around, but much of the time we were engaged in sex, which had the aspect of coitus interruptus, because the room, as well as the hotel, cozied against the switching tracks and watering tank such that no sooner would we passionately embrace than a locomotive would chug, railroad cars would begin to clank and bum, men would shout, and the building would shake and tremble as if collapsing.

Jill went home and we wrote again and again and decided to get married if ever I could get to Chicago on a three-day pass. Thus:

Dearest love,

How is every little thing? Still love me? Cut out the comedy and give me a serious answer.

Because I'd hate to marry a girl this coming Sunday who didn't. I think this is it, darling. I've just spoken to the 1st Sergeant who is arranging a three-day pass (maybe four), starting Saturday at one. If all goes well, I'll be on the "City of Miami" at 10:30 that night and loving you to death shortly thereafter.

Hank Dannenberg will be with me on his way to NYC to get a divorce - funny? -. I'm sure you'll find him an eminently lovable character, enough so to be best man. To facilitate recognition, here is a picture of him, all 225 lbs. of brawn and as light as a mosquito.

The 302 is an old battalion, the first one here, and they're a pleasant bunch. I'm giving a short current events lecture Wed. & Sat. at noon to the battery. I'm also rehearsing with the 306th dance orchestra. In other words, I have a few interesting things to do. But none so interesting as to keep me from longing & fretting for Saturday to come around.

I'll know for sure Wed. but am almost positive of the leave.

Imagine yourself, if you can, as a married woman, J.O., I can't quite. To me you'll always be someone I'm trying to make.

I've got to go, now. All my love and more. Will write right soon.

Your
Al

Love to all the family.

Thereupon we spoke on the telephone, a matter of my calling her from the PX, once I reached the head of the line at the booth. This and the other calls were not happy affairs. Too much was to be said, in too few minutes, with too much chance of saying the wrong thing.

JILL TO AL May 6, 1942

My darling -

You deserve some explanation for my awful indecision tonight; yet I hardly know how to give you one. I have turned the moment that should have been our happiest into something miserable and confused for us both. Yet why I don't know.

Do I want to marry you? The question should be - do you want to marry me, now? Al, I haven't changed. The things in me that made me undecided, quarrelsome, tearful before are still there. I yearn for things, the existence of which I can't define. I look frantically towards your love, and understanding, but I hardly know how to give you those things.

You grow furious with me when I call myself a neurotic - it's a smug, pat generalization, I know - but I think I am. And then my anxieties are intensified because I think or know I am behaving differently from other people.

You want me - and I'd like to, too - go into marriage high-heartedly, viewing it as the climax of all my hopes and expectations. That's the way some girls - maybe all - do it. But how can I, Al? God, for two years now we've fought, equivocated, contemplated infidelity - and loved - one another. We must have had reasons for doing all those things. Or I must have had them (perhaps, truly, I was the sole instigator of all this atypical behavior).

And now I am on the verge of getting married, and worried sick because I don't have the same feelings I think other people have when they get married. Yes, I love you in my way - that is - I can't imagine loving anyone else. You are the fixed point in my existence. And because I realize that, I am afraid to get married. I have this idea that people get married for reasons that I don't understand - not for my reason - that I am lonely and dependent on you. Even when I say I love you, I sometimes feel that you and everyone else have a secret knowledge of the words that I don't and never will understand.

You see, I take my trouble to you as I have always taken it, telling you everything as if you were a detached observer. Which of course you're not, which must make this letter something at the same time ludicrous and painful to you. I want your assurance - as if you were my mother! - that no, I'm not the least bit queer or different from other people, that everything will be all right, that of course I should marry you. And, as I write these words, I do want to do that. But again, the pain rises up in me - that I can never honestly be the sort of wife you need and want.

Shall I sum up what stands between us? It comprises all these vague yearnings, all this preoccupation with self - the chief characteristics of my mildly disordered personality. When I see you again, I shall probably swear that I am whole and perfect as a government stamped side of beef. But there will be nights when I'll weep and toss and not know why -

When I see you - and how much I want to - I'll not be able to say the things I've said. I shall have forgotten them by then, because I never wanted to say them. By then, we'll either do what we both want to do - I think - or else we, or rather you, will make one more of your gentle accommodations. You've been wonderful to me, Al, all these years. [Actually only two: but it had been a heavy affair] You've really put up with a lot of - well, the word is inappropriate in this context. But how much more can you take? I love you, darling, but God, do you really think you can stand being psycho-analyst, mother, brother and lover to me?

I'll get a room on the South Side for the weekend - for Hank

- but how about us? I am staying here you know. Why don't we get the room & let him stay with your folks? They suggested he could.

And there were all these other things that came to my mind when you asked me tonight - that I want to stay with my job because it's a good one, even tho all I have done is color counties red and blue. I was - and am - afraid that that's not the right attitude.

Please, darling, forgive me for all this crap.

Your

Jill

I sent your knife today. Watch for a small package from Field's. Hope you like it - it was the most expensive one in the store.

AL TO JILL MAY 6, 1942

Dearest love, *Wednesday*

I should be used to hearing what you said over the phone, but somehow it hit me awfully hard last night, probably because I was so happy over the prospect of coming home.

Most certainly something must be done. I can't go on having you as a wife but not in name. It is terribly unfair to you. Whatever you say about being willing to go ahead, I can't let you do it.

For quite a while and perhaps even now, you thought me hard and untrustworthy. If that is why you don't want to marry me, I am happy - first because neither is true and second because, if you believe it, it is something in me and not something in you. I pray that if we do not marry, it is because you think there are things about me you don't like. I pray that your reasons are not in yourself - either because of not confiding in me something that stands in the way, something that has happened, or some basic disturbance in your character and mind. If this were so, I would be really smashed in heart and spirit.

All I care for in the world is that you be happy and well-adjusted. I could stand it being with someone else. I can't bear to have you torn within by something not rational, meaning by "rational" a weighing of my qualities against someone else's or yours. My stomach shrivels when I think that you may love me but that I can never make you happy.

I'm sending this letter before I receive yours because nothing will change what I've said. When I receive yours, I'll send either a telegram or another special delivery letter to you. I'll be home but can't say exactly when, - Sat. nite, I hope.

During all the time I've known you, I've never been unfaithful; the only exceptions you can recite me were done for the reason I told you, because I loved you so very much.

I seem to recall us being very happy together for months. In fact, it seems that when we were together we had delightful times, jaundiced over only by the uncertainty of their duration. But, again, I am not you and I may have been wrong. Perhaps you had happier times before then which you could recall & compare to my disadvantage.

I beg of you to tell me the truth about yourself. Put me in my place and I'll be content. You can count on me for all of your life for anything; so please don't feel that by leaving me you will be alone.

This is no love letter, darling, as you know. I'm not recounting the infinitude of pleasures you have given me and telling you how much I desire you. I don't want to sweep you into a marriage of reciprocal sympathy. I want you to love me as I love you, not with troubled feelings and deep insecurities, but with a lover's light heart and boundless acceptance.

If you decide to marry me, I will be most happy. If not, I want to know the true reasons why you don't.

I hope all this is not hurting your new work too much. But I know it is. Well, this love affair has hurt my work in the past, too, if that is any consolation.

Please smile for me, darling, and say, "Well, that ape wasn't for me but we had a lot of wonderful times together and we both came out the better for it." If not that, smile to think of Hank & myself staggering off the train with drunken grins and smile at the thought of our future marriage.

     I love you,

          Al

JILL TO AL MAY 8(?), 1942

Darling -

I hope you'll forgive the awful paper and the scratchy pen but it's the best equipment I can find.

Your special came - very belatedly (you should air mail a special to make it really effective) and I noted pictures with interest. Hank looks like Herb Blumer - or does he? - and appears to be a fine broth of a man. I shall fix him up with either Rosable - the racy type - or Marion Gerson - the pretty, sweet (but intelligent) type. Marion is somewhat shy and comes from a very sheltered background, but she's a damn nice girl, far and away the nicest I know, with the possible exception of Gertie Goldsmith. The only trouble is that she lives at the Ambassador, an inconvenient location.

Sweetheart, I'm awfully sorry about our phone conversation and the letter following it. In a way, I'm glad I wrote that letter. That is the way I feel basically, I guess. But I forget that I also feel other ways. While I think that essentially I am a confused and - for lack of a better word - apathetic personality, most of the time I behave and react as a normal happy person does. I think that, given the responsibility of a husband or a job, I can behave appropriately. I think I know how to act, even though my motivations to action are weak. (Please don't misunderstand me - don't class yourself as a motivation and then get angry because you think I think you don't count ... I just mean that my most deep-seated wish is to retreat from everybody and everything, and sit in the sun. But as long as I don't do that - as long as I realize that there are things and people important enough to deny that wish - I guess I'll be all right).

If you're willing to take me this way, knowing that perhaps I am not entirely what a person should be - and I think my analysis of myself is correct as far as it goes - then let's get married. Certainly we can be happier together than we can singly.

But we can't get married Sunday. The license bureau isn't open. As that humorist in the County Building said when I called him, they're all in church - and we should be too (he said). I can get my test Saturday & call for it Monday (takes 24 hours). Oh, & I can't get the license by myself because we both have to bring our certificates. So - if you still want to - let's get married Monday. I'll be

> *able to take the day off if I tell them what for. I just hope I don't lose that lovely $40 a week job in the process of telling them. You can come to work Monday with me & then we can just walk across the hall & get the license. Hot dog! (Corny, ain't I?)*
>
> *Monday night I dragged one suitcase down to the South Side to look for a place to live. I went to the Harvard Hotel and such places, & got so overwhelmingly disgusted I hopped right on the I.C. & went back to home & mother! Jesus, I've been spoiled by our apartment. And guess what! They didn't rent it after all. Apparently, the people who were going to take it welshed on the lease. Anyway, there was a big For Rent sign in the window when I biked by. (I left my bike with Jane Tallman, having no way to bring it to the North Side).*
>
> *I'd like to take our apartment again. With the incentive of making a place for you to come home to, I really could fix it up nicely. (The incentive plus my income of $200 a month.) Your mother suggests that I wait upon your decision, wisely enough. Unless I hear otherwise from you, I'll delay the home business until you come home. As usual, I leave everything to you. But really, honey, the idea of a hotel room curdles my blood, & 5479 is so familiar to me that I wouldn't feel lonely in it while you were away. Not very lonely, anyway.*
>
> *I ought to mail this now.*
>
>   *All my love,*
>
> *Jill*

"Why should I get married?" I asked myself repeatedly. There were many reasons why the marriage should fail; like the bumblebee, according to the laws of aerodynamics, ought not be able to fly. "But," so went my line of thought, "we're coming near to the end of the world in a certain sense, something so big is happening that to refrain from an action, otherwise quite reasonable and called for to cement the most important relationship of our lives, would be cowardly. To cement it, to commemorate it, to celebrate it, would be fitting and proper."

So we did it. I hitched a ride to a town some distance away where the fast train from Miami paused and one could climb aboard. The train was full of bronzed slackers, big city slickers coming back from vacations in Florida, a hard-looking business crowd, both men and women, mostly Jewish, I noticed, with an embarrassment that they would not have felt, but my friends, the Oppenheims, the Gersons, the Hess's, would have, and old Hank was fit to be tied. I was disgusted with them and hostile. "Not my kind of Jew," I thought. "Where was the war? In their pocketbooks. Where's the Promised Land? Miami! Damn, don't they know what the War is about?"

I came into Chicago, it was Saturday morning, and we were to stay with the folks on Addison Street. Jill and I went downtown to get a marriage license and learned that we needed a blood test, so we had to find a doctor who would testify we were free of venereal disease, which this one, caught emerging from his office, granted could be deduced from the man being a soldier with a recent Wassermann test on his card and the girl looking too neat and prim to be down with the clap.

The Mom and Dad later joined in as witnesses, Hank having flown the coop, and we went over to the City Hall, where the problem now turned into a search for someone with the authority to conduct a civil marriage. Found: one heavy-set bespectacled dark-jowled Slavic type from the County Clerk's Office, who could perform the ceremony without a tremor of emotion, and free us after a few minutes to go out with the folks for a cup of coffee. Then home. I showed up late for roll-call on Tuesday, but the CQ covered up for me.

There was not to be an end to jealousy on my side, nor of lust. My large concession to fidelity was "not to go out of my way to look for women" and, when I did encounter an attractive female, I prided himself on playing with the lowest cards in the deck - no squandering of money or resources, no lying about my marital status, no promises, no dressing "fit to kill," no interference with my higher calling, whatever that would be. I did have a need to experience women, or, as they said in humbler quarters, I was not ready to settle down yet. Womanless, in the presence of mixed singles, I could not but compete, for that, too, sexual competition, was part of my make-up. Still I was in love as I had been for years, unceasingly, unfailingly ready to sacrifice anyone else for her, thinking practically of her alone as the object of love and sex.

It was before my marriage, for instance, that a dance orchestra came in from Paducah, Kentucky, with singers and dancers, and a beautiful girl danced; I cut around and through everybody with aplomb until I was alone with her, and had her dancing and scribbling down her name and address in Paducah; the Camp Tyson newspaper gossiped about my encounter with the hottest thing seen thereabouts since the Balloon went up in flames. I actually hitched there one fine Saturday, and inquired the whereabouts of her house at a barber shop nearby. On the one hand it was simply to ask for an address; on the other hand, it was a prudent bit of reconnaissance and intelligence, because I heard that she was married, that her husband was jealous, and that "folks heah ain't partial to soldiers cumin roun fixin to make trouble and gittin too friendly with the girls." So I wandered off after the butterflies of the pleasant Dixie Spring day.

And there was a strange moment on my first trip to Chicago, when I took a slow train and at this town where the train stopped, it was Galena, Illinois, I had time to kill and was in a hotel that had a balcony running around its foyer, where a beautiful woman took up a conversation - she seemed to be with a party, for there had been two men talking with her. Suddenly she threw her arms around me and kissed me passionately and I was entranced, wondering what would happen next, when she pulled away as from a lover in an Italian Opera, sighing and throwing kisses, and went tripping off down the stairs and out and I wiped off the lipstick and walked around some more and concluded that I could make nothing of the affair. A contribution to the War Effort, perhaps?

Nothing else, then, except the movies. I saw one a week at the Camp theater, one worse than another. The War Effort virus was infecting them more and more. And taking our dimes. I was paid $21 per month. Every dime counted. Yet at the same time money counted for little. You received your pay in cash, at an impressive ceremony, as elaborate as a marriage, in the Battery Dayroom, where you stood in line, in alphabetic order, and, advancing slowly but surely, ultimately arrived at the table where sat the Battery Clerk, the First Sergeant, and the Battery Finance Officer (normally an ordinary lieutenant charged with this detail), saluted briskly, received what was owed you, saluted again, executed what you hoped would be a respectable about-face, and retired.

Not $21 by any means, because deductions were removed beforehand: $6.60 for life insurance, to be paid to the parents upon my death, later changed over to my wife, several dollars toward the compulsory purchase of a Victory Bond, and the like. If a piece of equipment had been lost or deliberately or negligently broken, its cost would be deducted, as also a fine from a Court Martial. From the remainder, you would buy soap, lotions, beer, movie tickets, any article of clothing above the army's basic issue.

I was content with maximizing the army's hold on my property and was fully the G.I., in olive-drab from head to toe, inside and outside, heavy high shoes of leather with rubber soles, woolen socks, long-john khaki underwear, etc. with an olive-drab shirt, ill-fitting trousers and jacket with brass buttons, one horse-blanket overcoat, one overseas cap, two pairs of fatigues - the overalls issued for everyday wear, two khaki handkerchiefs, and a belt of canvas with a brass buckle. That was all. When I needed a piece replaced, I would turn it in upon the appointed hour to the Supply Sergeant, who of course had a Supply Corporal, and this one would issue me a new item, asking me to sign for it, or send me off to the central depot if the Battery inventory had a shortfall.

There were guys who had a little money and felt a little freer and more elegant if they bought the few articles authorized for purchase, whether at the PX or at the Army and Navy stores that sold official gear in the towns of the country. The men could wear watches and did so, if they could afford them. The Army issued watches as the need arose, and to the appropriate grades - not to ordinary dogfaces! Any private travel was, of course, paid for out of pocket. Cigarettes cost little, a nickel a pack at the PX, by the carton. A great many men could never have afforded cigarettes, given the tax and profit on them, were they still civilians; even now they would often buy tobacco in bulk to roll in papers or stuff in pipes; there were men who chewed tobacco, but it was going out of style, no spitting in the barracks.

You could barely scrape through the month if you wanted to go out for a night of beer drinking or whiskey, or buy a gift to send to someone out there, or buy books, newspapers and magazines, or eau de cologne, or chew too much gum, or have your woolens dry-cleaned. I washed my own stuff at the line of sinks in the large Barrack washroom; the Army didn't care if you were well-pressed so long as you were clean and it did a good job of cleaning up Battery A personnel within a couple of weeks.

Once broke, you could rely upon your comrades. Bumming cigarettes was epidemic as the month drew to an end. There would have arisen regularly a complicated network of indebtedness to be largely resolved in the hour following pay-call. The creditors skulked about the Battery Dayroom like wolves, letting no debtor escape. Gambling resulted in swift changes of fortune. I was a good gambler at dice, for reasons unknown. I could make them jump, bounce, careen, stop short, spin. Best of all, it seemed to me that with a scarcely detectable way of picking up the dice when my turn at dice came, and a way of palming them into the order in which I wanted them to fall, and a flat way of running them out over the blanket - that with all this more often than chance the dice turned up my way. It is important that the gambler thinks that he is luckier than he really is in order to generate the volume of bets he needs to win heavily, but yet not believe he is so lucky as to bet foolishly.

I was helped in both regards by Hank, who played some himself but was not a hot gambler, whereas I could work up a passion and enjoyed the orgasmic feeling of seeing the two faces of the dice reveal themselves like two lovers, but now and then as a rejection, or maybe only a momentary flirtatious turning of their behinds to you, so that you know surely on the next round you will set them down good and proper. And you do or you don't, while Hank held the money and collected for me one night when I began to beat the game, and Hank placed bets for himself as well.

There you had it: the dozen players, the dozen watchers, the smoothed out khaki blanket, wooden slat floor, bare windows, naked bulb lighting the space, the squatters, the benders, the standers, the ever-moving bodies, all fascinated by the action. And the side bets. As I played, I could hear the babble of voices:"1 to 3 he comes on the next roll, who'll take it?" "I got you!" "All faded?

Let 'em roll!" "Come on, sweet 7!" "Come on, snake-eyes!" "Damn!" You sense who is with you and against you, who is thinking you must be hot and is beginning to ride on you.

You pray hard to make your point, you squeeze it out of your dice, but at the same time you are thinking what am I going to do when I make it, should I pinch the pot, take the winnings, retreat way back to where I started, or let it all ride, go for broke? The smoke rises thickly, the grunts and calls get louder, somebody shouts thinking you must be hot and betting for your point to come, 2 to 1, while the unbeliever sticks grimly, going his own way, and keeps betting 1 to 2 on a crap-out.

Then straightening up and stretching your limbs finally when it is time to go, perhaps for everyone, or for the broke ones, or for yourself, whether you've lost as much as you can afford, or won as much as you think you can win this night, usually only a few bucks, oh, but there was that Great Night when I was hot as a pistol and Hank was booming right alongside of me and we cleaned up the blanket with fifty bucks apiece, two and a half months' pay, when a 29-cent stamp cost 2 cents and the nickel cigar and nickel beer prevailed. And friendship - probably it has inflated even more.

All in all, "A" Battery was a friendly 300-man aggregate, where over several months there were no fisticuffs in anger - so much for the idea that Americans, all the more when they were a melting pot of strangers, continually brawled. Our leaders - the officers - were practically unknown to us, and known only distantly to the non-commissioned officers who ran the company in proverbial army style. They were regular army, these non-coms; most had served as privates for years, their own old non-coms having been shipped into outfits going overseas or retired from the army. You might say they were a lot of Hillbillies and Italians and End of the Road farm boys and onetime riffraff from the big cities. They were supremely ignorant and narrow, but comforting in the very ponderosity of their behavior and in their conviction that the army will take care of one, if you just don't cause trouble, and keep your nose clean, and do as you are told.

The recruits in themselves constituted an ethnic and geographical fantasy, the main elements coming from an Italian neighborhood of the West Side of Chicago, a Jewish neighborhood of Brooklyn, with a scraping of Okies and of Indians caught off the reservation, remote Scandinavians of the northwest, and a dozen other types. Absent by the vagaries of assignment were Far-Westerners and Deep-Southerners. Blacks had been segregated, both here and everywhere; the Old Army had been racist and the Army would continue to discriminate invidiously until forced by the Federal Government and Liberal Opinion - and perhaps by an anticipation of high casualties - to integrate its troops racially.

Intellectuals were totally absent from all ranks up through the Post Commandant, so far as I could tell - all except Prof. Ziegler of Amherst College's Political Science Department who came, hated it all, and went to who knows where. We should have loved one another - and indeed we did communicate in the academic mode and code on several occasions - but your Private was no longer, not socially, an intellectual; I liked the guys around me, and intellectually I lived off my fat, plus a few books, and the letters from my love.

A dark-skinned Oklahoman, perhaps carrying along with his "white" classification the genes of Cherokees and Blacks, as do a number from that country, a cheerful stocky farmhand, bunked next to me in the big room of many beds. I had brought along from home a copy of Cohen and Nagel's formidable volume on *An Introduction to Logic and Scientific Method* that I had stolen from the University of Chicago Library. If anything could justify the period of Basic Training, I thought, it would be the mastery of this work. I left it laying upon my bunk one Saturday afternoon to toss a baseball outside, and when I returned a while later the Okie was reading it with interest. He handed it back promptly. "How did you like it?" "It's interesting," he said, "It's just like common sense." I could not make out whether the guy was disappointed that it was decipherable or pleased that he could handle it.

He had only an elementary school education. Hardly a man in the battery had been to junior college and many, including the non-coms, had not finished high school. They were not noticeably different from the Americans whom I had known, except from the academics and intellectuals, who are really the only distinct class in America, or were, until mass higher education and hi-tech industry swept over the country beginning in the fifties. In manners and considerateness, the men compared favorably with the business class of the American cities and the fraternity and athletic circles of the University.

With the gossip bruited about and my application for Officer's School before me, the officers could respond readily to national directives urging All Personnel to conduct orientation and education sessions for the troops. We were already viewing the war propaganda films that Frank Capra was directing from Hollywood on "The Nature of the Enemy." So on Wednesdays and Saturdays, in the mess-hall after lunch, I was on detail to lecture "A" battery, officers included, on the news and on the meaning of the war. I delivered discouraging news, reminding them that a Japanese submarine had fired upon Santa Barbara, California, oil installations and the enemy had taken over the whole of the Western Pacific and Southeast Asia.

What I could not tell them, because such news was kept secret (a mistake in mobilizing the country), was that a month earlier all Allied shipping had been halted by losses too heavy to sustain, 834,164 tons or 273 ships; that the Battle of the Java Sea was a serious defeat; and, also because it was not "battle-relevant", the first trainload of Jews had been shipped out of Paris, France, destined to die at Auschwitz.

I then gave them encouraging news on the progress of the War, which they already had known but liked to hear from the podium - that the Russians were holding fast, that American planes had successfully bombed Tokyo and other cities of Japan, and so on.

I would then scold them for being lazy and negligent citizens who had allowed the government to be isolationist, to divorce itself from world problems, and to allow the Fascists, Nazis, Imperialists of Japan and all of their minions in various other nations, including the USA, to grow enormously in power and influence, until the very minds and souls of people everywhere were being meanly controlled, along with their lives and fortunes. The enemy, having taken over their own countries, practically all of Europe and Asia, and even to be found in Alaska, Africa and battering at the doors of America and Australia, would soon target Detroit, Chicago, New

York and Washington. So here we are, I expostulated, going to fight thousands of miles away because of inattention to the world around us.

I was half-baked, ill-prepared, arrogant, dogmatic, but my act went over well. Everyone felt better. Americans feel better if they've been lectured; it's as if they've gone to church and heard a sermon. It's true, of course, that I had enjoyed a certain experience as a teacher, had experienced hundreds of lectures of all types, knew the background of the War and devoured the news daily, so I could be confident, which in the last analysis is what the lecturer ought to be, especially before troops, and which put me well ahead of the audience; no one else, from the captain down to the "sad-sack" recruit out of the Ozarks, had any idea of how to conduct such affairs and even if I had done well, they would not have had the self-confidence to judge my performance.

They might better appraise me as a Balloon Chief, for they had all started equally, and totally ignorant with regard to balloons. Few had ever flown a kite. Now a number of them had qualified for ratings as corporals and sergeants and would be training others to fly the balloons. There would eventually be a million promotions in the Army of ten millions, even if the casualty rate should be low enough to put a brake on promotions. But then there were the nine millions who never reached beyond Private First Class.

Modest talk of ratings entranced the men as they sat upon the wooden stoops in the warm light of Spring. To most of them a promotion to PFC, Corporal, or one of the several grades of Sergeant would have been a great leap forward. What couldn't be done with another twenty dollars a month! Soon they would get $45.00 per month, everyone would. What a great payday that was! It took many soldiers several months to raise their standard of living high enough to dispose of their surpluses.

It did not stop, however, the interminable argument of the barracks stoop as to what was the best grade to possess in the Army. Strangely, there floated an old myth that the best grade of all was the Warrant Officer! He was half officer, half top sergeant, got respect from all sides, appeared independent in consequence. No one had yet encountered one of the species save from a distance.

Argument proceeded, also, on the question, who made the best officers: Soldiers with battlefield promotions, men who had gone through Officer Candidates School, West Point graduates, Reserve Officer Training Corps products, or National Guard officers? The preponderance of opinion rated the five groups as West Pointers, first, then battlefield officers, then OCS, NG and ROTC. Considering the inexperience of the soldiers, the ordering was remarkably intelligent.

At first, unlike everyone else around, I was disappointed in my assignment. I wanted to have something to do with high explosives. I felt consoled upon learning that these dragon-like creatures were to be filled with hydrogen gas, after their first trials with helium, because everybody knew that hydrogen was highly inflammable and explosive, whether mixed with oxygen or touched by flame. The greatest care had to be used in filling the balloons from the gas cylinders and afterwards in releasing the gas from the balloon when collapsing it for transportation and storage. One day the biggest balloon in camp nearly got away when a little convoy balloon tangled with it. They poised together in the air for a minute, "looking" I wrote, "like two lazy, copulating carp. Then a tear appeared in the big fellow and he was hauled down rapidly."

We heard that the balloons were being used in London and on ships at sea, and the idea of being sea sick repelled me - I had been quite nauseated on a couple of trips across the Atlantic before the War began; I disliked, too, the sense of confinement I believed would be part of a marine existence, an idea that had discouraged me from applying to the Navy for a Commission when I might have done so. Furthermore, I believed in the ultimate supremacy of land-based power and that the United States, like the Soviet Union and Germany, was fundamentally bound to the land, unlike the British Empire. At any rate, I discovered a modicum of danger in these balloons and experienced with pleasure how they tugged like wild horses when you tried to launch them or moor them in a wind; I could picture how they might bring down or scare off a dive-bomber from a direct approach to my ship. Or, if such came at my boat crosswise, midships, they wouldn't be able to rake the ship well with their machine guns. It is remarkable how much of the time of

A Private in Paris, Tennessee

the soldier, so little of which can be spent in combat, is occupied in violent fantasy. The soldier must therefore always be something of a child. Unless he blanks out, a dullard.

Privately, I did not become reconciled to the Barrage Balloon Corps and the chief reason was that I did not believe that they could have much to do with winning the War. I was set, heart and head, upon fulfilling some function that would be dangerous without being fatal, and that was involved in the thrusts that would win the War. I did not see much future in the Coast Artillery for that matter and wondered, and would continue to wonder, why they did not shut it down, as it was becoming most unlikely that the Japanese or the Italians and Germans were going to come steaming up to our coastlines, blow up our cities, and land a mass of troops.

We were told, however, that it used to be the choicest combat arm, asking the most of the military brain to operate its long-range cannon, and affording the most luxurious life within its seaside garrisons. I could see none of this and even doubted it, for the Air Force was now the most technical branch. I had begun soon after arriving in Camp to plot a transfer to another arm. But meanwhile I had no alternative to entering the Coast Artillery's Officer School. They were seeking a great many new officers. The reason was soon made clear. The anti-aircraft function, the most technical type of artillery, had been given over to the Coast Artillery. And there were armadas of Axis aircraft doing great damage, which would have to be shot down.

It appeared that I was qualified to direct such cannons, and I was called before an Examining Board to determine whether I was inordinately ugly, improperly garbed, of sagging morale and lacking self-confidence, badly informed, and wanting in the judgement expected of one to be entrusted with matters of life and death. The Board's two lieutenant-colonels and single major were pleasant beyond what one might reasonably expect, given the burden laying upon them. They chit-chatted easily and comfortably.

How do you feel, asked one of the Colonels, probably not of German origin, about fighting the war against Italy, assuming, as it appeared from my name, that I was of Italian descent. I replied that Italy had begun the war, that fascism was no good, Mussolini a dangerous dictator and that Italians as a whole were unenthusiastic about fighting, especially against Americans, but that a lot of them would have to be killed before they would be able to extricate themselves, and that I anticipated taking part in the action. It did occur to me, who had achieved a certain subtlety in such matters, that it would have been quite useless, or, as the Army people came later to say, counter-productive, to object to the stereotype that lay behind the question. Here was a war in which about a quarter of the American combatants were of German origin and about ten per cent were of Italian origin, not to mention all the other Americans descended all or in part from nationalities, like Croatians and Ukrainians and South Irish, who were engaged by sympathy or conduct upon the enemy's side. (The prejudiced ignominies that were being perpetrated against the Japanese-Americans of Hawaii and the West Coast were far from the consciousness of both Board and Candidate.)

Nor were questions being asked about the more important sources operating against the war effort, the anti-communist fanatics, the racists who insisted that blacks be kept segregated and not allowed into fighting units, and so on.) Actually it was evident that the Board expected no problem with the answer, expected, in fact, rip-roaring chauvinism.

The question that actually stumped me was logical, clear and relevant: "How much dirt can a man dig out in a day?" I stared bewildered at the Colonel, who after a moment almost apologized for his question: "Well, you know, he said, we have to be practical," and smiled kindly. I smiled back and everyone smiled and I replied: "I am sorry, sir, I don't know but I believe that I ought to know." (Should I have said: "What sort of man, under what kind of conditions, working on what kind of ground?" and then admitted ignorance of that, too?) But it was the last remark of any consequence. I was elevated to the rank of Corporal, Candidate and Cadet.

Now it was a matter of waiting for the orders that would give me ten days of freedom in Chicago en route to Camp Davis, North Carolina, for at least three months in officer's training. I was by no means assured of winning a Commission, although I could hardly

A Private in Paris, Tennessee

believe otherwise. Hank and the gang were sorry to part with me but looked forward to an Odyssean return, when I might exact salutes and demeaning details from the non-coms on their shit-list. I was less sanguine about this prospect, as well as more forgiving of disposition. I had heard, and it seemed reasonable, that precisely in order to avoid this kind of vengeful hazing, newly commissioned officers were not sent back to their former units or even their former camps. Besides, the social barriers between officers and enlisted men would in most cases put the newly commissioned officer ill at ease with his former buddies.

The American Army was growing too rapidly and moving people around too mechanically for attachments to endure. The Camps were all much alike; it could hardly matter where one was dumped. They were equipped now with recordings and loud-speakers that sounded the various calls of the day on a technically flawless bugle: reveille at dawn, assembly, mess-call ("soupy, soupy, soupy..."), retreat and taps. Retreat was the favorite call, for it fell at the close of the day's work, and often as the sun went down, and the Stars and Stripes were lowered reverently from the flagpole: it is a call of peace and freedom. Too bad Retreat had to be sounded automatically, inhumanly. Hank and the others would even walk some distance toward the pole in order to freeze at attention and salute the flag as it descended.

A few bugles were still inventoried. One came to my hands as I was preparing to leave. I could play it; I had been bugler at a Boy Scout Camp at Berrien Springs, Michigan, one time; and you might recall my trumpeting. A cluster of G.I.'s gathered around my bunk while I sounded off various calls, with verve or with nostalgia, as deserved. That's it! That's what we need, they exclaimed, a live bugle! It even occurred to them that I might play the bugle at Retreat in place of the recording. Go ahead! Yeah! Sure! You sound better than that tin horn! Why not! A delegation, with Hank in the lead, went over to the Military Police and proposed the idea. O.K. Just this once.

Like a gladiator with his trainers and sponsors, I walked to the flagpole the same afternoon, late, and stood by. As the Flag Detail loosened the rope, I sounded Retreat. I had a powerful open tone,

I hardly needed the help of the amplifier. I sang out over the wooden barracks and Tennessee fields as if they stretched out from the Place de la Concorde. The soldiers stood around marvelling. THIS was the Army. Human! Caring! Friends! Peace! I blew beautifully; I didn't quite remember the second passage of the call; it is a complicated call; but I improvised well, elided nicely; Hank, who knew, said enthusiastically, you didn't get it exactly right, but it was wonderful.

I was surprised and happy at the shower of compliments afterwards coming from the cluster of men around the flagpole. They had stood as stiff as ramrods and saluted up and down as sharp as razors to lend my bugling moral support. It was the real-life restoration of the hoary tradition of the Army of the United States, in Its Imperial Majesty, as they dreamed of it and saw it in the old movies. It gave the recruits one up on their Old Army cadre, too, because those men of yore, when the days went nowhere into the future but interminably into the Retreats of each sunset, and the freedom of the evening afterwards, were deeply stirred, and they too talked of the real live bugling of Retreat.

They made plans to perform Retreat this way at least once a week, maybe on Friday or Saturday. I was catching the right spirit; I resolved to get hold of the Army Manual for the Bugle and refresh my memory over the melody of the summons.

But my Special Order was being cut at Camp Headquarters. I was destined for Camp Davis. The bugle was put to rest. I could not be sad. All I could think of now was the ten laughing horny days with Jill coming up, The Mom's great cooking, walking the campus of the University, drinking beer at the University Tavern, Chicago Schmalz and Smørgasbord. I was a Corporal now; to my mind it was a high rank, justly deserved, somewhere between Brigadier and Lieutenant General. It would bring more dollars on my next payday, on the promise of which I stood my friends a round of drinks.

BalloonChief...

Written on the back:
"I wonder if the Russians will recapture Smolensk?" April '42

CHAPTER THREE

A CADET IN NORTH CAROLINA

REPUTABLE historians have said that Allied Victory in the War was foreseeable by the fall of 1942, at which time I was ushered out of officer's training at Camp Davis, which is situated not far from the Atlantic Ocean and Wilmington, North Carolina. However, Allied Victory was not foreseen at the time by our enemies, who appeared to be doing fairly well; they would have to let many millions of people die and many more millions suffer through hell, and have many fine cities devastated before they would concede, by which time they would find themselves bunkered down in Berlin and Tokyo.

Projections of victory were not, I hasten to say, founded upon the fact that Our Hero had been enduring weeks of a grim regimen and was about to project himself upon our enemies, but rather upon statistics of manpower and production, allowing a fair margin - say, 10% - to the probability that the generals and soldiers of one nation were more effective than those of another nation. In a particular case such as myself, if I was indeed becoming a better soldier, the probability of victory coming sooner rather than later would be enhanced by one fourteen-millionth or so, much less if one included into the count the industrial soldiers who labored mightily in the War Effort - perhaps one thirty-millionth.

I did not think along these lines. If I was to suffer the tortures of the dammed, it was in order to make A Significant Contribution to the War Effort. I had declared, you will recall, that the Japanese and Germans, not to mention the Italians and several other nationalities, ere insane to go to war with the United States. If I was so confident of victory, why didn't I play cornet in the Camp Grant Band and let it go at that? My 1.4×10^{-7} or 3×10^{-7} of the required heft was hardly needed.

Instead, exaggerating my potential role and unaware of what was confronting me, I signed in and took up my bunk space at the Officer Candidates School of the Anti-aircraft Division of the Coast Artillery Corps, graduates of which were called Lieutenants in the Army of the United States and given a new Army Identification Number. They were also termed "Ninety-day wonders." The road to graduation was one of the rockiest of anybody's army career, not excluding direct combat.

Let me begin my story via a letter to my newly wed wife, despatched not long after I entered upon the scene:

> *Sweetheart,*
>
> *A ten-minute break brings you a letter, but it is perhaps a sad one. For I am hopelessly morose without you. And this is a hell of a life. Really darling, you can't imagine how much I love you because you can't see the feelings under the skin.*
>
> *We are all dead tired. No sleep and nagging officers every minute of the day. My baggage with everything in it hasn't come yet and I run to one place to borrow a razor and another to borrow a pin. My papers haven't arrived to give me the travel money owed me, tho I can neither get the time to cash a check or spend any money. So don't send me one yet.*
>
> *...This is supposed to be the toughest officers' school in the country. I can well believe it. My back is almost broken from arching it to the tune of an officer saying "Get your chin in, Mister. Stick your chest out Mister. Guide that rifle, Mister." Well, I'll write more details later.*
>
> *Your loving husband,*
> *Al*

No one was free from the regimentation of war, she would have me know:

> *I think they've rigged up a public address system just recently for the sailors across the Midway. Did you hear any untoward noises when you were here? Anyway, they talk to the boys every 5 minutes - telling them everything from orders to report to their C.O. to go to Pearl Harbor to enjoinders to wash their socks. Needless to say, every word uttered wafts in here, & I find myself leaping out of bed at 6:15 and hurriedly Lux-ing out my summer whites, before my higher centers have a chance to say "boo".*

My complaints were only beginning; they continue week after week, viz:

> *The foremost thing to keep in mind always is that I have a chip on the shoulder against anything that keeps us apart and since I can't take it out on the real culprits, the Japo-Nazis, I am very restless and unhappy. For truly I love you as much as any mortal could possibly love.*
>
> *But first the training and then the reactions of the men. Here's the set-up. The directors and officers are out to get the men. The tools are constant and close supervision, most exacting demands, perpetual driving and criticism, a terrific program of activity which I have told you a few things about in earlier letters...*
>
> *I've learned a good deal and relish these new things. The first week was composed of miscellaneous subjects such as these: map-reading and aerial photography, customs of the service, court-martial, motor transportation, characteristics of American, British, German and Japanese planes, anti-tank defense (we use anti-aircraft guns against mechanized & armored units, you know), first aid, and math. About the latter: I've learned a lot, now that I must buckle down to it. My knowledge right now is average in the class. Four subjects are tested, algebra, trig, logs, and coordinates (directions, azimuths, & a combination of trig, logs, etc.). I think I'll hit off the math all right in enough time and expect to catch on fast now that I have to. Maybe then I can hold my head up in speaking to you on the subject.* [She was good at mathematics and statistics.] *There is quite a bit required. Some of the firing mechanisms are marvelously intricate. Next week we study searchlights and they are beauts, then later*

machine guns, 90 mm. anti-aircraft guns (long, sinister-looking cannon), 37 mm. guns, Garand rifles, and so forth.

Meanwhile every day we stand rigid inspection which gets on the nerves of the men like nothing else. Such things as these cause demerits: bedding not folded to perfection, shoes not properly aligned, books on shelf slightly askew, a piece of broom straw beneath the bed, a smudge of dust anywhere, a button unbuttoned.

Today was the climax of the worst week of the course. At 11:00 a full-dress inspection was held. We had between four & five hours' sleep last night and before dawn were polishing and scrubbing the barracks. The whole morning we spent in rigid drill and classes, bolted lunch in 5 instead of the customary 10 minutes and changed to our clean khakis. Then we began to march, a whole battalion of over a thousand. The chief of the school was reviewing us. We walked at strained attention with our rifles for a mile, lined up on the concrete parade ground and stood for an hour while being inspected. From where I stood I could see the splotches of sweat appearing and growing on the backs of the men in front of me. Some looked as if they had wet their pants. I couldn't raise my hands to stop the sweat pouring down from my face onto my collar. I tried everything to take my mind off the agony of waiting, I thought of you, I thought of cold drinks, I tried to pick out the man who would collapse first, I tried to take my mind off the idea that I perhaps couldn't stand it myself. I tried to rid myself of the mutinous idea of yelling "go to hell", throwing away my rifle, and walking into a cold shower. Later, I asked several of the men what they thought of and they said they too were wondering how long they could last.

Finally the colonel came before our rank. I shot the rifle up but gripped it a little below the balance. Gigged! Well, so were a lot of others, I thought. [They called their rifles "gig sticks."] The rifle was a Springfield, and you remember that I formerly had an Enfield. I'm not quite used to a perfect manual of arms off this one (i.e. without glancing down).

We marched back again and had barracks inspection, short & sweet. When finally we were set free, I felt like a new man. Now, after a dinner with a couple of other guys at the Service Club, a weekly luxury I plan, and a cold shower, with a thunderstorm outside & the *barracks comparatively quiet and thinking about you I feel very comfortable and relaxed. Since dismissal, I've had four cokes, 2 iced teas, at least a gallon of water (really), a bottle of milk, a glass of lemonade and a glass of beer.*

The Coast Artillery is running this giant operation that graduates a new set of second lieutenants every week, and there is some doubt in my Cadet's mind about the usefulness of the whole operation, though I do act as if I must get through the dammed course no matter how, and I feel sorry but encouraged when each week a few men less belong to each class of the school and are replaced by men who have been moved back for having flunked one of the score of special components of the curriculum.

The curriculum consists largely of technical subjects until several administrative ones are studied in the last weeks. The math gives me trouble, the mechanics not so much as you might expect, given my life-long immersion in matters intellectual. I finish high in most academic subjects, in deportment, and in field exercises. In the final analysis, the curriculum is likely to be of limited use; a battalion ends up with an ordinance expert who is called to say whether a piece is easily repaired, should be sent to base ordinance, or should be junked. What, then, was important? The firing was important, maneuvering also, and communications, and intelligence, and planning. These were nevertheless slighted. So, too, were genuine training in the leadership of a group, in group relations and inter-relations, in coordination between platoons, batteries, and battalions, between infantry, tanks, friendly aircraft and the automatic anti-aircraft weapon systems.

A certain all-over atmosphere was nurtured. There was scant indication that it was intentional, but it probably was. Its core was a deliberately produced staggering fatigue, bringing a weakness of body and mind into which were introduced a tolerance for irrationality, a poignant desire to obey the slightest command to perfection, and a crowd complex arbitrating against comradeship, cliques, criticism and doubt.

Close order drill was fanatically pursued. The barracks platoon was the drill unit. The Lieutenant was the leader and Instructor, and after a time began to put us through the hoops. "Forst, front and center!" "March the platoon to the mess-hall!" "Yes. Sir!" Salute. Rightabout face. "Platoon, Shoulder, Arms! Left, Face!" And one hopes for the best. Cadet de Grazia should have done better. I hardly managed to scrape through. I had acquired stage fright. Nor had I any experience worth mentioning. My voice, ordinarily loud and clear, emerged uncertain. Here was a source of gigs, once, twice.

I would have had less trouble had I believed in close order drill. I thought it ludicrous for modern warfare. But how else do you get an organized crowd from one place to another? "Follow me!"? No; there was good enough reason to have an orderly procession in rhythmic motion to go between a number of points. I did, actually, begin to enjoy the marching:

> *(Y)esterday was very strenuous, but I don't feel it at all. We walked four miles in an hour with pack & rifles, very good time for a marching column or for anyone for that matter. Our platoon is full of good marchers & singers, so we really swing along. It is really a sight to watch us in action, no 'hut-trip-thrup-fore' is necessary. Two seconds and the column is right in the groove, swaying from side to side like a metronome.*

The worst of the experience was the continuous nagging and scolding from pre-dawn to lights out, and in the darkness of night, the shadowy men still fearfully, feverishly, working at shining, sewing, ordering gear, pushing a rag through a rifle barrel. The sleeplessness stunned the mind, five hours, six hours, occasionally interrupted by mock air raids, guard duty, special details. And upon the same minds were piled reading and lectures loaded with information; the memory reacted bizarrely, recalling only snatches, retaining facts only for short periods of time. As the summer deepened and the misery intensified, the commandant granted a few minutes' increase in the dosage of sleep, sounding assembly at a gracious 05:50 hours. Then came the heat - crawling up to 110 degrees at times - the rains, humidity, and mosquitoes, sleep murderers all.

DDT had not been invented. The mosquitoes prowled and swarmed. On the march, no one dared brush one off, less he be scolded and gigged. So many gigs, though a specific number was not to be known, and a man would be sent packing. You marched in perfect symmetry, stiff, sweating, shuffling in that peculiar U.S. Army military style so different from the British or the German, or most others of the day. Your eyes never shifted. They focused on the burnt neck of the man ahead, where you could see the mosquito alight, immerse its proboscis, swell up with blood, and swoop off heavily, as you dully, silently remarked the incident, helpless to aid, and awaited your turn.

Since it appeared most unlikely that the enemy would attack American shores with any force that would not be given short shrift by the Coast Guard, the top brass designated the Coast Artillery to take over the anti-aircraft function, and indeed the school was named for this, the Anti-Aircraft Artillery, more technical and complicated than field and coastal artillery operations, since it fires three-dimensionally against its target.

But how many planes can the enemy have? They are already losing large numbers of them, both in the Pacific and Atlantic Theaters. Their manufacturing ability diminishes from month to month so far as one can tell. The response to heavy enemy losses in the air is that anti-aircraft artillery should be used for ground fire as much as or more than for aircraft fire, and I finally wax enthusiastic when at midpoint in the proceedings we get some instruction on how to lower the 90mm, the 40mm, and the 50 cal. guns against ground targets such as tanks, bunkers, trucks, and attacking infantry. But the Coast Artillery Corps is speaking rather modestly in these regards, because if it moved whole-heartedly into field artillery operations it would surely incite conflict on the highest levels in Washington, and might indeed lose out to the field artillery.

Actually, by the time my class graduated with all due ceremony upon the blazing finale of August, a day when only a few men fainted from the heat, the CAC was already suffering heavy unemployment, and yet was swallowing up enormous resources for the production of weaponry and training of manpower, both of

A Cadet in North Carolina

which could be quickly turned around into gains instead of losses on the balance sheet, except that the organization costs were enormous. All the ideology, planning, ordering, assigning, transporting and so on of a half million men and their logistical support and weaponry were aimed at a war that no longer was happening.

This certain Cadet didn't spend too much time doing a full-scale study of what would have him court-martialed as a shadowy minor version of General Billy Mitchell; I was struggling to keep in line with the steers passing through the corral gates. I was neat as a pin, fast as lightning, clever at quizzes, silent and unprotesting. When the management, or let us say "Commandant" for that sector and age, passed out a form asking for self-criticism of the program, I knew better than to go to the heart of the matter; instead, I expressed myself strongly on an annoying habit of the cadets: so automated generally, still, when they were let into the dining room, they rushed to the tables and gobbled up everything in sight, without an if-you-please, generally behaving like exhausted boorish laborers at a rooming house of South Chicago. I said there should be rules about manners.

The management leapt to it and I was gratified to see a notice posted shortly to all cadets, warning them to behave as officers and gentlemen at table or else. To act snooty is much safer than being a conscientious "trouble-maker".

I was not, you may gather, fond of my fellow cadets. They appeared narrow-minded and unsophisticated, humorless, and desperately selfish, like drowning men. If I behaved toward them humanely, cooperatively, correctly, it was because I appreciated their suffering and was suffering myself. I wondered why there was so little camaraderie: it was the Command's fault. The cadets could afford neither ideals nor a critical attitude; they could not be charitable, could not extend sympathy to their fellows. I noted: *"A few days ago, the platoon applauded a lieutenant who announced he was leaving for overseas duty. That night, the Battery Commander rose and reprimanded us. 'You were heard applauding. That is the last I expect to hear. You have no feelings - you do not cheer, laugh, or boo.' He's a very popular fellow, you can gather."*

I made friends named Tom Powers, Hanrahan and Jim Fisk, all Easterners and of the 'auld sod, it would appear, plus a Rutgers man named Mills who enjoyed a large literary background. We would go roam together for a day in Wilmington or at the ocean beach. Or simply go over to the Service Club for a beer or food.

An acquaintance, Harvey Sherman, had come to Camp Davis a few weeks ahead of me; we had known each other studying political science at the University of Chicago. Harvey saw my name on the list of newcomers and came to find me; his somber face was for me good news. Harvey seemed confident and gave the best of counsel; that he was on the beam was demonstrated by his return, following graduation and leave, as an Instructor in the School. With him came and went my most valuable friend, and the only possibility of discussing world affairs and administrative management seriously. Harvey's girl Nebbie, who had been of the same group of students, worked in the War Department; her letters spoke contemptuously of the indolent supernumeraries infesting the place.

Other Chicagoans surfaced. After Sherwyn Ehrlich, there came Godfrey Lehman from the University. They struggled along, evincing the same symptoms as the rest. Lehman got the bright idea - and had the cash - to reserve a room at the beach for every weekend, and, although he was off-and-on a pain in the neck, his accommodations permitted me to spend two nights away from Camp. Money was a problem until the end came. The first weeks were made even more dismal by a delay in receiving my barracks bag from Tyson and by being broke. I remained practically penniless through the summer.

There is nothing to do of a week-end around here. A good number of the fellows go away, thinking thereby to ease the strain. I suppose it does but I can't afford it & probably wouldn't enjoy it. It costs about 10 bucks to get away overnight and do anything. I've got to keep expenses down as much as possible, spending my money mostly on cigarettes, cokes, ice cream & candy bars to ease the pangs of hurried and bad meals, and shoe polish. Going to show Sat night and perhaps the beach on Sunday are sufficient pleasures. I'd as soon cut out all weekends and get this damned grind over sooner. But then again I wouldn't be able to write you a long weekend letter such as I plan every Sat. & Sun."

I ask her to send money, though it must arrive late:

> Dearest wife,
>
> Just a note to say hello and to ask you for a little money. My baggage has not yet arrived and won't probably until next Sunday. That won't be too bad; I'm getting used to it. But I am down to a few cents & would appreciate a $5 bill tucked in a little love letter and sent air mail.
>
> I went down to the ocean today for a wonderful two hours of relaxation. The army provides a convoy of trucks to bring the men down & back. The ocean was pretty calm, the water not quite cold enough, and the beach very pleasant."

She jestingly confesses to me her "extravagances."

> Sweetheart,
>
> You at last have sufficient grounds for divorce - if you want them. "Judge - not only did she refuse to get up to make my breakfast, not only did she insult me bitterly when I got up, but - but, Judge, she spent all my money".
>
> Well I did - but I'm sure you won't mind. (Hah) Just remind me never to complain to you about money, a thing I do periodically I think, just for the hell of it. (Really, darling, I never actually worry about money. We've got lots - for us. But sometimes people start owing me a lot, and I just get sore.)
>
> Anyway, I just relaxed into a state of infantilism when I got your check. Maybe you'll feel better when you hear what I got. An itemized account is herewith forthcoming:
>
> | | |
> |---|---:|
> | One bond for us both (I guess I'd better put that first) | 18.75 |
> | One pair very high-heeled shoes (navy blue) from Joseph's (reduced from 8.95) for Al | 4.95 |

One blue & white silk dress from Saks	
(reduced from 11)	5.95
One Saks bag for Mom (reduced from 5 or 6)	2.00
One for me (blue to match shoes) " "	2.00
One fountain pen for me	3.50
One pair play shoes (white) which are going	
back to Saks tomorrow	4.00
	41.15

I feel pretty good 'cause everything I got is pretty-pretty, which you like, and everything on sale, which deludes me into thinking myself a sharp trader. I shall look very spiffy for early September when you get home. Fortunately all these things are too dressy to wear to work.

Saks is open now on Wednesdays til 9 o'clock for, quote, war-workers (that's a laugh) and career girls. That makes it convenient though. After I got thru I came up North & am writing this letter at your folks.

Is there anything you need or like? Incidentally, I raised my monthly bond deduction from $2 to $16, figuring that I really should give 10% as they say.

So, as you see, I'm feeling very opulent. Part of it is that I got a $90 dividend or rather, quarterly payment from home.

But I had worse problems than our personal finances; the lecturers were clear, understandable, but uninteresting, and I was tired; I had to watch myself carefully and continuously to avoid falling obviously asleep in the sultry classroom. *"The rat race here,"* I wrote, *"is getting almost ludicrous. Yesterday, during the showing of a training film, row after row of men dropped off to sleep, a truly amazing sight. I actually fell asleep today standing up, listening to a demonstrative lecture. I just got behind my sunglasses & lowered my lids, like an old plow-horse catching a few winks while the farmer's off to lunch. A grand melee occurs at every break in the vicinity of the Coke dispenser. I'm a raving advertisement for Coca Cola. It's all that stands between us & oblivion a good part of the day."*

I did rather well with the mechanical operations of the School. My only moment of embarrassment came one evening when I was supposed to dismantle the new Garand semi-automatic rifle while blindfolded. I could not do it in the allotted time and was left behind with the instructor, fortunately not the meanest of them, who tried to get me going on it and then decided not to harry me through to the very end; so I had a piece left over: I wondered afterwards if it was crucial to the weapon's operation. The Garand rifle itself is an interesting case, a complicated bulky weapon meant for long range and for accuracy, for the kind of war which was not being fought. Too few of the enemy were struck by it at rifle distance, the mortar and sub-machine gun being far more suitable for the scenarios of encounter. And the continuously pounding artillery for farther away.

The officer's .45 caliber Colt automatic was a fossil, supposedly the very thing needed for stopping an otherwise unstoppable Filipino gone berserk in the War of Independence of 1899-0. An anachronism. I doubted it was useful. So finally did the army, and, if you were up front, you got to pick up an officer's light carbine that could hit something at a fair distance with a .30 cal bullet and fire a few shots without reloading, or, better yet, for moments of surprise, an automatic tommy-gun.

Not then or ever had I heard reliably of, or witnessed, a bayonet being used to stick a live standing enemy; bayonets were used to herd prisoners of war, and on occasion to despatch a wounded enemy in violation of the laws of war. And, of course, to slice baloney and open cans. Yet they were standard equipment along with the gas mask that by universal tacit agreement was not worn at the front but had to be worn here at camp. I liked the bayonet:

> *"..yesterday we went out on short maneuvers and I enjoyed the vigorous activity and the freedom that can't be taken from a man who is crawling along the ground with his heart next to the ground and his eyes towards the enemy. I still like skirmishing better than anything else in the army. This morning we had bayonet practice and I like that too. I get awfully vicious when I have one in my hands and am pretty good at it. It's just like a good old free-for-fall, smash!, slash, butt stroke, jab, thrust and smash!"*

The Home Front was a busy scene all the while I was sweltering in North Carolina. Jill had a box seat: she was now employed in the Office of the Corporation Counsel of the City of Chicago, actually working upon political analyses and propaganda on behalf of the wicked Kelly-Nash Machine. Chicago, like all the cities of the country, held a grand preparedness and win-the-war parade, of which she tells:

> *Anyway, the only nice thing that can be said for today is that the parade is over. The* Sun *man did a much better job of describing it, for purposes of general consumption and public morale, than I am going to do. His prose was richer, his* Weltanschauung *a more lovely thing than mine. But maybe I saw more, in my weasely way. You may caption the following a worm's eye view of the Great Chicago Parade of fawty-two.*
>
> *I can state officially that it was a fine parade, undoubtedly, bigger, longer, better, with more floats, legionnaires and labor unionites than the New York Parade. It lasted twice as long (14 hours to New York's seven). And it probably got started twice as late and got behind schedule twice as easily.*
>
> *We arrived at the appointed meeting place at 10 o'clock. That was on Superior over by Lake Shore Drive. We milled around for about two hours, advancing two steps every ten minutes, until we finally reached Michigan Avenue about 12:30. Naturally there was plenty of opportunity in that time for members of our little band to detach themselves and forage in search of women, beer and sandwiches. I was pleased to note that none of the Corporation counsels got tight, unlike Some Other municipal employees I saw (Sewers, Election Commissioners). Several of them hugged women, others joined Licenses (Bureau of) in song. The latter department had several good Irish Tenors. Naturally, your own unique wife foraged and found in her own unique way. I admired several participants from either Mines or Health, I couldn't figure out which, who in turn admired me and allowed me to clap an oxygen mask on my face and inhale pure oxygen. It was a device used in mine rescue work, which they saw fit to carry in the parade. I got kind of high on the oxygen but it wore off very rapidly.*

When we finally got started it wasn't so bad, and it was singularly uneventful. Kelly was still in the reviewing stand at Congress St. when we passed by there at one o'clock. Little Hodes led our contingent manfully; it was a gallant thing to do, considering what a sloppy crew we were, in colorless civilian mufti, red-eyed from sleepiness and the big spot lights on Michigan Avenue. Our float was a lot of flowers and a girl from the stenographer's division who has very long platinum hair (natural) whom they dressed up in a white robe to represent Justice or maybe it was Sex. We got to 12th St. finally and Lundy and I started towards the I.C. We walked past our float to congratulate the stenographer, and at that moment, the driver emerged from wherever he was in the flower-covered truck and fell unconscious to the pavement, poisoned by carbon monoxide. Somebody gave him artificial respiration and they finally took him away in an ambulance. I hope he lives. I'm sure the Law Department was the only contingent in the whole parade whose driver got poisoned. And they're probably the only body in a position to fend off lawsuits successfully.

That was the great parade of Chicago, from where I was sitting. The floats were elaborate, the women beautiful, the men heroic, but the best thing in it was a sign on one of the Sewer Department trucks, namely:

> United We Stand
> Divided We Fall
> If You Want a Sewer
> Call the City Hall

And then, to boost civilian morale by fearful mimicry of Europe, the whole great Chicagoland rehearsed a blackout:

The blackout was a great success, from all newspaper reports. You know, they blacked out the entire Lake Michigan area, even as far as the Province of Ontario in Canada, and including the 1400 block on 60th street. At the last minute I became rather hesitant about taking a bath in the dark, so I just sat at the window and watched nothing and the wardens flashing about with their green lights. Like Carter Harrison, who gave out such a statement to the press, probably in imitation of me, I just sat and contemplated the glories of the past.

Besides, I was feeling rather enfeebled, since at first-aid class last night I played dead dog for a couple of ambitious artificial respirationers. One of them, a cute girl who attends with her cute husband, was very good about it, but the other girl who took over from her damn near bashed in my ribs. I am still breathing in long whistling sighs.

I begged for more letters, exclaiming at their indispensability. She puts a condition on such a plethora, however:

Darling,..

You must accept certain qualifying conditions if you are to reap the great joy of receiving a daily letter from me:

1) You must promise not to save my letters. Obviously, very few of these missives will contain much that is beautiful, true, enduring or touching. Most will be compendiums of the iconoclastic rubbish that passes daily through my mind, of my faulty actions, of my ephemeral observations on life as it is lived by a 9-to-5 gal. You would hardly want to carry these jerky missives through the Sturm und Drang *[What the hell does that mean?] of battle. And I certainly don't want to envision our little love nest of the future, with one room devoted to the De Grazia's and their four or was it six pups, the other ten piled to the ceiling with beribboned packages of early Oppenheima.*

... I am getting insomnia again, probably because I miss you so much, & am edgy as a fox. I got very disgusted with map making today & told everybody so & in general was disagreeable. I wish I had a job in the outdoors. I get so sick of being at a desk. I hope we'll be able to live in the country when you come back. I don't think that being a housewife would be so bad in the country. I would bike to market every day & buy sharply & well. Then I would paint the furniture, tend a garden, & maybe type your PhD thesis at night. I don't see why that isn't a good way of living, even tho I have at times intellectually rebelled against being dependent on a man. But despite all my intellectual protestations to the contrary, I'm not a careerist; at least, every job I've ever had I've viewed as a stopgap, certainly not as

> a career, & always end up setting up some other object (you!) as the end of life. I've got the brains, I guess, but not the temperament of a career girl. And I just don't like being indoors all the time.

I couldn't agree more. I was made to hate this country of sprawling barracks, trailer camps, swamps and sand, but I dreamed of a country like Glen Park on the Fox River where I spent my childhood summers, all shade, coolness, running waters, unspecialized farms, wooden cottages with screened porches, where there would be no drill-step. The affair of my bouncing walk is worth a few lines: it almost cost me my commission.

The de Grazia way of walking was a loping bouncing style that covered ground rapidly and was perfectly comfortable over long stretches of beach and road. However, it was not the ordinary nor the Army way, and in OCS there was one correct way, the Army way. The fault lay partly in being conspicuous. Everyone knew this and said it and rediscovered it every week: when a Candidate became obvious for some reason, standing out from the crowd, he was on his way down and out. The De Grazia walk was noticeable in the compact and perfectly uniform marching of the troop as it was drilled. Though perfectly in step, I bounced a little.

In a full marching battalion, everyone had to take the same measured step and raise himself off the ground by the same measured height and had to move his arms back and forth from the trouser side seam, and could not bend his knees any more than it took to reach the required pace; you had to keep off your toes and march on your heels, a flat shuffle that contrasted notably with the English, German and Russian stiff swinging. It was an insult to American manhood to have to march in a way that denied Abe Lincoln and Davy Crockett and all the people you see in America clambering along the ridges of Tennessee or Vermont or California, but there you were in the blazing heat of the Carolinas with mosquitoes sucking the blood on the back of your shaved neck and you had to march that way or else.

So I did. I wrote home finally that I had conquered the lope. It was paramount in a growing pattern of small triumphs, ever more resounding in the barracks now partly emptied and silenced by departing failures. I no longer wrote letters raising the subject of indignant resignation over the impracticality, psycho-social sadism, and false standards of the school, or implying that I may be thrown out. I was now corrupted and confident to the point of arrogance. I will be arrogant when I graduate. On August 1, I score in the top dozen of 360 cadets taking a 2.5-hour gunnery exam. On August 4, I write:

> *I'm in quite good health, something that a great number of the men can't say. Today the man in ranks alongside me collapsed right into my arms, puking the meanwhile. I awakened last night by chance and actually found myself amid a bedlam of mutterings and short cries. About six men were talking in their sleep at the same time. A large number of men are bothered no end by a heat rash which in some cases covers the body and limbs. I guess I can take any punishment they can dish out. In fact the only way I'll leave this hole which I hate worse than anything is with my bars or by polite and firm request.*

Yet the suffering continues:

> *You rant about officer's training, dearest, and you have my sublime agreement. Yesterday was a Saturday, the likes of which I hope to see never again. The usual early rising was followed by exercises, breakfast, furious polishing, and an examination in searchlights, sound locators and electricity. After that we were lectured and given a demonstration on 268, the highly secret radio locator which can spot planes at tremendous ranges.* [This would be the new radar equipment.] *It is no secret that with it planes can be shot down in utter blackness, to the surprise & dismay of the pilots. Following this, we had a bite of lunch, and rushed to form for inspection. For hours we stood on hot pavement that burnt right through our shoes. I was actually below ground level when the inspection was ended, so soft was the cement and so still did we have to stand. Every agony and despondent thought passed through my mind as the hot sun beat down.*

My girl back home is showing me how smart she is: she would certainly have no trouble with my exams and nothing else I was doing, for that matter, and how she would love the chance to go through it all!

>Darling -
>
>I am sitting outside on the Midway watching the sun go down in an eruption of pink clouds. Which puts an obvious time limit on my writing you since any minute it will get dark with a bang.
>
>My eyes are rolling around in my head like a pair of loose Brussels sprouts. I was over at Rosable's for dinner (part of our joint drive to live well at a price) and afterwards she starts to talk about psychological testing, so I says why not, and proceed to waste my time and substance in an exhibitionistic display of test-taking. I took a mechanical aptitude and an intelligence test. The results of both of which surprised me, in opposite directions. I ranked in the 98 percentile in both, which was funny, because I thought I was low in mech. ability & high in intelligence. Really, whenever I take a general int. test I am always sure I am going to get 100 and feel aggrieved at anything less. The source of this astonishing instance of self confidence I can't explain, certainly I'm not so sure of myself in other spheres of activity. I guess I've just got into the habit of knowing a little about everything and nothing about anything, and so feel that my territory is being invaded when I miss out on a piddling detail.

I have had enough of math and instruments and tests, but lust:

>....Lately, it has been occurring to me that much of the pother about words as weapons has its refutation or at any rate some relation to what I've been doing. The social scientists & semanticists fulminate against words with emotional overtones. Yet look here at the terms from a blueprint before me: screw, washer, lug, ring, window, adapter, nut, balls, hole, worm female (socket), male (plug), follower, retainer and many others. All of these words are double-meaning, some of them blushingly so, yet no one worries about changing the vocabulary of mechanics. The men who work with them are conscious, too, of the similes. Hypothesis: It is not the terminology, but the subject-matter of

> *a science which gives it difficulty with the emotions.*
>
> *The check came - merci, my sweet little one - but I'll try not to cash it. I think Saturday is when the eagle shits.*
>
> *I got the marriage certificate back today & have now folded it carefully into my wallet, so that when I look for money I don't find it but find something just as good....*
>
> *About my progress report. Darling, there is no doubt in my mind that I'll be a better officer than 90% of the men around me. I've cut out the bounce very effectively, and in the future will use it only to cover a long distance easily & hurriedly. With you. Among company, I won't use it. Many of the men have had official dressings-down, a thing I haven't experienced yet, I guess because I just naturally look like an officer.*
>
> *The major inspects us minutely. He glances at a rifle, over which a man lost a night's sleep. "Rusty rifle, gig him for inattention to duty." His handkerchief dangles from his pocket, his posture is that of a bar fly, his walk almost outbounces mine, and his attitude that of a county hall politician. Any of those habits would dispose of us poor candidates.*

She continues in the nostalgic vein:

> *I'll never forget how nice it was to be wakened by you when you came in early one Sunday morning with Hank. I had been waiting up for you til late that night before - very mindful of waiting for Santa Claus when I was a kid (well, I did), and finally, and with difficulty, I went to sleep with the happy knowledge that when I woke up you'd be there. And all of a sudden you were - & I got up, still more than half asleep and drooped all over you. It was a fine and memorable feeling.*
>
> *Jimmy Durante was on the* Baby Snooks *program and he affects me the same way as M. Fields and the Marx frères do, i.e., he kills me. He has that highly original, subtle-buffoo tho he isn't subtle, style that I snobbishly feel can only be appreciated by intellectuals. There is a song he sings called "Did you ever feel like going when you wanted to stay?" that is a masterpiece of what I don't know. If you ever can get to it, he sings it in* The Man Who Came to dinner -

> *and you've got to hear it.*
> *...I see by today's* Times *that Dorothy Dix advises people writing soldier boys to make their letters jolly. So many people write sorrowful letters to the boys and then the boys get sorrowful and Miss Dix gets sorrowful, etc.*
>
> *P.S. Can you send me one of those little Coast Artillery pins. Bill Cate's wife Jane wears one of the air corps, which he's in, and it's very pretty.*

It is remarkable that her letters did not irritate me with their expansive sociability. Hardly a day passed without her taking in visitors, female and male, or traipsing about the city with them, when it wasn't all of these. To wit:

> *When I got home from work yesterday afternoon I raced down to the lake, where I spent the afternoon pleasantly chatting with John and Polly Hart and swimming. Then I dropped over to Tallman's to see what she was doing for dinner, the idea of eating alone appalling me, and we went to Morton's which has re-opened in the style* moderne *and stinks, and I had lobster tails. The joint is very expensive now, too, besides being pretentious looking. But I felt fine after an eight-course dinner because I had begun to sicken of my sardine-on-bread suppers. Then I went back to Jane's house to get my bike and all of a sudden all the fairy-foot men she knows descended on her and lo there was beer and a party. Somewhere in the midst of all these covert and overt homosexuals, Johnny Wiggins showed up. We rushed out into Jane's lovely garden and had a rousing game of night baseball until I lost the ball; then we took an extended trip on the bike to fill up the tires with air, during which I lost my keys which necessitated another extended trip to find them. Johnny has only read Freud and Damon Runyan, and it gives his conversation a color not obtainable elsewhere. I think he is a good guy, do you?*
>
> *A boy named Sid Rolfe was at Jane's too, and we had a protracted conversation about you. He told me to tell you that he has gotten a candidacy, straight from civilian life, to the School for Military Government at Charlottesville, Va. (I wrote this all down, dutifully)*

and that this school is for administrators of occupied countries after the war, and that if anybody in the world is qualified for this work, you are, and that if you are interested, the man he saw and that you might contact is a Lieut. Col. Joseph Harris. It sounds pretty good to me. This boy has had some experience in public administration. He is also running for some minor office in Lake County. He is beyond doubt a Commie, and was under the impression you were, too, an impression I promptly dispelled. John thought so too. I tried to explain that you were more iconoclastic than anything. As a matter of fact your position, or rather lack of it, is difficult to explain to other people, although I feel it instinctively and can pretty well know in advance how you are going to stand on various matters. But you even refuse classification as a New Republic liberal. As Sid said, it must be sort of funny being a man's wife and not being able to explain his political views. I said I didn't think it was funny at all, and besides it wasn't the case.

Of course, we talked about the war and it was nice to discuss it with an informed person. I read him a passage or two from Buzz's [my brother in Washington] *last letter to me which will interest you too. "It turns out that American equipment in Libya, both tanks and guns, is very good, despite Axis propaganda to the contrary. The British defeat was due mainly to a tactical blunder it now appears. All sorts of reinforcements have been rushed, especially air, & the Br. have been blasting away like hell ever since. Claude the Auchinleck has been doing some fast thinking & acting. Monday at lunch we had Seversky, Nash the New Zealand prime minister, and Commodore Perry of the* Graf Spee *battle. Seversky & Perry agreed that the* Graf Spee *battle was probably the last purely sea battle. Seversky, speaking broken English, seems to know his onions, but the Commodore was simpletonish & oh so sweet & conservative, & so pathetically appealing in his self-awareness of his conservatism. Nash was neutral ... etc." Interesting, what?*

Somehow, despite Russian reverses, I can't help still feeling that the war will be decided in this year, with the next as a melancholic afterlude....

I had gotten into the habit of mirthless recitals:

A Cadet in North Carolina

> *We are beginning to lose a few men. A number will be dropped next week, too. A couple left from nervous prostration, a few from illness, and now some for flunking courses and not meeting the "leadership" requirements. A guy across from me who has a degree in Civil Engineering is leaving soon. It's so senseless. His talents should be utilized in more than a non-commissioned position. But he can't bellen out his commands and doesn't cut a military figure.*
>
> *...Incidentally, if you happen to see Gordon Hall, collect $5 from him, lost to me when the Germans didn't take Moscow in June. Sneer, too, while you count the crumpled bills. I would, if I could be there...*

She apologizes for not being sufficiently sentimental and romantic:

> *Sometimes I wish I could write love letters. Rosable and I were talking about that this morning. I know I never really say anything to you that could possibly go down in the history of fiery epistles, and it must be disappointing to you sometimes. The most I ever get off is some bright little remark about missing and/or loving you, and that I never do in any particularly original way. You, on the other hand, could be very adept at love letter writing and are, frequently. I guess you know I love you by now, but you might possibly like to hear it in a different form, now and then. But how can I speak of romance when this goddam typewriter slides all over the place, for one thing? (I lost my pen.) And I guess I really don't much care for love letters, for some reason or other. I probably got the idea in my early adolescence that they were mushy, and never have gotten over that post-pubertal embarrassment at either receiving or sending them. I don't like movies about love either, although I don't mind reading a good psychological novel about the subject. I guess it's because the ordinary brief expression of the love motif, as in movies or letters or most short stories, tends to be corny just because of the necessity of condensing the whole thing into a few black and white symbols. But tell me you love me - that I like to hear. Shit on this typewriter!*
>
> *Your loving wife,*
>
> *Jill*

To read my letters, you might get the notion that affairs were in a deplorable state at Camp Davis:

> *Due to the large number of cases of heat prostration, Sat. afternoon inspections will now be held on Sat. morns. Probably Sat. Aft. off, I hope to do a little pleasant reading of the* New Yorker. *Bill's battery had a dozen men faint last week on the parade ground. A little jeep was kept busy scurrying about the ranks to collect them....Nor do conditions improve:...Everyone is depressed this week. It is very tough academically, in addition to the usual pother about polishing and shining. More guys have flunked and they feel pretty low. Several have moved out of the barracks for reasons of academic ineptitude or "leadership". Tom Powers, next to me, feels badly because he just got a letter from his mother assuming he would graduate & he has flunked gun gunnery. I hate the whole goddam setup so much that I have constantly to hold myself in check.*

My war continues relentlessly:...

> *This week we are firing the guns over the ocean at targets drawn by planes. It's tough to hit the damned things. Sea-coast artillery is pie compared to it. Our target speeds are ten times as fast and we have a third dimension to cope with. You can understand how elated we would be if a tank lumbered at us. We'd depress the 90 mm barrel and blow it to hell.*
> *We swim every noontime. I think I'm on life guard duty tomorrow, duty consisting mainly of blowing a whistle so that each man can grab a buddy who will keep an eye on him.*
> *Harvey, another looie & I had a long talk last night about morale & relative fighting effectiveness of German, Jap & U.S. troops. Harvey is convinced of the all-importance of morale. Despite my predilection for problems of morale, I'm not at all so feeling on the subject. Mainly I define morale more broadly, and feel that there are things that compensate for a fanatical politicalism -- ingrained aggressiveness, physical self-confidence, etc.*

A Cadet in North Carolina

For her, politics is the order of the day, "McKeough for Congress," it develops, is the big push of the machine.

> ...I didn't write you Tuesday night because I got started working out some scheme for promoting McKeough to the housewives of the state and all of a sudden it was 10 o'clock. The scheme was one of those cards for housewives to post in their kitchens giving the list of foods that are price-controlled - it's been done by OCD [Office of Civil Defense] but not very decoratively - and also leaving a space for writing in the food bargains of the week which they could erase slate-like. However, Rubin put thumbs down on it for a reason that was good but that I can't remember now.
>
> I'm working pretty hard these days for me. I've gotten up a leaflet instructing absentee voters and service men on how to vote, and also enjoining one and all to register. And also some letter forms that absentee voters can use to send in for their ballot applications. It was my idea - the leaflet was - but I notice that I don't get any credit for it since it all goes through Rubin's hands. I don't care much, since that's the way publicity and advertising offices, or any kind of office for that matter works, and I am past disillusionment. And besides it's nice having something else to do but maps. I still haven't finished the ward maps yet and Hodes is on my neck every day. But I do hope that when the time comes when Hodes says to Rubin, what the hell good is that girl for anyway, Rubin will assert my usefulness, paltry as it may be. They've worked up that story book business I did on Curly Brooks into a very cute little booklet - a professional production man did the job and didn't change my copy too much and added a lot of humorous touches. We all hope it gets into print, since it is a very whimsical and new form of campaign propaganda. However, we do know that the professional politicians from the central committee aren't given to as much whimsy as our office....

I continue to gripe:

> The petty discipline goes on and most of the time I ignore it. Curses on the forces which make a man go through this to be an officer! The buck private is the only man that can look himself

squarely in the eye in this goddamned army. If I obeyed my impulses I would be in the guardhouse half the time and a good fighting soldier the other half. All this nauseating concern over shiny shoes, conventions of courtesy, debasing rigmarole will never win the war, but sometimes I think that I am one of the few persons concerned with that little matter.

...A bare thirty days to go. Wowee! 96 men flunked the course in Directors; I got thru OK. 300 took the course.

...You would love to see these guns go off. The firing point is a continuous bedlam. Our classrooms (we are in class drawing up and solving firing problems part of the time) are about 50 yards from the big guns, farther from the 37 mm, 40 mm, .50 and .30 cal machine guns. An aeroplane drags along a target sleeve continuously and everything that can shoot opens fire. The building shakes, we put figures in the wrong squares, & the graph squares look like ticker tape. I keep a wad of cotton in my left ear which is next to the window in order to keep it from ringing. We fired the 90's at a horizontal target today on the water. The blast from the guns whips back one's trousers and scares up a lot of sand. The splash can be seen on or near the target. It probably would interest you to know that in cases where tank armor has been too heavy to pierce with the 90 shell going at 2700 ft per sec., the shell has ricocheted and the impact was so fierce that sufficient steel splinters are knocked off inside the tank to demolish the occupants.

Since anything would be a welcome relief from my grumbling, I give you more of life on the Home Front, courtesy Jill de Grazia:

Darling -

...My inner man, which was never dissatisfied in the first place, now satisfied, I can settle down peacefully to ponder on the day's events with you. The war news looks terrible and I challenge you, in your usually unflagging optimism, to make it look any better than it is. Naturally, all we hear about is the second front up here - and then editorial shut-ups from the newspapers. I honestly don't see why they don't do something about invading the continent - anything would be better than a predominant Nazi victory in Russia - even a Dunkirk.

[The German armies were moving in upon Stalingrad.] *Oh well, as the papers say, the military authorities know best. But it would be a ghastly page in history - Russia's fall while we stood by doing nothing.*

Johnny Hess just called to say goodbye - he is leaving tomorrow. He sends you his love - that's just what he said - and I bid him what will probably be our last goodbye for the duration. It seems improbable that he will get any more leaves before he goes over.

...You know, when we lived down on the south shore of Long Island when I was a kid, I used to watch them target-practice, much the same sort of thing you're doing now. Those rickety old airplanes of the 1920's used to drag cones up & down the shoreline. I never saw any hit but we could hear the guns very plainly. Fort Tilden, where they had the coast artillery, was about five or maybe less miles from where we lived. I guess I told you about the time, or maybe it was times, I used to bike up there & look at the soldiers, to the great dismay of my family & nurse. I was nine then, but a sexy girl withal. They had the police out once looking for me.

I felt pretty proud of myself last night. I borrowed some tools from the garage around the corner & took the wheel off my bike & patched that big hole in the tube. While it wasn't a very workmanlike job, because I misread the directions on the can of patching equipment, the tire is holding up fine & the wheel is back on the bike without any parts missing. Of course the bike has a decided list to the starboard now, but it was one of the pleasantest hours I've spent.

I should hate to detail the thousands of deaths by war, famine, and massacre on this day - like every day in these parlous times, but did not Jesus say something about "not a sparrow falls.."? And so in Chicago, Grim Reaper of Mother Nature: we listen:

Darling -

I certainly feel foolish, considering the circumstances under which I am writing this letter. I ran out a moment ago to buy cigarettes, with the intention of having a quiet drag while I was digesting my supper (bacon, eggs, tomato & garlic - and very good too) and writing you. And what should my keen nature lover's eye espy on the ground in front of the house but an adolescent sparrow, out cold.

Perhaps I ought to furnish a little meteorological background to this latest report of St. Frances of the City Hall. It's been raining and storming like hell all day - in fact, the lights in the City Hall went out at 4 and we all got to go home early when they showed no intention of going on again.

Anyway, it's apparently not fit weather for birds, because this little chick is lying there, wet and ugly, like dead. I pushed him with my foot and he stirred a little, so I rushed upstairs, rooted out a small box & paper & put him in it. At the nonce, I am sitting on the john seat writing this. Box with bird is on the bathroom floor, where it is always hot as hell, and where I trust he will dry out so I can release him. However, the chances are that he will die before he dries out.

I just arose from my writing to administer a stimulant to this miserable creature, consisting of one part sugar water, one part Black & White. He tried to bite me, which I take as a good sign. Incidentally, first aid teaches us never to give whiskey as a stimulant, only tea or coffee, but I'll be damned if I'll brew a whole pot of coffee for some miserable bird.

...Generally this has been a bad week for animals. On Monday, the Brookfield Panda died. Tuesday, there was an awful fire at Ringling's circus in Cleveland, & nearly two score beasts were burned to death. Wednesday the City Council passed an ordinance that women can no longer stand or sit at bars but must be served at a table.

The last-named catastrophe moves me not at all, although all sorts of feminist slogans have been burning in the skies since the Mayor & Barney Hodes handed down the word of God. Obviously the law will protect soldiers to a certain extent from whores & consequently venereal disease, the rates for which have been sky-rocketing recently here, & even if it doesn't, it will appease the prohibitionists & military officials who might otherwise make Chicago a restricted area. Personally, I don't give a damn whether I sit at a bar or lie down when I drink - as long as I can.

I certainly hope this bird dries out by the time I go to bed. While I am fond enough of all living things - fond enough of them not to let them die when there is anything I can do about it - I do not count birds as being among my special friends, & would just as soon not spend the night with one. In the first place, I think birds are funny looking.

I am having quite some fun doing a special analysis of the 18th Congressional District for a guy named Butcher, the Democrat who is running against that Trib bitch, Rep. Jessie Sumner. I hope he wins but the figures look bad. I really like my job a lot better now than the first couple of months when I started. I enjoy saying hello to all those silly men who sit behind the throne, & being known by the elevator operators, & answering the phone for Rubin and in general - the feeling that I'm sitting in on some half-important doings...

Enough of her Chicago politics. I reminisce of family:

Darling Jill,
    Tomorrow is Buzz's birthday and I recall those easy days as boys when that was a big day. Buzz and I would be dressed for the occasion and a select crew of little hoodlums would be invited for the occasion which usually broke up in a free-for-all with toys breaking liberally over everyone's head. The climax was blowing out the candles, but being unsatiable kids, one climax wasn't enough and the candles were blown out and blown out until mere shapeless hulks remained. Mrs. Erickson always baked a tremendous sponge cake for our family gatherings and various womenfolk dashed about the house doting on our avarice. We'll have to have such splendid parties for our children some day after we settle down from our lengthy honeymoon without child. Meanwhile a couple of nephews will suffice.

    Gosh, the mortality rate here is terrific. We've lost a number of men from the platoon for a variety of reasons. Out of sixteen men in my row of beds, only four (including myself) have flunked none of the courses. Most will have to take an extra two or three weeks of school before graduating. The school to all intents and purposes is now more of a 14 than a 12-week affair. Some of the men who get through don't deserve to do so and vice versa. It's all a great rat race.

    Speaking about rat races, at Wrightsville Beach Sat. night they had a roulette game in a miniature Coney Island there. A poor harried rat crouched in the middle of the whirling disk and finally dashed into a hole of some color or another. If the color is yours, you are the winnah. The rat never wins. He goes round & round and never comes out.

  We groused around at great length, drinking pop, beer, & cubalibres. Mills had a hotel room full of men and whiskey. Later, Mills & I went swimming & then, since he had no place to sleep, we arranged a mattress for him at our room.

  Mostly we sat around, ate pretty good food and swam. There were a lot of girls on the beach & I don't mean women. The Southern belle is like the rodent plague. She disappears at the age of 16 and is never seen thereafter. Oh, there were a few whose breasts were apparent but words confuse them so. The fact is that I would rather write you a letter than speak to any woman in these parts.

  .... So long, love.

        Al

P.S. Did the sparrow die?
P.P.S. They invariably defecate on one's hands when picked up.
P.P.P.S. I know, I sheltered lots of them when we lived on Hill Street.

No! The bird is not done-in, she reports:

  Oh, that sparrow got to his feet that very night, and even took a couple of spins around the room. I took him downstairs then, because birds in rooms make me very nervous indeed, but he was disinclined to do any more flying. So I took him upstairs again - he was perched on my finger all this while - and made him a little bed on the window sill. Pretty soon he went to sleep, with his head tucked under his wing in authentic sparrow style, and when I woke up in the morning he had flown away. Since then I have been leaving bread on the window sill, in case he comes back. Incidentally, when he dried out, he turned out to be a full-grown adult sparrow, not a baby the way I thought he was when he was all wet....

A Cadet in North Carolina

The month of August nears its end. More and more time is spent on the automatic weapons and there are intimations of a happy ending:

> *Dear love,*
>
> *The imminence of graduation is here, unbelievable and soul-stirring. Smiles are more frequent on some faces, others are a little more drawn. Every day someone thinks of something else to measure Der Tag in terms of. - Fifteen more bottles of milk, two weekends, six more double-timing exercises in the morning, one more dirty laundry list, etc.*
>
> *I still can't say anything for sure, nor can anyone else. The chances are good that I'll light out of here like a scared jackrabbit come the morning of the fourth....*
>
> *Down at the firing point we shot the 35 mms at a sleeve towed by a plane. I was a gunner and every time I kicked the pedal there was a great bang, a whistle, and a nice red tracer shooting out into space...*
>
> *I just got the news of the big Commando raid.* [The Dieppe raid in which half a Canadian force of 6,000 was lost, to no gain; the defeat encouraged pessimists over the prospects of landing successfully an army in France.] *Very interesting but too early to analyze its significance. It's hard to believe that tanks would be risked in a transient skirmish. Perhaps the feints are beginning....*
>
> *Today we were down at the ocean again and did a lot of firing. I got off a beautiful blast in my turn on the machine gun, Browning 30 cal., 250 rounds at a towed sleeve without a pause. That's more firing than most men ever get in the army. It's one complete ammunition belt. Usually the guns stick or jam for a second after a few rounds & goodbye airplane.*
>
> *Later on, we switched to the 40 mms. and again potted at the sleeve with the heavier gun. It was like all hell breaking loose. There were a whole row of 40s, 37s and machine guns shooting away at the same time, and some bigwig got the ingenious idea of making everything hyper-realistic, so a big sound truck parked in the middle and blared forth choice phonograph records of dive bombers, bomb whistles, and sundry explosions.*

> *About that time I was on the director of the 40 mm, with my eyes glued to the telescope, tracking the target and I could see all the tracers converging on the target. But it was hard keeping my attention on the eyepiece when it seemed as if the ground were being blasted away beneath my feet. Tracking is a delicate operation, you see, the slightest jerk of the hand and a big rate is set in which will take the gun off the target completely. Tomorrow we are firing on the anti-tank range about 50 miles away, reached by our favorite conveyance, the horse car,* soixante hommes *et no* chevaux. *That should be fun too.*
>
> *The general of the school was out today to watch us, and expressed an unfavorable comment on the state of our knowledge of the innards of the 37 mm, with only a couple hundred pieces to learn in four days together with the other guns we have to learn. Unhappily, the instructor asked questions of a guy who has slept through most of the last ten weeks. The poor fellow is just yearning to get back to Alaska where he can cool off.*

But some pine needles were flashing in the Southern light:

> *Just now, Hanrahan, the Fordham flash, sitting next to me, is talking me into seeing some show with Betty Grable and Vic Mature in it tonight. I'll probably go if only to kill off a couple of the hours remaining between us.... Chicken Little, the sky is falling! This morning, for the second time, we didn't have to double time before breakfast. Instead, we had a short arm inspection, which didn't appeal very much, apparently, to the inspecting medical major who had to examine 150 penises before breakfast. I can say, though, that that's the easiest test I've ever had in this school....*
>
> *I must dash down to shave now before the latrine gets too crowded. The classroom latrines are really a sight, lines of men at all the bowls and the rest of the room crowded with men smoking & drinking cokes until you can't move around at all. I shall probably expire from delight in the quiet seclusion of a tiled bathroom.*
>
> *Don't bother about the tidiness of the house, Darling. I'll automatically rise at 5 and sweep, mop, dust, shine all the shoes, arrange the closet, fold the blankets and sheets and turn out in the hallway for reveille....*

> Also yesterday, I learned that officially the reason the Americans surrendered on Bataan was because of disease, that they could have held out much longer but for lack of proper food and pills. That almost everyone had scurvy or malaria or severe dysentery or combinations thereof and that the men simply couldn't coordinate their movements because of a lack of vitamin B, and suffered night blindness because of lack of vit A; they couldn't see more than 150 yds away any time. [Here we come upon an important piece of news, without the implications and lessons being afforded the cadets, nor, as we shall see, was there ever enough attention given to the prevention of ill-health and disease as a primary duty of officers. Disease, prevention, morale - sometimes it appeared such words were tabooed, insults to "tough guys," to their machoism - a word not then used - or excuses for "goldbricking.".]

To continue my story, which softens with every passing day:

> Today was easy enough; we spent most of the time examining and taking apart a beautiful 40 mm gun that the U.S. is now producing in copious quantities. It's a Swedish gun adopted by the English & turned over to us. We also fired 30 cal machine guns at toy balloons.
> Around 11:30 we were allowed a swim, though I was life guard half the time allotted. The other guard was a Cal man who guarded maidens & men at Long Beach in the past.
> Next week I'll purchase the remaining bare essentials of an officer's wardrobe. That will include socks, shoes and a khaki suit for the remainder of summer. The rest you can buy with me. Sometime this week Rogers Peet will have my suit ready for try-out. I don't know that my pants will hang on; you can see how much depends on a hearty breakfast when I'm home. ARE YOU PREPARED? Ready or not, etc.

Five days later, in a relaxing mood, I am telling Jill that "Betty Grable is in camp today and causing a great to-do."

> *A number of men from my barracks dashed over to the "lucky" adjoining battery where she was sharing mess with the boys. They came back with glowing accounts of her ravishing beauty, blondness & figure. One even described her as having an ankle bracelet which finished her for me. I already had a pretty good idea of her in my mind,, flashy, high heels with a beach outfit, much make-up, long blonde locks and paunchy jowls with a raucous voice. Exactly; I saw her later while she was eating and, all joking aside, I know ten "26" girls who would pass as her beautiful young sister. In all fairness to the men, they weren't as much enthralled as they were curious. Anyway, one day in the life of the hapless second-weekers she visited went a little swiftly. There's just no comparison between the Betty Grable type, and women like Bette Davis, Joan Fontaine and Katherine Hepburn....*
>
> *I've a lot of letter writing to do. Stouffer* [Professor Sam Stouffer who directs morale research for the Army in Washington] *wants another morale letter but I have so little free time. I must write several other letters here & there, and periodically I worry about the income tax I didn't pay. Could you inquire about the amount and pay it for me?* [This boy has a social conscience!] *I really should do something about it, and I don't think there's any point in asking for a delay for the duration.*
>
> *About the duration and its length, I can't help but be stirred by the bad events in Russia* [the German Army had reached Stalingrad], *but nevertheless persist in a "watch the cat in the bag" feeling, though this may be all too mystic for your caustic, sophisticated soul....*

We even deserve a decent meal:

> *We had a wonderful breakfast this morning for one thing; awakening to an amazing Sunday with the final week ahead. The good cooks were out en masse to give us Freshly Fried Eggs and crisp bacon with JAM and PLENTY OF MILK. I thought I was still dreaming when I finished eating. It was all so good. Those of us who went to breakfast were startled and overjoyed. It seemed as if the Good*

Lord had provided for us this morning with special indulgence. The morning was cool for sleeping and the paper boy came early for a change, a combination of circumstances that reminded me of the wonderful ritual we used to follow of a Sunday morn.

With all of this, I recover in one thrilling moment the full and ringing voice that I had lost early in the game. Now, put in command of the platoon and full battery for marching maneuvers, I call out across the length and breadth of the drill field - "Left, Oblique! Right, Face!" "To the Rear, March!" With splendid precision moving the robots.

Photographers come to take a picture of the battery of stern-faced, strut-backed candidates. All who remain know now that they will be commissioned. I write with friendly hauteur of a visiting West Point cadet group that cannot handle the guns and miss their targets.

Finally, the Army, taking with the one hand and giving with the other, discharges me honorably from the ranks of the enlisted men and, on September 4, in Special Order 121, names me and a lot of others to be members of the most expendable rank in the army, and commands Second Lieutenant Alfred Joseph de Grazia Jr., O-1043313, from Chicago, Illinois, to report within three days at Camp Tyson, Tennessee.

Here I was, ready to lead a panzer division against Rommel, yet back to the boondocks and to the flatulent air-cows I was being forced to go.

Friday morning came and, with it, the departure of a newly fledged Lieutenant. The event went unnoticed in the huge encampment, except that the MP at the Gate, passing me out indifferently, had to cast at me that all-important salute. To which I responded in kind.

CHAPTER FOUR

TEXAS AND THE MOHAVE DESERT

NEWLY vested, smoothly tailored, burnt brown, ramrod-straight and stiff-gaited, I flashed my bars upon Camp Tyson. This earned me a barely furnished, unpainted room in a fresh wooden barrack, on the walls of which a previous occupant had pinned up graphics of nudes and chorus girls, which I now tore down and replaced with pictures of airplanes and a map of the world. I wrote Jill that a fine space remained for her, *"now that all the messy girls déshabillé [sic] are gone."* I also received my new dog-tags, on which the Army had inscribed 0-1043313 and I had substituted "Non-sectarian" for "Catholic;" further I had named my father next of kin rather than my mother, because, as I explain, "he's less likely to go into hysterics if I try unsuccessfully to hit the little man who wasn't there."

I want my wife to become a camp follower:

> *Remember how we lived the first months of our love, moving lock, stock & barrel every week? Well, I think our life in the army would be something like that, footloose hours and many hours of separation when you'd be on your own, quick moves with little baggage, grabbing some things on the run, others at a snail's pace, all very much in the 20th century pattern. Join me and see the country, I say. Cure your neuroses by the super-neurosis-induction method. Knowing you as I do, I'd say you'd like it a lot... Well, Butch, I'll be seeing you...*

I don't see much of my old friends. The segregation of officers from men is both functional and social; they live apart, they make incompatible friends. And some of them have to attend to their wives. Hank Dannenberg has re-married as soon as he got divorced and brought his bride to camp; she is a diminutive, smart and sufficiently attractive Jewish nurse from Buffalo; they drove down in his car for about $50 and live in a room in Paris for $6.00 a week. Gigliotti has dovecoted his cute Irish wife from Pennsylvania in Paris, too. The Lieutenant across the hall is becoming a friend now; he is a curly, black-haired officer called Pinkerton. We play poker, eat at the Officer's Club, see movies, and read. I write long letters, and peruse Jill's longer letters, but I am not up to killing time.

> *Last night was really the time to write you when the air had the coolness of fall and the clouds were hustling by in thick clusters. Instead I waited until now* [the morning] *and spent the evening poring over some materials I have here on tactics and psychology. I'm in the process of drawing up an extensive, rough outline on the subjects of leadership, discipline and morale... The morning has dawned very cold, around 35 degrees, and the hot coffee and pot-bellied stove in the mess hall felt very nice. The news seemed rather cheery, too, with the Russians holding very well at Stalingrad.*

I joke about the self-censorship to which we are exhorted. *"There is xxxxxxxx of xxxxx around here, leading me to believe future global strategy moves into channels other than xxxxxxxx. Don't relate this bit of information, even, to anyone. Can't be too careful. An astute spy system puts everything together like a jig-saw [puzzle]."* Though assiduous scanners of the events-manifold, we have no idea of how much the Army, backed up by the Free Press, was withholding from us. The opening of a Second Front in France is already a perennial concern: the Soviets are in a desperate situation; they are battling 240 Axis Divisions while the Allies in North Africa occupy 15 of them. (Of course, the Allies in Asia are engaging a score of Japanese Divisions.)

As she remarks,
> *I think I should lay off newspapers altogether, if it weren't for my job. There is little comfort that a democrat, using the term generically, can take from the trend of the times. Despite W*[endell] *Willkie, our Russian allies do not love us. This country's strategy is apparently more and more coming under the control of the military*

> *instead of the political (i.e. New Deal commissariat), & I really think that all the Army wants to do is to build up the hugest, and consequently, most un-maneuverable, un-supplyable land force of all time, with the consequence of obliterating Hitler on his own ground being forever negated.*

She is becoming paranoid about draft-dodgers and amazed at the contradictory ways of obtaining officers' commissions in the Armed Forces:

> *I ate at the Commons.* [Hutchinson Commons of the University of Chicago.] *It's amazing how many young men are still around - and also some very young ones, about Ed's age.* [His Brother of 15.] *However, some of them may be boys taking C.A.P. training before induction into the Navy Air Forces. Such was the case with an old office boy from Science Research, who I also met at Int. House while cooking for Beatty. My gosh, they sure are taking some awful specimens if he's one of them.*
>
> *And those were the words of Barney Hodes today too. One of his assistant counsels got a commission, Lt. j.g. & has been waddling around the office in a uniform. Hodes says that he is the most incompetent guy he ever knew - he even filed a suit once in the wrong court! And just got his commission in a breeze, it seems. Hodes says he, Hodes, nearly dropped dead when he heard of it & tho he's glad to get rid of him, he despairs for the Navy.*

The political campaign takes a turn for the worse:

> *And as for politics - the New Deal Democrats are taking & going to take an awful licking. Including Mr. McKeough, I fear. And I must tell you this in private because you are my husband & should share these confidences, I'm beginning to think our candidate is a dope. He's no brainstorm to begin with. And he has come forth with absolutely no promises of positive policy since the campaign began. Stand by the President is the watchword - and the only word, unfortunately. But you vote for him anyway, see!*
>
> *I hope letters to soldiers in the U.S. aren't censorable cause*

> *if they are, somebody's baby is going to be in the brig. And I am your baby, aren't I?*
> *I do love you so much...*

I dutifully vote by mail, weeks ahead of time:

> *I voted two days ago, mostly for men about whom I knew nothing, confirming my long-standing favoritism for the short ballot. By the time you get this letter, all that could be done will have been done. Then, like us, you'll be singing, "Praise the Lord, and pass the Ammunition." Whatever the result, it won't materially change the course of mankind which, as you know, is destined to end up in the bosom of the just and merciful Almighty anyhow. I voted "yes" on all the propositions for reasons known only to myself.*

Our friend - hers more than mine - Johnny Hess, had received his commission at the Tank Corps OCS and heard that his outfit may be going overseas soon. Johnny had been two years in the army and was still training, saying now that he was finally learning what he needed to know; she forwarded a letter from him. It replicated my experience, past, present and future:

> *...I arrived at this northern New York joint without the faintest idea of where to go, what to do, who to see or any of the general data that one ordinarily has in mind when arriving at a destination for which one has trained for months. I didn't know a damn soul, which was o.k. with me because I didn't come here for improvement of my social standing, or even for the lark. When I found the right place to report to, I strode in and began an era of signing papers, vouchers, identifications, and all that has lasted to this day, even though I've been here a month. I got here at noon on a Thursday and on 3:30 Friday morning an ill-tempered leprechaun woke me up and told me to join my company, which was then in the field on a tactical problem. After a day's journey in a light tank, in a jeep, and on foot I found my company in bivouac, reported to the commander and had pointed out to me five well-camouflaged, giant "medium" tanks and was told that was the first platoon and that I was in command of the first*

platoon and that we attacked at dawn the next day. I said yes sir, which is what you're supposed to say. As if all that wasn't dazing enough to my whirling and horribly inadequate mind, they decided to move us into attack position that night, which meant a blackout drive. That was at once one of the most exciting and confused and frightening events of my life. I was supposed to know what I was doing, and I gave some orders, all right, and generally managed to come through alive, but the sensation of riding in the turret of a lunging, bellowing, firefarting steel monster, at the head of four others just like it, not able to see a god damned thing, me in upper New York State in a 30-ton tank with a crash helmet, goggles, and a 45 pistol to glamorize my costume, and with a map I couldn't see to guide me to an attack I didn't understand .. leading some 30 men I didn't know ... The uniqueness of all that has thinned now, and after a month of it (almost all of it in the field -- I've been here on the post on a relatively few days and nights) I'm accepting it as if it were normal and getting along reasonably well. Right now they've made me supply officer, which ordinarily is only an extra-curricular duty, but since this division is moving out for maneuvers the 26th of this month, all property of the company (and there's hundreds of thousands of dollars worth of it .. each tank, for instance, costing the taxpayers 70,000 rocks) must be inventoried, booked, and accounted for with the proper figures, forms, documents, etc. It's a job I relish not one bit, having always felt that bookkeeping and property accounting was definitely not my line, but it must be done, and now I'm sitting around the supply room pretending I'm straightening things out, while the rest of the company continues its work in the field . . . In general it has been vastly informative .. I've learned more here than in my previous 15 months in the army .. and rather exciting, too. I can easily see, though, that constant repetition of even the best of it would wear badly. My company commander was a first sergeant for some 15 years before graduating from the first OCS class at Knox, and his unpleasantness, unimaginative insensibility, and loud-mouthed, ignorant "toughness" bear out that record in more than real tradition. I think if he hadn't been a first sergeant, or an army man, for so long, he might have been a pretty good guy, .. and I don't find him too hard to get along with as it is. I think he's fairly able, and won't mind having him as boss for combat. It may even be a break.

When we present ourselves to German or Jap gunners I don't know. As far as I can find out we go to Tennessee on from 4 to 6 weeks maneuvers beginning, as I said, September 26th. We are told we will not return to Pine Camp, but are given no further information, the implication, I suppose, being that we will shoot off to a port of embarkation. Maybe and maybe not. I don't much care. The outfit is a good one, and the boys are generally capable and trained and tough. And I feel almost ashamed that we have done so much loud talking and boasting here in America and have let others fight the war for us.

I have no idea where to send this. I don't remember your address on 60th. I'll have to send it to the folks, and have them send it to Al's folks and have them send it on to you. I imagine Al gets out of his jail pretty soon now, and should be ready to assume the titanic social responsibilities of a 2nd Lt. Please pass on my very best to him and try to soothe what angry moods he has stored up for me for being an absolutely worthless correspondent. To show him that I'm penitent, I'll write to him from a slit trench somewhere in Tennessee, with a stick, soot, and some birch bark if I can find them. Let me know when he graduates from School so that I can acknowledge the event somehow.

But the Army was adept at keeping friends apart. With whooping joy, Lieutenant Alfred J. De Grazia, Jr., 0-1043313, obeyed new special orders to quit Tennessee and haul-ass down to Tex-ass, where a great ensemble of forces was in training at Fort Bliss, close to El Paso and across from Juarez, Old Mexico. There, a comfortable old Cavalry post has been encumbered by an air field and a training base, a mechanized new cavalry, and an anti-aircraft automatic weapons center, all in wooden G.I. design.

I was pleased to be assigned a tent on the far edge of the vast base, elevated so that I could view the planes taking off and landing, the sunrises and sunsets as they created orange and purple mountaintops in the distance, and some of my happiest literary efforts were spent describing the concomitants, such as:

Needless to say, dearest, how much I miss you. Numerous

> *small animals share my couch, but it still is not the same as sleeping with one I love. Even though they cause me considerably less bodily wear than you around the face and neck. The most monstrous looking creature crawled in with me last night and I could have sworn the DTs were on me. I killed him outright but this morning encountered another monstrous-looking one in the sink. It was a different species and I can't understand how two totally different insects could both appear equally wicked. Anyhow, this one was having a lot of trouble, poor fellow, since he was all wet & couldn't get any traction. At lunchtime he was still there trying to dry off, but I removed him to terra firma and he ambled off to frighten innocent babes and women.*

And more of nature in the raw a few nights later:

> *Monday night*
>
> *My dear love,*
>
> *You may not believe it but at any moment my whole establishment may come tumbling down on my ears as I write you. A wind, rain and thunder storm is raging overhead, much in the manner of the fabled battle between Wind & Sol. The wind is saying 'I'll blow his tent down!" The rain is jolting it down furiously, and the thunder is trying to shake it down. All in all, they're doing a damned good job. I've done everything I can, and they can go to hell, however. I've put all my belongings on shelves & table, removed my clothing to the center of the room, and climbed up on the bed myself. The tent roof & sides are whipping away frantically and I've stuffed my bedding roll against a crack in the door flap thru which the rain had driven halfway across the tent floor. Last night an only slightly worse storm almost blew away my home and I'm getting damned sick of this supposedly gentle clime. Just about all the other officers have quarters in town, but I really like to stay out here even though the wild winds blow occasionally...*

The larger environment, say I, is "funny."

> *Just now my life down here is a funny affair. El Paso is a great soldiers' city, and the bachelor officers, in whose unhappy ranks I fall by accident of politics, follow certain established patterns of*

behavior. *When I finish work at night, I usually go into town for dinner, preceded by a drink or so. We naturally settle on certain hotels and bars and I generally see my friends over and over again at the same bars and lobbies. Incidentally, I was sitting and chatting with a couple of officers in the Hotel Cortez lobby yesterday before dinner and who should appear but Pasquale Di Cicco and Gloria Vanderbilt. He is in Cavalry intelligence, a corporal waiting to go to OCS, and a strikingly handsome fellow. All the hotel's girls are mad about him. Gloria is what you would call a "stunning" creature, exquisitely groomed and very shapely.*

Well, we gathered ourselves together when a couple more arrived and had a round of beers at the Hilton Hotel and then had dinner. The streets were thronged last night, every man with an eye out for likely prospects. You are going to be chased to death, darling, when you get down here. There is no scarcity of women but there is a sort of continentalism about the country that makes every man's eyes loose in their sockets. I think you're going to enjoy spending some time here. The enlisted men seem to have the edge on the officers as far as the women are concerned, e.g. Di Cicco and wife, and the officers, most of them, fume and cuss against the restrictions that separate them from the ranks. The reason is that a lot of the enlisted men have been around for a long time.

I'm writing this letter from the rooms of three officers in El Paso. We're going to Mexico to see a bull fight this afternoon. This evening I must prepare a lecture on methods of combatting air-borne troops (paratroops and transport-landed troops) to deliver to the officers' class. We take turns delivering lessons...

Must go.
Love as always,

Al

[in the margin, in a different handwriting]:

Dear Jill, Just a line to let you know that Al has been enjoying himself (in the right way). Bye Now. Fred
(That was Dougherty. Now Eubank wants to say hello:)
Hello from me to you. I hope it is as good here when you get here as now. An apartment awaits you. Hope to see you soon.

After exploring Juarez, I promised her trips to Mexico, deep into the country, too. Though it had a couple of nice night clubs, Juarez was largely an ugly town of junk jewelry shops, lowly beer joints, and whorehouses. My companion had been an aging captain whose intentions were always more or less pornographic but whose behavior was naive. It was no problem to steer him away from the primrose path, though he got quite high on Tequila. I thought I had a great idea for Christmas presents, to wit, purchase many of the great variety of cute little bottles of whiskey, liqueurs and cordials made in Mexico and send them to our friends. I bought 6 little black bottles of coffee-chocolate liqueur. I offered to send them to Jill, an offer she ignored. So drank them, and that was the end of that genre of drink for me.

I crossed the border on a Sunday to witness a bull fight. Bullfighting was forbidden in America. I paid for a cheap seat; the seats were divided into those in *sole* and those in *sombra*, the sunny ones costing less than the shady ones. The show was gay and gaudy, full of epaulets and bespangled horses, with Spanish-garbed señoritas in army jeeps adding a "hands across the border" touch. The affair was bloody: four raging bulls were killed, two by an accomplished matador and two by a not so accomplished Mexican general on a beautiful, spirited horse. I sat next to one of the *peones* on a busman's holiday - the "peones" being the men with capes who enrage the bull and let themselves be chased about the arena - and listened to pointers about the sport as they sat in the hot sun, drinking weak beer and smoking Mexican cigarettes.

Lest we forget, there was more to the setting than señoritas and bulls; military training, for instance:

> *The day goes roughly like this: up at 6:15, orientation lecture to the men by a staff of lecturers at 7:00 (have to march them over). 8-11:30 artillery drill or teaching men a variety of subjects, foot drill sometimes, rifle drill at other times; battery administrative business interspersed throughout. Afternoon the same thing, usually ended by retreat parade at 5:20. Then there are personal problems. A few men aren't in the game at all; they're recalcitrant and non-attentive. One poor old guy of 45 told me his troubles today. He was drafted from a*

very rural area in Missouri and left "ten acres of wheat, 20 acres of corn, etc." to be harvested. The poor fellow was justifiably worried. A corporal sent him to me to discipline because he couldn't keep in step, but the old guy just couldn't lift his feet fast enough. He was only a plodding farmer. Another old man in my platoon saw 5 major battles in Wd. War I and is back for more. I have a young corporal who is a crackerjack and my candidate for top honors. We four officers have a chap as batman (orderly) who is perfect for the job. He loves his work and really keeps the home fires in shape. Lucky for you your housekeeping never made an impression on me or he would seem an adequate substitute.

    I get magnificent food at the battalion officers' mess across the street - i.e. magnificent in quality, quantity and type. Good fresh tomatoes, corn, potatoes, steak, bread & butter, cherry pie and cocoa for dinner today, e.g.

    Tonight I took over another officers' job so he could get home to his wife, and visited the library for a while. I've brought a book home and will read a while before turning in. The searchlights (also referred to as the moonlight cavalry) (and incidentally our 1st sgt Camaretta, calls the cavalry contemptuously, the "shit-kickers") (P.S. I agree) are making a pretty pattern in the sky tonight.

I really liked this job. I commanded a platoon that operated four 40mm automatic cannons and the same number of .50 cal. machine-guns. Still, I was attracted to the new airborne formations. I was among the dozen officers who volunteered, attracted by the *"bang up outfits, armed to the teeth with grenades, tommy guns, pistols, machine-guns and knee spikes for close-in dirty work."* When I did not receive a transfer, I cocked an eye at the Air Corps.

To her, I admitted that I was a Seversky fan: "Victory Through Air Power." (However, in urging the book upon her, I granted that "the author's bias is sometimes too crude and blind.")

She lent me the requisite moral support, not without qualms.

    Darling--   *Monday*
    I feel like a heel not writing you the past day or so, but I have been a) busy (well, that's no excuse) and b) sort of stopped by the

necessity of helping you decide between airborne troops and flight training. But then your letter came this morning telling me you had applied for flight training, so it seems to be all decided.

I hate to sound like a milk and water wife, but anything you do is O.K. with me. Trusting as I do in a destiny that will probably permit you to live a hundred years or at least to cause my prior demise beneath the wheels of my own bicycle, I don't worry much about what is euphemistically called the future. And I am not the least bit jealous of the competition I'm going to get from your flight instructor. And as for moving around, why, that's fun. (Heh, heh).

Meanwhile, my parents were exposing unknowingly how mankind ought to be letting out its aggressions:

Yesterday, while I was home, your maw & paw went mushroom hunting in Glen Park. They came home with 3 huge shopping bags full of mushrooms - cauliflower & the small kind - and also a bag of watercress. We've been eating mushrooms ever since, & your mother is exhausted from canning them. Your dad gets such a kick out of "hunting." We ought to get him a farm some day - or install him on ours.

I initiated an application for flight training but heard nothing farther.

I was growing ever happier with my own outfit, the 531st Anti-aircraft Automatic Weapons Battalion. My Battery was led by Captain Love, a soft-spoken Georgian, proper in deed and word, conscientious and sober, ready to listen but also to command. The other platoons were commanded by Lt. Roach, a hearty, open northern urban type and Lt. Davidson, small, quiet, and sweet-smiling, giving me somewhat the impression of a Scotsman. All three were among the founding cadre of the Battalion. The Battalion Commander was a rolly-polly, mild-mannered Kansas farmer-businessman, his Executive Officer, Major Long, a robust, fast-moving Californian. Several had their wives nearby and they were glad to know that my own wife was due to arrive before Thanksgiving: they were planning a feast at their Officers' Mess, which was housed in a small building next to the Enlisted Men's Mess hall.

The Enlisted Men were something else again. The draftees came from the Great Plains and South West. The cadre, and hence the non-coms, were regular army men, early cast-offs of the Great Depression, a rough, cynical, ready crew, careful of their own interests and masters of the art of pleasing officers who did not understand them. They rarely used the second person in speaking to an officer; instead they employed the antiquated third person: "Sir, if the Lieutenant wishes, the men can be assembled for the First Aid Lecture." First Sergeant Camerata strolled about twirling a whistle, with a removed look upon his swarthy visage, exemplifying the ancient Chinese sage who said "Do nothing and all will be done."

My own Platoon Sergeant, Burdine, come out of the border-state hills some years gone by, pretty-faced, small and careful of eye, waited hound-like for cues from me. When he saw that he had an officer who was tough on the men - or so it seemed - he began to put more pressure into their training and inspections. His platoon won first prize of the battalion for hits scored in the next firings, but I was the first to confess that this was none of my doing, which is to my credit, because it was true.

Lt. Roach and I maneuvered our platoons against each other, changing commands at mid-point to allow peculiarities to manifest themselves. We practiced ground warfare and camouflage. With the one pursuing the other, I discovered that ten minutes were enough for my platoon to swing about, take cover, deceive, and receive the pursuing "enemy" with cannon and machine-gun fire point-blank. Considering that our pieces were truck-drawn, not self-propelled, the elapsed time seems in retrospect scarcely credible.

I was an energetic officer, perhaps too active, too ready to innovate, too ready to engage. I thought officers, in addition to their special superiorities of staff and line, should be able to achieve within reason what they asked of their men (this would be an enduring puzzle for me, for most thinking officers and men, in fact); I am speaking of small matters, as well as large: I was leading the men through an obstacle course one day, permitting the weaker ones at one stage to climb a pole rather than jumping up to catch a horizontal bar and swing over it; I had been taking the tricks in turn, but this time I couldn't hold onto the bar without pulling my trick shoulder out of joint, but kept trying, not willing to admit I had a bad shoulder, until my non-coms yelled at me to climb the pole, which I reluctantly did. They were embarrassed more than I was; they did not want an officer getting mixed up with all the nonsense that an enlisted man had to go through.

Or, on one dark night when I was Officer of the Guard, I claimed to be dissatisfied with the vigilance and training of the guards, and, taking Sgt. Berdini with me, went about sneaking in or crashing in upon their posts, testing their nerves and wits. This was going too far. It could lead to accidents, even though the men carried unloaded guns. Perhaps Sergeant Berdini, who was a coarse gossip, related the adventure to First Sergeant Camerata, who mentioned it to the Captain in his offhanded manner. At any rate, Captain Love heard of it and mildly reproved me. Like a smart dog, I took criticism seriously; there was no more of this.

Sgt. Berdini, if he were the informer, had his comeuppance. He was the three-stripe gunnery sergeant of the platoon. The pieces were firing at a towed sleeve. There was lots of racket and smoke. The Sergeant was in direct command of the cannon and machine-guns, standing directly back of them as they blasted away. I stood a few yards behind the Sergeant and the guns. I shouted to the Sergeant to cease firing; I wanted to realign a gun. The Sergeant shouted, no sir. I shouted again. The Sergeant was turning from the guns to the officer and back. He did nothing. I turned to Captain Love, who was standing within earshot and witnessed the action. "Sir," I called, "The Sergeant refuses the command." "I heard," replied the Captain. "Stand aside, Sergeant," he said. The Sergeant obeyed. I took over. The firing was ended. Nothing more was said on any side. The next morning, in the orders of the day, Sgt. Berdini was demoted to Private.

I felt sorry for him. He reminded one of Jimmy Durante. He had a good heart. When the Sergeant, now Private, approached me on the Battery grounds several days later and said he was sorry about causing the trouble and wanted me to know that he did not take the matter personally, I was glad to shake hands and become friendly once more. The old regulars were used to the ups and downs of their ranks; a fight, a drunken binge, AWOL, backtalk, a sloppy barracks - and they would be broken. Only to get their stripes back later on: they were the security blanket of the officers, a link with the tradition of how things should be done and the crazyquilt new army. Berdini was soon enough promoted to his old rank. His long hitches and devotion made it embarrassing to keep him among the raw recruits.

Something rather worse happened to me when the brigade went off on several days of maneuvers. I had my mind fixed upon ground artillery, perhaps wisely, even more wise than the leading generals, and drawing in my mind in effect two curves, one depicting the decline in the Japanese, German and Italian air fleets, the other picturing the exponential rise in Allied aircraft production and fielding. There was no doubt of the result, to occur shortly, and before my outfit could even be committed: there would be few enemy airplanes to shoot at from the ground. So I, faster than anyone else I knew about, studied the ground-fire capabilities of my equipment.

I couldn't wait to try them out. When loosed onto the open range with our guns and an "enemy battalion," advancing and expected soon to come within range, I had my guns emplaced, and muzzles levelled for ground fire. The "enemy" advanced; I ordered fire. An umpire came up, Major Strong, the Battalion's Executive Officer, wearing his white armband and riding a jeep, shouting: "What in the world are you doing?" "Sir," said I, "The enemy is advancing and I have ordered my guns depressed for ground firing." "But those are friendly forces," exclaimed the Major. I had just realized the fact for myself. I ordered the guns elevated and changed the command to an aircraft alert. Since I had not suffered defeat by the "enemy," I did not lose points in the maneuvers, but forever after I was sensitized to the deadliness of "friendly fire."

Back at base, I was an obliging stay-at-home most evenings, such that fellow officers with wives in town treasured me, for I would take up their duties as Officer of the Day, inspecting the Guard from time to time and settling such crises as would arise, a sick man, a quarrel, an accident, a midnight arrival. The free ride would end for them when Jill arrived and I was, not without prompting, advising about her wardrobe.

> *People here are wearing San Francisco clothes, not too heavy during the warm days, not beach clothing at all or resort clothing, but warm coats at night. Your green outfit is just the thing. G. V.* [Gloria Vanderbilt], *when I've seen her, looked a little too formal, high heels and long hair and expensive wraps. You'll be able to wear sweaters very well. But I don't see why you are concerned. You'll do very well with your present wardrobe.*

I put my mind now to stabling my filly upon arrival. A tent? No. A trailer? No. An apartment? Where in this crowded land and for what period of time? A rooming house? Demeaning. A hotel? Yes, perhaps a hotel. But what hotel? El Paso may not be a one-horse town, but it's a one-Hotel town in the view of a Northern City Slicker. The only hotel worthy of the name is the Cortez, so I approach the desk there and request a room. No rooms available. Not quite. There is the Bridal Suite. It is at the top of the Hotel. Pat di Cicco and his wife Gloria Vanderbilt just vacated it; he had to check in to officer candidates' school elsewhere. "I'll take it," I say. (Having mentally calculated the thirty-day cost at our total income for the month minus a few dollars. It's no more than she deserves; she has it over Gloria V. any way you look at it.)

She arrives on schedule. The airport, well... The uniforms, well... El Paso, well... I myself, buddy boy, my man, ready to go, here we go! The Hotel Cortez, O.K. What's this? The Bridal Suite? Don't worry, sweetheart, it's O.K. (Actually, it was nothing but a large room and anteroom, and bathroom, drably and darkly furnished, but what a great view, and quiet, and then, you should have seen the other rooms!) Nothing doing. "Oh, Al," she exclaimed a few times despairingly, by which I inferred that I had not landed the coup of the year.

The next morning, after I went off to my battalion, she began a search of the environs for something suitable, comfortable, likeable, and affordable. She found it, and on the third day we dumped our suitcases into a typical humble rancho of the great Southwest of America, a rambling affair descended from the mismating of a chicken coop with an adobe hut, and graduated in material status as the inhabitants of the region accumulated aspirations and wealth. The ramble was halted at a dissection that extended into a room and bath; this was for us; the rest was occupied by the washed-out, watery-blue-eyed landlady and her likewise little girl, the Army husband being long gone to far places. Jill loved it. She liked its scraggly yard, its view of the mountains far off, its unpretentious I-ask-nothing-of-you, don't-bother-with-the-dishes-or-anything-else, would-you-mind-Sissy-while-I-go-shopping, your-man-reminds-me-of my-man conglomerated boredom. She could have spent the whole war there in quiet happiness, turning a hand as a waitress in a local diner, or a scribe at the post hospital, if given the chance or the need.

No need, no chance. Within weeks came the order for the Battalion to go nowhere, more precisely, to head for someplace referred to as "Desert Maneuvers," across the Arizona into California, somewhere south of Death Valley in the Mohave Desert, where we would find the Sixth Armored Division if we looked hard enough. She packed her grip and headed for Russian Hill in San Francisco; that's where her brother Paul and his wife Ann Whittington spent the while, sailing and dancing.

I stuffed my bag, collected my platoon, and cut into the convoy that headed toward Parker, Arizona. How I loved to convoy: "O.K. Let's get the show on the road!" And out the vehicles towing their cannon would pull, roaring onto the highway from the sod, then purring and finding their distance, stretching out like an old-time wagon train, always in the sweet air of the southwestern dawn, interspersed with whiffs of gasoline exhaust.

When we arrived in nowhere, we set up pyramidal tents by the score. There was a set pattern, a veritable town plan, here the tents of "A" Battery, here its park for guns and vehicles, here its office tents, here its officers' tent, and so on to the conjunction of "A" with "B" Battery and so on to the full 531st Battalion, thence to the Brigade pattern, then the Regiment and the Division. The whole spread its parts uniformly over a great stretch of desert, never (almost never) a light to be seen at night, never a campfire. As I wrote to her in San Francisco:

> The division encamped fulfills that bustling picture Tolstoy describes very well. The encampment is enormous but with the enormity of a mount of ants. There are thousands of details, yet all is swallowed up in vast space. One striking difference for your imagination. Tolstoy writes of the numerous fires. But nowadays "blackout" is a vital word, and every encampment is constructed to exist without lights that are apparent. So only occasional searchlights or truck lights play about the darkness and no materials are available for campfires, even if the soldiers thought of lighting them.

Every Monday at dawn the Division would strike out on maneuvers that would end with a return to its encampment on Friday night. The site, the conditions and the training were chosen and formed to emulate the kind of desert warfare that was occurring even then in North Africa, where the Italians, British, Australians, New Zealanders, and Germans had been chasing each other back and forth since 1940.

American and British armies had just disembarked at several points extending from Casablanca in Morocco to Bone in Algeria and were clearing the last of sporadic resistance from French troops loyal to the Pétain Government in Vichy. Meanwhile, new German forces were pouring into Tunis. Unless we could make it over there soon, there would not be much need for desert training in itself.

One important gap, I realized, existed in the training: there was no air force, whether friend or foe. Two of the most important elements of modern warfare were missing in the mock war: friendly planes to reconnoiter and bomb the enemy panzers and troops, and the planes that gather intelligence from the air and dive-bomb your installations and columns. The accompanying ground-air coordination could not be practiced, either. The same was true at Fort Bliss where there were a great many planes that could properly train with the troops. Southern California was also loaded with aircraft in training and readiness. When on maneuvers, the anti-aircraft batteries had to practice against sleeves instead of live targets. The shock and surprise of the piloted plane descending upon you from nowhere are inimitable; they were missing from the otherwise elaborate simulation of the desert campaign.

Nevertheless it was probably the best training that the Army afforded, and I liked all of it except the part that kept my wife far away, first in San Francisco, then with our old friends from University, Bill and June King, who lived in Hollywood. Bill worked for Walt Disney, helping to draw an infinite series of cartoons on winning the war; his studio was the greatest single workshop of domestic propaganda. My nearest geographical reference was an ugly desert stop called Rice; you got there by hitchhiking on some passing truck; a train labored through there around midnight on Friday and could be caught up with at a trot, whence, after it halted at Palm Springs, a bus could be found that ultimately arrived at the Greyhound Station in Los Angeles sometime Saturday morning. Then a taxi could deliver you to June's Hollywood ranch house and your beloved. After a few hours of food, sex and talk, considerately arranged by June, the first in her large kitchen, then in the spare room, finally in the living room, all had been done, the Other Life had been renewed, and it was time to start back, reversing the order of travel. On Christmas, the Command indulged me with an extra day. Other soldiers had the same idea and the trips were not only complicated but also crowded, forever being delayed.

On my third trip, busing in from Palm Springs, a drunken soldier lost control of himself, and started up a continual stream of invective directed at the world, suggestive remarks to a pair of women behind me, and anti-authoritative generalities that I might have taken personally, since no other officer was around. I turned and told the man to shut up. To no effect. As the bus pulled into the station, I stood up and called out: "All military personnel stay where you are! All civilians please disembark." No problem. The bus driver sat by, the civilians descended in good order, the soldiers sat where they were. "All military personnel will disembark now, except that Man there, pointing!" No problem. The military descended in orderly file and disappeared as fast as they could. To the last of them, I said, "Send the first M.P. you meet over here double time, get it? You, come with me!" I ordered the man. "You are under arrest!" "The soldier made no attempt to escape. He began to plead innocence: "All I was doing was sitting there looking out of the window." He whined and protested like a character out of Dickens. "Never mind that! Stand where you are!" The M.P.s came up and saluted. This man was causing an obscene drunken disturbance, they were told, "I want him in jail." "We can't keep him, sir, unless you come and proffer charges." "O.K. Here is my phone number, call me in an hour." Away they went, and I arrived late at the Hollywood cottage. The M.P.'s phoned as they had promised. "I will not proffer charges," I told them, "especially if you let him cool his heels for a couple of hours." The incident was closed. The man would hardly have time to get drunk again before having to return to his Post.

Less was left of my brief leave, for that matter. Was it worth the trouble, I asked myself; I thought so. Yes, I know, the world was blowing into smithereens, people were dying every minute, what mattered a small breach of discipline, who was I to establish order and justice? I had as many problems with moral choice as the next man, more so, since I was inclined to philosophize. There was this to be said about moral responsibility, Army and civilian: civil life had practically given up the concept of *noblesse oblige,* while the Army had held on to it, though less and less; an officer, any officer, was responsible for a soldier, any soldier, in the absence of the immediately responsible commander. In the faded memories of the medieval estates and the old common law of citizen's arrest could be located the notion, but now almost never the practice.

On the way back to my encampment, the sorrow of parting was obliterated by the military vision when I left Rice in the pre-dawn. There, in the gloom surrounding the road, could be perceived through the headlights of the car the first elements of the Sixth Armored Division, blacked out, of course, unlike the taxicab, and ghostlike. As the sky lightened, more and more reconnaissance cars could be seen, half-tracks, and then I could hear and smell the foul snorts of the steeds of war. The tanks began to show up and spread over the dunes - as far as the eye could see, which was farther with every minute of dawn. I knew the order of battle, I knew the order of march, I knew that my own battalion was in the rearguard, practically the last unit to move. I had time to arrive at my tent by the dirt path, pull off my clothes, dress in camouflaged fatigues and arm myself, and find my platoon, with its trucks beginning to warm up, its cannons hitched to them since Saturday.

I was now Executive Officer and, lo!, there came my Battery Commander, portly Captain Dorset, waddling out of the morning mist, receiving salutes. Captain Love had been promoted to Battalion Exec, a good choice by the Colonel. Dorset had come in new to the battalion and battery; he was from Maryland, with a commission from college, and promotions somewhere in irrelevant commands. I and, by a first all-around consensus, the rest of the battery, hadn't liked him at first, had thought him a panty-waist, with his fat and his porky pouting face.

I felt better about Dorset now. Dorset had shown guts and decency. When the Battery took off on a long hot march, I and the others joked that he was in poor shape and couldn't make it, huffing and puffing, red-faced, through the sand. But he stuck it out. That was one thing. Also, despite his sulky face, he was fair-minded and did not pick on anyone. That was remarked.

And he let it be known that he was not antisemitic, that he had some Jewish in him along the line. It might seem strange: why should this come up? It came up incidentally and without my prompting. I just said I didn't like antisemitism and that was it. But it came by way of comment on the running noisy quarrel between the Battalion Medical Doctor, working out of his ambulance, happily named "The Butcher Shop," and the Battalion Dentist, with a covered truck of chairs and infernal devices. The one was named Belosky, the other Berman, both of them lieutenants, the first dark and handsome, of Polish-Italian descent, with a booming large barytone, the second heavy-set, of round soft features, wearing round glasses, tenor-voiced, of Polish-Jewish origin. The voices are mentioned because Lt. Belosky would frequently start up an argument with Berman, who would vigorously respond, and usually the argument would end with the two loudly calling each other, respectively, a dumb Polack and a dirty Jew. No matter what the source of conflict, it would end up the same way, whether a missing analgesic or a hand at cards.

I would endure these scenes as did the other officers of the battalion, craftily lending respect to Berman's assertions where otherwise Belosky might think himself ahead. I was content that my fellow officers did not take sides. Yet it was remarkable that no one tried forcefully to put an end to the nonsense, especially to the strident assertions of Belosky, that usually started up the fracas. Perhaps we thought little of the annoyance, and no one wanted to squelch anybody. Perhaps there was this, which was important: that Americans, being such strong individualists, do not regard such defamatory exchanges as collective debates, involving the community, but as personal disputes between two men, with nothing larger at stake. The Medic developed no following whatsoever, a fact supporting this theory.

Anyhow there was a lot of cantankerous interaction, what with the sandstorms, the boredom, the drinking, and the aggressive card games that were set up each evening in one or another of the pyramidal tents. We find Our Man describing the scene to his Sweetheart:

> *Last night the B Btry officers' tent was full of card players and I was inveigled into losing some money. They were playing a lot of odd games where skill is no good to anyone. I rarely lose at straight poker but lost some heart-breaking hands last night at a game called, fittingly enough, "Son of a Bitch". I had intended to read and write letters, including one to John, but will do that today instead. About 10 o'clock we stopped the game for a few minutes to eat some kosher salami Berman has brought back with him from Chicago.*

I did not mention that sometimes, inspired by alcohol or not, an officer would take a shot with his automatic at one of the bolder of the desert rats that would scamper in and out. A dangerous shot. Nor was it nice. But it was better than playing Russian Roulette.

> *The nights are freezing out here and by 1 a.m. we were huddled shivering around the candles and lamp that lit the card game. When I did turn in, the bedding roll stuffed with two blankets and two quilts was just enough to keep me warm. Some of the men are*

> *buying sleeping bags for about $9.50 and they swear by them. I just hate to purchase anything so bulky. I wear the army woolen underwear constantly, for though the days are bright and sunny, there is a tang to them which creeps through a cotton suit, especially when riding in an open car.*

Sleeping bags? A premonition of things to come. My most congenial friend in the Battalion was the Chaplain, a Methodist, who believed in the Social Gospel. So did I. And he became a kind of spiritual consultant:

> *The chaplain's going into LA tomorrow to purchase some records from the Chaplain's Fund, a slush fund the army gives the chaplains to make religion more comforting. I've given him some names & numbers of symphonies and other music, including the recordings of the Red Army Chorus, to buy, both of us being in a conspiracy to not cater to the lowest common denominator of tastes.*

My wife in Hollywood, whether influenced by Sunset Boulevard or the venal Christmas Spirit or simple stark need, was also thinking of purchases to come:

> *I window-shopped extensively & have come to the following conclusions:*
> *Daddy, I want a brand-new:*
>   *yellow thin wool scarf*
>   *" cotton sweater*
>   *Pretty dress*
>   *" hat*
>   *Mules (bedroom slippers)*
>   *Cotton quilted housecoat*
> *Could also use:*
>   *Compact (not really)*
>   *Bubble bath (not really)*
>   *No camera. Just lost interest.*
> *What do you want?*

I must not have been reading her letters with my customary literal rigor. Nor was I near to where these things were sold. So when the time came, and it seemed as if I might get to her by Christmas, I pondered the question of gifts, visited the under-supplied Desert PX, and walked out $9.50 poorer but with just what she (he) needed: a Sleeping Bag! Perfect for the Camp Follower. And she was such an Outdoor Girl! It could even hold the two of us in tight embrace the whole night through! I carried it with me when the time came to make the harrowing voyage to Hollywood. I said to her, look what I've brought for you, Merry Christmas, and she did what was quite foreign to her nature: she burst into tears. It was extraordinary, that sleeping bag; it was never used, almost forever, but I encountered it whenever a move was to be made, looming in my baggage and hers like the hull of a boat turned turtle. And then finally it was worn until it dissolved into a frayed rag, in circumstances that can await the telling.

I was happy enough myself in my thick blanket roll that I spread on the desert floor when night fell. I liked especially to be detailed to reconnoiter for the Battalion. Then I might leave in the evening and sleep alone under the immense desert sky, careful to find a furrow or obstacle that a tank or vehicle would not dip into or climb over. Nighttime traffic in the desert was heavy, off the road, and poly-directional. Stories of rattlesnakes crawling in to share the warmth abounded; not much could be done about them, except to move over and give them room.

Then came the light of morning over the dunes, ever more beautiful, re-sketching daily the sharp rough edges of low mountain ridges by filling in a background and foreground composed of oranges, reds, yellows, finally blues, and tan sands, punctuated by a cactus or a Joshua tree; then, unless the movement of vehicles was destroying the limpidity of the air, a brilliant sun arose, to be experienced happily at its coolest during these days of its lowest course. It would be hot as hell by springtime.

I was thoroughly at home in this environment - military and natural. I had been nominated for First Lieutenant. I felt that the future was proper, too; the Sixth Armored Division was ready to go; it could go only to where I wanted to go, to North Africa. An order came in that fortified my expectations: Go through your rosters and consider any soldiers who might have evidenced sympathies for the enemy and would not be fully trustworthy; when such are found, process them for discharge from the Armed Forces. The order excited a certain amount of soul-searching and casting about for likely spies or deserters. Battery "A" finally was able to focus its suspicions upon an ugly blonde farm boy from North Dakota who had been heard to say that the War was unnecessary and, anyhow, we had no business to be wasting ourselves overseas. I was looked up to on such matters, as I should have been. What do you think about Private Fred Hermann? I pondered. I talked with Hermann. Hermann smiled secretively and shook his head when he was asked whether he believed in the war. He was embarrassed at the attention he was receiving. He was one of the sloppiest soldiers in the Battery. For its part, the Battalion should probably evidence a serious effort at fulfilling the terms of the order: at least one man in a thousand should be found to be unpatriotic. So it was determined that Private Hermann should be processed for discharge. He departed for home, looking a little embarrassed, but with the same secretive smile.

My days, too, were numbered. Mysterious forces in Washington, D.C., were at work. On the 16th of January, 1943, a Special Order 16 of the War Department appeared in the Battalion mails. It was most impressive, printed, no less, rather than mimeographed. A Copy was especially marked for 2nd Lt. Alfred J. de Grazia, Jr., 0-1043313 and a single line encircled in Paragraph 10 read cryptically "rel'd 531 CA & det to 2 Sig Rad Serv Section (Psychological Warfare Unit, Camp Ritchie, Md.)" At the end came, "By Order of the Secretary of War, G.C.Marshall, Chief of Staff."

The Headquarters officers and men of the 531st stood stock-still in their sandy shoes and stared fascinated at the document. It was like the Hand of the Lord reaching down and tapping you on the shoulder, saying: "You are Called!" They acted as if it said: "You are Chosen." Since no one knew what it was all about, not the least I, they could regard me with awe. The Colonel told me that I might depart any time I pleased.

Whatever it was, I felt ready for it. The clarion calling me to a challenging new duty, however, had to be harmonized with personal interests; I was getting in the habits of an Army Regular. I had fallen to contriving means of taking along my Frau and of laying over in Chicago en route. She looked up the trains, although I intended to drive a fictitious or maybe real automobile at an unreal 35 miles an hour (the formal recommended speed limit for cars) from the Mohave Desert to Camp Ritchie, Maryland. She duly reports:

> *Well, here are some statistics. The Southern Pacific route through San Francisco, which takes approximately 41 hours from there, adds up to $224.54 for two persons. That includes the 15 dollars extra fare per person for going on a streamliner, also a roomette which is the minimum satisfactory accommodation for two persons. Presumably, we would not enjoy sleeping in two separate berths or together in one lower berth. Tack on about $15 for meals, drinks and tips for two. That adds up to about 241 dollars for the trip to Chicago. The Santa Fe Superchief, which leaves from here, is the same price. Sweet monopoly. That takes 41 hours straight through. The airlines come to $231 for two persons, with no extras, of course. (Our employees positively do not accept gratuities.) Oh yes, except baggage transfer, and I do not know how much that is. The City of San Francisco leaves every three days, and the Superchief sails on Tuesdays and Fridays. So there!*

So we went by train on the *City of San Francisco,* up the sunny California Coast to the Golden Gate, across the Sierra Nevadas, along the marvelous gorges rushing across the Rockies and swooping down upon the Great Plains leading into Chicago, where all trains stopped, and then, after embracing the Home Folks and Friends, proceeded on our familiar streamliner, the *President,* to the Capital of the Free and the Brave. And never regretted it ever after.

The picture that would have graced Mom's dresser, had I not come back from the war (notice the background of painted trees - evoking the Elysian fields)

This would have been more realistic....

Chapter Five

A SPY CAMP NEAR WASHINGTON

AT CAMP Ritchie they said, go to Washington. In Washington the address given me belonged to the Office of Strategic Services. I reported to a suave gent named Earl Looker, a Colonel. This one's appearance and manner suggested an advertising or media executive, an acquisition of OSS directly from civilian life. Looker introduced me to a Lieutenant Martin Herz and that ended Looker's role in my life. It was Herz who did say, on one or two occasions, that Looker had bought De Grazia as a Second Lieutenant, not a First Lieutenant; he wanted to reserve any promotions to himself. Too bad, he had to accept the orders when they came through: score one for Our Hero. Second, Looker wondered why it took me so long to get from California to Washington; but he failed to interrogate me personally, a mistake, since Herz gave an understandably garbled explanation of what was byzantine logic to begin with, such that Looker gave up the inquiry. Not that there was a mountain of work awaiting me, once my job was detailed.

Here was the set-up, according to Herz. OSS was not Part of the Armed Forces, but then again it was: the Highest Officials were continually disputing over this question, and no answer had been or would be shortly forthcoming. (Herz had a hacking laugh, which chopped the air on matters like this.) The missions of OSS concerned intelligence, espionage, counter-espionage, and dirty tricks against our enemies. Since the Army and Navy, not to mention the FBI, Treasury, Immigration and Naturalization, and the State Department, were also in the same business, or could be, were they so inclined, OSS might step on many toes and did so do.

Still, in the present case and as I entered the picture, OSS and the Army had agreed to mingle their personnel, uniformed and civilian, and their resources to devise, staff, and equip a special outfit - an exceedingly complex company it would have to be - to reach out to our enemies by propaganda. This company, to be called deceptively the First Mobile Radio Broadcasting Company, was even now forming up, and we, the two young lieutenants, would be responsible for the analysis of the psychology of our enemies in the theater of operations and for preparing the messages to be delivered.

I found the prospect most engaging, even before I knew more than this. I could see that Herz was on the ball, honest and straightforward, at least with his peers, serious, objective, using a curt rasping voice and speaking a proper exact canned English. His wiry frame and thrust-back head passed him as a soldier, whether he had been much of one or not before the present operation began. He had black hair, snapping black eyes, and a hooked nose. His movements were somewhat jerky, but he could repose calmly when there was no reason to move. He seemed to be the type who was always quite busy, and, in his case, usefully, or, at least, intelligently.

"How did I get here?" I asked him. I happened to meet your brother, Sebastian, said Herz, at a little conference. I told him that we were looking for someone with military training, a knowledge of propaganda, and an acquaintance with Italy and the Italian language. I said that we had the authority to procure a transfer. He said, my brother would be right for you. Herz was himself bi-lingual in German. He had been born in Austria, where perhaps he had learned to laugh and play with words, and had been working on international money transfers at a New York firm before induction.

As a newcomer, I didn't feel I should tell the whole truth. Yes, I had the needed military training, I had the rare tutelage in propaganda (I was, incidentally, now hearing a term being used as a synonym - "psychological warfare") afforded by Professors Harold D. Lasswell and Nathan Leites at Chicago, and, yes, I had traveled in Italy, but, I had to inform Herz, I didn't speak, read, or write Italian well. Fact was, although I didn't say so, I was totally incompetent in the language. Herz had no intention of questioning a language deficiency in any event. He was delighted with finding a genuine soldier who was an officer and more than that, an intellectual, and even versed in the field of public opinion.

We have two platoons, he said, one dealing with German matters, the second with Italian. I head the one. You can head the other. That's the understanding of the Commanding Officer, Colonel Oren Weaver - he's at Camp Ritchie, you'll meet him. Then we have a printing section and a radio transmitting section with three 1KW transmitters. The whole company numbers about three hundred soldiers, almost all from the signal corps, or recruited directly from civilian life, especially in our sections, with high language capabilities.

I lacked a marvelous quality that the United States Army bred in its Regular Officers, an unruffled acceptance of command over matters of which they knew nothing. I felt it was unconscionable to be falsely ticketed as a linguist. It was not my fault, but I must do something to redress the situation. Upon leaving Herz I hastened to the room that my wife had found for us in the comfortable Victorian home of Mrs. Singleton, a pleasant Southern lady whose husband was an attorney and who was happy for every indication of getting closer to the War. Taking Jill by the hand, I escorted her from one phonograph store to another around town until we came upon a single unsold set of Linguaphone in Italian. We brought it back to our room, I closed the door as a security measure, and, unwrapping the cellophane cover, placed carefully upon our portable gramophone Lesson Number One, then listened attentively as the needle scratched it out: *"La Famiglia Bianca: La Famiglia Bianca e'..."* Mrs. Singleton could not help overhearing the strange phases in that beautiful language; when I met her in the hallway, her eyes lit up excitedly, I had to warn her to secrecy; she was delighted additionally with the stamp of a secret. Her home was a staging area for the invasion of Europe! Unfortunately she could not have her nice young Lieutenant couple for long. Before I had finished *"Lezione Quattro,"* I was ordered to Camp Ritchie, along with Herz.

What else had I done while in Washington? Between *"La Prima Lezione"* and *"Lezione Quattro,"* I had plotted the invasion of Sicily. Everybody was wondering what might be the next step after the defeat of the Axis troops in Africa. I figured that Sicily should be next, not Greece as Prime Minister Churchill would have it, or France, as Stalin wished: Greece could be counterattacked from every direction even including the South from which the invasion forces would have to arrive and be supplied. The Dieppe disaster showed that the costs of landing now in France would be enormous, unacceptable, unless the leadership there had been faulty. Not peninsular Italy directly, because of the lack of air bases from which Allied planes might protect their ground forces.

My plan for Sicily was unorthodox. It popped into my head as I thought how to conquer Italy. Like most of my ideas, beginning with the fantasies of infancy, it assumed a visual completeness in my brain immediately, as if it had been there all the time waiting to bolt out like Minerva from the brow of Jupiter. I had toured the Island five years before, and I could picture its features vividly as I pored over the fine maps that the OSS library provided for me. Mt. Etna, so prominent on the Eastern half, obscures with its grandeur and fame the presence of another notable feature of Sicily, a high central plateau around the small city of Enna. The road network of Sicily, well developed, as was its railroad network, created two patterns. The first circumnavigated the Island, along the beaches and seaside cliffs. The second consisted of a spider web whose center was around Enna.

The Allies had most of two airborne divisions in North Africa, battle-hardened, and could reinforce these. They would soon have aerial superiority over Tunis and control of the sea. Malta held. Pantelleria would fall. They had aircraft carriers. Of the enemy, there would be large numbers of Italian troops, mostly of low morale, a large part of them recruited in Sicily. The Germans had few Island forces, but, even in the event that they did not lose all of their African Army (as they did in fact by May 12), they would have been able to bring only several divisions to bear in Sicily.

I inquired about who might be able to listen to such a plan in OSS and pass it along. I was referred to Dr. Gengerelli, who had been Professor of Psychology at the University of California and was engaged here in intelligence and planning on Italian operations. Gengerelli was surprised and wondered whether there was a leak in security. Not at all, said I. The target was obvious. I explained how the airborne forces could be dropped on the undefended plateau, could seize Enna and the towns around, in a triangle that included Caltanisetta. The airport there could receive supplies and reinforcements. The Axis forces could move only by routes around the Island, which would get them nowhere and subject them to continual air and sea attack, or by thrusting up one or more of the several roads leading to the plateau. But they had nowhere near the forces needed to carry them up any one of the roads, and difficult minor mountain roads would have to be traversed to bring their forces together without going back to the sea and climbing along a single route. If they accomplished this feat and were able to push back the Allied force from the central plateau, there would be no second Axis force that could block its withdrawal, and they could readily embark and depart on the Allied fleet. But this was a worst case scenario, because I had in mind that, as soon as the airborne force was landed and the enemy started up the roads to the interior, an army would be landed on the South-Eastern beaches, headed for Catania and Messina. The enemy army would have to surrender or flee by the northern coastal road. The Eastern enemy troops would have to be driven up the coastal road to the Messina ferries. There they might surrender or be destroyed by land and sea artillery and air strafing and bombing.

Having persuaded Dr. Gengerelli that the plan was worthy of consideration and extracted a promise to move it at least one level up, I left it with him and departed satisfied. I heard no more of it, nor did I expect to. It didn't help that I volunteered, according to a footnote of the memo, to join the expedition. Meanwhile I disposed myself for the move to Camp Ritchie, where Jill, conveniently introduced, had taken up quarters in the home of a cousin of Mrs. Singleton.

If Camp Ritchie, now Camp David, has become a retreat for the President and his entourage, I would be able to explain. The area was hilly, abundantly supplied with trees. It was speckled with cottages and small settlements, flowers blooming among them with the first sign of Spring. Its brooks were poetically exact, with the proper gushes and gurgles, the right proportions of accelerations and decelerations, glistening beds and warm banks of pebbles and sand, rugs to the barefoot. She and I tripped along a stream lengthily and dreamily until her and my bodies fell down together upon some sandy niche, nor did we rise up until shadows fell upon us from the low bluff behind and we had finished dissevering, one by one, the sounds and lights of mild exterior Nature from our own orgasmic explosions. There was more of this in the sanctuary of our large-windowed wood-framed room, but Cousin Singleton could not have been surprised, after what she would have heard from Mrs. Singleton. However, something was happening to us that we did not now realize.

I warmed to the Camp itself, too. It nestled in the mild hills, with buildings here and there, not uniformly spaced. Paths wandered hither and yon, unlike Tyson, Davis, Bliss and the Desert encampments. Most striking was the absence of large formations. Rather, at any time of day or night, you could observe human figures, from the many singles to the multiples, typically from a dozen to a score, moving this way or that, sometimes armed, sometimes carrying strange packs, sometimes scurrying about empty-handed. If you could have infiltrated the thousand minds, you would have located a dizzying lot of schemes whose ultimate denouement would occur in a Malayan jungle, a Baghdad consulate, the Spanish Steps of Rome, and the Old Port of Marseilles. Oh, yes, too, in Palermo, for someone here was thinking about sneaking some patriotic mafiosi into Sicily to rouse up local interest in an American victory, and actually did something about it.

I found my Company, the 1st MRBC, scattered about, the Radio Station crews setting up and taking down their transmitters on one field, clusters and couples conversing in several languages around a set of offices, men off by themselves quietly reading an intelligence report of interviews with prisoners or a manual on the portable Mergenthaler offset printing press, or, for that matter, one of a score of books that I already had well digested, which helped persuade me that I was well equipped for my job. What job? There was no manual, no routine, no training program, no tests, nothing but serious talk and good fellowship, it would appear, for the forty intellectuals of the Company. We should have been, but were not, being trained in the interviewing of prisoners of war, of politicians, of ordinary civilians, in the production of certain kinds of reports on the political situation as known to or believed in by respondents and informants, in map-reading, and in propaganda analysis and propaganda policies. Never mind the manual of arms, firing of small weapons, booby-traps and mines, vehicle driving and maintenance, and in the actual preparation of propaganda. Snippets of all these things did come our way. Russian Front leaflets were passed around, cleverly written, well designed and illustrated: Herz was of the opinion, which I accepted, as did others, like Hans Habe and Hans Wallenberg, but perhaps not Peter Viereck or Klaus Mann, that Soviet propaganda was too political, too ideological, too demanding. The mentality of the German soldier was too Nazi to believe the message; the practical tactic and consequences for any German soldier who might accept the message were not made explicit. My favorite Soviet leaflet had the Nazi leaders in comical poses, with headlines: "The German G.I. has it good!.." following with: "Hitler thinks for him!.. Goebbels talks for him!..Goering eats for him!..Ley takes care of his girlfriend!.. He need only die for himself!" showing him stuck bleeding in a snowdrift.

There was a Headquarters staff consisting of a red-headed, red walrus mustachioed, cheerful blustery Executive and practical Commander, a former advertising man named Caskey; there was, too, his Assistant, a full-cheeked, resonant-voiced Captain Rathbun who knew some Italian because he had studied opera singing, a Lt. Jerry Stern who had been a radio programmer and was now personnel officer, a Lt. Zimmerman, who had been a radio announcer in Milwaukee, a Lt. Tommy Anglin who had been and was, well, a nice guy. Two facts were apparent: the 1st MRBC stood high in priority for shipment overseas, and the 1st MRBC was in a state of happy confused ineptitude.

Rarely to be seen was Lt. Col. Oren Weaver, the Commander, who appeared in jump shoes, paratroop uniform, and beret, out of the skies, so to speak, a former CBS radio man from Chicago, exuding confidence, smiling, teaching nobody anything, although, to conjure up excuses, he may have been helping to develop and obtain equipment: he had to be doing Something! Supernumeraries and redundancies were structured into the Army brain from the time when every cavalryman led a couple of spare horses.

The designers of the 1st MRBC were myopic. Two major operations, and the equipment and training requisite therefor, went overlooked: loudspeakers for delivering messages to audiences across the lines, and the system for distributing leaflets by artillery. They would have to be developed in the field. For that matter, not a single leaflet was written and printed at Camp Ritchie as a sample of what would be effective for dissemination among civilians or enemies at the front.

I wish that I could relate to you that I moved in effectively, was cordially received, and in the short weeks remaining, transformed the outfit into a Mark VI dreadful monster of the mind. Not at all. I was cordially received, I did my bit, working almost entirely with Herz, to evaluate and integrate the two-score propaganda soldiers, and I even drilled them and helped them to fire rifles. I was ashamed to parade them, but kept them off on corners of the fields and bypaths of the Camp.

They were a charming group, whatever their military bearing or fire-power. The Company had been granted permission to commission several of the men from the ranks, and their designation had been left to Lts. Herz and De Grazia. Consequently, I personally interviewed them all, beyond the normal variety of contacts.

At that time the most conspicuous officer candidate was Hans Habe. He was older than the ordinary lieutenant, tall and confident, with a confident manner, ready with a big smile, cordial, almost effusive. He was born Janos Békessy and had published a novel. His Hungarian accent was scarcely noticeable. His complexion ruddy, his hair reddish-blonde, maintained by dyes. A *bon vivant,* he could be indulged and indulge others, especially Captain Caskey, with drinks and dinners, for he had married a rich woman, the heiress of General Food Inc., one Eleanor Post Hutton, old and ugly some young sports might say, quite nice said many another. She was already his third wife. He wore custom-tailored khakis and fatigues, the only private in the US Army to have been known to do so. He was ever so clever in human relations. He knew Central Europe very well. He had written an early article on Hitler and was anti-Nazi. He had volunteered to fight the Germans in a French foreign regiment and been taken prisoner. He had escaped the Paris internment camp of Drancy together with wife number two, and fled over Portugal to the United States. He was rational, i.e. not addle-pated, or distracted, or visionary. You could imagine him operating a system consistently without breakdown. We agreed, and Captain Caskey heartily concurred, on Habe.

In fact, we agreed on all three candidates who were to be finally commissioned. Peter Viereck was very bright, a poet, a dedicated anti-Nazi and liberal. His father, rumored to be a bastard grandson of German emperor Wilhelm 1st., had been the most famous of pro-German Americans in World War I and had spent time in jail as a traitor of sorts. The mark of this (in)justice was clearly upon Peter, in his clashing determination and hesitancy of manner. (A pedestrian psychoanalyst would venture, aha, there's one who wanted to kill his father but couldn't let himself do it!) Physically, he did not cut a dashing figure; he looked as if he had just escaped a concentration camp. He seemed quite uninterested in managing others, though was fully cooperative at work.

More ambitious and a fine figure of a man was Corporal Costas, who told the Lieutenant, with a strong Greek accent, that he was expert in seven languages, but in none better than English. He had a way with Germans as well, he recounted. His calling card when in *the Reich* carried him as Alexander, Graf von Costas, Sparta, Greece. The Germans swooned at this. A true Spartan!

Sergeant de Lattre taught French at Northwestern University. He was a large, fleshy man, whose bullet-head put him credibly in the ranks of the French infantry in Morocco as he claimed. He was heavy-handed, obstinate, opinionated, endearing because of his good will and of his harmless role of the moment. He had the war all figured out, of course.

This could not be said of Corporal Grigis, who kept his own counsel, obeyed instructions promptly, and exhibited a judicious temperament under incitement. He had the manner and speech of a Near Midwesterner and there was no question that his stocky body could support a heavy load over long distances. He showed no obvious source of his knowledge of Italy and Italian, which was satisfactory; "I've always listened to Italian radio programs, " he said. There were Italian-Italians in the platoon, Jewish refugees, Fabio Coen, Raymond Guetta, and Kaminski, a version of Viereck; all were young, bright, intellectual, congenial, and militarily untrained.

Hans Langendorf was an older man, lean and depressed of temper, a German refugee whose perspective upon the War and the World were those of a political extremist from a worker's party. He gave no sign of capacity of leadership, or of caring about managing others. In this he was like Klaus Mann, who was even more depressed, with sunken, haunted blue eyes, which were those of his father, the great writer Thomas Mann, whom I had visited with Jill in his home in California together with Mann's younger daughter, Elizabeth, and her husband, Giuseppe Borgese, a Professor at the University of Chicago. Klaus could be voluble on occasion. His knowledge of what had been occurring in Europe, historically, and his mastery of German prose were unsurpassed in the Company. He had a beautiful intelligence.

Hans Wallenberg was a short stocky pugnacious-looking Prussian Jew, baptized Catholic along the way. His father had been a leading publisher in Berlin in earlier years. Hans would never lose his strong German accent, but he spoke clearly, like Henry Kissinger, and was naturally authoritative. He was not out front among the men. He led from within, by his forceful personality and competence with ideas. Of his self-sufficiency and hardihood, there could be no doubt.

So there you have it, the candidatures. Besides Habe, the choices were Wallenberg and Grigis. Their names were seconded and duly forwarded. It was time to turn to other matters. Ready or not, the Mediterranean Theater of Operations was beckoning the 1st MRBC. There was a large army of German and Italian troops, hard-pressed, but well-situated to put up an extended defense of Tunisia. They should be suffering a barrage of propaganda. Elements of the

1st MRBC should already have been flown over by now and be in action.

Instead, the orders to move came at the beginning of May. This had given my wife and myself time to get a preliminary opinion - positive it was - on her pregnancy. The occasion could not be fully decided. I thought it was the sandy bower of Spring flowers brookside. She, who was contracepting in her typical unreliable way - or was the unconscious wish creating unreliability? - believed the conception to have occurred on Cousin Singleton's bed with the breezes of April blowing the light curtains into the room over our heated bodies, or even in their airy bedroom in the Maryland hills.

Howsoever that may have happened we reversed, almost without discussion, our long-enduring refusal to grant any neonate the privilege of our parenthood. We even felt that it was the best thing that could have befallen us at this moment in time. We wanted to commit an act of reproduction, to bring in a unifier who would serve to defy our fateful separation. Since we were not sure of the conception curves, its chief indicator being a by-passed menstruation, unless you want to consider a loss of appetite and a slight illumination of the senses and skin, we spoke of it to no one.

No one would have listened, anyhow. All were busy packing gear, drawing an issue of new shoes and clothing, polishing and greasing vehicles against the salt air, writing their families despite the rule to keep any troop movement secret, redrawing wills, and arguing about our unpreparedness when, as was anticipated, we would be cast to die or survive on a battlefield of grand scale.

We boarded trains that reached Newport News, Virginia, somewhat after the arrival of several cars of wives and sweethearts. So much for the secret destination. Everyone knew that the Nazi SS wanted especially to kill enemy propagandists; this was evidenced in Russia in thousands of cases. Also, we knew that the sea lanes were hardly safe for the Stars and Stripes; the truth of the matter, unknown to us, was that convoy losses were heavy, 21 eastbound ships having been lost in one engagement with submarine packs in March, 13 westbound ships from an April convoy. May would be a better month, watching the sinking of only 264,852 tons. In June, (we could not know) the situation would dramatically improve, with

Davy Jones' Locker in receipt of only 95,753 tons.

Jill and the others registered at the Hotel Warwick. There, like high-priced courtesans, they were visited furtively and in haste by their consorts. Jerry Stern was an important runner. When everyone else was locked into the great dock area, he had to go out on logistical problems. On May 6, in what was guessed to be a last contact, Jerry was given a letter for her, which, *inter alia,* said:

> *Certainly we haven't had much leisure in which to reassure each other of undying fidelity and love but I feel such reassurances not very necessary, even though very nice. I have no intention of giving you up for any girl in the world. I have every hope of creating happiness for both of us in the not too distant future. Even under the stress of these uncertainties of the day and the to-morrows, I am growing more delighted and expectant over the probability of a child to come. At the same time I pledge a successful resumption, and this time an unfrustrated one, of romance as we know it - and we do know it intimately, from breakfast for two to breakers off Santa Monica. You need never feel that you are being forced to create a world of yourself and a child. I always love you and you always have, barring sleepless nights and nerve-racking departures, a gay blade with an open heart & a boon companion.*
>
> *Well, wish us luck and carry the torch high. Maybe, I'll get home sooner than we think, the way the African battle is going today. All my love.*
>
> *Al*

[in the margin is written] *P.S. You might as well leave tomorrow sometime, inasmuch as we shall be departing tomorrow. This looks like it. Goodbye for now, love.*

But there is more to it; it's an operatic ending. The faithful Jerry (who is not missing the chance to see his own cool, combed beauty of a wife), brings back a note from her, with a coda.

> *Darling,*
>
> *Jerry just told me the news and gave me your note. I hope I'll be able to see you at the gate in the morning. If I do, no written words*

are necessary. But if vile fate intervenes once again, this will have to be our last goodbye, for the duration + six months anyway.

To say I wish you all the luck in the world is redundant, almost silly. I know we'll see each other again - that we'll both be as we always were, only there'll be more of us. I'm not sorry for anything - that we married in wartime, that you're going over (I still wish, impossibly, that I could too) or that I'm having what we hope will be a baby. And - and this may annoy you, since it marks me as a dupe of propaganda - I am and always have been, very proud that you were in the Army - from private up.

Come back soon. There'll be lots of us waiting for you.

Early the next morning, at the dockyard gate, silent around save for the guard and a couple of soldiers passing, I did meet her. We held hands, kissed, especially we looked at one another for a few minutes. Then, when we should have been trudging off back to back to the tune of Lili Marlene, we say things like "Don't forget to.." and "Tell Buzz that.." and "Watch your step when.." and "Have a good time with Liz and Bill at Quantico," and, most ridiculous of all, "Don't forget to write.." One more kiss.

My description in a letter that I slipped to a stranger going ashore, which reached her when she arrived at the home of Miriam and Sebastian in Washington, says it better:

You were sweet when I saw you last, quite wide awake for such an early hour. It was a nice, brief way to say goodbye. When the parting is prolonged, the thought of how much I love you grows more and more oppressive, and the pain unbearable. All my love, baby, may we be together forever soon.

On the 9th of May the convoy finally got underway. My Navy transport, with a Captain for the Ship's personnel and a Commodore to rule the Army crowd, seemed to ride in the middle of the files. Its log, according to me, contains the following entry to begin with:

We had little sleep to commence the great journey. I had a hasty breakfast after a brief nap, and then packed my laundry into my snappy grip, which, incidentally, has aroused much favorable comment. All my buckles had to be tightened, my straps slung and my cartridge clips filled, before taking off. We were a staggering lot, borne down, in my case, by a knapsack, jammed with small articles & a raincoat, a gas mask, a belt with compass, first aid kit and cartridge container, a pair of binoculars, an ammunition sack pregnant with .45 ammunition, a dispatch case full of essential papers, and a tommy gun. Plus the helmet.

The men were similarly laden with a barracks bag in place of several of the above items. Le tout ensemble tottered for the mile or so to the trains, the weaker dropping slowly behind. Every now & then I would carry a rifle or a bag for one of the men [particularly Viereck]...

That night I lay in my bunk, my fellow officers no more than a spit away in every direction, and thought of convoys and submarines, and Jill driving northwards in Martin Herz's car towards Quantico to visit Bill and Liz Evers, then to Washington where she would stop with Sebastian and Miriam before going on to New York to see her sister and others, turn over the car to Martin's mother, and then head home to Chicago for the duration.

The duration, I thought, could be as much as a year. The nation had been at war almost a year and a half. I was trained well for some things, but not certainly for what could well be coming, and I felt that all about me were men who were much less trained. Who is in charge of this show? What in the world is this crazy company going to do? It would be weird to run it up to the Front with its panoply of equipment, its gibberish, its bedlam; it would certainly startle the enemy into some response. No other combat unit would want to be near it.

In all my Army time I had done about 300 hours of learning and training; the rest of 3000 working hours had been wasted. And of these 300 hours, only perhaps a hundred represented skills and knowledge that would be used. In the 14 months before I was transported to North Africa, I cost the army about $800 in cash and

$500 in keep, and then my share of the low-cost training and my pro-rated part of the use cost of some equipment, the most expensive of which would be 1%, say, of the cost of eight 40-mm cannon, on whose sales their Swedish developers had grown rich while preserving their neutrality.

I might have been sent overseas ten days after I was inducted, a day for clothing and shots, a couple of days to explain a batch of equipment and arms that were to be draped upon me and carried overseas, and several days of military intelligence about the front to which I was being sent. All the rest could have been learned, and a lot more, especially concerning the environmental factor, in and near the action, or behind the action getting acquainted with the people I'd be working with. I could afterwards have been pulled out from whatever outfit I was with for my special work. Feeding in, that's the way it should be done: feed the recruits into whatever units, British, Russian, Indian, Senegalese, Jewish, etc. that were in action, American, too.

It was important to build up cadres quickly, to train men to train and lead groups of men. Place men as individuals and small groups wherever they might experience the environment of warfare, get the taste of it. Training by huge encampments and then organizing by full divisions, corps and armies, so that no one dampened his shoes until a half-million could do so at the same time: this was hugely wasteful in irrelevant and unusable motion, interaction, and of precious time. Perhaps all units should be conceived and basically organized as modules, like organisms begin as an undifferentiated cell, and they should be limited in growth like *bonsai* trees, until you have a large number of modules with incipient specializations that should be kept intact until they win or are destroyed. These could be formed into as many different kinds of larger units as might be required. What I was getting at, never having been to a General Staff School, was the concept of the Task Force, that was making its way in military circles. To my credit, perhaps, was my envisioning the process as radical, going back to the beginning of all military training, so that there was no other way to operate from the beginning than through Task Forces, and therefore, when the special Task Force was called into being, its personnel would possess an intense concern for communications, liaison, information exchange, three times the intensity and effectiveness of the ordinary experience. Nobody foresaw it, but that's what happened inefficiently to this tiny special function of the Army called psychological warfare, and, finally, combat propaganda. What actually took place at the end of the line, at the front, bore about as much resemblance to the way the whole thing was conceived and put together as the fat larval slug to the svelte butterfly. A metamorphosis occurred.

The Army, like the school systems of the nation, did not prepare one well for what would happen, the real thing. Were the other soldiers on the boat even less well trained? Or perhaps their jobs were simpler. But that's not what bothered me. It was the lack of agglomerative flexibility that was just mentioned. And, too, it was the failure to emulate the environment of logistics and battle that affected the individual's behavior and thence the outcome. Were American troops really acculturated to this environment? How long would it take for them to test themselves and adjust the difference?

But there is more to be quoted from my extensive log of the voyage out:

> *The 1st MRBC was only the beginning, the advance party, the first sprinkling of men. The long lines* xxxx ["too much information on page 5-6" scrawls the Censor; he even forbids telling the name of the ship, which is lost in memory and in a square mile of federal archives now] xxxx *in the hold where the air is foul and dark. The bunks there are packed four deep with a thread of space in place of an aisle, line after line of them, in or around each a barracks bag, two blankets and a rifle. The occupants sleep a lot in them, but otherwise shun them. They clamber up the ladder to the deck, girded with the padded life jacket which is the laissez-passer to the world of sea and sunshine. Some hardy gamblers stay below and shuffle their cards and clink their coins in a shaft of light which enters from a missing board forty feet above.*
>
> *At the first signs of darkness the order comes from the loudspeaker to "Prepare to Darken Ship" A few minutes later comes the order "Darken Ship!" The smoking lamp is out on all weather*

decks. This means no smoking except in prescribed places inside the ship. From then on, one stumbles in darkness, feeling his way up and down ladders, into staterooms, along cluttered decks and into dark latrines. I have suffered my share of hard knocks, funnier to discuss than to endure. First a crack on the head from an overhanging assault boat which didn't hurt as much as an excruciating bang of my knee against a bulkhead.

Lately, I have taken to sleeping topside in the open. The air is so much cleaner there than in our tiny compartment where nine men breathe the equal cubic space of a room at International House. It was very cold last night outside & I'm making more adequate preparations tonight. I carry my cot up with blanket, my life belt and my tommy gun with some ammunition. The compensation is drifting to sleep with the sky and sea stretching immeasurably around me, with the other ships in the convoy lying away gently into the darkness and with the whole world being put to sleep naturally instead of artificially by a flick of a button. Whether at sea or in the desert, sleep in the open is, like reading a book before falling asleep, an unconscious denial of the regimentation that now it is time to sleep, ergo sleep. You remember those very pleasant nights when neither of us was pressed by the morrow and we could lie in semi-darkness talking affectionately and agreeably at ease.

Some of the men grouse around each night for a place on deck to sleep. The sailors are crowded too and they crawl into all sorts of places to sleep when twilight comes. They sleep in the assault boats and on all the decks except the top one. Despite the small size of the ship, its domain, so to speak, there is a kind of nomadism about these boys in their prowling around and changing of lairs in the evening, and in the way they shimmy from here to there to no seeming good purpose. You get the same sensation watching monkeys in an outdoor rocky cage. They still are wanderers and migrant citizens.

There isn't too much work for anyone aboard the ship, and frequently a group is composed of both soldiers & sailors. There is a great deal of friendliness on all sides with an astounding display of courtesy on both sides. The most irritating things are passed off with great good humor. Painful encounters in the darkness, many dull questions, terrible crowding are passed over in a most gentlemanly *fashion, befitting well-fed, housed and slept persons of strict Christian upbringing.*

The men don't have too much to do. The food is good but the hold is stifling and the deck space is limited. There is a little reading, a considerable amount of card-playing, but mostly there is rail-leaning hour after hour, rewarded by the sight of other ships, some flying fish, a scout plane now & then, the great seaweed bed, and once a whale. Conversations are endless. The men are already planning their return trip. Some are looking forward to the women of North Africa. The length of the trip, seasickness, incidents of the sea and ship are all favorite topics.

Some of the group clusters are striking. A dozen or so, clad in coveralls and a padded life jacket, unshaven and unkempt will stand around listening to two or three champion BS's ["bull shitters"], or to a soldier strumming a guitar, or watching a young sailor painting a post with patient, unexcited interest.

The officers are fortunate in possessing a wardroom which, when the tables are cleared, serves as a smoking and reading room. It is a great asset, since even our rooms are too cramped to bear for long. It is here that meals are served by efficient messmen in white jackets.

The life of a naval officer is soft and pleasant. They have very little to do with the men. They have their quarters which are far more comfortable than any in the army. Their food is superior. Their linens are clean, on the table & on the bed. The lieutenant commanders have spacious rooms with private baths. All of this goes with them to the last battle. They go into the fight living & eating & sleeping as gentlemen. They come out of the fight with the same blessings. How different from the soldier who never has a home, a place for his possessions, bathing facilities or a constantly good food supply. If he is lucky, he goes into battle on a tin of food and exists for days on less. He is exposed to the rains and snows, to heat & cold, to great noises and great confusions. There is something of finality about his absence from home, whereas, to the sailor, home is never more than several weeks away on an order that may come at any time....

The chaplain aboard ship is from the Univ. of Chicago where he took some work in Sociology. His name is Phillips. Perhaps you can recall him -- a slender, medium-sized man of about thirty with a small mustache, glasses, sparse blond hair & a receding chin. Most ships haven't chaplains but this is an exception.

I've read several books during this voyage. Appeasement's Child *is excellent - calm and learned. Massock's* Italy from Within *is likewise good. I've done some conversing in Italian and am able to get along pretty well, as well as a person who has spent a couple of years in Italy, according to my partner in conversation.*

Have you ever read Not Peace But a Sword *by Vincent Sheehan, U. of C. fellow alumnus. He is really good, a clearer thinker than Schuman on what lay ahead, I believe. He gives out on the kind of socially conscious writing I like. I mean that he makes it a part of the whole fabric of life - not some monstrous and all-consuming Marxian whole. No doubt his mind, and he is only human, would tend that way, but he has that trait of mixing with life, of wading in the currents that drives obsession from actions or thoughts related to actions, if not from the original fort they hold in the ideology; to mince platitudes, he is a "practical idealist" - words that ordinarily mean nothing.*

This is my fifth crossing of the Atlantic and the experience is as it was always, boring much of the time. Despite the lack of women, dancing, swimming pools, many flunkies and scrambled sweetbreads for breakfast, it is not a worse voyage. The ever-present danger lurking around us night and day gives some zest to the trip. But I suppose it is again the abnormalities which one always finds in war which afford the chief interest, the efforts of men to adjust, to find meanings, to take or avoid responsibilities, to explain unknown fears, to pass the day and night, the way they bear discomforts which always cause one to ask himself "What does unbearable mean?"

Midway in the voyage, a soldier dies suddenly in a great fever. Spinal meningitis. A dreadful plague was feared. Several contracted jaundice. The dead man was buried at sea; the Reverend Phillips prayed and a goodly company assisted. One of the MRBC men was stricken with acute appendicitis and operated upon; he survived. Let the log resume:

You may have noticed indications here & there of this letter being compounded over a period of days. This afternoon, after several days of good weather and slick seas, a heavy roll hit the convoy. All the ships are pitching mightily, nosing up great puffs of spray. The stocky cruiser, especially, is bucking and tossing like a bronco. Appetites were not so sharp this evening and pale, wan smiles are common. The land had never so much to offer as now.

Another day and less change. A convoy passed us at a distance this morning, homeward-bound. It looked to be chiefly cargo ships. A funny sight in a way, that crowding of masts and hulls away off. One felt like exclaiming "Ahoy, the Spanish Armada," or "Lo! The Carthaginian fleet." I realize the thrill a look-out must have had in those days of visual communication.

What an ordinary beautiful day this is. The sea is again very calm. I have read more. I have read several short stories by Aldous Huxley, again admiring his masterful techniques and condemning his approach to his subjects, poor things. They are certainly flailed unmercifully. And I have read some absurd pastoral by Thornton Wilder called Woman of Andros. The pastoral is typically an attempt to sugar-coat nonsense so that it will be swallowed easily. Prurient sex becomes charming & cute; drivel becomes mystic and corn goes rustic....

We have been giving news programs to the ship's complement & troops twice each day. The idea was put out by Herz as a good exercise & a way of getting the men out of the hold. The talks are very successful & are heard throughout the ship. It was by means of this loudspeaker that the men learned the cheering news of the fall of Tunisia, the great diplomatic activity everywhere, and now the brilliant RAF assault on the Ruhr dams. The news has done a lot, I think, to take the men's minds off the submarines. Zimmerman has been doing an A-1 job of announcing. He is as good as any I've heard. I've found that I've lost none of my editing skill & can cut a thing to pieces & put it together in quick-time. Most of the time I let my extreme critical faculty rest & allow ordinary, decent presentation to get by. Funny, though, how little effect an "abased" life has on one's mental processes. Habe is pretty good at handling the relative importance of items. He has a little of the Hollywood about his literary efforts, however.

> *Several of the men have been giving language classes to the officers of the ship. a nice way of taking up time & learning a little. Peter Viereck and I have had a chance to converse at length several times. He is, to my mind, a brilliant man, an American Shelley, a writer full of epigrams and wit. I expect him to be writing famous books some day. He is as nervous & thin as a reed, wonders where the war against Fascism is, and rather too constantly is complaining and railing. I reprove the latter behavior by forcing him to admit that to me it is old, old stuff - I know it & I agree but so what & T T* [Tough Titty = it's hard to feel sorry for you] - *but he can't help himself and says I have no right to be an intellectual, because of my stability.*
>
> *Great indign* [line missing] xxxx *destroyers, disturbed at the* [words missing] xxxx *into our march of pomp & circumstance across the broad sea. I have read much, too, some short stories, a biography of Churchill and now, with great voracity, Thomas Wolfe's* The Web & the Rock. *And what a delight it is. I recall now why I treasured* Look Homeward, Angel *in those rather bitter days in New York...Yet I know that my writing would never be of his type. I am repressed. I hate to blurt. I cannot confess so completely in all detail, though I be ever so conscious & full of these details.* [line missing to the censor] xxxx *lands of blue waters & perpetual sunshine - old Mexico, Southern California in their pristine state - white buildings set like jewels in mountainsides. And now after more blue water, our port of disembarkation, a great cluster of white houses, some looking quite large through my binoculars. It is a marvelous day - a flat sea full of tiny wrinkles & glorious sun and land!*

Peter Viereck has been writing, too, in this and that crevice of the ship. The *New Yorker* publishes his poem shortly thereafter:

> *We grumble up the gangplank to the ship,*
> *Zigzag past periscopes toward history,*
> *And know that in each squad of twelve, one man*
> *Wears doom, like dungarees, and does not know.*
>
> *He will not see the Brooklyn Bridge again,*

> *No, not though all his buttons glow like planets,*
> *Shining like prayers to intercede for him,*
> *Though he ban sins and wrinkles from his bed*
> *And scrape his mess kit clean with sand and soap –*
> *Not even this can coax a soldier's furlough*
> *From death for one who strolls among our twelve.*
>
> *This morning we,*
> *Because not knowing which of us he is,*
> *Swore twice as gruffly at each other with*
> *That soldier's gentleness we won't admit.*

I would have quibbled over various lines of the poem, mostly their melodrama, but stayed fond of fierce-feeling and gentle Peter. Warfaring needs poets. It needs the leadership of the phrase and word. This is not said in praise of war. Concentration camps need poets, too.

With Jill at Camp Ritchie

CHAPTER SIX

AFRICA, FROM ORAN TO TUNIS

ON THE thirteenth day, the ship docked at Oran in Algeria. There had been alarms, but no submarine strikes. Near the Azores, an old Spanish tramp had labored near, been warned off, and changed course. Corporal Tuero, a Cuban who had fought in Spain for the Loyalists, would have liked to sink it with shots from the ship's large guns, now lightly covered against the heavy spray. He wished they might invade Spain instead of Algeria, and was certain that all their movements were reported by Franco Phalangists to the enemy.

The convoy, faithful to its orders, swung nicely into the Mediterranean Sea below the great rock of Gibraltar. Nor were there further alarms before landing.

The Company disembarked, its vehicles were unloaded, and it rolled off into the hills behind the city. The hills were burnt and bare and the facets of the great Sun's diamond flashed upon them. We encamped. We set up pup tents, boiled water for Nescafé, and, even while we blessed *terra firma,* lamented the lost sea breezes. Nothing to do, nowhere to go, no escape from the heat. Weren't we a conquering army? Why shouldn't we have pushed into the comfortable houses of the city? And let the inhabitants, the indifferent Arabs and the Vichy French, double-up, shift for themselves. "Protect yourselves!" cried Sgt. de Lattre, "I know this heat. I was a soldier under General Lyautey. You will get sunstroke. Cover your heads!" I looked at his bare bald head. "Cover your head, Sergeant," I suggested. But the Sergeant said he was fine because he had gotten used to it. We tried crawling into the tents; the Sun was blocked but the heat was worse. *Tout passe,* and the Sun at last draped itself in orange and left for the night. The next morning the head of Sgt. de Lattre was a startling red and he complained of a bad headache.

All were up by dawn, each with his own hopes and fears for the day. There were no orders to move along, or to find some better place in the area, or to pick up large tents. There was an order, ascribed to General George Patton, our Commanding General, to wear woolen uniforms, the olive drab, not the summer khakis. It was because of the sweat drenching the cottons and the cool nights causing chills. You can argue the point; it was, in any case, going from the frying pan into the fire. An immediate wholesale adjustment occurred. All empty vehicles were used to transport men to the relative comfort of town, where the most notable monument seemed to be a huge sign in a Greek that even the unlearned understood: PROPHYLAXIS. The other vehicles became refuges if they had generator-operated fans, or two-storied shelters with their canvas tops and beneath their chassis. Some men dug deep holes in the rough soil beneath their pup tents, and lay in these.

I lead a party back to the sea. There, off shore, not too far for strong swimmers, lay a gunboat battered by shot and storm, half under water. I dove in and around it and with a tire wrench tore out a gauge from the torpedo tube and a second brass meter from the control room, and took them ashore. (They were to be sent to my wife, who must soon know, if she did not connect it with the Mohave sleeping bag, that either I have poor taste in gifts or there was nothing to give that didn't rely to please upon the spirit of giving.)

Herz and I lost no time seeking out prisoners of war to interrogate, beginning with two Germans captured before the mass surrender of Tunis and an Italian from a captured hospital ship. No one thought the Axis could win. The Italian believed most Italians to be anti-Fascist; I did not like the Germans. The Germans were friendly and harmless, politically apathetic. Themes to be repeated in a hundred interrogations to come. We went again and again to

Africa, from Oran to Tunis

the camp, and wrote our analyses down studiously, as if there were someone somewhere whose mind would be formed by reading them. Afterwards, we found a restaurant that fed us liver and noodles, with wine, a welcome change of diet. The population was not starving, but even the better restaurants barely excelled the Army messes. The unique genius of the 1st MRBC was beginning to reflect itself in our life style; a score of veteran travelers spread out over the landscape on intelligence and reconnaissance for *la dolce vita*.

My own specialty was biota and seashore, both of which I searched for my wife as much as for the Company:

> Sweetheart,
>
> Today I shall direct my propaganda to my audience; there have been tremendous developments in regard to a "bug-eyed" view of the world. Just now, for example, a steady stream of ants is winding across my tent floor, fortunately only battalion and not brigade size. Another army not far away is carrying off everything but the GI soap. They are not alone - there are weird little things that would bewitch, drive your pretty nose into the ground & befoul our romance - scorpions & daddy-long-legs, fat funny beetles & a horde of nearly invisible things of all kind. Yesterday, some winged little beast hit me in the back & almost knocked me down. There are lizards scampering about, interesting little snails, toads and turtles. They all hop, skip, march or crawl through our encampment en route to some great destination beyond.
>
> But down at the sea yesterday! How can I describe it? I swam out around a point off the cove, where short, sharp cliffs descended into the sea and found dark, murky little caves with shiny rocks & the sea beating in at them, with dark and skulking crabs that slithered into crevices. When I approached, I could see little shell fish imbedded into the rocks, snails that crunched beneath their fancy shells and little red globs of jelly that packed things into themselves.

For his part, dashing Sergeant Tuero (he'd won a promotion) had discovered Spanish settlers, and he brought me one day to a hill above the sea, there to eat abundant fresh fish and drink homemade wine. The French sailors who had picked us up and driven us there donated the bread. At twilight, after driving crazily along the cliffs and beaches of the seaside, we visited another Spanish farm where we took a cool bath from a pump and drank freshly-drawn cow's milk, mixing in lumps of sugar. Another time we went to a village restaurant run by yet another Spaniard, who fashioned for us a grand *paella*.

Supreme in pelf and procurement, Hans Habe took us to visit the home of a friend who presented us with a full French dinner, Cinzano and Armagnac included. The occasion coincided with the arrival of the special orders commissioning the three Lieutenants, and with the news that the world Communist Comintern had been dissolved. We took this news as a clever and proper gesture of the Soviets, making communists everywhere seem more nationalist and unrevolutionary, but doubted it would mark the end of the idea of a communist world revolution.

The Company found itself a farm upon which to base itself more comfortably, but orders quickly arrived to proceed eastward to Algiers. We were needed! Conniving ghouls had already spotted persons and machines in the Table of Organization of the Company that they wished to detach unto themselves. Early next day the convoy snaked along the desert road. I will not arrive, however.

As the column passed through an Arab village, an officer up ahead somewhere recalled some stern admonitions against espionage and the uncertain loyalties of the Arabs, and, thinking that the enemy might very well profit from knowing that his misinformation of the future was right now on its way to his men, shouted back to us to shut down the hatches and doors. I was riding in a radio van with a tight soundproof door, opened to catch a breath of air, and was clutching the edge with my right hand to keep from falling out as the truck rocked and bumped along.

My favorite private, George Glade, dutifully jumped from the assistant driver's seat and slammed the door, painfully trapping my third finger, squeezing off its flesh, but, because Glade alertly and promptly reopened the door, he did not wrench off the flattened bones. Grimacing, I dosed myself with sulfa powder from the first aid kit on my belt; inquired of oncoming traffic where there would be a hospital big enough to provide morphine and amputate fingers, and had the Private drive me there. We sped ahead to a British hospital under tents, off the road some miles ahead of the convoy, and to the admissions tent. Where, all in good time, a doctor stopped by to take a look. "We'll get back to you as soon as we can," said he, "messy, isn't it?" No morphine; the pain was aspirin-sized, a big throb as if the nerves were mostly dead and the surviving neurones had gathered together for mutual consolation.

I am lucky. By the time a number of worse cases are disposed of and I have had a spot of tea, the gory mess had begun to reassemble as a finger; the bones were together, the tendons had relapsed from threads into tendrils; only the flesh was weak and largely absent. Let's give it a while to find itself, I was advised, and I joined a hearty if not hale group under canvas for the night. As I picked my way to a cot, a couple of ambulant patients were helping a leg-amputee to escape the premises to go in search of the alcoholic beverages that had been forbidden him. They were gone for hours.

The other patients of the tent idle about, swapping tales of Old Blighty and the States and Africa. I had my first immersion among British soldiers; I had felt guilty because the Germans and Italians had had to be fought off, in the West, largely by the British, and I secretly appreciated that they were decent enough not to exclaim: "Where in bloody hell have you been all this while!" That they did not razz me for the defeat and flight of Kasserine Pass in February that cost them ten thousand men.

They told me that the Germans had incomprehensibly surrendered just now in Tunisia; that they appeared to be in good order, well-equipped and supplied, and could have held out for some time. That it wasn't like them. Perhaps the Eyeties had urged it upon them. The amputee hopped back in to the tent, soaked to the gills, to the consternation of the staff that had been looking around for him.

The next morning, the injured member, swept clean of sulfa dust and examined closely, half-promised that it may heal. I bade my friends goodbye with a promise to bring them some of the partying materials that are in short supply and in infinite demand. Within a couple of days I managed to collect sausages, cakes, whiskey and wine, and jazz records, and brought them out for a celebration.

I had meanwhile discovered my Company respectably encamped on the outskirts of Algiers, while I was being sought out for a project shaping up. I was authorized a room at the Psychological Warfare Hotel, the *Hotel Corneille,* in the City, with a Mr. Brooks, an English literary agent and editor, who spent four years in a German prison camp in World War I. He could not talk of his job so it had to be with the black propaganda station broadcasting in German. He was neat, inconspicuous, quiet, daintily mustached.

Food was poor at the "Corny Beef" Hotel, as some of the British called it. I saw at table an extraordinary assortment of faces, washing down a dull fare with carafes of wine: about half of them were civilians, and, of these, half wore civilian clothes and the other half uniforms without insignia; the English were mostly older than the Americans; the garb, even the uniforms, were colorful and varied; there seemed to be no Muslims; there were several women - English and French - and there were French officers and civilians. All together they supervised the press, radio and movies of North Africa, and figured out ways of feeding their propaganda into Europe. For their cues, the British turned to England and Cairo, the Americans to Washington. The PWB operation was under the Allied Forces Headquarters, also set up in Algiers. It was not responsible for the American or British correspondents, who related directly to the Army commanders. You learned by gossip. No general orientation was provided by lecture or booklet to this American Lieutenant and his Company.

My return from hospital coincided with a reception at night for the officers of the 1st MRBC, and particularly to honor the newly commissioned men. Our Commander arrives, Commander, in fact, of all of Psychological Operations in Africa and new Fronts to come, Colonel Hazeltine, a short, stocky, full-bellied watery-blue-eyed specimen well along in age, wearing cavalry boots half his height and the insignia of the U.S. Cavalry. He slouches about, guzzling whiskey liberally, muttering incomprehensible trivia, tells the story all had been alerted to expect, how he had been appointed to his job and only then had heard of PWB for the first time, and had no idea what it was all about. He felt proud of this.

Africa, from Oran to Tunis

It did not keep him from exercising - and soon abusing - his authority. He gets drunk, "was drunk" say some, "is always drunk" say others. Looking around him blearily, he fixes upon tall, slender, dandified, jovial Hans Habe, questions why he should have deserved a commission from the ranks, insults him as a foreigner and remarks contemptuously that he is too well dressed and pretentious for the work of a true soldier. Hans is indignant. So are the other officers. Not a one sides with the "shit-kicker," as I thenceforth call him - to his back of course. Captain Caskey, first in line to protest, says not a word. No one dares object. The tyrant is quite capable of putting one into a hole, somewhere, or sending him into a replacement depot for the next flesh-dealer who sends out a call.

All, civilian and military, all nationalities, all ranks, agree that he is an incompetent drunken bastard. Yet there he will remain forever, boasting that he knows nothing of psychological warfare, that he is a cavalry man and proud of it, further that he is the most senior colonel in the American Army, and resents the way his juniors, Patton and Eisenhower, have been promoted over him. He doesn't shout all this muck, he says it in an ordinary voice lacking affect, which makes what he is saying the more unbelievable.

Among the Army's many problems, which in turn lead to many other problems, was how to get rid of incompetents and destroyers of human relations. Attack someone like Hazeltine, and he will poison you from Washington and Capitol Hill, or deal with you summarily if he gets wind of it, so there is no way for a junior officer to do this. Still, it was astonishing that all the non-American officers and the American and British civilians of high rank in the organization, with all their connections back home, could not or would not take the necessary steps to get rid of him.

He should have gone before a retirement board of his peers, not easy, because he outranked everyone in seniority, which is as good as gold in the Army, even if it is by a week. He should have been given appointment as Ambassador to Nicaragua, fief of the Somoza family. He should have been sent on "Mission Impossible," but shot beforehand, just to make sure. His appointment to be chief of Psychological Warfare was as much of a disaster as one could possibly wreak upon the newest and most complicated organization in the European Theater. Compare the brilliance of Dr. Goebbels, commanding both domestic and foreign propaganda for the Reich, with this clown and his tricks, and you have one more reason why it took a while to win the War.

It cannot be said that there were not those who were pleased to have an evil misfit in charge to justify and conceal their own ineptness. There were even some Englishmen who thought that Hazeltine was satisfactory, for they could operate free from top control or coordination - it was not difficult to deceive him, even though he was paranoid - and, if lazing or bumbling on their jobs, might seem quite competent to those who would compare them with their American model.

Only a few, the more useful characters, of the Company were in Algiers, the rest of the troop was encamped at the large hacienda in the countryside. Theoretically I was still in command of a platoon, of which there were now three, commanded by Rathbun, Herz and myself. With me were Lieutenants Bell and Wallenberg, the one a good routine soldier, the other essentially a propagandist. I was relieved of practically all duties, but kept my censoring job; the men were permitted to choose their censor and I got the most choices; they must have known that since I wrote many letters myself I was unsympathetic to excessive censorship and besides, I had to scan their own mail fast.

Algiers was then the only French city in the world of any considerable gaiety. Undamaged by bombings, a fine European City up front, and an Arab city behind, complete with an intriguing casbah. Without effort, I fell into the sociable life of an easy-going espionage agent, planning and waiting for the Italian operation. Josephine Baker, otherwise active in Algiers as an agent of counter-espionage, came to sing blues, hot jazz and ballads, throwing in French songs as well. She had a ten piece French band accompanying her that played *le jazz hot*, which I called "corny."

I encountered Henry Kaplan, from the University of Chicago, expert in French, conversant with the area already, and together with an Algerian plainclothes policeman, we got on a private tour of the great casbah, touching in upon bars, shops, tiny restaurants, and a brothel, just to say hello. I addressed Jill about the tour:

> Do these views strike interesting chords: "a wavering Arab drunk in great good spirits struggling up a steep street with a bloody basket overflowing with a ram's head, wild and alive-looking. What a dinner the Arab will have." Or "an Arab cemetery, full of small graves bearing the half moon, with olive, almonds, pomegranate and fig trees shading it". Or "a brothel with ugly women who bring you in to where two Arabs play on a piano and tambourine and sing Arab songs." Or "a drunken sailor of unknown nationality swinging a huge club down a narrow gutter of a street with perfect abandon." Or "a little meat shop in a grotto where entrails and other meats are sold & where a huge, quivering sheep's heart lies on the table with two great green flies sucking at it." Or "streets that are only passageways & stairways over which centuries old wood and stone structures rot." Or "a mosque in which several Arabs are kneeling or lying in the gloomy coolness." Or "a working class section where on some wall in each block is inscribed the hammer and sickle." Or "a beautiful church on a great hill dropping down to the sea." Or "a gruesome stench of burnt flesh and garbage, human manure and sewage, of filthy bodies and unaired holes."

They did impress her, for she wrote to inquire in an uncritical but concerned way whether I had taken my brothel visit seriously. I replied no, and felt complimented that she was anxious about me, perhaps even jealous.

Pastor Phillips of the U of C Divinity School, "dapper Dan," had turned up aboard another troopship and sought me out. We exchanged hospitality - the genuine roast beef on the ship's table staggered me - and we walked the deck, from which we could view the City above, more beautiful than close-up, as he pointed out when we took a walk around. I thought of my clerical friend as a member of the numerous "true" circles whom I knew at the University, friends quiet and not flashy, loving the campus, the Midway, the rocks of the Lake, even to eating early breakfast at Steinway's or the Commons.

I arranged a car for the beach and the rocks and shore were indeed beautiful. We came upon a husky American soldier playing western songs on a banjo and a little old scrawny Englishman with a walrus mustache who was tap-dancing crazy Limehouse steps to the music. He boasted that he was classified B4, physically deficient, but then stood on his hands to the cheers of the crowd gathered around. Dressed in a towel and an oversized pair of military shoes, he danced to all the Country Western pieces.

Hans Habe and I had become fast friends and were thinking of taking rooms together, perhaps because we both were arrogant, or because I was outspokenly hostile to Colonel Hazeltine and the rest of the useless lot hanging around the Corny Beef and 1st MRBC, or because I had the bearing and dash of a "real" officer, Central European style, or was more of a man-about-town. Habe and I spent an evening at the house of a Viennese lady friend of his who prepared meals for no more than ten persons, authentic Viennese food. The other table was occupied by two U.S. Navy Captains, and a Commander, Gene Markey of Hollywood, who recognized Habe from a party at the Soviet Embassy in Washington, and we end up as a jolly single table once we all sense where the others are coming from. The Commander's first wife had been Joan Bennett, his second Hedy Lamarr - "the Austro-Hungarian Connection!" Upon leaving the jolly crew, Hans did his lady friend a favor: the duller of the Captains had come once before and had left with a bottle of excellent brandy without paying for it; what shall she do? Don't worry, said Hans, just put it on his bill and don't mention it. It worked.

On June 13, 1943, 240 cameramen, under the inspiration and orders of Mikhail Slutsky, spent 24 hours at 140 different filming points of the vast Soviet Front, gathering the raw data of "A Day of War," ultimately shown in eight reels. PWB was hardly in the same class. It was devoid of imagination, and underemployed. As a matter of fact, just about the time when the Soviet cameramen who survived were going to bed, there took place a rousing party among the Corny Beef crowd and our Hero got drunk, danced madly, borrowed the trumpet player's instrument, and played with the band for an hour until everything in the room was reeling and he decided to call it a night well spent.

True, we are only doing what is permitted to us. I got Peter Viereck properly placed, for instance: "He is so weak personally, despite his sparkling intellect. Now he should be much more happy, at least for the time being, doing analysis and living a more intellectual life." Martin Herz arranged a number of excursions to prison camps, where I, devoid of the linguistic excellence of the others in our crew, listened to an interpreter and studied the prisoners, their bearing, eyes, expressions, the details of their personal care, their musculature. There is much to be told of a person without understanding what 99% of his words mean. I listened so closely and sympathetically to the story of an Italian Major, about how he walked three times the length of the desert from Egypt to Tunis without proper equipment, weapons, and food, and how glad he was that the war was soon to be over, that the guy ended up by giving me his insignia to send home to his wife. He explained to her: "He was very happy about his changed situation, so it is in no way like the gold out of a dead man's tooth." The Germans this far from the front did not believe in victory, either, it seemed. They had passed masses of American equipment and troops on their way getting here, and were impressed.

The interrogators discussed the advantages to be derived by sending back prisoners to their own lines, there to tell of the terrible weight of Allied arms. However, what seemed at first to be a clever idea, was discarded for at least two reasons: many of the freed prisoners would be imprisoned or killed if they were in any way suspected of deserting or surrendering easily, and, in any case, they would be threatened with dire punishment should they ever disclose the impressive wealth of weaponry, vehicles, and soldiers of the enemy.

A team was formed for the first phase of the invasion of Italy. It consisted, first, of John Whitaker, a famous American journalist, and Lt. Archimedes Patti, who were OSS cloak and dagger types. Then came a tall American naval officer, Lt. Senior Grade Livingston Hartley, who was usually looking downwards through his bifocals like a stork, was Back Bay Boston, studied at Eton and Harvard, and had busied himself with League of Nations affairs, do-good groups, and the Committee to Save America by Aiding the Allies (my group, too), and whose wife was a beauty and an actress, which got him to talking of the plethora of Jews in the stage industry reproachfully, because his wife had been now and then accosted, harassed, and/or involved (one could not be sure of his grounds). He was always dressed for parade with a visored, braided hat.

There came then four Britishers. Two were very blonde types, the one stocky, Captain Reyburn Heycock, the other slender with a mustache, Major Galsworthy. Add one little Englishman, dark with a small mustache, a journalist and civilian named Barney; he had worked in Italy for years. The fourth man was a Scot (or so he said when talking against the English), Ian Robertson. This last one, "Robbie," became my closest friend, eternal source of amusing stories and commentary, a bachelor, veteran of the trenches in World War I, three times wounded, with ugly scars along his legs and arm, twice torpedoed in trying to get to North Africa, of which we were to hear much in good time. He was brusque, and had a severe look, until you looked into his warm brown eyes. He pretended to stand on his dignity as an old fighting officer and gentleman. He had moved to Italy, where he worked a tuna fishery off the Island of Elba.

John Whitaker, thanks to OSS's secret slush funds, had a villa above the city and the group of eight decided to convene there each day to talk about the Italian situation and what they would like to do in Italy. I would be trying to systematize something but no one seemed interested in any planning, just in having tea leisurely served to us and talking about Italians and their culture. We took turns leading the discussion but it was a silly show.

Heycock and Galsworthy were a close pair. They had just returned from the Front. To me, they appeared to be up to something, maybe discussing means of assuring control over relations with the Eighth (British) Army Command. Whenever I came upon them, they froze, until finally I confronted them and said, look, this is a joint show, and you are obliged to keep me informed. "Poppycock" said the slight blonde; "Balls" said the stocky blonde. I turned on my heels and walked out of the room.

They must have conferred, because, a while later, apropos of nothing, they said to me that they had meant nothing derogatory by their remarks and quite agreed that it would be splendid if they and I shared information and worked together fully. I was surprised.

The two of them, with Robbie and myself, we did work closer together after Whitaker and Patti retired, thick as thieves. The English didn't like them, this famous American correspondent, whose book, *You Can't Escape History,* had just appeared, and his saturnine poker-faced sidekick Patti, whose name derived no doubt from the town of Patti in Sicily. Perhaps they were cosying up to the American Headquarters, the Seventh Army, whose help they would need if they were to be operating in Sicily. There was already something of a competition between the Seventh and Eighth Armies, and certainly no love is lost between Generals Patton and Montgomery.

Without any formal orders coming from anywhere, or so it seemed, I found myself committed to the British Eighth Army. Somebody had cut the appropriate orders; else I would be called back; moreover the address on some of my mail was changed to go to Eighth Army HQ. It was all a jumble. Where did Hartley's orders come from? Who was this ancient archaeologist from Egypt, who seemed to have withered in the sands to look now like a leafless branch and who joined us from time to time? Was Barney sure to come, or just taking an extended vacation out of reach of any authority? They all acted like moles when it came to divulging the location of the holes from which they emerged and where they were about to dig next.

For a moment it would seem that Richard Crossman, who had turned up in Algiers, would want to go on the expedition. But then he was designated as a kind of head of the Brits at the Corny Beef, and began dueling with Colonel Hazeltine, so the group did without his energy and bustling. He was not liked by the core foursome that I mentioned, nor did they, military men, want any civilians "buggering about the Front." Besides, they were Conservatives while Crossman was a Socialist.

There was also a British Colonel McFarlane to be accounted for, another handsome dark Scot, who seems to have a hold of some kind over the foursome. He was able enough to be loaded with important cares, but was destined for some useless job connecting the PWB operators and the Operations Branch (G3), Eighth Army. (In the American Army, propaganda operations were given over to G2, Intelligence. This was a mistake, though I was in no position to judge such questions yet.)

Somebody somewhere, probably Captain Caskey, was told by Hazeltine, who had been reminded by one of his civilian advisers, alerted to the imminence of warfare in Italy, to cut orders and get this new outfit over to Tunis, closer to the war and out of the HQ which was crowded enough with all of its types - more of them, too, being shipped over by the Office of War Information all the time to do God knows what.

At this point I decided, if I was to be Eighth Army, I must look like one of those snappy British staff officers, so, to quote me addressing my wife: *"I've had very little to do this morning except to be barbered at length by a very excellent French barber in the neighborhood. I've had my curly locks shampooed and now look very sleek. Just think what you're missing - my fine, tan skin, my black hair and a very black mustache of recent vintage that my friend Barney tells me makes me look like one of Ireland's famed 'black brood.'"* But, that's, of course, what Barney looks like.

So it happened that we found ourselves on the road to Tunis, convoying with some of the 1st MRBC. The latter would be doing POW interrogation and then move up if the need should arise. And others of them would be working on the fake Italian language broadcasting station, called "Italo Balbo," in honor of Italy's most famous aviator, whose planes had flown the Ocean and descended at Chicago under my very eyes when I was a child. The little team rode along in two jeeps and a trailer, the several officers, less Whitaker and Patti who disappeared, less Captain Heycock, too, who had gone ahead to find us a home. On the way, a friendly warplane buzzed us and, believing it enemy, we were scared; it might easily have knocked some of us out, and I realized that in all the hard training I had gone through, never had anyone thought to arrange for me to be buzzed by airplanes, in maneuvers or otherwise. The main defense was a periodic placement of anti-

Africa, from Oran to Tunis 165

aircraft batteries along the main roads, constantly alert. Barrage Balloons would have helped for this purpose but were never to be seen. Lacking active help, it was well, if uncomfortable, to remove the jeep tops and lower the windshields; one could at least stop and get out quickly, then. Was this lack of training the fault of separating the Army Air Corps so completely from the Army ground forces? And a failure of combined training? No doubt. So simple it would have been to provide such training; and the same for the pilots: how had they learned to strafe troops? But the worse was yet to come.

For three days, we were on the road over the mountains to Tunisia. It was already June 25. I had missed the fighting in Tunis. Heycock, the Sandhurst Graduate, had, however, unerringly selected the best villa of a set of them along the sea north of the City of Tunis, at La Cram, not far from ancient Carthage. Bachelors, fops, and culinary incompetents notwithstanding, all must pitch into housekeeping; I prescribed it with a duty roster duly posted. There turned out to be eight men around the place, and several jeeps and drivers.

We all ran around in shorts. Inspired by Robbie, we were calling the stately Hartley, "the Admiral" and the strutting barrel Heycock "the General." One day a couple of GIs wandering along the beach approached me lolling in swimming trunks by the door and asked whether I could lend them a bottle opener, whereupon I shouted, "Admiral, do you have the bottle opener?" and Hartley yelled "No," and hollered at Heycock on the beach, "General, do you have the bottle opener?" and the soldiers sidled away, so that when I got inside and appeared shortly with the found instrument, they had disappeared.

Then Heycock and Galsworthy finally got around to telling the others about their experiences in combat propaganda. So here, now, for the first time, I learned that the principal combat effort of psychological warfare so far was to write and print up propaganda, stuff it into emptied smoke shells, and get them into artillery pieces to fire and burst over enemy positions, scattering down upon them like confetti cast from a window upon a parade. A Captain Foster, whom I would meet, had been credited with developing the technique. The stories enchanted me for I was an artillery officer and what lay ahead was familiar. They had preliminary firing tables, worked out for the chosen weapon, the British 25 lb cannon. Its range covered the Front lines and well back. When tables were worked out for the American 105 mm cannon, it would become the standard means of delivery of frontline propaganda. The British had tried before El Alamein to send a small truck through the lines tossing out leaflets, but the operation was given up after the vehicle was captured by the enemy.

I was shown several leaflets that had been showered on the Germans. Thus, over a score of meals, and by evening's dim light, and driving along here and there, I picked up their knowledge, the first in the American army to do so. The other tasks of psychological warfare were to reveal themselves, at the time when I would be forced to address them, "learning by doing," my old pragmatist educators would say. But I had roughly in hand the main combat propaganda medium of the coming campaigns.

I exchanged visits with my American comrades, encamped up the line, who were not sure at all to get in on the Sicilian operation. Some of my mail was still coming in through 1st MRBC channels. Too, cagily, I extracted from the American ration allowances food that could be brought to my comrades by the sea - who were also, *tutti quanti*, living on British rations and the Italianate supplements that Robbie and the others were able to solicit from the environment (like the spaghetti made by a neighboring Italian lady in return for giving her an equal portion of flour for her own family).

On the Fourth of July I was naturally to be found in the American encampment, where a feast, in bulk if not in quality, was conducted, and before and afterwards the ritual game of baseball was played. My spectacular patriotism was not to deny my all too frequent aspersions cast upon the behavior of my countrymen. I was disgruntled with the War Effort, despite the mountains of materiel forthcoming.

The news from the States isn't too good and I wonder where future improvement will come from. Do you think people realize what

> *stupid representatives they have in the Congress? They have managed to settle none of the great, pressing problems, save on reciprocal trade, and have generally mislegislated on things. The strike sounds bad, but I don't think it is too important. The removal of price subsidies and the refusal to tax sound much worse, as well as those silly personal quarrels which take up time, energy and news space. ...I won't bore you by getting completely wound up on the subject.*

I waxed wroth over accounts of race rioting between whites and blacks in Detroit. I felt that the cure for strikes and racism was to put all offenders into uniform and ship them overseas. Hardly an original idea, and not even a good idea, considering how long it takes to get even a willing inductee into fighting condition, and what of their families, and who would make the tanks and guns and all of that? Well, on occasion I would sound like any regular Army officer. In her letters, my wife eggs me on, too. Moreover, I am irritated at the unused military and industrial manpower in North Africa, both French and Arab.

I did have a flash of insight into one matter at home, though. A Gallup Poll was put out reporting that the American people were becoming less isolationist, an encouraging sign to liberals. But, I thought, "a mere sentiment is not enough. In fact it may show a dangerous and evil sort of imperialism and interference rather than a desire to cooperate. We shall know better *après la guerre.*"

For war news from around the world, the Le Cram lodgers relied upon the British Broadcasting Service that entered our home with the resounding chords of "Hearts of Oak." It was at least as reliable as news from any other source. The American service exaggerated and wasted time on enthusiasm; the German service was becoming ever less reliable in the face of defeats, and the Italian service was desperate in anticipation of invasion. We got a lot of intelligence reports without any planned profiling of our needs. Robbie subscribed to the airmail microprint edition of the *London Times,* for its crossword puzzles, he insisted.

Dapper Major Galsworthy, formerly of the Colonial Office and Private Secretary to Prime Minister Winston Churchill, was the perfect liaison, and the Le Cram lodgers were treated daily to the news of the build-up and the impending invasion. It was to be Sicily, of course, and he was trying to get his little team into one of the first boats, but there was a lot of competition to be among the first to land. The Army Staff did not understand combat propaganda yet, didn't really want to, they were interesting in killing the "Boche." They were suspicious, more than the American Command, of men who knew too much about the places they were targeting, and might have a vestige of free speech left, worse, a command of means to get a contradictory message back. It was decided that I would be the sole American officer in the group. Liv Hartley will come later. Herz, Habe, Wallenberg, Grigis and the others were trying to get confirmation from the Seventh Army for their inclusion at some stage.

In the mail they held for me, I learned that the war-baby was on its way. There was only one letter to me, dated June 15th, then another on the 25th. The first since leaving the States. The pregnant woman writes from Buz' house in Washington:

> *Despite all the tempting alternatives - the Waac, a $2600 job as ass't technical editor at Fort Monmouth (a telegram came for me at Buss's this week - that's all I know about the job) - Lockheed, etc. etc., I'm awfully happy about the baby. I must assure you again of that, because maybe I didn't give you that impression when I last saw you. The idea just grows on one, and now I wouldn't lose it for anything & can't wait til I get large & complacent. I've been whoopsing some, but that will pass, & besides it isn't hard for one who whoopsed her way through college.*

She forgot that I hadn't had a medical resume and gave me one:

> *Oh yes - I saw the doctor today. That test he took was positive, all right. However, since you didn't give me his home number, I called his office that day in Washington & got the wrong message. He's awfully glad it's a baby, & says I am well & should lay off ice cream. I am already abstaining from coffee, coke, cigarettes, alcohol (except when I'm forced) candy, spaghetti, fried anything and root beer, so I see very little point in eating at all, since the range is so narrow.*

I can't even have as much milk as I want. Incidentally, that long list of prohibitions is self-imposed. I'm just naturally averse to all those items. I'm glad you're not here, at least at mealtime. I would sicken and die at the sight of your filling your sweet face with goodies. I wish to hell you were here the rest of the time, tho.

I brought Martin's car back today, as I shall presently inform him. I'm telling everyone about the baby now, as I come to it. There's no point in keeping it a secret & it gets people to carry my bags for me.

Darling, darling. I wish I'd get a letter from you soon. I love you so much - it seems a shame we can't be together now somehow - either me there or something.

On the 10th of July the first soldiers landed in Sicily. The Eighth Army Team packed up, left the villa to Barney, Grigis and Hartley, and drove down to Sfax looking for their boat, any boat - it was not systematic or even formal. We found crafts of all sizes and shapes, coming and going. It seemed every unit had a tail that had to be curled up into the last bit of space. Enemy airplanes were rare.

I memorized some old English songs croaked by Robbie and several tippling visitors from Army Headquarters. Thus,

Frigging in the rigging, frigging in the rigging, frigging in the rigging, there's fuck-all else to do...

and:

Oh, I stuck my finger in the woodpecker's hole, the woodpecker said "God bless my soul! Take it out, take it out, Take it out-Remove it!"

which, in the final verse, went *"Take it out, put it back, take it out, re-volve it!"* and then my favorite, *"They shifted Pa's remains, to make way for ten-inch drains,"* which after a couple of verses, proclaimed that

> *Father in his life was never a quitter,*
> (all: *never a quitter,*)
> *I don't suppose he'll be a quitter now,*
> (all: *quitter now,*)
> *So when the job's complete,*
> *he'll haunt that shit-house seat,*
> *and only let them crap when he'll allow,*
> (all: *cor-bli-mey*)
> *Oh, won't there be some frightful constipation?*
> (all: *fr..con..*)
> *Won't those shit-bound, high-brow buggers rave?*
> (all: *bu..rave*)
> *Its no more than they deserve, for having the bloody nerve,*
> *to bugger about with a British workman's grave, corblimey,*
> (all: *to bugger about with a British workman's grave.*)

The sirocco blew like a blast out of hell. It penetrated the very wood of the doors and shutters. You cannot find words to describe it, it is awesome.

Robbie was getting impatient. He said to Galsworthy: "Come on now, let's get aboard. It's time I had a new kit." This was *à propos* the story I mentioned above. In World War I, young Robertson had lost his greatcoat in the course of a battle, and, despite repeated pleas, the Treasury refused to recompense him for the loss, saying that it was his fault. He nursed a grudge over the many years between wars. Then, his ship was torpedoed by a submarine on the way to North Africa. This time he held onto his greatcoat, but upon being rescued he filed an application for compensation for the loss of the coat, and received the money; so, he boasted: "I finally got even with the bloody bastards."

He was not so pleased at the etiquette on torpedoed boats. A confirmed bachelor and somewhat a misogynist, he ranted at having been forced to stand back with other men like heroes, while a crowd of nurses was being escorted into the life boats. He declared that he would much prefer to sail on a German ship "where the wretched women and children come last."

Finally a tank-landing craft came in and the loading master gave it the word to take us aboard. The boat was of the design made famous in World War II for descending upon hostile or undeveloped shores, with an armored forward prow to cut the waves; yet the prow wa split to open up quickly as it neared the shore; a vertical water-tight door contained behind it then opened from the top and dropped down to become a platform to let out the men and machines.

The sea was fairly calm and the voyage was undisturbed by the enemy. The several officers aboard ate together in a handy little mess-hall topsides. The enlisted men - "other ranks" one should now say in the 8th Army - eat here and there. It is a slow boat, the voyage surprisingly long, we sleep aboard. My bunk was the latest in over half a hundred different sleeping spots since I became a soldier, an average of one every ten days.

On the prowl, I discovered that a ladder was fastened to the vertical door and went down to a pit between the door and the false prow. With each dip of the prow the seawater rushed into the hole and was blocked from entering the hull by the door. I took off my clothes, calling to the others, and descended the ladder into the pit. There I stood, and as each wave broke into the false hull, it lifted me up and I thrashed about. The water rushed out as the bow rose and I stood in happy expectancy of the next surge. Heycock tried it out, once or twice, and gave his tight approving smile of the adventure. There came another, and another, all morning long.

The outlines of Sicily rose along the horizon. Not an enemy plane to be seen. The landings of the British had not been difficult. The problems encountered in the past forty-eight hours, some serious, were of their own making: confusion and amicide had begun to take their toll. The leading column had moved up from the beaches and passed through Syracuse.

The LST entered directly into the fine old harbor and sidled between a smoking sunken hospital ship and the Fountain of Arethusa. I scampered onto the quay. It had been about 2600 years probably since the first of my ancestors had landed here with the Greeks, following upon natural disasters that had struck the natives. Here now it had been the Allied bombers. But the Fountain of Arethusa was still flowing and people of Syracuse were filling their jugs from it. They politely let me cut in, to fill my tin cup, and drink of the water.

From left: Hans Habe,* me, Martin Herz,**
Grigis, in front a Tunisian well.

* Hans Habe (1911-1977) Austrian/Hungarian writer, novelist and newspaper publisher.
** Martin Herz was political attaché at the US Embassy in Iran (1963-1967), US Ambassador to Bulgaria (1974-1977) and Director of the Institute for the Study of Diplomacy at Georgetown University..

CHAPTER SEVEN

THE INVASION OF SICILY

THE warlike invaders look beyond the Fountain of Arethusa and its real water and thirsty people; no other tourists are to be seen. No sounds of bombs or firing at the moment, a faint noise that might be artillery in the distance, but you cannot always hear well for the noise of lorries being loaded and banging their way into and out of the Port area. There are few ships in the harbor, considering its presumed importance in the invasion. The men ashore tell the propaganda team that the enemy has withdrawn promptly to the North and is resisting pursuit on the roads to Catania and all along the Southern flanks of Mount Etna. The Yanks are somewhere off to the West.

The port is wrecked, the train sheds in shambles, the ancient city still standing, the population not much in evidence - where are they? - *sfollati,* fled to the countryside and to the great quarries, but they are beginning now to trickle back into town.

Once outside the old city, in the quarries and caves, and scattered over the hills and in cottages, you could view people by the thousands. Without binoculars and unless you got in close to their poverty, you would have imagined a panoramic picnic, a county fair, a collective harvest.   In these same ancient quarries had labored the surrendered army that Ancient Athens had sent to conquer Syracuse, a myriad degraded to the status of slaves following their defeat. The Italian and German prisoners of the moment were much better treated. Half the Italians, who, it develops, were Sicilian, were simply dismissed, or dropped out and went home.

The region had been somewhat deforested, the springs become less abundant, the population grossly swollen in numbers, the fish less plentiful, over the millennia. Syracuse had become a backwater town with superlative monuments, sublime ruins of Antiquity, a Cathedral of the greatest architectural beauty, a castle of the most brilliant of medieval Emperors of the Holy Roman Empire and Sicily, Frederick II. Fine old Baroque palaces and town houses crowd the little ancient island of Ortygia, which is the oldest part of Syracuse and embraces the old Port. They were now all damaged to some degree. Robbie and I took up two small apartments of a rather newer building; the rest of the advance party had gone forward to work with the artillery and interrogate German prisoners; they were trying to get surrender demands over to the enemy, without much success; their problem was their English exclusiveness; they wanted a small party, Colonel Head of G-2 agreed, indeed suggested that they hold off bringing in more professional people on the printing side. There were several good chances to fire leaflets or get them through by patrol. A loudspeaker would have been dangerous but useful.

The Syracuse party got some messages conveying a measure of what was happening. Again, there was no plan, no scheme, no knowledge of the technology available; still, like muskrats going instinctively into a new swamp, Heycock and Galsworthy got busy with the Operations Staff and Robbie and I set up shop in Syracuse. We found a printing shop, undamaged, with some paper, and began to print what we called the *Corriere di Siracusa*. It became the first Allied paper published in Europe. Robbie was Editor, I was Co-Publisher, member of the Editorial Committee, and Production Manager. As we were about to go to press with the First Issue, a Capt. Charlton showed up: he was the cheerful fast-moving one-man (cum batman) publisher of the *Eighth Army News;* he had started it just before the Battle of El Alamein. He had a good claim on the paper stock and press, and might have beat us out for it, backed by his vain boss, who commanded all the hardware and territory wrested from the enemy.

But Charlton was clever enough to see advantages in collaborating with people who knew the lay of the land.

Furthermore, he recognized the need to get the civilian population lined up; too, he latched on to an additional source of news. And besides, he was a decent chap. So we made a deal to publish the two newspapers together and swap news. The Italian printers stood by during all of this negotiation; they were pleased to be part of something new. There had been no newspaper in Syracuse hitherto, and they were glad to know that an American was involved, for where there is an American there is money. That was the way Charlton must have felt, too; there was a hint that a part of the small subsidy provided him by HQ, 8A, could go into subsidizing his whiskey ration as well. No one bothered paying for the paper or presses or anything aside from the food and money needed by the Italian printers, who were eager to put out the newspaper.

This was another "first," as they say: it was the first Free Newspaper of this part of Europe since Mussolini, Franco, Stalin and Hitler turned out the lights. Handset, and hand-printed on the old press by a youth on extra rations, Numero Uno of the *Corriere di Siracusa* appears on 14 Luglio 1943 from Via Minerva no.3, in one tabloid-sized sheet, Italian on the one side and English of the *Eighth Army News* on the other.

On the Italian side there appears a stern warning against hoarding and hiding food supplies from the hungry populace. It recognizes the existing Italian money and also proclaims the legal tender of the new Allied bank notes being used by the troops and for civilian purchases by the army. It carries brief notices from the Sicilian fronts and reports a Russian advance near Kursk. (The greatest battle of the War was then taking place in Russia, a battle from which the Wehrmacht could not fully recover.) The *Eighth Army News* headlines that the roads to Augusta are cleared. It bears a snappy portrait of General Montgomery in his beret, Mussolini-sized, and highlights his visiting the troops; it reports as well the battle news from the American sector.

On the 26th of July the headline is "Mussolini has Fallen!" Both the Italian and the English sides of the page print word for word the latest BBC slow-speaking broadcast of the night before.

Next the paper split and the Italian and English newspapers went their separate ways. The *Corriere* carried a great speech by Churchill to the Italians assuring them ultimately a secure role in the new Europe, if now they surrender unconditionally. (Obviously this was hardly an unconditional surrender.) A long editorial told readers that Sicily had been partially destroyed, but that it will rise again thanks to the hard work and willpower of the Sicilian people and the good will and assistance to be rendered by the Allies. Then the foreign coverage went around the world from Kiska and New Guinea to Orel, USSR.

The people began to trickle back into town but were still afraid of bombings, now by the Germans and Italian aircraft. Planes did come over, not too seriously. I was printing the paper when bombs started to fall and ack-ack went off and a crowd rushed the print shop for shelter - or for comfort. I pushed the door shut to keep the shop from getting mobbed and messed-up and to keep the presses going, and I was scolded for my heartlessness by the people banging against the doors. I shouted at them that there was no danger, but they knew better: odds on safety are subjective.

Enemy planes came at night and many people crowded the shelters, including British sailors. I was abed, trying to kill fleas, or at least to calculate the missiles trajectory, saying an occasional Paternoster and Ave Maria, for their soporific effect, and listening uneasily to the explosions and the artillery. Robbie was in his own apartment, no lights, but sailors came up, arousing him and he came across the hall to the me and said: "Would you go down with these boys, like a good fellow, Alfred? There is some damned trouble, I don't know what, in the air raid shelter!" No use to say: "Call the police." Italian police and carabinieri retained their functions but could not be expected to discipline the troops of their conquerors; fact was, the Military Police had a hard enough job doing so. The civilians had lost respect for their own uniformed authorities as well.

I drew on my trousers, slipped a 7.65 cal. automatic I had confiscated into my pocket, took up my flashlight and went down with the sailors into the darkness where there was a lot of screaming and cursing. One or two inebriated sailors were beating up on people, mostly women and children, or that's what it seemed like in the near blackness, and the one who was most disorderly wouldn't budge and seemed crazed, striking out in all directions with wild strength at the several buddies who were tugging at him, so I rapped him on the back of the head with my automatic, and the sailor who had called me interjected: "You'll hurt him, Sir!"- "No, it'll just stun him a bit," and the lug did roll his eyes perplexedly at his assailant and quieted down enough to be dragged off. The same sailor met us the next day and apologized: "he says his head doesn't hurt at all."

Next night, another gang of sailors came charging into the flat building where I was staying, intent upon taking it over. Again Robbie called me to help, himself disappearing into the shadows, and I had to draw a gun on them - which hardly impressed them, but they did sullenly depart.

I could not but notice a shapely young woman in pumps and black dress, true, most were wearing black, which made soldiers think they had suffered heavy casualties, but it came from their traditionally very long mourning periods, and she had long black hair and was well-stacked, slender-legged, and pretty and her name was Nuccia; she gave me the eye, no more than that, but paused also to give me the time of day; she was easy to talk to and friendly and even had an apartment of decent taste where we could cook up a passable pasta with a can of corned beef and some tomato sauce.

Thus I found myself unthinking, unrepentant, and quite ready for sex in Syracuse, never mind the general state of affairs, or the ever-present longing for a love five thousand miles away. I passed a couple of hours with supple Nuccia. Her fine ivory skin was one thing. She fitted to size immediately, without fumbling and jostling, not all elbows, knees and hipbones like some women. I was not so naive as to fail to bathe thoroughly, but, in my vanity, did not ask whether she needed compensation beyond food, drink, cigarettes and bedding down on my bedding roll unrolled. She asked for nothing, taking with her a pack of American cigarettes (worth three of Bengal Lancers, the British ration, which were so bad, said Robbie, grinning with his big teeth under his natty brush, "the Italian prisoners of war in India rioted against their distribution, invoking the Geneva Convention").

We smiled and said *"Buon Giorno, Come' stai"* in passing, and had another heavy date a couple of days later. Then, as I and my driver Hank were parking in the narrow street after a day's trip, I saw Nuccia in a cute flowery dress entering her doorway, a few steps away from mine, with a handsome British naval officer in tow; he was spruced up for a party, ruddy-cheeked, happy of expression and carrying a sizeable portion of his boat's larder, and I did then realize that Nuccia had a living to make and others who appreciated her more, and I had better get on with my mission in life - as if other officers had none, but I supposed that I was much more of an ideologue than practically anybody in the war, let's say more than 99% of the combatants, wherever in the world they were.

Robbie and I decided to charge money for the *Corriere* on the idea that I had picked up in America, that people only appreciate what they have to pay for. Robbie was delighted to discover that he was actually selling all that we could print, employing an improvised distributing group of urchins and Italian army deserters. Captain Charlton was envious because he could not charge for his paper, but the difference was that he would have embezzled his funds, whereas Robbie only got a Scot's satisfaction out of the money, which he saved up, despite its becoming a burden, until finally he could dump it into the PWB treasury the first time a paymaster came through. Meanwhile other officers convinced him that a few occupation lira could be spent to add greens and fruit to the bully beef ration.

Robbie and Charlton were the chief sources of news, except for local matters. Robbie listened to all the broadcasts in English and Italian that could be heard on our radio and to occasional German broadcasts in English, then summarized them for composition at the printing plant. His best source was the BBC's slow-spoken, clearly enunciated shortwave broadcast that he took down word for word. He longed for some word about his own tunnery on Elba; he hoped to return there some day. No news. No prisoner from Tuscany had yet put in an appearance.

Charlton brought in the communiqués and gossip from Eighth Army HQ and let the American use it as he composed it for his own newspaper. Pictures! I saw Charlton locking one into the type. Where can they be obtained? This was an exciting one, and

Charlton offered me more, "any number of them, at the Fascist Party headquarters." The exciting picture was captioned: "Soviet Soldiers attacking encircled Germans at Kharkov." Helmeted figures were seen leaping with bayoneted rifles through flames upon what appeared to be rooftops in the light of the fires. "Wonderful, and up to date!" I was enthused until Charlton told me it was really a photograph of Fascist troops conducting war exercises some time in the dim past. "That's what we call yellow journalism, Charlton." He just laughed: "So do we."

Later he gave me a manuscript to criticize that he had written on the history of his *Eighth Army News*. It is duly read and returned. "I have seen better," and "Charlton, you are better than your story about yourself." Self-conscious, as written by a man in uniform, as I in many of my own letters, written under the internalized eye of the censor, and as a matter of fact the *Eighth Army News* had to pass the censor. The PWB team were both writers and censors. We were, of course, devoted to the policies of Roosevelt and Churchill and reconciled them as best we could, without much trouble, and there were directives coming from here and there that were to be followed, but we had wide leeway because of the veritable political and psychological ignorance of those who might have set themselves up to censor us and to dictate to us, the "experts," the generals, the assistant chiefs of staff for operations and intelligence; the heads of PWB were so far away from most operations and so engaged in quarreling amongst themselves that they were hardly even considered, unless they happened to descend upon "the people out there," as they would do once in the while, and I must recount to you how.

Robbie and I, prompted by expectations of reinforcements and "visiting firemen," located and seized a large pallazzo with a great dining hall, and move into it out of our smaller apartments. It was a fine baroque construction of the old town, Ortygia. No one was in charge, no one had to be ordered out or chased.

Hardly had we set up than there appeared a Lieutenant-Colonel McFarlane and a Captain Beauclerk. They were not so bad, congenial enough, with some skills to offer; moreover, McFarlane had the brass to hire an excellent majordomo and superb chef from the local *Hotel Splendid,* and bully beef was banished. John Whitaker jeeped over from Palermo to exchange recipes; he looked tired and weak; Patti had come down with malaria, he and a great many others; why couldn't they have developed a shot or a cure - meanwhile, use a net if you can and grease yourself with repellant oil.

But then came none other than the Chief of the Psychological Warfare Branch, AFHQ, Mediterranean Theater, Algiers, Colonel Hazeltine of the United States Cavalry, accompanied by the man who was pushing himself aggressively into the top-level leadership on the civilian side, under the auspices of the Office of War Information, C.D. Jackson, of *Time Inc.,* a tall handsome figure, especially by contrast with Hazeltine. They came in arguing, disposed into their bedrooms, emerged for dinner when they began to argue again - about little that could be termed intelligible to the others around the table - who should be placed where to do what in Algiers - while here they were in Italy! - and there occured an interlude while the enemy came over and bombed, which they watched with interest, and then they resumed arguing, with everyone having left the table, and nothing but shouts echoing through the late night of the Pallazzo, Hazeltine, of course, drunk. In the morning they departed for Algiers, there to report that they have seen the Front and it is Ours.

The Sicilian campaign as a whole was notable for ill-feelings, arguments, and recriminations among Allied Leaders. Quite apart from their costly badinage, their tactics, actually going back to the strategic conception of *Operation Husky,* were deplorable. I was hardly aware of the range and depths of the mischief and mishaps: I was, do not forget, of impeccable morale, and took every occasion to believe well of General Montgomery, General Patton and the rest of the gang. Still, by the time my own less respected top leaders left the Island, a number of events had occurred or were about to occur, with the exception of a depressing finale, that would have made me wonder, which is about all a soldier can do, wonder: anything else would have been against regulations at the least and at the most, conduct unbecoming an officer. What had been happening?

The Invasion of Sicily

The landings were successful, almost unopposed, from which surprise was deduced, but it was not so much surprise as an inability and incapacity of the enemy to respond. The would-be defenders of the Island were largely immobile, outnumbered, and vastly outgunned. They had lost air superiority even before the invasion began, and promptly began to withdraw their aircrafts to peninsular bases. A great number of planes were reported to have been destroyed on the ground, but this may have been in many cases because they could not get off the ground.

Italian submarines were completely inactive and the Italian fleet at Taranto and other bases refused to attack the invading convoys and their hundreds of armed vessels. The Italians numbered on the whole of the island 200,000, mostly unequipped coastal defense forces; the Germans amounted to about 60,000. with elements of two armored divisions. Over half the Italians surrendered quickly or in batches as they fled and were ultimately overtaken, they being on foot and not giving a damn. There were rare instances where an Italian unit displayed high morale in the face of the landings; notably, a battalion of their only top Division, the "Livorno," decided it had to put on a good show, and fixed bayonets and charged on open terrain against a Ranger battalion defending the left flank of the beachhead at Gela, and were mowed down, which took care of that problem, until the next day, when the scenario was repeated.

German units reacted too slowly to counterattack the two main American beachheads as these formed up, and there was fear on their side at one point that elements of the renowned Hermann Goering Panzer Division would panic. The German armor and infantry descending upon the American beachhead at Gela were repulsed finally by a conglomerate of disorganized forces, including especially large naval guns. The personal leadership of Col. James Gavin catalyzed the morale of individual soldiers and small groups of paratroopers and 45th Division wanderers with the effect of defending the crucial Biazza Ridge until the enemy withdrew, frustrated.

Upon the failure of the Axis counterattack, the American Seventh Army moved swiftly and relentlessly northwards, ultimately reaching the Coast, where General Patton turned West for a personal triumph in Palermo, losing precious days from the pursuit of the Axis forces along the North Coast toward Messina, their only escape to the toe of Italy. This flamboyancy, all agree, was counter-productive, a serious error; among other consequences, it let a new German division from Italy come across the Straits and get into position to block the Americans when they did get around to pushing along the coastal road to Messina.

Perhaps the impulse to "liberate" Palermo was incited by a personal slight. Patton had been blocked by the Commander of the Invasion, British General Alexander, shortly after the Americans had broken out of their beachhead, at which moment they could have employed a good road to the Northeast; there was one that turned upon Vizzini, a picturesque hill town (and setting for the opera of *Cavaleria Rusticana*). The irresolute Alexander allowed jurisdiction over the road to Montgomery, who was doing badly enough on the Eastern roads and had his forces stretched out and disorganized by several disastrous incidents. General Bradley, serving under Patton as a Corps Commander at the time, urged Patton to protest more vigorously. But Patton was in hot water with over-all Commander Eisenhower, as a trouble-maker, an obscene loud-mouth, and an Anglophobe; Patton was afraid to get into a quarrel with Alexander.

As it turned out, he came close to being relieved later on by reason of the press coverage that followed three instances of his cursing and/or slapping soldiers who were *hors de combat* and in hospital. Medical personnel and the Press got after him; only the combined efforts of Eisenhower, Marshall, and Secretary of War Stimson saved him from disgrace and dismissal. That he was also a show-off, publicity-hound, poet, and mythomaniac hardly caused him harm. He was a misfit among Allied generals. His untypical frenzy for the attack is what made him useful here and later.

General Montgomery played upon a terribly modest image, the opposite of Patton's, a devout man of God, but he was as schizophrenic as Patton. For a couple of days he looked to be the dashing relentless aggressor, but then he subsided when he should have been well on his way into Catania and headed for points

The Invasion of Sicily

North. He let his troops be spread out against an even thinner enemy. He sent thousands of them far to the West, but, of course, you do not envelop anybody's troops by climbing up and over the shoulders of Mt. Etna; you just go back East where you came from and join with the coastal drive. He walked his infantry into battle to the point of exhausting them; he could have transported them by truck. He did not call upon the tremendous Allied fleet to bombard the Axis troops and installations along the whole of the East Coast and on the toe of Italy. True, for this, he might have had to call in Churchill himself, but that was precisely what Churchill could do best. (This is a story told one evening at dinner by Major Galsworthy: Frustrated once too often by the Admirals when he proposed a reform of the Navy, he then being Lord of the Admiralty, and hearing the exasperating words: "But tradition will not allow it, Sir," Churchill bellowed at them: "Traditions of the Royal Navy, Bah! Rum, Prayers, Sodomy, and the Lash!")

I will tell you later what this failure to bombard cost. You may well ask, too, why the two great navies did not literally cast themselves into the breach between Sylla and Charybdis. They would have had some of the best hunting of the war, and gone a long way towards winning the upcoming battles of Salerno and beyond. Perhaps that is what most of them were doing now, resting and refitting for the invasion of peninsular Italy, that is, Salerno.

Four airborne fiascos had accompanied the Allied landings, two on the Gela front, two on the Syracuse front. Because of high winds, poor planning, and pilot inexperience, an American regiment, landing hours before the seaborne landings, was scattered over a thousand square miles. It could not thereafter operate as a unit. Making the best of the situation, impromptu squads transforming into guerrillas spread surprise, fear, confusion and inflicted much minor damage. (Granted that in warfare, much minor damage can add up to major damage.) The largest element landing intact, a meager battalion, did assume an important role in blocking attacks upon the beachheads.

On July 11 when the beachhead was getting into shape, following the repulse of Axis counterattacks, 2,300 paratroopers were flown to the beachhead. Nervous anti-aircraft gunners at sea and ashore mistook the planes carrying them for the enemy and began a crazy fire that knocked out or damaged many of the aircraft and killed or wounded about two hundred men. More men were killed and wounded and more equipment destroyed than in the total landings proper. Fault was batted from one headquarters to another. To no avail.

The British could not brag of a difference. Arguably, the glider disaster that came on the eve of the invasion may have been worse. An incredibly makeshift collection of aircraft was assembled in Africa to transport a couple of thousand men, never fully trained, and inexperienced in night flying and landings, to the area around Syracuse, aiming at taking up and holding the strategic points to let through the main invading forces that would follow the next day. High winds and widespread incompetence crowned an adventure that was perilous at best. The miracle, as at Gela, was that a small unit landed, almost randomly, by the main target, here a bridge, and held it as envisioned. An Italian military launch picked up over a hundred of the drowning survivors from the sea and the wings of crashed gliders, brought them ashore, and surrendered.

British ack-ack batteries enacted the same scene as their American counterparts in the West when the First Parachute Brigade endeavored to land on the plains of Catania. They were abetted by Axis batteries. The force of 126 troop-carrying aircraft and 19 airplanes towing artillery-loaded gliders was destroyed: only 395 of the 1856 soldiers of the force landed in the neighborhood of the central target, Primosole Bridge. Again, as in the case of the American elite troops, they fought on, even as partial squads. Survivors were shipped back to Africa.

Elite troops of the two armies thus were practically thrown away. They could only show bits of their capabilities; individuals and small groups picked themselves up from the miserable scene and tackled important jobs well. Men are not equal. Soldiers are not equal. One of such men, properly used, is worth several ordinary soldiers; a squad of them is worth disproportionately more.

It would be instructive at this point to describe the adventures of the German parachute units sent down into Sicily, which landed more or less where they ought to and caused the

The Invasion of Sicily 185

Eighth Army much trouble. Their losses were heavy but more "rational," that is, brought on by necessarily high risk and enemy action. The German First Parachute Division arrived organized, stayed so and fought on continuously through the campaign and in Italy.

Amicide might have figured worse in the Sicilian campaign than before or thereafter elsewhere. Yet "friendly fire" remained always a nemesis of advancing troops. In fact, even as the Sicilian campaign progressed, across the world on Kiska in the Aleutian Islands, Japanese defenders abandoned the Island when faced with the certainty of a large American invading force; eighteen days later, the Americans suffered 300 casualties assaulting the shores against a phantom enemy. The fog had been heavy.

Your Hero was out of range in these actions. I learned something of the Gela episode, circuitously, via the British Navy, the Intelligence Section of the Eighth Army, and Major Galsworthy, coming back to camp. No doubt I would have learned more if there had not been so much to conceal on the British side. Strangely I did not feel at all lonely with the British. There were several Americans now with my team - Brown Roberts, an OWI civilian photographer from Tennessee; Sergeant Leone came in, Corporal Laudando, and a couple of others. Generals Patton and Lucas were angry at the absence of any American officers on the staff of the Army Group, commanded by Alexander. I did not even notice it, nor the similar vacancy on the Eighth Army staff.

The British were still quite insular; they did not wish the show to be stolen by the Americans, it would seem. Too, they generally had a low opinion of American military prowess, at least on the command and general staff levels. Even while I was writing letters praising the British soldier, and more so the American soldier, the British leaders were in some cases wondering how to prevent the Yanks from botching things. No doubt one of the reasons why my British comrades became so devoted to me was that, while being bold and confident, I did not brag about how quickly we, the Americans, with all our superior qualities, would settle the war with a little British help.

At any event, it was time that I propelled myself on a trip to the interior, because from this there originated activities of a non-bloody type that would have meaningful effects. With everything in order at the newspaper and now endowed with a jeep with a driver, I decided that I could derive some useful intelligence in the neighborhood of the ancient village of Licodia-Eubea, birthplace of my father in 1882, and could discover, in the first place, how it had survived the battle raging around the Island. I had dropped in on the town several years earlier with my brother and Danny Phelan, who were piano-player and traps-drummer respectively of my jazz combo, that played aboard ships in the summer. It was only a couple of hours' drive from Syracuse, up through orange groves and vineyards. The tomatoes had ripened and been picked and were being dried in the hot sun on walls, patios and verandas everywhere.

I stopped for the night at Vizzini, to examine the heavy damage done by the planes and close-in fighting there, and to visit with the Allied Military Government officer who had already moved in. He was an intelligent and diligent man, American, who was the political head of the town and its chief provider of goods from the outside, from wheat to medical supplies, for the time being. Recognized promptly by them as a super-*podesta* or *sindico* or mayor, he got excellent cooperation from the Italians. He had had a few instances of errant Allied soldiers, Canadians, who, under the influence of, or looking for, liquor, broke into places, like bears. He had a great many Italian ex-soldiers foraging for food and beating about the bush, and was trying to get Eighth Army to feed them, whereas Eighth Army would have liked him to feed *them*. Take them prisoners, he said. Let them go free, Eighth Army said. Give us our daily bread, say the Italians, civilian and soldier alike.

I drove around the mountain and down the cypress-lined road to Licodia only several miles away. Practically no damage there. I knocked on the door of a little stone house on the quiet main street, and was greeted with astonishment by my aunt, Francesca, a Franciscan nun in dark brown gown with white coif, her bundle of large old keys clanking at her waist. She was a tiny woman, chirpy, cracking jokes, but businesslike, too. Long ago she paid for an authorization to "go secular," and since then has taught the children of the first two grades of elementary school and lived alone in her ancestral house. At the sight of our jeep, townsfolk crowded into her living room; she chose and regulated the sample that would be allowed to enter to sit upon the many little padded wicker chairs. But I did not even stay the night. There was a lot of coming and going. At intervals I went up to the second floor to look up and down the street from the jutting wrought-iron balcony. Hank was minding the jeep in the shade across the street, watched carefully in turn by several urchins.

I heard a string of stories in short order. An American soldier was killed, and given temporary burial. He was the only casualty. He was entering the town from the south, from the road from Vittoria and the beaches beyond. A ruined castle at that end of the village looked down from a rocky eminence upon the road. He was killed by a German sniper who had been the last of the German rearguard. Our men would come for him, I said.

A large landholder, a *"pezzo grosso,"* entered the nun's little house. The farm tenants were in rebellion, he complained. They were refusing to pay rents or give up shares of the crops; they said that this was the way the Americans wanted it. Was it true? Had communism now arrived? No, said I, it is not true, but I refused to attend a meeting to tell the world that it was not, the AMG (still called AMGOT) officer in Vizzini was in charge of such problems. I found the landlord distasteful; he probably deserved his troubles; he looked quite greedy.

Everybody was happy, said a politician, because the real reason that the Americans (whom they assumed, even in this zone, were in charge of the *Inglese*) had come to Sicily (instead of Italy) was to announce a separate Republic of Sicily; it was the Italians' fault that the war started and the Sicilians never wanted it. I reminded them that the Sicilian invasion and liberation were part of a Total World War for One World and Democracy: they should not think of dismembering Italy.

It didn't take many experiences of this kind to teach a major lesson of warfare, that every soldier was a propaganda machine wherever he was in contact with civilians. The American troops were less experienced than the British in both warfare and civilian relations, but because they came from an ethnic melting pot (a significant percentage of the invading Americans were of Italian origin), and also because they had suffered less from the Italians and from the War generally, and, finally, because there had been a deliberate educational campaign by the American Army to prepare the soldier for contact with the civilian population, the Americans were probably superior as "psychological warriors."

I returned to Syracuse feeling that I should do something about this strong separatist sentiment that might well bring on civil war, and I was, furthermore, of the opinion that most responsible Sicilians were in no wise persuaded of the value of independence. The sentiment was expressed in the Syracuse newspaper and again later on in an editorial in the *Corriere di Catania*. The editorial declared loudly: *Sicilia e' Piccola!* ("Sicily is small!") and then went on to reproach all those who believed that if they could only free the great Island from the exploitation by the mainland Italians, they would prosper; it scolded the population for believing that somehow the whole World War was directed at liberating Sicily. It exhorted them to patience, to cooperation, to working for a unified world, because Sicily was small!

The battle was raging around Etna. Catania at the southeast slope incurred heavy damage. It became our next home. The newest arrival from Africa, Captain Beauclerk, went into town to find us shelter. He found an excellent villa down toward the City Center, but it lacked the furnishings required by our group and we moved into a villa farther out. It was just as well, because the first one harbored a large time bomb that blew it away a day later. Little was made of the deadly near miss. Captain Beauclerk was embarrassed and more frightened than the others because of the decision he had almost made.

Sergeant Leone, erstwhile Philadelphia schoolteacher, took charge of the new urban villa, with its typical lush Italian garden where one could walk at dawn as if the world were at peace. He came down suddenly with fever and chills: malaria. Thousands of men had contracted the disease in North Africa just before embarking; here the number quadrupled; by the end of the campaign both armies had lost more men from malaria than from all casualties incident to battle. There went the equal of all replacements for all battle casualties: pffft! And many units landed without mosquito nets, tantamount to landing without anti-aircraft guns. Remember the AA Officer Training at Camp Davis, where endurance to mosquito bites was rewarded, but malaria was hardly mentioned. How to put it: the Ancient Myth that War is a Struggle between Armed Men Befogs All Sense and Reason in All Types of Behavior.

Leone did not want to go to the hospital; he was a Christian Scientist. So was Captain Heycock, who nevertheless ordered him to go for treatment and sent him off in a jeep. I was turning into the driveway of the villa the same evening when I saw Leone walking up the road: "Hey, Sergeant, what are you doing here? You're supposed to be in the Hospital!" "It wasn't necessary. I am O.K. Lieutenant, I am well." I felt his brow and pulse. No sweat. No shakes. The guy was cured. And he stayed cured. Heycock had grit; a letter from England told him that a downed German plane had crashed into his garden in England. Later, he heard that his little son had chopped off a finger with a scythe. Not a word of complaint; only mumbled phrases of sympathy accepted.

Captain Beauclerk, the type of the tall, bony, ruddy Englishman, complete with a slight royal lisp to emulate King George, wanted to edit the newspaper that was to be recommenced in Catania. For my part, I insisted upon handling the job. Robbie supported me, letting me lie about my experience, which had to be collapsed into a period when I must have been a student and, yes, I was active (which I was not) on the University daily paper that was the size of a typical English wartime daily.

Beauclerk, encumbered by his nearly fatal choice of villa, and embarrassed at the pathetic wartime British newspapers, is nevertheless a *bona fide* English newspaperman and ranking Captain. He bides his time. He knows I will leave as soon as the road to Messina is passable. And he will live there happily ever after. Only fools want to keep moving up, or men like Robbie who have an interest, a tuna factory on Elba.

The *Corriere di Catania* is named after the Syracuse paper, and is printed in the offices of the preexisting newspaper which shut down before the invasion and was, of course, of Fascist persuasion. Now how do I find non-fascist, if not anti-Fascist, journalists? Obviously there would be none, after many years of Fascist dictatorship and censorship. Once more, to begin with, Robbie is editor, I publisher. We clean up the wreckage and litter of the plant. We look to see who is skulking about, printers, yes, and they will work well. A Seventh Day Adventist from Turin appears, named Palma, about as marginal a character-type as you can find in Catania, and he is hired as an associate editor because he has been publishing religious tracts. Then an apparition appears in the form of a well-dressed, well-set-up woman of a certain age and decorum, who says that she is a writer of features of all kinds and seeks work. I hire her, and Sicily has its first victory for Woman's Lib. "Fosca of Agrigento" she calls herself. She writes calmly about life on the eve of the invasion, on the problems of women, about attitudes toward war, and she helps fill the paper and gives it a little class, as they say, and a sense of warmth. Robbie, the misogynist, is amused; it offers him grounds for scornful remarks.

Next, there occured a political crisis because there did show up on the scene a true journalist and editor, a Giuseppe Longhitano, and although I quizzed him about his prior life, I found there no indication of fascistic activities or beliefs. I liked him. He was square-cut, had an Italo Balbo goatee, moved fast, was about forty years old, quiet, low-voiced. He quickly revealed himself to be an excellent editor and publisher. The job of running the newspaper slipped off my back.

Then I was told by informants that Longhitano was a former notorious Fascist journalist. I interrogated him again. I inquired about. After some days of investigation it developed that there was a Fascist newspaperman named Longhitano, not so uncommon a name as one might think. So far as I could discover, the two were different characters. He was left in charge when we left. He ran the paper under an owner who had reappeared and this Signor Ardizzone, it developped, also was not a committed Fascist and so could be brought back into the picture; the two of them got along; so, within a month or two, Catania, the most progressive of the Southern cities, had the best newspaper. Or at least, such rumors did come to the ears, and no one gainsaid them.

Mt. Etna presented major difficulties to envelopment. Both the Americans and the British were working their way over roadblocks and traps, through bottlenecks and ravines, beneath blasted bridges, avoiding mines. And under persistent fire. I went up now and then and the desolation was pitiful. Corporal Ignatius Laudando was driving, and the jeep slid off one of the roads along a rib of Mt. Etna one twilight. No serious harm done. I stood by the road watching the curl of smoke above Etna and smelling the renewed air of the evening, pissing, then shifted position as I discerned, emerging from the dusty debris, the helmet and face of a German paratrooper. I muttered: "Excuse me." It all inclined me to pathos. Thus I was writing to Jill, describing the Desert Rats of an artillery convoy:

> ...Men are men in war as in peace and they hold onto their precious little objects - things that no one would ever bother to pick off the street at home, cans of odd sizes with annoying jagged edges, a piece of inferior cord, a pencil stub, a ragged blank letter-form, a loose match with a non-matching scratcher, a broken glass lamp cover.
>
> It's a sight to watch an old army on the march, all the pathetic evidences of men constructing a life around a gas engine. And the engines themselves, like old faithful horses, not coughing with their original uniform noises but with a variety, with an individuality induced by age. There are bullet holes and cracked windshields, bent fenders, missing pieces of iron, added pieces of canvas, exposed parts gasping for air, makeshift upholstery of Arab cotton, Italian pillows and army canvas - a deadly procession of okies.
>
> And the men cling to their vehicles like children to their mothers' breasts. They look as if they might fall off easily, but they can't. There is a magnetism about the body of their machine. And what queer unorthodox gear - old helmets, some with camouflage netting, some without, shirts open at the first or the third button, with or without leggings, tams, berets, neckerchiefs. Each man, as if to demonstrate that he is a man, not a machine, carries his particular loot, more pitiable than condemnable, some bought, some raided, a crate of ruffled chickens dangling from a gun barrel, a bad picture of a pastoral scene, a battered German helmet, odd implements not

> *conceivably useful to anyone save a soldier, a pot or can to boil tea, and a mattress tucked into a crowded corner. Each has his own favorite piece of loot and the story behind it, a fat candle, a weird mug, an old fork, an atrocious undergarment, a cherished book, an old magazine... Our victorious armies sweep on in this way and not in martial procession.*

There was little loot to be found. The country revealed itself in dire poverty, rendered grim by the dry summer, acting all the poorer, hiding everything possible in the face of the rampaging troops. I know a chateau that might be looked into, I tell Laudando. (I don't tell him that it is the house of a distant cousin, a Baron Centaro.) We approach it, near Vizzini; it is hidden by carefully piled up brush, the driveway is blocked by felled trees. No matter, we charge up the hill on the jeep, and lurch into the courtyard. The residents look out, startled, wondering at this tour de force. The Baron is away.

When we look around, we see no one who is suspect or hostile, nobody has been carting off the marble statues, the paintings, the embroideries, there is no sign that Front or Rear Echelons have visited, but into the cellar - what, not even a bottle of wine? No. But then the pungent odor of cheese and the sight of a shrouded wheel, grey on a grey shelf, a true parmesan! Off we go with it, with the acquiescence and to the relief of the household staff. Robbie, Galsworthy, all of us, we are delighted. Now the C-ration canned hash and the English bully beef are spiced with garlic and sprinkled with grated cheese of supreme quality. There is some wine to be had. Robbie has spoken up for that, and we eat gratefully and laugh and talk late into the evening. When, we ask ourselves, shall we go across the Straits?

Large political events were occurring in Italy and the Allied High Command was considering what to do next. They appeared to be doing nothing for the time being.

What happened was this: As mentioned, the Italians removed Mussolini on July 26. He was finally held in custody in a hotel in Abruzzi. The Badoglio government would have liked to let in the Allies and let exit the Germans. No such luck! The Germans were

The Invasion of Sicily

moving heavy traffic through the Alps into Italy, starting on August 6. On the 12th the Germans began to withdraw across the Straits of Messina. Apparently they had no intention of giving up in Italy, whatever the ultimate decision of the Italian government. Italian forces were scattered in a dozen countries from the Soviet Union to France. They had lost most of their planes, tanks, and cannon. Their fleet might be used, but to what end? The people stood by, watching with approval the mass melting away of the troops. The civilians in Sicily revealed little but pity and sympathy for their surrendering and deserting soldiers. A general strike could be called in Italy to block the use of the rail and communication facilities by the Germans; but it was against the ideology of the Italian military now in command. If the Italian forces could hold only one area, perhaps Rome itself, the Allies could move in; this was considered, but the Germans moved first. The plan to send in airborne troops to Rome was abandoned.

On August 15, General Castellano in Madrid got in touch with the Americans to offer surrender. It took three days for Eisenhower to answer. The next two days saw the last of the Italians and Germans leave Messina by ferry to Italy and the first Americans and British arriving in the destroyed city. For a week the British reconnoitered and bombed the toe installations to no purpose, for the Germans were speeding North along the coast. British troops then landed and the pursuit began. On the same day, a secret surrender document was signed. On September 8, Eisenhower and Badoglio issued separate announcements of the "unconditional surrender," which was not that at all. The slogan had served to delay matters. The true agreement was that the Italians promised to do everything to work themselves back into the good graces of the Allies, including opposing the Germans at every stage possible and setting up a democratic government. It might have been better to designate a heroic exile or a Fascist prisoner, instead of defeated generals, to run affairs. The Italians were told that they would get such aid as may be available to combat famine and disease, and restore basic services.

The next day, at 03:30, Allied forces of the Fifth Army land on the beaches of the Bay of Salerno, well below Naples. (Minus the

General of their Tenth Corps, Sir Brian Horrocks, who at dinner the preceding evening in Bizerte, Tunisia, had stepped out "to watch the fireworks," and had been killed by a bit of "friendly flak.") Simultaneously, a British Airborne Brigade landed in Taranto to take in hand the Italian Navy and installations there and shortly move across to Brindisi on the Adriatic Sea. Everyone was confused, from the top down.

One cannot review the events of these days over sixty-five years later without wondering whether truly the political leaders and generals knew what was happening and what to do. The announcement of surrender was postponed to what was thought to be a shrewd time to strike, as the American and British troops were going ashore at Salerno. The effect, however, was to paralyze the Italians, to clarify for the Germans the exclusion of the Italians from their reckoning of sources of support, and to confuse the Allied troops as to what to expect: an easy walk in the sun, a time-out, an armistice while the Germans withdrew, a possibility of seizing strategic positions here, there, everywhere, or, of course, nowhere.

Actually, everything that can happen does happen, to some extent. Italians and Germans came into conflict. Allied troops could not be sure of how to react to the presence of Italian troops, but then learned to ignore them or use them in different minor ways. The Italian troops dissolved up and down the Peninsula. Abroad, they had to stay together, and become prisoners of the Allies in some cases, of the Germans in others, of partisans in still others. In many areas they remained in encampments, as in Sardinia. Sometimes they disarmed themselves, sometimes were disarmed by former foes on both sides. Upcoming was a rearming.

On September 12, Skorzeny's parachute task force freed Mussolini from captivity and Il Duce set up a new Fascist Republic far to the North at Salo. The news dismayed and infuriated me and many others; the daring trick won the equivalent of several divisions of troops and police to struggle against the Allies. After failing to drive the Allies into the Sea at Salerno, the Germans moved up through Naples on the first of October, and drew a new front line across Italy, abandoning Foggia with its enormous air field.

The Invasion of Sicily

On October 13, the Badoglio Government, having waited for no good reason, declared war against Germany and took up the status of Co-belligerency, a second-class membership in the Allied Club. On October 31, an Italian 1st Motorized Brigade actually joined the Allied Fifth Army. And I need not go on from here, especially since I have not picked up from where I was last seen: My comrades and I were then encamped among some bulrushes, enjoying ourselves, discussing the campaign just ended and contemplating the next moves.

The American and British troops had hooked around Mt. Etna to join up in Messina on August 17, concluding a thirty-nine day campaign. The day before, the last of the Germans had motored across the Straits. For a week, a masterful escape had been under way. German and Italian shipping officers had managed to ferry to the toe of Calabria about 60,000 Italian and 40,000 German troops. The Italians, it may be surmised, were non-Sicilians who took the opportunity to get closer to home before calling it quits. What we saw in their escape was that the Allies were completely incompetent, for here was no desperate fighting retreat. It could be perceived in these figures that the Germans withdrew more troops from Sicily than they had there to begin with. The German forces were doubled in size (despite casualties) during the Sicilian campaign. It was maniacal, but they did it.

Why did the German High Command decide to risk losing excellent divisions in a hopeless attempt to hold Sicily? The answer was to be found in comparable situations elsewhere in the War. The German Command was ruled with an iron hand by Adolf Hitler, who hated to give up positions, witness Stalingrad, Tunis, and Hungary. (And more to come.) But at the same time they were masters of withdrawal, a technology probably well-honed in Russia and Africa by now, but always a signature of highest professionalism.

The Allies had their own kind of problem, which was that they let opportunities slip by; they let the enemy out of traps. Unlike the Italian refugees, the Germans will live to fight another day. They will immediately appear opposite the Americans landing at Salerno. The Hermann Goering Panzer Division will be heard of again and again, the First Parachute Division also.

But how could any and all of these escape, given the overwhelming sea power and air power of the Allies at the scene of action, and pursued by two huge fully-equipped mobile Armies?

Victory was trumpeted by the British and American Generals and by the media. The Psychological Warfare Team, which should have known better, celebrated as well; Robbie and I and the rest were right in there tooting our little tin horns too. The troops believed that they had waged a highly successful campaign and triumphed against odds.

Victory is a poorly defined term, designating the holding of a battlefield after a conflict. When the utter failure to seal off the Axis troops from all flight to the mainland, which was not only a possibility but practically a surefire operation, was added to the many other blunders and misconducted operations from the planning state in North Africa onwards, it was difficult to use the term victory in any but its most narrow sense of possession of the battlefield.

The statistics ordinarily employed are crude and misleading to the point of deception. Some 20% of the Allied casualties were self-inflicted. Probably 30% of the Axis casualties came from the destruction of Italian troops whose intentions were unclear or who simply got in the way. The campaign of thirty-nine days might readily have been one of two weeks, had Montgomery concentrated on pushing up through Catania to Messina immediately, putting a shielding force on his left flank until the Americans would arrive in a day or so.

General Patton, once his Army had repelled the beachhead counterattacks, within three days, that is, could have struck the Northern road and cut off all Axis forces in the West of Sicily. He could then have despatched a force along the Northern seashore road to unite with the British at Messina. The weak German forces would have surrendered there, and any airborne brigades sent over the heads of the encircling Allied forces would have been doomed.

But they would not have been sent down for such a futile task; their despatch in any case was a mistake. It was apparent on the second day, as soon as the weakness of the Axis on the ground, in

The Invasion of Sicily

the air, and on the sea was revealed, that Sicily could not be held by them without a massive infusion of new well-trained troops. These were quite unavailable.

The Axis would have done as well to pluck out the best of their troops, no more than ten thousand, and let the Allied armies blunder about, "shooting themselves in the foot" and assembling for major offensives. Victory in Sicily would have then befallen in thirty-two days instead of thirty-nine.

I should revert, however, to the mind of Our Hero, as he was then, fully persuaded of the excellence of the Eighth Army and even more of the Seventh, and marveling at the lightning victory. I could not wait, in my enthusiasm, to leave for wherever the Front might be, and proposed a scouting trip to the mainland of Italy. I promised the others that I would return soon, brimful of information, and forthwith departed.

With British Intelligence officers in bivouac near Palermo
(I am at the far right)

In Chicago:
My brothers Vic* (14) and Ed**(16) protecting Jill (seven months pregnant)
* Vic will become Deputy-Governor of Illinois (1972-1976)
** Ed will become a noted civil rights attorney, professor of law, defender of the First Amendment, author and playwright.

CHAPTER EIGHT

ITALY TOE AND HEEL

THE Germans were retreating along the instep of the Peninsula rapidly, fearful of being cut off by an amphibious landing before they arrived wherever they were going. The Brits' Fifth Division went after them. It could not possibly catch up. The coast road, the main road, was one of the most precipitous and gully-clefted highways in the world. Every bridge, every traverse, every angle has been deftly and deeply blown. Then liberally mined.

I fitted Brown Roberts, Private Helms, myself and a jeep into an amphibious truck at the Messina docks and crossed the Straits. At Reggio's harbor, Italian soldiers - you could not call them prisoners since they were held not by guns but by a daily ration, but you could not call them anything else just yet either - were unloading ships and repairing bomb damage of the weeks past. They were revealing the mines that had been laid to hamper pursuit.

We drove up the mountain and joined the interminable column of trucks, artillery, and soldiers headed North. We slipped in and out of the traffic when we could. There was a bottleneck every kilometer or so. I wondered why we were not cursed from the vehicles - "ye bluudy fookin' bastards" - but no: unlike ourselves who had a mission, to take over media and search for intelligence and useful personnel, the soldiers in line gained nothing by pushing ahead, and lost little by lagging. The precipices were frightening, the roadsides here and there mined. Weaving in and out of sight along the mountainsides ahead and behind were the beaded threads of a thousand cars.

The trip was going to be unproductive. It would take days to reach the next large city; in fact, it would be Salerno. A couple of hundred miles away. This day was the Fifth of September. The landings on the Bay below Salerno were four days off and the plan to land there was still secret. It would take another week after that for the Eighth Army to make juncture with the Fifth Army on the beaches. And the advance engineers were far from having cleared up the intervening obstacles. I turned back.

Better, I imagined, to go up to Catanzaro, a small mountain city of the instep of Italy. The First Canadian Division had been climbing the mountain roads in that direction, to protect the main column's flank and clear up Calabria. When my jeep caught up with the forward elements they were shivering from the cold. Some had found a Fascist warehouse containing blackshirt uniforms, and were wearing them under their cotton khakis. Some wore the stuff openly and played the clown. Our roads were blocked too, but rather quickly the jeep wove its way into Catanzaro, a fine, decadent, depressed, undestroyed old town. We left some propaganda in the town hall. There was no press or communication facilities worth seizure. Maybe a couple of amplifying systems and cinemas. The people were so happy to see the Americans that they needed dosing with pessimism more than bucking up.

I saw that it might be possible to get to the cities on the Adriatic and therefore turned the jeep around toward Messina to fetch the others. Italian soldiers were scattered everywhere about, most of them trying to find their way home and to survive meanwhile. (Upon the very day of the crossing, unbeknownst to me, General Castellano and General Eisenhower had met in Syracuse to sign unconditional surrender documents - why sign if the surrender is unconditional? - and agreed that the news would be kept secret until the Eighth of September. I met a crowd of "prisoners" at one point, and a despairing British soldier in charge asked me how to handle their surrender. The prisoners knew that they were supposed to be fed. That was one of the reasons they gave up, they claimed. I said to the soldier, tell them to go down the mountain another mile to where a prisoner-of-war canteen and camp have been set up. (I recalled having seen it.) They objected, saying that they were collapsing from fatigue and hunger. I exhorted them to the last mile

Italy, Toe and Heel

and, with that air of distress, resignation and humor that is so Italian, they picked themselves up and ambled toward the promised meal.

I re-crossed the Straits to Sicily and arrived at the bombed house in Messina where I had left the others. I portrayed for them the situation. Then the Italian surrender was announced. We listened to the radio stations broadcasting in English, Italian and German. What a mess! The Germans were furious at their betrayal by the Badoglio government and gave every sign that they would try to take over Italy and every other place around the Mediterranean where Italian troops were standing. Within hours, I and Robbie were at the airport greeting an Italian bombing plane whose pilots were surrendering according to the plan. There were not many like them; the opposition to the Italians' surrendering was heavy; their actually joining the Allied forces was dangerous and unlikely. There was on the one hand the understandable fury of the Germans at being left to fight a desperate war alone, and on the other hand the equally understandable disgust and fatigue of the Italians at the disastrous course of events. They were less militaristic than ever, economically down and out, witnesses to their beautiful country's piecemeal destruction, and ashamed of their faith in the dictatorial figure of two decades, Il Duce, whose face still glowered at them on giant-sized posters pasted upon every wall and edifice. Nor were all of them pleased to change from cooperating with Nazi Germany to cooperating with the Allies. They had ten divisions in Russia, now trapped, more divisions perilously exposed in Yugoslavia, Greece, a score of islands, France, and of course in Italy itself.

I urged my comrades to take the route of the Canadian Division as far as it had reached, and then to proceed on to Bari where major Italian press and radio facilities required securing and operation. They agreed. This time the first team was made up of Robbie, Heycock, Laudando, and me. We had a tough trip. We overtook the Canadian spearhead and proceeded ahead of it. The bridges were generally destroyed and at one point we had to retrace our route by many miles to find a smaller road that took us through.

The territory was officially enemy-held but we saw no Germans. "How does one know where they are?" one may well ask. You find the faces of people that seem to be most sympathetic and reliable, often female, because they are more disposed to help avoid bloodshed, also natives rather than Italian soldiers, because the natives of the mountains or of anywhere notice who is passing through and where they could possibly be going, and they will do a better job of telling what these unknowns were carrying, and how they were getting around, than soldiers would do in the same circumstances.

We finally drove down onto the plains of Basilicata, amidst the quaint neat *trulli*, the round white beehive stone cottages. There were many roads here and one had to stop and ask at every opportunity. One knows when there is an enemy about because the place is unusually quiet. It is like a Hollywood Western: the people disappear when a gunfight is in the offing.

We entered Bari amazed at the completeness and normality of the City. As we drove along, we were noticed with rather more favor than astonishment. There were a number of Italian vehicles, civilian and military, on the streets. Italian soldiers were to be seen under arms. Asked questions, they responded helpfully; the experience was dreamlike. Our team looked for the best hotel and found it, *Albergo Imperiale*. It was new, undamaged, magnificent, looking upon the sparkling waters of the Adriatic. We were covered with dust, grimy, helmeted; our guns protruded; our radio was popping with static; our jeep was an eyesore against the shiny civilian-type cars. We stomp in our boots over to the elegant reservations desk, already visualizing ourselves immersed in gleaming bathtubs and dining at a splendid table, shaven, in clean uniforms. Not that we could be a match for the admirals and colonels and generals lolling about the lobby, dressed splendidly, like victors taking their leisure from a distant war. There was some curiosity and eyebrow-raising about the newcomers.

More turned their heads, because Heycock had started sputtering and gasping in fury; his face was apoplectic red, and he was waving his tommy-gun around as if he intended to use it. In fact, he was saying that he would. The desk manager had just informed us that all the rooms were occupied, so sorry, Signori. I did fear that Heycock would shoot up the place and tried to soothe him while trying to get across to the clerks that they had better get rid of a couple of admirals because we had every intention of spending the night in a comfortable suite.

At the critical moment, there floated upon the scene the familiar face of Sgt. Guetta, last seen in Tunis. All action froze: as if a movie director had called "Cut!" while we exclaimed surprise, greetings, and explanations. Guetta was here with Major Ian Greenlees, "good old boy," and Mr. Williamson of OSS, "don't know him," and another officer. They had landed at Taranto with the First Airborne Brigade and were living not far away at a place less conspicuous.

"That's all very well, Guetta, but explain to these bloody fools here that we must be given rooms." "Sure I can," said Guetta, "the Director is my cousin." Two large rooms magically emptied. Bellhops leapt to carry the rolls and guns upstairs, and shortly we found ourselves precisely where we had hoped to be, in steaming bathtubs. After which we descend for cocktails in the fine barroom and thence into the dining room to be served a dinner. Greenlees and Williamson join us and chuckle at having beaten us to Bari by way of the air. They had arrived two days earlier with the first reconnaissance platoon, and had discovered that the Germans were gone. The Italian government of Badoglio, a farce but for the symbolic presence of the King and Crown Prince, was in Brindisi. Harold Macmillan was soon to be there, maybe was there now. He was chief of British Mediterranean political policy. General Maxwell Taylor also, the only American. They were all in a state of confusion. They were talking big about making major decisions, but events were beyond their grasp. The Italian armed forces should now be purged and supplied with equipment for battle on the Allied side; nothing was done, a battalion, a division, a corps - nothing of anything.

The Germans had been driven from Bari, following a brief battle, by a task force organized on the spur of the moment and led personally by an Italian general. The General had been shot, and proudly displayed to his new friend, Signor Maggiore Greenlees, his arm in a sling. At night there would still be occasional shooting here and there, but they slept well and had been busy and were "happy to see us" and "needed us" and the rest of the advance Eighth

Army team from Sicily as soon as possible.

Around the table now sat all the Allied forces there were in Bari and points North except for the aforesaid airborne platoon, which was commanded by a lieutenant. Greenlees was effectively the Commandant of the City, which was on the Front Line and in a State of War- who with whom? - without curfew, with electric lights, running water, orderly traffic, and ships riding at anchor.

Greenlees was admirably suited for majordomo of this mad scene. A rich literati. Handsomely tailored. Stocky, erect, large headed and curled to look like the bust of a Roman Emperor, crisp in speech and low of voice, elegant of manner, thoroughly conversant with Italy, longtime companion and lover of Norman Douglas, who wrote superbly of his walks through Calabria and also the novel *South Wind,* about the Isle of Capri, where Greenlees possesses a villa. He should have been in charge of the Italian surrender. He would have squeezed out an effective political force for collaboration.

Greenlees convinced the paratroopers to patrol and to drive around conspicuously in different formations, now wearing helmets, now berets, to give the impression of an occupation in force. As his comrades from Calabria arrived, so had a tank platoon from Taranto, and this helped greatly to give the population a sense of security and of the beginnings of a new society. Then we, the propagandists, had to let everyone believe, for we were being asked all kinds of questions, that the Eighth Army was swarming northwards and eastward from Calabria like locusts.

The limited size of the British force in the Taranto area was well known since it was the Headquarters of the Italian fleet and in touch continuously with Bari. The Italian forces, whether naval or ground, were under no orders to join the fighting forces of the Allies. Few at that moment could imagine the possibility. However, reorganization for the other tasks could have begun immediately to good effect, but the top leaders had only asked themselves whether the whole force could be turned around, which it obviously could not be, and, given a negative, had ceased to plan for a very large and possible redeployment, especially in logistics and combat support units, road-building, engineering, and other special contributions.

Italy, Toe and Heel

Sicily, and now Southern Italy, and eventually Central Italy would be liberated but millions of Italians who could have served in one capacity or another, spent the rest of the war unemployed, economically and militarily. The Italians were now in the hands of the uninspired and unimaginative, of their own kind and of the Allies. President Roosevelt could readily have thought to send Fiorello La Guardia, Mayor of New York, to catalyze the elements, as indeed the "Little Flower" had done in World War I, in the uniform of an Army Major, when the Italian warring capability was faltering. His assistant had actually been my Department Chairman at the University of Chicago, Charles Merriam, Captain Merriam he was in World War I.

As matters stood, the small PWB Team, numbering perhaps six officers or equivalents thereof from OSS and OWI and six enlisted men, plus Italian staff that were being hired, was in receipt of communications from various branches of the Italian government addressed to the Allied High command, yet, to all practical purpose, these presented problems that could be handled just as well by the team, and so they were handled by the Team, which assumed an authority both imaginary and effective. Personages entered upon our premises, escaped and released Greek, Serbian, British and American Prisoners of War. The German consul was in our care. The Team also directed the press, cinema and radio.

I was brought an Italian corporal-driver-interpreter by Corporal Laudando along with a new Fiat, so that I could take in hand the Italian press. The Italian came quite handy but was arrested by the Italian Military Police for being absent without leave and disappeared. Laudando found out that he had been brought back by the Italian MP's to his outfit, and with another Italian soldier as guide, he took me to the rescue. We drove into a large post, that looked rather more attractive than Camp Tyson, and plucked the man from his barracks. The scene gathered a crowd, of course, that had nothing better to do. They followed the jeep to the entrance, where stood the Commanding General and his Staff, more curious than angry-looking. I thought that I had better pay my respects to authority, so I had the jeep pause in front of the General, saluted him, explained that I had been using the man, thank you very much, salute again, and Laudando let out the clutch and roared off.

I was supposed to supervise a large daily newspaper, the *Gazzetta del Mezzogiorno,* which now printed news of the King's doings. It referred to him as the King of Italy and Emperor of Ethiopia and Albania. It was not an important article, but it gave umbrage to me, who had to show my authority and teach them about the new order of affairs: these unlawful conquests were not to be given any semblance of recognition. I caught some on the newsstands and the rest undistributed and ordered them all destroyed, snatching several out of the very hands of the startled purchasers.

I hastened to remove my gear from the *Albergo Imperiale,* for the British Royal Navy was wetting its shorts to set up a sweet nesting spa in Bari. Of course, the port grew busy right away, and if they would have spent as much time guarding the rapidly growing fleet in the harbor as they had in feathering their nest, they might have imagined a German attack, for the Germans still had airplanes to the north and east, and on the Second of December sent in thirty of their precious few bombers to loose their loads upon the glut of ships, sinking no less than 19 of them, beginning with two ammunition vessels. One blasted ship carried mustard gas, that burned hundreds. But by then I had been long gone from the scene of this awesome carnage.

Moved out of the *Imperiale,* I joined the rest of the enlarged team at *Albergo Maggiore,* a perfectly comfortable hotel in the center of the city. My seniors, the Brits, were, as indicated earlier, woman-shy, and Greenlees, in his flippant fey way, foisted upon me the task of clearing the rooms of the hotel for occupancy by their growing numbers. Evidently a simple order passed along by way of the Italian concierge was not working. I discovered why, after giving the sternest of instructions to the Manager: a knock on his door introduced a beautiful young woman, smiling, call her Letitia: *"Mio caro Tenente,* I understand your problem, but surely we can arrange for a small room for myself, and even yourself, when you need it." No, no, *mi dispiace,* we need all the rooms. Many officers are coming, you understand. Of course, she understood: all the more reason for her keeping a little room. *Impossibile,* I had to say, suppressing all note of regret. She left. Another knock, another entrance, tears this time, beautiful again. And then the loud-voiced indignant one: accusations of cruelty, hard-heartedness, *ma,* more kindly, there must be a way out, no? No. I sneaked past them as I skulk down the stairs. They were packing, talking to each other in despair. I was pleased at my own fortitude in the face of the invitations and imprecations, but annoyed at having the dirty job inflicted upon me; they were, after all, humans, whores, so what, beautiful, courtesans, mistresses, prostitutes, still I was not evicting disabled old ladies, no, but this was harder, no, they would do extremely well, if only they knew, in the coming days and months, getting rid of their money-poor Italian majors and soliciting the wave of bill-wagging British and Americans. So I broke up as handsome a circle of ladies as was to be found on the Continent, despite every reason they could give for remaining, including connections with high officials, friendships with rich provisioners, promises from members of the police force, and, of course, free trips around the world whenever I could tear myself away from my work.

Hardly was this scene enacted when I was given the message from Greenlees by the Front Desk Manager to the effect that the Committee of Italian Liberation from Fascism was soon to arrive and that I should carry on with them until his possible late return. And here they came, a dignified, formally attired half-dozen gentlemen, several of advanced age, looking forward to the occasion, believing Greenlees, me, our Team, to hold all directives needed to extricate Italy from its predicament.

I explained the delay; they were nonetheless pleased. A Signor Giulio di Giovinazzo, who seemed to be their chairman, presented me with a remarkable photograph: it was of our predecessors of another war, World War I, in Bari, and sitting in the middle of the group is Major Fiorello La Guardia, now His Honor, Mayor of New York, as big as life. A couple of faces were the same, after a quarter of a century of Fascism. It was an excellent preface to the meeting to come and I began to hear what they had been up to, wondering also whether I should not invite them into the salon. These were the people to bring democracy to Italy, not the monarchical idiots of Brindisi.

I could not attend to what they were saying very well and was growing uneasy, because a half-dozen men in Allied battledress, without insignia, reporters probably, have burst into the small reception area near them and were berating the Desk Manager, who, his apologies and genius failing him, finally turned upon me and the men at the same time, saying "you will have to speak to the Lieutenant, please." They were indignant and pounced upon me now, who was generally irritated from my unusual labors of the day and was feeling an acute embarrassment before my Liberation Committee; they were shouting and demanding rooms from me, telling me that these people, embracing the Committee, to whom I was giving my undeserved attention, had damned well lost the bloody war and ought to be thrown out the door - taking off generally upon a series of insults directed at them, not listening to me at all saying that the Hotel had been requisitioned by the Allied military and was restricted, and they would have to go elsewhere, but exclaiming at all the woes they suffered in fighting their way here from Africa, with an insistence upon the rights of journalists over the rights of the bloody Italians. In exasperation, glancing uneasily at my listening Committee and essaying a bit of psychological warfare, I exclaimed that "If these people had really wanted to fight, you might still be there," whereupon the burly self-chosen ringleader, shouts "You're a disgrace to your uniform, that's what you are," which was not a well-conceived description of a young man who was coming to think of himself as a one-man army and therefore became excessively inflamed, and found himself impelled to shove, push and send the man sprawling, and to escort brusquely the lot of them into the street, declaring "Get out, get out!" then turning to the Committee and continuing as if nothing had happened - I am very sorry, but you know, *si capisce,* this is the way we behave - and soon Ian Greenlees came marching in and took over the proceedings in the salon, His Excellency of Bluff.

Actually, had they spoken to me politely, I would have tried to help them out, or if they had expressed themselves indignantly to me, I would have still borne with them and tried to guide them to accommodations, even though as correspondents they were supposed to be taken care of by a special staff of the Army

Headquarters and should not have to go blundering about like a gang of hooligans. But they had misinterpreted the situation that they came upon, and I had lost my temper, already high-strung from the day's events.

In any event I had put the incident out of mind, but that evening, as we sit at dinner, an American correspondent comes in, sweet as pie, asked for me, and was invited to sit with us, which he did, and then let the cat out of the bag, saying that he was going to tell this story that had been told him - of an officer knocking down worthy members of the press, abusing them, denying them a place to rest their combat-worn heads, siding with the Italian enemy - to the people back home and "the public will not like it." To which I angrily retort, with more learning than prudence, "As Jay Gould once said, the public be damned," and this, too, says the correspondent, will not go down well with the people back home. The dinner party broke up, the correspondent persisted, until Heycock finally ordered him out of the building.

The incident was not to be, as I believed, just another brawl. The reporter did file the story and the army censor scotched it. My friends were not without informants, who reported that the ringleader and the others denied that they were drunk, as I asserted - which would imply that they acted that way normally? - but did not want to press the matter, except that this American correspondent, whose name, they said, was McCarthy, wanted to take it up. Further, it developed that he was a correspondent who was regarded as most troublesome, an isolationist and Anglophobe, here masquerading as a friend, and, in fact, at a Press Conference in Washington, President Roosevelt took time out to present him with a German Iron Cross Medal for damage done to the American war effort and civilian morale. This, too, nonplussed the reporters, for the downed man was British and the American Lieutenant, your servitor, was backed solidly by his British fellow officers.

Still Army Headquarters liked to sacrifice lieutenants who make waves and I was lucky to be the only American around, hence doubly useful. Major Greenlees was delighted over the incident; he chuckled over it and recounted it periodically. He was quite fond of the Committee of Liberation and me. In later years, while Director of the British Institute in Florence, he would embellish the story to match his appetite for getting at journalists, until he had me knocking the gang of them about; quite untrue it was, though a slight domino effect could be discerned once they had stumbled into reverse.

Only two other Americans of appropriate rank were in Bari at the moment and Army Headquarters put it upon them to deal with the case. One was my new acquaintance Williamson from Delaware's Eastern Shore, who ranked high in OSS, though a civilian. The second was General Maxwell Taylor, commander of the 82nd Airborne Division, who was looking into the local situation after returning from Rome. (He had landed secretly there to determine whether his outfit could take over Rome when the Italians would announce their surrender, but had been shown by the Italians that the Germans were reacting too fast and had already moved in two divisions. It was a dumb idea anyway because Rome would have suffered grave damage, and local Italian forces were poorly equipped, there as everywhere.) Williamson knew Taylor and introduced me to him in a chance encounter as we walked along the street. I gave him a Class AA salute, and Williamson said jocularly: "Well, this doesn't look like a man who would go knocking people down, does he General?" (Actually, among paratroopers, bulk is not highly esteemed for physical prowess, so the remark probably is off-target with the Number One paratrooper.)

Taylor was not as friendly as Williamson, but at any rate they struck a deal later on, whereby both the correspondent and the officer would return to Algiers; I was assured by my friends that I would only touch base in Algiers and they would get me back to the Italian Front soon, in the West where the next big scene was to occur.

We may suppose that the British correspondent principally concerned, last heard of relaxing at a bar in Algiers, also found his way back later on. The idea was that the Army could protect itself by pointing to some action, rather than a cover-up, in case the issue of the brawl were raised again. I considered the matter and decided that I would indeed prefer Naples and points North, where Greenlees and the rest of the team would soon be entrenching

Italy, Toe and Heel

themselves.

I took no chances on missing Naples, however, and decided to head over there right now, so cut orders to Foggia and Naples and drove with Cpl. Laudando over the Apennine mountains by way of the town of Benevento. These fell to the Allies around the same time, as October began. We encountered one destroyed bridge after another and it was tiresome, because we could get across gullies and stream beds only by searching for passage up and down the river banks and over fields and through woodlands. I was determined to avoid the land mines that I was sure lurked beneath the stream bed and the rubble alongside the destroyed bridges.

After one particularly trying detour, when we sank in mud far from the road and had to persuade farmers to help extricate the jeep, I told Laudando that at the next blown passage we'd stay close to the bridge where we'd be sure not to get stuck again, and, as might be expected, the next little blown bridge was only a couple of hundred yards down the road at a bend. As we crawled up to it watching carefully the road for signs of planting, we were taken aback by an explosion; truck parts, tires, seats, and duffle bags went flying into the air from the channel bed.

We grasped quickly that it was not the Germans, but an American convoy, proceeding through no-man's land from the opposite direction, a Company of Combat Engineers at that, which had gotten to the bridge just ahead of us, and had let the half-ton lead vehicle carelessly go down upon the stream bed. Had they been Germans, of course, we would be in trouble. So we laugh in relief at our own escape and at the crazy sight, despite that something bad had occurred, and the Commander, walking up to us, did reproach us, saying: "You know, there is nothing funny about this. Men have been hurt!" But he could not be too nasty; our jeep had Army HQ markings and he would not have wanted it known how his men had plunged into a probable minefield. I apologized. We gave the Engineers information on the terrain that lay ahead for them and wound around the mountains to Napoli.

There a German-planted delayed charge in the central Postoffice, Telegraph, and Telephone Building had just exploded, killing and injuring many civilians, and anti-German sentiment had risen high, bouncing directly to America now via the press corps that has come in with the liberating troops; it relished to tell of innocent women and children being hurt by rotten Nazis. The 5th Army combat propaganda nucleus had settled into a billet, and we check in and spend a day and a half exchanging information around town before heading back to Bari.

One of their men, Fred Faas, had been shot in the ass, a painful wound, taking long to heal. It happened at Salerno while he was stooping outside a doorway to take a shit. Charlton, too, had arrived via the route of the 8th Army from Salerno and was publishing the *Desert Rat News* again, so our departure was delayed by a bottle of Scotch.

How do we find these people? - simple: we go to the presses, the radio station or wherever communications or intelligence are involved, or Army G-2 and there somebody knows where they are. Laudando (literally: *he must be praised*) was a prolific information source on food, billets, army and civil gossip; while you were doing something else, he was never slumping in his jeep. The huge Chicagoan was even born in Naples; he spoke Italian fluently, he was Figaro with a Neapolitan accent. We encountered a pretty little girl, Maria, daughter of a Neapolitan Viscount, who he knew was beyond his barbaric reach but who seemed to admire me and wondered why I didn't pet her like I petted her cat. Laudando said he wondered, too. But I had all I could do to write letters home, what with all this dashing about.

The Brits of Bari found Laudando indispensable, and I realized that I could not hold him. But they would appreciate the Corporal's strengths and tolerate his foibles. He was a rough and cheerful guy, who conducted himself with rare prescience and gentility toward officers, who was reliable in reporting on the state of the masses, and a genius at living off the land. He did get into trouble later on, but the incident can wait the telling.

We headed East by North to return to Bari and struck en route upon the great air base of Foggia, that had been found untenable by the Germans, wrecked by countless air raids. We arrived at pitch-black night in a downpour, the field was empty, a British patrol was huddled in one corner of a building. I did not wish to be blown up by a mine and would rather sleep in the rain, so made up a tent of sorts beneath a piece of wreckage. In the morning we went through the city. It was in poor shape as well. I assembled a cursory intelligence report for the Naples and Bari people. Then back it went to Bari and on to North Africa.

Very little could be expected of the Italian government. Already there were tough problems over the admission of all or some parties to the coalition that was to run the civilian offices of the government. Actually the country was in the hands of foreign armies; the Allies addressed the Naples-Foggia line from the South, the Germans were dragging their heels while organizing resistance north of a Volturno River line.

Why the fighting and most of the British forces should be shifted to the West puzzled me. Along the Adriatic coastline, there runs a better plain for driving North and there were many fewer Germans in opposition. But everyone had eyes focused upon Rome. It hardly occured to the high command of the Allies, who were little different from ourselves on larger strategy, to conquer Italy from the East. As a matter of fact, the Allied 15th Army Group would offer for the first time in history a conquest of Italy from the South. (I do not really believe this, but that's what General Alexander and the historians have said.)

Ah, yes, they would most likely be saying something like this: "If we move rapidly up the East Coast, the enemy will come over and cut us off." But the Allies could wreak havoc upon any sizeable German forces moving across the Apennines. Furthermore the Allies could then reinforce the West by sea or air. You could not move the Germans' equipment-poor army back and forth across difficult mountain roads, such as I and Laudando had just driven through, especially with demolitions everywhere. And if they swung over to block or trap the Allies, would they not find themselves in even worse danger of being snared themselves? A law of warfare, from grand army to patrol, seems to be: a) logically, the one opponent can trap the other, like two wrestlers, b) the better equipped, trained, aggressive, cleverer and more numerous, wins, c) but, not content with thus explaining victory, the winner claims to have performed a brilliant flanking movement.

On October 9, I cut my orders, got them signed by Greenlees, and headed for the small Bari airfield. There I found a DC-3 leaving for Catania with a load of sick and wounded men for the evacuation hospital. I climbed aboard. The night was stormy, visibility nil, the men anxious, myself included. The interior of the plane nothing but a metal cylinder with strings of wires, with metal bucket-seats and a ragged rug on the metal floor, so that stretchers inclined this way and that, and the men sat as best they could, holding whatever part of them hurt the most as best they could to ease the painful bumps. The noise, the smells, the groans, the thunder, the lightning, the dips, yaws and jolts - almost like continuous collisions.

The other healthy passenger aboard was a flight lieutenant of the RAF, born in the West Indies, graduated from Yale, named Kennedy, a man who had spent a year in the Soviet Union and spoke Russian - a good man for dinner-table in Catania, I thought, whatever that may be like now. At Catania I found my villa - the same that we had taken possession of, it seemed, years ago. Only Beauclerk and a couple of others were old faces among the dozen there now. But their welcome was hearty enough, and the cuisine had continued in the respectable tradition set by Captain Robertson and Company.

The next day, I lucked onto a plane to Algiers, so bade all goodbye and flew smoothly to Africa. The people in Catania were really enjoying the war, it seemed, but life was even better in Algiers. Sometimes, you know, at odd moments for some, most of the time for others, not only these characters, but soldiers even down to where the other guy's machine-gun can be heard, say: "I pity those poor bastards back home; they don't know what they're missing." And they really mean it, at least for a couple of hours now and then, maybe even for the whole long time they're gone.

Chapter Nine

ALGIERS AND PALERMO

AT THE Algiers airport, I phoned to the Headquarters of the First Mobile Radio Broadcasting Company, using the handy list of the Military Police, and shortly a jeep arrived to fetch me home. It was home. I was still on their roster. And they were even drawing rations for me because nobody at the rations dump asked the pertinent questions. They were glad to see me, with my news of places they said they would like to see, if the circumstances were pleasant: what gold-bricks!

They were already apologizing for why I had not been promoted to the rank of Captain. They claimed that I was recommended for my captaincy on September 23. Who would be blocking it? Among themselves, but not to my face, so maybe I was imagining it, they could say: "He got in some brawl." They did not tell me, but they were all up for promotion and before long they would be sprouting double bars and maple leafs. It was inevitable: if you didn't stay close to where the promotion orders were cut, your chances of being passed over were increased. The swines, as Heycock and Galsworthy liked to say about such types. Better, the farrow: they stayed close by the teats.

But they were not hiding or deliberately shirking. They were just what remained of the Company after its useful elements had gone warfaring. And it just so happened that the remnants were two-thirds of the Company. One side of me was envious: just look at Tommy Anglin, the poster picture of an American Lieutenant, and just as nice as anybody could be; and take a look at Jerry Stern, too, his uniforms, like the rest, laundered and pressed to a fault, shoes glistening; Captain Rathbun, booming away cheerily; and Major Caskey now, his mustache brilliantly red and flourishing. All the way down to the last private.

Caskey was about to return to the US to activate and train more companies of the same type. He had not heard a shot fired in anger nor spoken to an enemy prisoner, nor even visited a forward zone - in fact little that would qualify him for his new mission, so therefore (foreshadowing the Peter Principle) he was elevated to perform the task and ordered (what a euphemism an Army Order can be) to return to the Great PX. Were he honest about his experience, he would say, well, we are a kind of a stockroom of parts, most of us junk, both ourselves and our equipment and what has been done with us has been to cannibalize our outfit, taking the best parts and personnel as they were needed, leaving the rest of us to cool our heels and monkey around with the junk left behind. There was this to be said for Caskey: he was not a wicked man or a martinet. He let his people relax and enjoy.

Waiting for someone up there to tell them some day what to do, and meanwhile living high off the hog. Vehicles, spanking new and well-maintained, with mileage more than ample to take them on excursions and into Algiers. A few were assigned to jobs in Algiers and stayed in town most of the time, using the Company as a weekend residence. No K-rations, C-rations, here, but the best that the Quartermaster could provide straight from the States, supplemented by locally grown fruit and vegetables. Refrigerated steaks from America. Fresh coffee beans by the sack, too. The whitest fine flour for bread-making and pie-making. Native Algerians to police the kitchen and the grounds. Sandlot baseball, puttering on the radios and motors. Drinking and card-playing. Concerts and spectacles.

To these worthies went the comforts and pleasures of soldiers whose tedious and tiring training days were distant in memory, whose fears of the Front were languishing, whose anxiety over transfer to the infantry were still non-existent, even while the generals of the European Theater were being told that they had better postpone plans for a Second Front because the rate of induction of civilians into the Army had been rather slower than expected.

All of this weighed against an occasional boredom, mixed with a gram of bad conscience, thoughts more or less poignant of a lagging education or career back in the States, nostalgia for families and friends and old neighborhoods and even wives in a couple of cases and American girls in many cases, mostly imaginary film starlets. The imbalance of risk and suffering in wartime, let us admit, is outrageously unjust.

The USA was winning the war on its production, on some daredevil or grim pilots, on some unusual platoons of some reluctant divisions, but especially on its production, whilst I and my friends were cursing the lucky guys, fully unionized, making time-and-a-half for overtime, and going home to their games and pals and families, fifty-three million war workers.

Their immense production of ships, guns, vehicles, planes was approaching its three-year peak, whereupon it would avalanche upon its enemies. In the main, the armed forces were camp followers of the small number of special types that found themselves in critical actions, a beach, an island, a river crossing, a strong-point, a vital target. All of them were in a real sense minions of home-front production. Bomb the hell out of the foe, blast them with cannon day and night, and then take them over: thanks to the war workers.

So overwhelming was this force, that slowly but surely the American psyche was coming to feel insulted when men actually had to die in any numbers, and the public and in the end the troops made a great fuss over it and the censors went to work to hide casualties. Also slowly but now more rapidly there emerged the related practice of the destruction of civilian centers, at first "to destroy military targets", then war production, then civilian morale.

Yet, although the troops on the cutting edge were angry in principle with the production teams who were winning the war by working under conditions by no means ideal - a great part of them ill-housed - jealously angry really, because they could not be among them, the same frontline troops were surprisingly not so upset over the millions of supernumerary soldiers abroad and in the military camps back home. Yet, again, the feeling of sympathy for the unlucky ones who were at risk was in itself the reason for the enormity of the train of provisioners - civilian and uniformed - behind the Front. It took several times the resources and personnel to get an American soldier to where he could fire a rifle or cannon than it did to get an Englishman there and ten times more than in the case of a Russian soldier.

At this point in time, the Great Teheran Conference of Roosevelt, Stalin and Churchill was imminent. Now hear this: The President and America's top diplomats, planners and military leaders rode the Battleship *Iowa*. FDR loved the Sea. The Destroyer *Porter* was one of the escort vessels, and about 350 miles East of Bermuda decided to practice its torpedo launchings. After its last patrol, it neglected to clear its third tube. The tube was now aimed at the *Iowa,* its #2 ammo magazine, just for practice, and fired. It was a bad shot, for the live and fully-armed torpedo missed the *Iowa* by 1200 yards to stern. What would have become the War's most spectacular amicide failed. Would the U.S.A. have won the War with its top leaders draped in Sargasso seaweed? Unequivocally, yes, says this chronicler. Why? For the aforementioned reasons: its massive war production, its morale (arising in large part from its productivity), its unlimited new troops, some of whom, at least, would shape up well and would have all the tools needed for their job, together with the high morale those inspired. Henry Wallace, rather than Harry Truman, would have become President, consequences of which occurrence would have been significant but too complex to unravel in a few lines here.

I have gotten a little ahead of my story in order to mention this near amicidal incident: I was still living in October, and will in any case never hear of the near-miss to my beloved leaders - censorship, you know. My chief danger of the moment consisted of falling into a life of dissipation and social dissolution. So beguiling the temptations, so contemptible was the operations setup of PWB, AFHQ. Not that I had been doing too badly, on the balance, in and out of the "Real War." Looking back, I have been miserable and at risk more than the average, and one has to count as risk, the reasonable anticipation of something bad happening to his head or flesh. A coward dies many deaths, the old saying goes, but a brave man dies at least a couple of deaths - and there are all the gradations in between for those who are ordinary or unfeeling.

The witnesses of War are not good judges, the more so the farther removed they are from the immediate risk. The folks back home believed my risks greater than did the lackadaisical comrades of the First MRBC here, but these exaggerated the dangers of my experiences too. I might write a book on how the authorities, the generals, the politicians, the pastors, the womenfolk, the workers, the soldiers just behind the "lines," the press, and Hollywood fashioned (consciously and unconsciously) the scene of war on land, on sea, and in the air to suit their own wishes and morale. The truth of the scene - what was it, then? - it was hard to fix, record, remember, recall; hardest of all was to proportion the reality.

So the people of the *Hotel Corneille* had a foggy notion of "up front," also. So I could swagger a bit around the place. I preferred the City and the Hotel and moved into a room there. Around the corner were their offices and after a decent interval of days I called upon the effective Director of PWB, C.D. Jackson, whom we last encountered in mortal combat with the Head of PWB, the shit-kicker Colonel, across empty dishes and wine bottles at the Eighth Army Team's Apartment in Syracuse.

By now, I was becoming prickly out of my own contradiction, for I began to see that I had profited from an act of censorship, just or not, whereas I had always been a foe of censorship. It was like being an anti-slavery slave-owner. I wished I had coldly accepted the tirades of the journalists instead of tossing them out.

Well, said C.D. Jackson, as I stepped into his office, you know you have given us some trouble. This was perhaps not the thing to say, especially since Jackson may have been given the assimilated rank of Colonel, but lacked the arbitrary powers of a military commander. I became angry, and demanded: "What do you mean 'trouble'? I am here, but I don't want to be here. I can't stand this place. I shouldn't have come. I came to make things easy. I want to get out of here as fast as I can. When can you get me back?" Jackson didn't respond badly. He was a little afraid to talk to "real" soldiers. What could he say? This adamant type facing him might spark an argument with Hazeltine or even with his buddies. Perhaps, but as I saw it, Jackson was not a shit like Hazeltine. He really didn't know what happened except that I was supposed to have gotten some correspondents down on him and, as a member of the press, was both embarrassed and defensive. So there was little for him to say except, just keep ready and you'll be sent back soon.

I, appeased, went to the dining room and got to talking at the table with some people I had not known before, including a chap who had been a screenwriter, hardly cutting a military figure, but unpretentious in civilian khakis, and the words "sweet," "funny," and "smart" began to jog my mind, so I looked closely at the round face, and especially at the beaming, uncannily familiar Baltic blue eyes, and I determined that I must be talking to my wife's first cousin, Jerry Ross, who, of course, it was. So it was hello again, and let's celebrate (he was a mild, non-boisterous civilian, there was no hell-raising with Jerry, but it was nice to have an intelligent guy around; also a kind of relative, and most of all someone who knows and can admire my beloved Jill.) It was hard to figure out what use he would be in Italy, since he knew the country neither politically, linguistically, nor militarily. But never mind, there was the rudimentary Peter Principle at work again: he was going as a high officer with a salary thrice that of the same Army officer. In this case, I felt no pain. A relative of Jill was a friend of mine.

Furthermore, it had to be deemed a demi-sacrifice, because Jerry would have made loads of lucre writing scenarios for the many romantic and war films Hollywood was putting out, with an enormous captive audience in the troops, and really among the civilians, too, because what else could people do, without gas for their cars?

Anyhow I made no attempt to find out what Jerry Ross was doing; maybe he was writing American scripts for broadcasting at home (though why there should be any need for more buncombe despatches back there was a mystery). We went on excursions to the Casbah to gawk and reflect upon Arab culture.

More important to my state of mind, I took up with a young

woman who worked for PWB at menial tasks, cleaning up. She was surprisingly pretty, considering the job she dutifully performed; she was using the job to get rations, PX supplies, giveaways (people were always leaving for the West or North), decent treatment (the Americans and British were so much more kind to the help than the French - here and everywhere), and relatively high pay. She had an unpretentious apartment not far away, clean, airy, simple, comfortable, where I learned to let myself in whenever I pleased.

She was even-tempered, didn't ask for anything, and got very little from me - who ever did? - at least so far as one could tell, certainly not in a material way, and there were no promises, no confessions of love. She was French, *pied noir*. Who was she really? Where was her family, her man? She was too attractive and altogether too nice a person to have no suitors or lovers or husband, not to mention her sexuality, for she was a gentle and appealing lover, in and out of bed. Perhaps her husband was in some far away place, possibly in a German prison camp, or one of the blockaded units of the Foreign Legion. There was nothing of the masculine in or about her flat, nothing fluffy feminine either. Perhaps she was just what she looked like, an independent, prudent self-contained person, and there was nothing else, and I was an interlude in her life as she was an incident to mine. I hoped that she was not growing too fond of me, because - but she must have known- I would not be with her long.

I do not know, I cannot figure out, whether a woman is much stronger than a man when it comes to giving up a lover, or some women are resigned and able to take such events in stride (while others blow up in anticipation, from the very first moments, or as the affair begins to close down). Cécile was her name, "Cecy" or "Sissy" I called her. She liked her nickname. It made her proud and distinctive and intimate.

Before my British friends could set up shop in Naples and get to me and before the Fifth Army Team realized that I was available (Herz and Weaver were there) and could get itself together, the Palermo office called for somebody to become their Political Intelligence Officer (what a gas!) and off I went, my weeks of "rest and rehabilitation" over with, winging to Sicily upon a deep blue

October day. Nor was I to have any but fine Sicilian early winter weather from now on, even though I came in on a bumping aircraft: they all bumped when they came to fly through the narrow pass between two rocky peaks on their way down onto the Palermo airport. The weak-nerved closed their eyes when the plane went swooping in, swaying its wings to brush one or the other peak.

I checked in with Capt. Cosgrove, a large con-man with a full-toothed yard-wide smile out of England, we struck it off well, and Cosgrove could hardly wait to show me the mess. It was worth bragging about. The decor was elegant, the service superior, the wines excellent, the food was the best of Sicilian cuisine, most of the Team's rations having been exchanged in diurnal transactions for authentic local products. As you entered the restaurant, you were greeted by the parrot who had given to the famous restaurant its name, "Il Pappagallo." The parrot got in the first word. *"Buon Giorno!"* he called to one. *"Buon Giorno,"* you automatically responded. But, *"Come sta?"*, he added, as if he really cared. And so on, with a paltry bag of phrases and witticisms. "Wait, now hear this!" said Cosgrove to me, taking my arm. *"Come sta Mussolini?"* asked Cosgrove, no longer a non-speaker of Italian. To which the blue and red beast shrieked: *"Mussolini e' cornuto!"* - Mussolini is a cuckold, the favorite insult of Mediterranean Europe.

I was delighted, and, like everyone, was subdued whenever the bird seemed off his wonted aplomb, and stuck his head beneath his wing, morose, silent. I was happy, too, with the Palermo gang, although I proceeded continuously pained by my absence from my wife, on one occasion doing an elaborate calculation of the number of days I had been with and without her from the very moment of our meeting in June of 1940; I charted it; I mailed the chart to her. It exhibited the unhappy fact of our great love, that, for one reason or another, although I, and probably she, suffered from and resisted our separations, there had been more separations than togetherness over the whole period of time. This might have been admissible in Nineteenth Century America, when Yankee Clippers sailed around the world for months, and wartime campaigns on foot and by horse and boat took up long periods of time, and a girl in Boston would be kept from her swain in New York for years until he had made his mark in the economy and had furnished a house. No more. The new Americans, even before the War, demanded instant response, repulsed any excuse for separateness, made the cause of it into an evil.

But we were here in Palermo. Walking down the street one day soon after arriving, I bumped into Professor T.V. Smith, who was to become Professor of Philosophy, Politics, and Poetry at the University of Syracuse (a title he chose himself) and who taught me modern philosophy at the University of Chicago, but appeared at the moment to be Director of Education for AMGOT, the Military Government still ruling Sicily. A fine choice, this tall and smooth-talking Texan, a Pragmatic Philosopher, an antidote to the influence of the Church in Italian education, a poison pill to Communism, a comprehensible successor to Fascism, which had at one juncture declared itself pragmatic because it had nothing else to say to explain its destructive activism and violence. More than anything else, and including all this, he was an enemy of the formality of the Italian schools and their curricula. I let loose a blare of recommendations, of course. How I wanted Colonel T.V. to turn the whole show around! Quickly to revolutionize the educational system! That was like me, to wish powers upon people whom I liked and with whom I agreed and to overestimate the capacity of the system to be changed. What I could do if only I had the power myself!

Among the Italians, significant numbers, many more than in America, and most of officialdom, South of Bologna and including the Sicilians, of course, were past masters at the art of evading conditions and demands that put disagreeable burdens upon them. The compatibility of Italy with modern existence and economy came largely from their considerable personal energies and voluntary generosity as individuals. But their effusive guarantees of compliance were evidence of defiance, I came to believe. The Sicilians did not, any more than most Italians, believe that they had unconditionally surrendered. They had long ago already surrendered in their minds, and therefore no gap existed that had to be filled with newly conceived or learned reforms, rather only those that they had had in mind secretly all the time.

As a birthright. Because they, like most Europeans, were not discovering radicalism or reform or new ideas as a result of liberation; Sicily employed an elected Parliament in the Thirteenth Century along with England; it had experienced everything within and from without; the ideas and the practices were known to them, and indeed they had been fighting over these ideas amongst themselves, which was precisely the reason why Fascism succeeded, by saying: "Stop this haggling and debating! Order, and a single man to command is what we need," or, as a precursor of Fascism, Professor Count Vilfredo Pareto, said: "Let us not waste words on 'representation,' poppycock grinds no flour." The humiliating finale of which was to be found by the American troops plastered on all of the walls of Italy: *"Mussolini ha sempre ragione!"* Mussolini is always right.

How lucky were the Sicilians with the British and especially the Americans, unhistorical freaks, invaders who were well-intentioned and undemanding except of reforms that the people knew in their hearts were what they needed. But the Allies could not make up for decades of misrule, not to mention a deteriorating economic situation going back to the Eighteenth Century. The country was, when you paused to consider it, not only beautiful architecturally and in nature, but profoundly rich and cultured; and basically, it was rationally organized to feed everybody somehow during a perennial economic depression. So they were by no means a hopeless case, even though faucets did not pour water, toilets did not flush, and the ice for ice cream came still in part from the ice caves of Mt. Etna. But the Allies did bring in some good people during the interim period, when they were in charge, and took little after having destroyed much by war, and gave enough to reconstitute at the least the *status quo ante bellum*.

Another good man who appeared before my young critical eye was Philip Hammond, who was on leave from Harvard University as a Professor of Classics and was here delegated to help conserve Sicilian art treasures which were truly enormous in number and scope, and which stretched in time from the Neolithic through every age down to the present. He cared every bit as much for the Sicilian heritage as any poverty-stricken and funds-straitened

Curator on the Island. The destruction of the artistic, religious, and archaeological treasures of humanity had been, if one was to speak in dollar-language, in the scores of billions.

Joining the "Pappagallo" mess, along with his crew of Sicilians from the schools and faculty of the City, was an astonishing character, already looking ageless with his dry white pinched skinny features and near-baldness. He had the glittering eye of the fanatic. They ate at their own table and talked vigorously and seriously through the meals about their assignments and questionnaires, and then they walked about the city, into the slums and into the fine bourgeois apartments, asking the citizenry about their attitudes and needs, their housing and eating habits, feelings about crime, opinions of the Allied troops (sic), awareness and support of the Badoglio Government, and conjectures about the future. Their leader was Professor Stuart Dodd of the University of Washington.

I had in two years practically forgotten about the nuts and bolts of my academic specialty, which was supposed to have been public opinion analysis, and here weirdly in Palermo I found Dodd dividing the country into interviewing districts and training and sending out interviewers to ask people of all sorts what they thought about all the issues that leaders of a government should know the opinions of their people about. I was impressed; this strange man was a culture hero: how did he manage to get into the military, how did he manage to get overseas, how could he believe that he might get across this notion of public opinion as something to be measured, here of all places, here when in America, where this science was just being born, it was the butt of jokes and censure among politicians, newspapers, and traditionalist professors.

He did it; working with incredible insouciance and dedication, sereneness of belief in the task, sense of mission of the New Social Science; his workers were devoted to their tasks. His protocols, which were examined with disbelief by your servant, quondam researcher at the University of Chicago, were professional, neat, complete. He was a veritable Ignatius Loyola, they were his Jesuits. I, being a "real soldier," a trencherman and companionable boozer, was regarded with respect by Captain Cosgrove, who was relieved and half-believing when I told him that Stuart Dodd was not a dangerous queer or subversive, but putting to work a new hi-tech system for governing a population sensibly and avoiding disturbance.

Hubert Howard turned up, a tall rather tense but sweet Englishman with the air of a perpetual bachelor, expert in matters Italian, of an Italian mother and an established English Catholic family that managed to pull through the bloody Reformation and Civil Wars without losing all of its sundry heads. His job it was to be generally informed and aware of the politics of the region; that is, he was an accomplice of my "D section" friends, Greenlees and Robertson.

An ex-correspondent, Hadfield, also English, was present, an American journalist named Lee, and a young man whom I had managed to detach from another outfit while at Camp Ritchie, and made sergeant, Kamenetski, an Italian Jew like Guetta, more Italian than the Italians, a pure scholar by character but now running the programming and news of the Palermo station.

Very soon after greeting and reveling in the new circle, I originated various tasks for myself. The first project that I suggested to Cosgrove, who exulted in the energies of others, was to set up an Information Center for things Allied and democratic, a modest enterprise, costing next to nothing. It was actually the archetype for the American Information Centers that would be established around the world in the decades to come. I collected a few books, met with several local artists to buy their paintings, gathered some propaganda published by the Office of War Information, printed more of it, arranged for cultural meetings to be held, and hired a sidekick, a pretty young blonde and blue-eyed maiden aged twenty-four, Carla Puleo, whom I put in charge.

When I introduced her to the privileged restaurant of the Team, Cosgrove was mightily impressed. "How does it happen," for he is a man with an urge, "that you should find such a beautiful young woman in this burg, where I hardly see a one worth chasing after?" Or words to that effect. Well, I should say, Cosgrove, you are a fright to a young maiden, and Palermo is full of shutters, intermediaries, and dodges for evading males. But I didn't, because Cosgrove was really a decent chap, despite his loud and gauche ways. Luck, I said, just plain luck, you know. But this alone, putting a woman in charge, a young one, without sexual compromise (oh, I may have kissed her once or twice), marked a break with tradition even in this, in some ways highly sophisticated, stubbornly old-fashioned city. Carla got mess privileges, a little cash to work with; rather soon, a cultural circle formed around her and thus the cultural and information center.

I hired a crippled little red-headed painter, Gianfallo, to draw a great map of the World on wood, which was then cut and nailed into a giant-sized unit that was mounted above the shop entrance. It hinted to the proud Sicilians the appropriate size of the Island amid the Earth's land masses, and became a conversation piece in local society. I met Carla's father, the Baron Puleo, whom I regarded with respect, not alone for his dignified bulk and courteous manners, but for not having asked to meet me earlier, for not having put conditions upon my friendship with and subsequent employment of his daughter, for having trusted her, for behaving like a modern father should behave. From Gianfallo the painter I also purchased several pen and ink sketches that I mailed back to Jill and she liked the stone walls and olive trees of the countryside of Sicily that they portray and that most G.I.'s had come to dislike in the course of their campaign in the dry hot summer.

Economic affairs were not in order. The country was near to starving. I noted how my visitors and companions of various social levels habitually carried a briefcase; when they opened it to remove or insert a document, a lump of bread, and perhaps a piece of hard cheese, could be seen resting there, to be gnawed upon sometime in the course of the day or evening, if there was nothing else to be eaten.

I was enlisted to arbitrate labor disputes in the film distribution business on questions of pay, of licenses to operate theaters, of claims over archives of film. I acted, too, as a film censor of an evening, viewing Fascist propaganda films and ordinary films that could be labelled fascistic and anti-allied. This was a waste of time, although I would not be aware of it yet; the audiences were so sensitive to and derisive of the old propaganda that such a film would not be played anyhow.

Ordinary people and the military talked a lot about the black market and the mafia and the crime wave. The story was making the rounds that the U.S. intelligence agencies had received help from the mafia before and during the military campaign. This may have been balderdash, but many Americans and Italians believed it. And it certainly profited the mafiosi, whatever the truth, to claim that they had been anti-Fascists all along and collaborated with the liberators. I could nott hope to discover anything on this account from my friendlies, for they would be covering up any connivance with criminals. Even though I would be interested in hearing directly from the mafia "partisans" myself, this was not the purpose of my modest investigation. I was interested mainly in the structure of the overall problem; what should have been the attitude of the liberators and new Italian government? My own position needed clarification.

Most people were more paranoid than not and therefore prone to believe in large, unseen, mysterious conspiracies governing the world, particularly if they lived in closed societies or societies governed socially by hierarchical and authoritative religion. So I was reasoning, but had little knowledge, and wondered whether the mafia was truly organized or whether it was largely a word to cast over the whole body of largely dissociated criminality.

I went to the police, examined their blotters, gathered some figures, talked to a few businessmen and informants, and arrived at the half-baked conclusion that the mafia so-called was a way of life but not a single organized criminal network. That there was a lot of crime was evident; there were big shots and punks; where crime is rampant, even by the modest standards of those days when drugs and alcohol were absent from the picture, a pecking order is established; "you had better not get in the way of This *Pezzo Grosso,* he bosses a tough gang."

Thus, like an oligarchic market economy, crime organized itself into behavior patterns, which, if you were not a particularly expert observer, you might see as a single monster organization; there was therefore no single head to decapitate; this was actually why the mafia or mafiosi or other gang systems could not be hunted down for once and for all time. It was built into the social system, as every culture had its own typical criminal system or underworld built into it.

High unemployment, strong extended family organization and responsibility, widespread economic distress, a hierarchical and authoritarian ruling system, and a dissociation of local culture and morals from a centralized national police system all combined to foster the endemic high crime rates, especially associated with the West of Sicily, as well as with other parts of the world with similar conditions, or with situations like New Jersey or Chicago or Marseilles that constituted a benevolent reception system, like a biological laboratory soup in which the mafia phenomena could prosper. The mafia seemed to be united, I felt, because they did know of one another, kept in touch benevolently or malevolently with one another, had the same characteristics socially and demographically and culturally, and killed each other when in conflict and under threat.

The mafia, therefore, was a difficult condition to eliminate. Crime is something to be fought piecemeal, and, at the other extreme, through reforms in the most general structure of the society.

My brief report circulated here and there among occupation officials and police of the occupying powers, the municipal police and the carabinieri. It had no discernible effect, much less a ripple effect; it is claimed that you cannot fight crime piecemeal because the petty crooks get off with the help of the bigger ones and the corrupt system of justice. As for the Reform of Society, it is impossible, as it has always been. Some people asked whether I was afraid of reprisals, but I had not named names nor given any indication of being party to secret information; getting after me would have been a purely gratuitous act, to which the mafiosi were not inclined. In anticipation of my departure, I turned over my ideas and papers to Hubert Howard, incorruptible, brave, but as remote from J. Edgar Hoover as a dove from a gander.

It was true that dysentery, the "G.I.'s," (actually, a slang name for the soldiers themselves, from "general issue") struck me down around this time, but it was not fear, nor poison, but rather an enormous Thanksgiving turkey dinner that provoked the attack, and I was soon well enough to move on, to Italy, where there had been occurring a tug-o'war for my talents, on the one side my friends in Naples of "D Section," on the other the Combat Propaganda Team of the Fifth Army, commanded by Lt. Col. Oren Weaver, whom I hadn't seen since April and then in Washington D.C. Fifth Army won, with the stipulation that I also help out "D Section" with political intelligence reports from the Front. On December 6, having dallied in Naples for three days, I was cheerily hello-ing Buck Weaver, Martin Herz, and the others under the palm trees of the Royal Gardens at Caserta.

Camera-shy officers of British D-Section
Ian Greenless, Edmund Howard, Ian Robertson,
Hadfield, Denham

Chapter Ten

THE BATTLE OF CASSINO

THE Royal Palace of Caserta contained both Fifth Army Headquarters and Fifteenth Army Group Headquarters. It could have swallowed the Algiers AFHQ for the Mediterranean Theater as well. It was a monstrous encampment, worthy of the enormous military bureaucracy and its equipage. Lt. Alfred de Grazia, AUS, CAC-MI would never get to the end of it, whether by foot or car. The Bourbon Kings of The Two Sicilies built it of a rich ochre stone in the Eighteenth Century with the grand and marvelous flourish of a Versailles. Its large gardens and exotic trees shade noble walks along which military officers might amble while deciding how to wrest Italy from the Germans.

To me the set-up was dismaying. It would appear that the Army had been taking on a long, long-term, a decade-long lease. Luckily for my morale, the weather was turning bad, the mud was beginning to climb to the tops of my boots and lick at my leggings, and the combat propaganda detachment was bivouacked on the fringe of the palace; it occupied a couple of olive-drab pyramidal tents.

I was out on the job every day contacting the units of the line, which was at the Volturno River when I first started up; the line then was forced in a score of bloody engagements to the outskirts of Cassino, where it got stuck. As the year drew to a close, I was awaiting news of the birth of my "son," and hung around the tents excessively, or so it seemed to Lt. Col. Weaver, himself tent-loving, who asked me courteously whether I shouldn't be out making the rounds of the Front. This embarrassed me a little: that I could have been imagined as slacking or lazy or afraid; yet I did not want to confess a real reason for dragging my feet, that I believed any moment now might bring the Message from the Red Cross.

Devotedly I detailed my existence to my Wife, saying little of the baby as the fateful date, December 29 - my own birthday, too - came and went; it was a crisis, and I did not want to put a wrong construction upon the absence of news. On the First of January I described the day before, December 31, 1943:

> *The New Year has started out as a howling banging affair. A wind blew up last night and even now twenty-four hours later is threatening to deprive us of our means of support. As I write I feel that my eyes have run amuck; it seems as if the tent grows bigger and smaller, constantly. Very disturbing and very true. It does grow bigger and smaller and the wind comes in great breathtaking swooshes that leave one to marvel that the pegs are still grounded.*
>
> *I spent a most bitter day and still have a few shivers left over. The rain, sleet and wind crawled into our very marrows. The Army is perfectly miserable. Wretched soldiers, drenched to the skin, their tents blown down or the rain blown in, a sea of mud and a welter of newly created lakes, the sides of the roads raging torrents and snow in most places a few hundred feet up.*
>
> *I went down to the dump to get some shells fixed up and found complete devastation. The crew were huddled in a little room in a stone manger* [shed?] *looking on the hostile outside dejectedly and miserably. Not only had their records blown away, but also their tents, leaving a pile of messy trash half buried in mud. The chaos revealed a cornet which was being reclaimed by one of the boys, and with an eager lip I tried it out. I suppose that it was strange to play "Stardust" out in the open like that, with numb lips and fingers, but it was only a small absurd bit in the whole Krazy-Kat scene.*
>
> *Hundreds of trees have blown down, many of them olive trees and hardly expendable. It is a conspiracy of wind and rain. The rain softens and the wind gives the mortal blow...*
>
> *Last night was spent in the tent. We drank a little rum and wine, opened and fried a tin of tongue which I believe Mom or you sent me, and sang a few songs. At midnight we fired our guns, adding to the general impression of a giant night battle with tommy-guns, rifles,*

> *pistols, BAR's, and even a machine gun which I could have sworn I heard. We came in and drank some coffee. I stayed up a while cleaning the guns and about the time I went to sleep, the wind began. Out of the daze of slumber, I remember various articles tossing about the tent and scary blasts which one could hear starting in the trees far away and which came towards and through us in a final rush like huge breakers...*
>
> *If one takes to signs, the year will be mighty and awful. It may be good, too, because I saw a beautiful rainbow in the midst of all the rigors today.*

The four officers - Dabinette, Foster, Herz and myself - slept in one tent. The office of the detachment was in another. An account of it made up most of another letter a week later (still no word of the baby):

> *Perhaps, in view of your expressed hatred of offices, I can describe what an army field office looks like. First there is the tent, dark green or camouflaged, and then inside, instead of beds, you have folding camp tables which hold hardly nothing except a pencil and a piece of paper. If you are lucky, you also have a chair, barring that a stool or box or anything that will stave off collapse. With this table you must execute masterful maneuvers to open maps which are peers of anything Standard Oil ever put out, including as they do every house or former house, and everything down to a machine gun in size. Every once in a while a wire crew comes in to put in a phone or take it out, which doesn't mean much since it never works, except of course to add to the confusion. The phone is a tantalizing instrument, you must admit. Half the time you get a whisper, which leads you to bellow enthusiastically into the mouthpiece, rising in a great crescendo on the margins of comprehension and resulting in two messages at least, neither understood or correct. Or there may be three or more, depending on how many other units become attached to your wire meanwhile. If the other members of the "office" have not been driven to seek out the enemy in hand-to-hand combat by the confusion and concussion of the phoning, they are having a merry time with their maps and overlays. (The overlay, for your information, is a heavy, semi-transparent paper*

that when placed in a certain position on part of the map, will show you strange and interesting things that somebody in a different staff section has found out about the war.) The tent can hold one man waving a map and overlay about, but more then two is hell, more than a man can stand. One of the results of this map-waving activity is to camouflage the stove which is strategically placed in the center of tent where you can't help tripping over it. Of course, the stove is well-tended. Every once in a while, in this closed-in canvas, sealed from the frigid air, an attendant lifts the lid, puts a mixture in, and a great, thick, black and oily column rises and covers the tent down to within three feet of the dirt ground. The attendant is coal-black in the oriental tradition.

A few moments later, it is safe, though unhealthy, to raise yourself from the prone to resume work. Whatever you were doing need not lay as you left it however, because the clerk, profiting from the demoralization and cloaked by the smoke screen, has gone about putting what is laughingly called the "file" in order. That means sweeping off all the odd bits of paper on the desk into a clumsy wooden basket labelled "in" or "out" - no difference. Some days later, when there is no comic magazine or copy of the Stars and Stripes available, he may perform a ritual called "putting the file in order." He takes the basket and a handful of used folders, already used for three or four subjects a temps perdu, including Italian social security taxes, Fascist Gioventù and the PWB vehicle record, and places the papers from the basket into respective files, putting most of them in the thin files and none of them in the fat files. In cases where the logic is inescapable, he makes the choice appropriate, such as incoming personal mail in the correspondence file, etc.

Knowing how hard-pressed for time the clerk has been, very recently an assistant was solicited from a replacement center. The assistant might have done well if he had tried, but since he is little and ugly, he works like Goebbels to establish master propaganda plans. Today, due to the fact that the rest of us, forewarned, had seized all available vehicles and rushed to the Front, the Colonel was cornered by the new man who has made long extracts from the Bible which prove among other things that the Germans can't win. He wanted to shower the enemy with these convincing, powerful words. Out of nowhere, the colonel was inspired to state that it might seem sacrilegious if the Germans then used the leaflets for toilet paper, as they are wont to do with extra ones. Highly impressed by this reason, the fellow retired to a corner of the tent, muttering something about making the paper rougher.. He is a holy terror. I gave him a note to someone down the line and he put it in an air-courier pouch bound God knows for where. One can only say that he has a certain utility in applying band-aids to people who burn themselves on the stove.

Odd people come around too, visiting firemen from the occupation team who want to get the smell of powder in their nostrils or to feel what an army is like. Or someone from Counter-Intelligence may call up to find out whether an Italian we have is a secret agent or is spying on a secret agent or just wants to become one. Our intelligence man can best answer that, but he is secrecy reductus ad absurdum and doesn't know where he is himself.

Then the mail comes in, which doesn't disturb the lack of routine at all. A package is opened and the walnettos spill out. The caramel gets stuck to the desk or some confidential papers and they are forever confidential. When the unlettered ones begin to curse loudly and the din is too much, Herz gets up and delivers a fiery oration on the need for quiet. But by that time, it's late enough for lunch anyway.

We retrace our steps to the matter of the baby. "He," " she" - I think "he" because my own mother, Kate, has borne four sons and no daughter - had been subject of a call from the American Red Cross well before Christmas. For no good reason, I received a garbled message contradicting my Wife's advices. The Secretary of Dr. "Jack" Greenhill (he is the eminent gynecologist who is also Lt. Johnny Hess' step-father) told them that the baby would be a girl and would be born in January. Remarkable on both scores, fifty years early in sex-prognosticating method, weeks late in length of term.

On January 13, I wrote:

...When I got back from the Front, I found a message to call the Red Cross. I did so, and a barely audible voice told me I was the

father of a girl infant. He said both you and the baby were doing well and I could ask no more.. It looks as if I shall spend the future beating off suitors. That ought to be fun. When it comes down to it, I am just as happy with a girl as with a boy. Think how much a girl can accomplish in reference to the rest of her sex compared with a boy... I think we'll make her an all-around girl, swimming, cerebration, and socializing. Herz has already asked for her hand but I've told him, with your presumed approval, that she doesn't want to have anything to do with an old fogey.

She had of course written profusely, but the mails were slow; I wrote on January 24 that a batch of mail had been arriving, dated December 24, 25, 27, 29, January 3 and 4, chock full of details on how to give birth to babies, a difficult birth it had been, many hours long, the head was too large and was squeezed thin and had to be helped through by an incision, but Jack Greenhill did a masterful sculptural restoration afterwards with his strong skilled hands. Worse than anything that I had been suffering: Motherhood! Jack Greenhill tried to hold things off, he jested, to give her the same birthday as her father, but, what with everything else happening, he had all he could do to bring forth the strapping bawler at over nine pounds.

So now all of our correspondence would be carried on over the head of this infant, so to speak, enough about her in it to fill a pediatric textbook, avant-garde because there was so much love in it. We called her Kathryn and Esther, after the paternal and maternal grandmothers.

The worst campaign of the War - West of Russia, though some even doubt that - proceeded regardless. The soldiers could not believe that it would last so long: they kept expecting a breakthrough on some other part of the Front. The vast fleets of Allied tanks and vehicles could hardly be employed in the mountains and the mud. Italian mule companies had to supply the French, Indian, and Polish infantry, trying to conquer the German bastion from the Northeast massif; most of the animals were killed or plunged to their death off the slippery trails.

The terrain and the immobility made it a battle of riflemen, mortar crews, sappers, and machine-gunners. (Riflemen were actually equally automatic-weapons men and grenade-throwers, and learned to employ bazookas to explode bunkers, where these failed against the too-heavy German tanks.) Among the Allied troops, the casualties were practically all in the infantry battalions; and in these battalions, each starting with about 400 rifles, 80% of the casualties were riflemen and lieutenants. Murderous to medics, too. The evil weather and incessant cannonading made life unbearable for those not hurt or diseased. Nor did you rejoice in the hurt and death around you. A Special Forces soldier sitting on the body of an enemy while poking C-ration from can to mouth: no insult intended, it was better than sitting in the mud.

Seven months passed, incredible, November to June, in an Italy that gave to fighting troops the lie about its famous climate, food, pleasures, and comforts. Its people remained human despite continual misery and misfortune: there were women who hung their wash within gun range, making soldiers feel foolish. In the middle of this period, in case anyone should wish to know, Lieutenant de Grazia has come and gone and come again.

The Campaign had its several phases, which I associate with the nationality of the troops principally engaged. The Fifth Army Command was American, under a British-commanded Army Group that controlled both it and the Eighth Army to the East. The troops were the most polyglot of the War: British, American, Canadian, New Zealand, East Indian (Hindu, Sikh, Gurkha, etc.), Polish, French (Continental, *Pieds noirs,* Algerian, Moroccan, Tunisian), Jewish, Brazilian, Italian. The American Headquarters Guard was Spanish-speaking, Puerto-Rican. One may mention more specifically Scottish, Irish, and any number of quasi-national contingents. Disgracefully, past racist policies kept American blacks out of combat whether as segregated units or individuals, though they supported part of the logistical chain from Naples; the French and British, in contrast, did embrace black African combat troops. The supplies, the equipment, the arms, were increasingly and mainly American and brought up by American transport.

Contacts with the Adriatic region were bringing in Yugoslav partisans, and I had by the end of 1942 been converted to support communist Tito's Partisans rather than the royalist "Chetniks" led by Draza Mikhailovich. Why? Because my intelligence sources had brought in one report after another to the effect that Tito's men were doing much more damage to the Nazis and Fascists than did the royalists. Anyhow, I did not like Kings. "D" Section in Naples, my people, have swung over to Tito, and, as if by some concatenation of intelligences, Winston Churchill had decided that Tito was the man to support. So, when a couple of vigorous Yugoslav partisans were introduced to me, I said: "Any friends of Tito are friends of mine."

The first phase in the gruesome winter-long Battle was the series of struggles to reach the Gustav Line, pivoting on the Town of Cassino and on the huge Benedictine Monastery towering above it; American and British would argue about who did most to arrive at this point. The Rapido River Crossing, fought principally by the 36th American Division, of Texas National Guard ancestry, was the larger part of the second phase. The 442nd Japanese-American battalion, later regimental combat team, began to play its distinguished role. The American 34th Division also was launched into the impossible, and lost half its riflemen. Whose defeat was worse, the 36th's or the 34th's? Who failed? Before long, every fact would be known about both episodes. But, where every fact is known, the truth acquires a multiplicity and complexity never to be resolved into an answer. One thing was sure by now: a frontal attack upon Cassino was madness. Still, the Command ordered such again and again.

I regularly visited these units and the 45th and 3rd Divisions and 1st Armored Division, hearing and spreading gossip, examining their situation maps, which were better locally than those at Army HQ G-2. The next propaganda operations were planned. I asked them to shoot certain leaflets over selected targets, explained why, gave them copies and English translations of the material to be exploded over the Germans, and shared whatever information I may have had about the results of past firings.

They liked to hear my opinions about how the war was going generally and when it would end: I was a live source. They got their news regularly and ordinarily from the *Stars and Stripes*. They got letters and clippings from home. But Americans do not write much. They heard an occasional short-wave broadcast. Men came back from leave in Naples and told what they had heard from other soldiers there.

I supervised the conversion of smoke shells at the little ammo dump which my Team maintained, and told the artillery ammo trucks where and when to pick up and deliver the shells. In each shell were about three hundred leaflets carrying general and specific messages; as the shell which was set to explode at a certain height over enemy pathways or positions went off, the leaflets spread out in a pattern and drifted down to where they might be reached and read by the soldiers. It took about 15,000 leaflets to cover a division's front, about 50 shells. A single burst, about 100 yards up, on a windless hour, would usually bring the message near anyone below within a diameter of 150 yards. The Germans were told by their officers that they should turn in enemy propaganda without reading it, but they read and often kept it, even if, to the minds of Allied troops and the Propaganda Team for that matter, they seemed hardly responsive. They would have been showered with the paper at dusk, so that they could observe the fall and pick up the leaflets after dark, safe from both enemy and friendly fire.

Then, along the way, I sometimes visited infantry units and got their ideas of what might bother or affect in advantageous ways the conduct of the enemy, and I talked with prisoners or prisoner interrogators for their information about specific weaknesses and details that would lend authenticity to the propaganda when received by the enemy. This information went to the Team, the intelligence and ideas to Martin Herz and Hans Habe. Unfortunately, Habe caught jaundice and then contracted pneumonia and ended up in a hospital to the rear. When his Christmas gifts arrived from home, his friends saved the finer little pieces for him and devoured the rest, as he had bequeathed it to them, though they felt sad and a bit ghoulish doing so. Herz, too, contracted jaundice, which seemed to be endemic, but stayed on.

Like any profit-seeking businessman, I must explain to Tom Crowell, civilian printing manager, what was happening to his product in the course of processing and delivery. We discussed the crushing power of acceleration on the rolls of paper and tred to locate stronger paper that would stand the initial explosion, would not catch fire, would not be shredded when bursting out of the shellcase in the secondary explosion over the target. Tom had his operation camouflaged under canvas and it had to be seen to be believed. He had discovered in Africa a German tank-carrying truck, given up in the general surrender in Tunis, perhaps the largest non-trailer truck ever to have been manufactured. He had collected in it a Webendorfer offset press, a Miehle letter-press, a composing machine with linotype, a full hand-setting array of fonts, a ton of paper, and a paper-cutter of large dimensions. He painted the name, the "Gutenberg Special," upon it in large letters. He and his three soldier assistants lived in the truck.

The Team quickly developed an operating system that was professional, that is, that had routines, rules, standards, criteria for evaluation of results, testing and research. It was quite different from the organization, methods, equipment, and division of labor foreseen by the designers of the First Radio Mobile Radio Broadcasting Company a year earlier at OSS in Washington and Camp Ritchie. Proof of this came in a manual of combat operations for an army team, called *Functions of the Fifth Army Combat Propaganda Team,* the first ever achieved and the model for all to come. My hand was heavy in its writing and editing. Tom printed the book up nicely and bound it with glue. It was sent to Army units around the world. As part of its preparation, I worked on the perfection of firing tables for the typical American weapon, the 105 mm howitzer, for the weight of the removed smoke-canisters was different from the weight of the leaflets and the settings on the shell had to be adjusted accordingly; further, the wind operated on paper differently than upon smoke.

I also thought of producing effects upon the morale of more distant troops by the use of larger cannons. The 155 mm howitzer was used for longer range and larger bursts, as well as for short ranges where profitable. An artillery officer told me of seeing a dead German half blown away by a 155 mm shell but with a hand still clutching a leaflet captioned, fittingly: "Now things will really be in earnest." I borrowed from the artillery a 155mm gun, together with

The Battle of Cassino

its crew. I had its smoke shells converted to contain leaflets, five times as many as the 105 mm shell held. Then the piece was dragged to the foot of a long gully, and set up. I climbed up the gully to approximately where the shells would burst, and took cover. Then a prearranged cannonade with various settings brought about bursts and leaflet showers around different points that could be mapped. Thus I could prepare a kind of firing table to substitute for the normal tables of cannon of this calibre. I assured, too, the readability of the available paper stocks upon explosion. After a third round was fired, an American vehicle came bouncing down the trail; they thought that they were coming under enemy fire.

The amphibious landings at Anzio were really a third phase of the Cassino Campaign, tied in clumsily with the 36th Division Attack of the second phase. Early in the month, Herz and I are told of "Operation Shingle." A strong force was to be landed at Anzio, to cut the German lines running south to Cassino and perhaps trap the divisions now at the Front. Buck Weaver and the others figured that, if they were able to unsettle the minds of the German soldiers at Cassino a bit, they might give way more readily in the face of the coordinated attack along the Cassino Front. They might even be bottled up.

Secretly and carefully the leaflet was drawn up and printed. It mapped the landings, told the readers that they were in danger of being trapped, and recommended the usual ways out, all colored in the terms and mood of heroic pessimism: slacking off resistance, retreating, letting oneself be taken prisoner at the first opportunity.

On 22 January, Allied troops landed on the beaches of Nettuno and Anzio against insignificant resistance; even the minefields were a negligible problem. On the Cassino Front, I had made my arrangements with Captain Peterson of the 34th Division artillery, which covered the central Front. Two days before the landings, a typical fire plan was mapped. The projectiles were set for air bursts every hundred yards from the first positions on back for 800 yards. Then, on 22 January at 15:50 the leaflet was systematically exploded upon the startled German soldiers: they learned of Operation "Shingle" before their commanders did. Total surprise, the dreamed-for element of all battle, was achieved, on both Fronts.

But General Lucas, in command at Anzio, exhibited no hurry to dash for the arteries of communications and their protecting hills. For that matter, he hardly attended to the chance to sweep right into Rome, which was weakly defended and had a population eagerly expectant. As soon as they encountered significant resistance, his troops were ordered to dig in, to await reinforcement, despite their vast superiority in organization, numbers, artillery, and air power. Despite, too, the fact that they had a powerful navy off shore, which could defend them if they were forced back, employing the same kind of deadly fire that broke up the Axis counterattacks against the Gela beachhead in Sicily.

I was disturbed to hear that the operation had been checked by counterattack. I hurried to the Map Room of G-2 of Fifth Army. I was astonished by what I saw there. The invading forces had identified at least two-score enemy elements. True. But they were scraps of this and that. The Germans were halting every *landser* going or coming on leave or from hospital, any vehicle, gun, unit - no matter of what division or special designation or competence - and throwing them together into a makeshift "Army," and pushing them forward against the Americans and British. The Allies waited; better German units arrived; the Germans counterattacked incessantly, as they were doctrinally commanded; and the new Anzio Front froze.

The Germans were so proud of their performance that they prepared their own leaflet, something rare on the Cassino Front. They reproduced part of the Allied leaflet, then placed a tiny dot alongside the beach on a map of Italy, far from Cassino, and crowed: "Here is their bottling up *(Kesselschaft)*!" I wrote to my wife that the Beachhead "is like a bird-cage into which the enemy can poke his finger anywhere. But already he's been bit, and bit badly."

Third Division, P.O. Box Anzio, asked for somebody to talk sense into the enemy. Martin Herz volunteered. I was willing to go but it didn't take much persuasion for me to concede my part of the job to a new comrade, Infantry Lieutenant Joe Ferla, who had a gentle smile and a willing heart, and felt that this was his dish of tea. They went by boat, bearing with them the loudspeaking equipment needed to talk across the lines. With local help, Herz and Ferla set up. The amplifier was sneaked forward - to within sniper's range of the enemy. They left it there and followed back the wire they had laid. Then they started to talk into a microphone. What they said was deemed obnoxious, apparently. Or perhaps it was too seductive. An 88mm artillery shell explodes nearby. Martin Herz is blown about and scratched up. Joe Ferla is struck by shrapnel in the guts and hip. He holds his guts in and tries to roll under his jeep and is hit again, this time by a 50 cal machine gun bullet. Martin calls for help and they are evacuated. With some surprise on all sides, especially his own, Joe survives and begins the long journey back through the chain of hospitals that ultimately ends with the Big PX. And here I wonder whether I ought to have gone and done the job right, which, translated, means, whether they would have had better luck had I gone myself.

Joe met nursing friends in his second hospital. They had been guests of the Team below Cassino. The Team was now on a field, well-drained, with a large cave alongside, complete with giant wine barrels without wine. They turned this into an officers' mess and club for all personnel. Otherwise they camped on stones or in the mud. "Club Rainmaker" inspired a party or two. Of this one I am writing ruefully, swearing that I hardly ever have behaved so.

> *Tomorrow is Leap Year Day and I regret deeply that you won't be around to offer me some sort of amorous inducement. Herz is in an even worse position since one of his few golden opportunities to snatch a bride is wasted on the tent and myself. I thought I denoted a note of rancor in his leaflet today. For most of today, I felt I had been clubbed. The assailant was the demon rum, the dissolving agent at a drinking party last night. The party was a classic of stag drunks, a group of men all with hidden talents that came out as the cognac went in. There was singing (shouting), violence to property and person, and some remarkably good specimens of solo dancing. Everyone at one time or another was ushered onto the dance floor by his guiding spirit and committed to the dance. Tom Crowell and Jim Clark were best, Tom with a complete repertoire of old burlesque songs and soft shoe steps, Jim with a gay, graceful Sprite of Spring affair. The publisher of the New York Post, whose name has slipped me at the moment made a*

>*most beautiful partner for Tom in a couple of steps straight from old vaudeville. I can't possibly describe how funny they were, typical old New York specimens. My modest contribution was bit parts in a couple of spontaneous and united buck and wings. I did somewhat better on the ballads, and was pretty good in the knife-throwing contest, though when I broke the bone handle of my knife, the latter degenerated into chair-throwing. Finally Tom, who had been sweet and jolly all evening, knocked Hindley down, which sobered up Hindley who was then able to drive our car. We got lost, infuriated a guard and finally got to bed. This morning I didn't feel so good.*

Back in December, I established a daily routine. Each day I crawled out of my bedding roll, usually first one up in the tent of four officers, brew coffee in a heavy tin can on the pot-bellied stove while shaving, and began my rounds of the Front. I could not tell at the beginning of a day how far I could get and whom I would see. I could be sure of seeing the barren hills, the exploding shells, both friendly and hostile, the dug-in companies, the destroyed farmhouses and bombed villages, the peaks of the Apennines turning white in the first snows of winter, and roads that were sometimes asphalted and pitted with shell-holes, at other times dirt roads and often only paths. I drove a Willys jeep that had lost its exhaust pipe against a stone and could cause nearby soldiers to dive into ditches when it backfired; I got it fixed at a motor pool down the line, so I could drive in peace with just the ordinary noises of warfare, the continuous booming of cannon from one point or another of the compass, the artillery shells that shrieked, the crazy jackass brays of the six-mouthed *Nebelwerfer* mortars. I almost never heard the small arms fire, being a safe distance away (I hoped), if only because they signaled an attack or counter-attack and were accompanied by deafening cannonading and occasionally by aircraft diving and bombing in support, always of the Allies, never of the Luftwaffe.

I was continually uneasy about land mines (over a half-million actually were dug up around Cassino alone); I hated the thought of getting my legs or balls blown off. The refrain of the song: *no balls at all, no balls at all, she married a man, who had no balls at all.* Mines seemed to be everywhere at first, but as the front stabilized they were discovered and deactivated, and besides I tried to keep to familiar paths known now to be free.

Captain Foster had a similar job with British Corps on the left flank to the Sea. They had their tea-times on occasion. *"You know what I'm doing now? Sweating out a pot of tea with Foster. Foster is jumping up and down besides the stove watching the water begin to boil. It's very important, the process, to the British. They make a gay, childish fetish of it, towards which I feel very sympathetic."*

When my wife asked about my health, I replied that I was *"very healthy, hardly ever miss a full meal, and even, strange as it may seem, visit my favorite toilet regularly. That last is a laugh. One of my victory aims is to get established on a familiar toilet seat once more. Vulgar, isn't it? But not, if you've visited the great number of inquisitorial devices I have. It does make one versatile and agile, anyway. The present one is a wood crate, worked over by some reluctant EM who apparently had 1) either a grudge against the power-wielding class, 2) or a very tiny bottom. In Foster's words, it's like trying to pass a camel through the eye of a needle. And in the cold dawn, a half inch of frost doesn't help."*

One time Foster came in quite late because he had been held up at a bridge under fire, which the German guns could not hit in just the proper way to collapse it, and finally they quit; but he was mostly impressed by a dead civilian without a hat, "without a hat," he said repeatedly, and one couldn't fathom why this detail should so obsess him. But then I recalled the old Lancastrian song I had been taught, which in dialect goes something like this: *Nympt te moor pah thet, o nympt te moor pah thet, o mympt te moor pah thet,* sung as medieval church dirge. *Else ye shall catch thy death o could:.......* repeat and refrain *then we shall av to bury thee ....then'll cum th'wurms and et thee oop.... then will th dooks cum et th wurms....then we shall kill and et te dooks...so we shall av to et thee oop* and of course it ends as it begins, "don't go out on the moor without your hat."

Foster had worked with the first leaflet-cannon in North Africa, a 25-pounder that he drove around with its crew, firing upon targets of opportunity. Now the peddler's little business had expanded. It was big business in which they were engaged in, a business that prospered when times were bad but capital was available, climaxing on the Cassino Front between January and May of 1944. The analogy of combat propaganda with a business enterprise could be carried far: research and development, industrial design, licensing to sell, sales territories, raw material purchases, processing and production, warehousing and distribution, advertising, customer relations, volume of sales: all of these had highly analogous operations in combat propaganda. The work was subsidized, hence not conforming to the private capital model; but if a percentage of incoming surrenders and breakdowns in morale were toted up as sales and paid for on delivery, the operation, if cleverly and efficiently conducted, would be quite profitable on the whole.

There was a psychological and ideological difference, very important, such that no one, I, Habe, even Weaver, would ever have tolerated the business analogy: our operation was intimate with the State, with the sacred symbols of government, with all that makes war so interminable and inevitable, the "participation" of gods, sacrifice, honors, martyrdom; war is a sacred activity to the Great Body of Society, never mind the poor devils unwillingly at high risk.

The Team moved out of Caserta to consolidate the operation and to catch up with the Front, leaving Buck Weaver behind for Army liaison, still our Commander. We located in the ruins of a farmhouse, camouflaged, and out of range of all except heavy artillery and aircraft, from which there was apparently no threat. That's where "Club Rainmaker" was.

Visiting firemen were ever more common, from units across Italy, from Army HQ, from Naples, from North Africa, even from London and the States, for the slaughter, misery, and legends of Cassino were becoming famous by word of mouth, soldiers' letters, newspapers, and film. It was the only European ground show where the Westerners were admitted. To hear the artillery serenade, to see bombs bursting in air, occasional dogfights in the sky, and the famous bleary-eyed bearded characters of Bill Mauldin's cartoons: that was the ticket. I sometimes carried a visitor along, warning him not to appear curious about what he was seeing and not to attempt joviality, prayers, or righteous wrath, nor optimistic forecasts about the end of the war or the waning power of the Germans.

Lt. Commander Livingston Hartley was irrepressible. He was so different, in his braided peaked naval cap and naval insignia, that soldiers were bemused. After all, his business was boats, which they vaguely realized were separate and distinct ways of winning a war. Liv came in one time telling of watching across the lines to a farmhouse under fire and of "a funny little German running in and out crazily." It appeared that every visitor formed his own peculiar indelible memory.

Not long afterwards he was riding with me, who was going up a road taken often before without being fired upon; but suddenly large calibre shells whistle overhead and begin to crash nearby. Hartley leaps out and runs for the ditch and rubble, I behind him for I have to stop the jeep before jumping, so I am struck by the absurd sight of this lanky naval officer in the flapping huge long greatcoat and the visored cap skipping along the side of the road. I blamed Hartley for the incident. The same German observer, who had watched me on various occasions and thought me too insignificant a target to waste some precious shells on, spotted the braid and thought, now we'll catch ourselves a General!

I did a little visiting on my own, to Naples where I bedded down with "D Section" at the splendid Palazzo Caracciolo. I joined in the general elation at the news from Algiers that Col. Hazeltine, our detested Chief of Psychological Warfare Operations, had been summarily relieved of his command on December 24; C.D. Jackson was temporarily running the show until a military Commander was designated. There were now new English arrivals to meet, John Reynor, a media executive; John Vernon, a more typical aesthete and scholar; and Edmund Howard, rather like his brother, Hubert, except that he had a more distinctive and wry sense of humor and was more of this world. (A third brother, Lord Howard, was G-2 with Eighth Army HQ.) There was talk of my coming back to join them; I, more militaristic of mind, was hoping for a breakthrough by some means. Whereupon I might do another Bari caper and be one of the first to arrive in Rome. Just imagine its plethora of media-control challenges! And other joys!

I fixed up a ground hut for myself alone out of a mosquito net and the canvas of two pup tents, sleeping on a canvas cot, shaded by bulrushes. I was practically sewn into my long woolen underwear, and slept rather like a pickle in a herring roll-mop, four blankets and a quilt inside a canvas roll. It was from here that I now left upon my daily milk run. The weather was bad, the troops in a poor mood. The Army was stuck; one could add brightly: "But the Russians are doing great." This Front was beginning to look permanent. New things were being added. More and more ammunition and artillery and airplanes arrived so that the enemy was subjected to practically continuous bombardment and dared not move about in the light. As if I didn't know, a leaflet told me: "We are firing twenty shells to your one and, if we need to fire another five, we can do that too!"

The Army Quartermaster had moved up an ingenious system, a mobile bath and clothing exchange. Soldiers proceeding along the main road, Highway 6, South of the front lines, were directed by a sign to where they could strip off their clothing, hand it in, take a hot bath, receive a set of fresh clothing, get back in their vehicle and go on their way. I was favorably impressed by it. Americans were dirtier at the Front than the English: I recalled Heycock in Sicily bathing daily out of his helmet, using a large sponge that he treasured; Heycock always walked after a meal, too, as if he didn't walk the rest of the day. I came upon several Germans, just surrendered, one morning; they had emerged from days of a filthy inferno; one blonde sad lad was picking dirt from another like him, and combing his hair with the carefulness that monkeys use on one another. Maybe Americans learned as children to punish their mothers by dirtying themselves. And now they were punishing the Army in a way that was hard to prevent.

There was a lot of dirtiness among the troops, despite directives to the contrary; trench foot was common; no one wanted to take off his boots and socks in the cold and muck and what the hell, so a guy spends a few days in the hospital... he needs the rest anyhow! Let them cut off a toe, for that matter; it's better than going back to the foxholes. Foot disease was the Cassino campaign's equivalent of the malaria of the Sicilian campaign.

I have a small problem, impetigo, dirty, no, an itinerant barber, wandering among the soldiers cutting hair, scraped my cheek with an infected razor. It itched and spread. I applied salves, stopped shaving, began to look like Bill Mauldin's famous cartoon infantryman, G.I. Joe. The nuisance clung and spread. I chaperoned a truckload of men down to see what Pompeii was like; it happened that at this very moment Mount Vesuvius was erupting. We watched it as we drive along, shooting a column of tephra flaming into the sky, exploding white steam clouds, carrying a delicate white collar of snow, red beads of lava trickling over it and down its flanks. The men were impressed by the Roman pornography; I had seen it before the War.

My face still blotched and itched, and now my neck. I stopped by an evacuation hospital and there met Dr. Stillerman whom I knew at the University of Chicago, who said Kupperman is here, too, so there were now these two acquaintances who said why don't you stay for a couple of days and clear it up. I sent Pvt. Long back to bivouac and climbed into a bed under canvas. I was awakened near dusk by a monotonous loud drawling voice saying: "There's a real soldier. He sure looks like he's been through hell. It's awful to have to live that way," and poking a long nose this way and that from the gloom of his corner of the tent, like a groundhog sensing the air, seeing who was listening, nobody, judging from the motionless lumps in the beds, with their own world somewhere else, except for me, who was embarrassed; I hated pretense and was proud of shaving regularly; I did not approve of G.I. Joe's couture; I stirred visibly to signal the long-nose to shut up. "I reckon he's waking up now," the man said, raising himself on his elbow, his horse-face sympathetically pointed my way. "How do you feel, Lieutenant, not so good, huh?"

"I'm O.K."

"That's good. It'll be time to eat soon." He espied an orderly outside: "Hey, orderly, what about some lights in this tent?" Then: "That orderly is a real funny character. He's got a good deal going for him. You know, he goes into Napoli every week. He picks up medical supplies and he spends the night there every time, he has a regular girl. I told him, 'Hey, boy, you better watch out who's laying your girl the rest of the week, a big buck nigger, I bet.' And he says to me, 'No, sir. I have her scared with my medical supplies. She thinks I can tell when she's had a man.'... This orderly took a blood test from her when he first met her and had the lab give him a report with her name on it, so she thinks he can check her up any old time. Ain't that a bitch?" There are several amused sounds. "I tell you, it's something! He said it to me, too. You know that creek down the hill right over there? Well, here were these soldiers coming into the hospital with V.D., they get treated, but when it's time to leave they still have it. It beats the hell out of the medics how come. You know what? These guys, when they were let out to walk around, they headed down to the creek where these Italian women are washing clothes. A couple of these have the clap, and give it right back to them." He laughs, but gets serious. "You know, whenever I get next to one of these Italian girls, I tell her, now don't you go around with any niggers, you understand, you hear me? They say, yeah, sure, O.K... but they're just pigs, they do it anyway, .. they say, 'Capitano, you crazy,' pointing their finger at their head."

Nurses apply ointments, sulpha, but I had already done this. I played volley ball with the medics; they were good at it. I watched the two doctors operating on brain wounds. "Kupperman," I said, "I saw a letter from you in *Private Maroon,* the alumni magazine." He raised his eyebrows questioningly above his white mask; he didn't remember writing. "Well, it wasn't much except a thank you note." He remembered.

Back in the ward there was a flurry and the orderlies brought in a lieutenant who was laughing loudly and put him to bed, saying, stay there now until the doctor sees you. He had been sitting with several men that night in a half-destroyed villa, he told the other beds, listening to the sound of an airplane overhead. (I know the place, the very house, on the lee of Mt. Trocchio.) Then there was a whistle, an explosion, and all his natural functions stopped dead; when the smoke cleared, there rested in the middle of the room a large armed bomb breathing heavily. He dove out a window and began running wildly he didn't care where, mines or no mines, until they caught up with him and brought him to the hospital. He giggled and chortled as he talked.

I was disgusted with my own case and moved to a backup hospital farther south where I was given anti-biotic injections and the volcano was beautiful by day and night. I healed quickly and amazingly. I shaved and revealed the miraculous radiance of a Saint. So I departed for the Front, finding it just as I had left it. Worse. Civilians had been finally evacuated for good, under military escort. Maybe the combatants just couldn't feel like proper warriors with the women hanging out their wash and the men plowing.

The holidays had passed, the Anzio trap had failed, the cold was unending. The world-famous Benedictine Monastery of Montecassino stood nobly on Montecassino above the town of Cassino. Most of the priests had withdrawn. Italian civilians were known to have taken refuge inside. The Germans claimed from Berlin and Rome that they were respecting the neutrality of the Monastery and safeguarding its treasures.

As I bumped along on my milk run, I heard different stories. I heard reports of helmeted figures appearing in windows, of firing from the gardens, of binoculars flashing. I knew practically nothing about the dramatic events inside - the rescue of the art treasures, the occasional death and wounding of civilians, the negotiations between the Germans and the priests, the increasing number of civilians from the village and country around who had begged and forced their way into the Monastery. I looked often, but saw nothing untoward through my own glasses. I said so to my comrades time after time, because the whole Army was becoming agitated over the question: were the Germans using the Monastery for gun emplacements, a reserve encampment, and artillery observation, or were they not?

The troops' mood was ugly. You scarcely dared say that the Monastery was not full of Germans taking their ease. One day I was at a natural rock fissure and path by the Rapido River to note the day's catch of possibly interesting cases, and several German prisoners were being led through by two Moroccans with fixed bayonets. A short Texan of the 36th Division appeared, a lieutenant, and said: "We should kill these bastards!" (actually I was wondering at their good fortune in not having being killed by the goumes already). "They have been firing down on us all day, the sons of bitches!" he says. I hesitated; I couldn't be sure how determined the officer was; he looked mad: so I said, diffidently: "Well that's why they're there, you know, that's their job, too," and the other lieutenant glares and snarls but let's them pass. There would probably be trouble with the goumes anyway; they were expecting a bounty for bringing in live prisoners.

But that was the mood along the Front. Pretty soon there'd be no prisoners taken, and then we'd have the German expending his last cartridge before giving up and it's the last rounds that kill the most, and Allied prisoners will disappear, too, on the way to the Rear. So thought I, and it was one of my biggest discoveries. Like a traveling salesman who after many wearisome trips "on a shoeshine and a smile" happily formulates the most compelling of sales pitches. I put aside most talk about obtaining deserters by propaganda, which was the first idea occurring to everybody, and said in a pessimistic, low-keyed manner that the idea behind the leaflets was to weaken resolve in specific ways. The effect of the propaganda was measurable by the number of rounds of ammunition left unexpended when a position was abandoned; by the minutes, even seconds, earlier at which an enemy withdraws or surrenders; by the minutes earlier of the hour when the truck driver pulls over to sleep, by how much rest he imagines that he needs; by how exhausted he feels; by whether he believes he has already done more than his share; by the number of times the thought runs through the enemy's head that, while we may not lose, still my family will be needing me when all this is over.

The War did not look so hopeless to the German soldier. (Their Generals would go on fighting forever, of course. It was a goofy error of Allied strategists and propagandists not to threaten the German Generals directly, saying: "You know damned well that this War is lost to you. Your men and women do not. If you do not bring it to an end you will be considered criminally negligent on their account!" The ordinary German, up to a high rank, is a docile infant in the face of authority, and will believe and follow it.)

But see all the reasons for a soldier to keep up his overall faith in victory, especially given his masters' assurances. So far as the German soldier is concerned, the Western Allies had been destroyed at the Dieppe landing, in Norway, and very nearly in Africa and Italy. The richest, most productive part of Italy is in their hands. They are so deep into the Soviet Union that any reverses there can be deemed temporary and not so significant. (Stalingrad is hard to deny, however. Tunis was the Italians' fault.) Germany holds the Baltic States; Sweden and Switzerland are cooperative. All of Eastern Europe is held, Greece, too. Millions of workers from everywhere are "voluntarily" producing goods for the war. Every Eastern German Division has about 2000 volunteer semi-soldiers doing everything but shooting at their own Soviet soldiers; but there are a million Russians and East Europeans who are actually fighting the Russians, too. There are French, Belgian, Dutch, Spanish and Italian troops fighting on their side. Spain is supportive. Italian Fascism is reviving, following Mussolini's rescue. The Germans are looting the European Continent and hunger is unknown to their people. There are great plans for rebuilding Germany from the wealth of the whole world. The Japanese, finally, are winning one victory after another in the Pacific Theater, and will soon turn upon the Soviet Empire. Add to all of this, a confidence in one's top leadership much greater than that enjoyed by Allied leaders, and a belief in the Nazi ideology, which, whatever its perplexing points, promises them and their loved ones a thousand years of comfortable hegemony over the whole World.

No, the Fifth Army Combat Propaganda Team, correct in believing in Allied victory, realistic by contrast with most other experts, was nonetheless optimistic in order to keep up its own morale, and was continually frustrated in finding the key to the ordinary German soldier's mind - except at the cat's hole at the level of the floor: these men refused surrender out of immediate affection and loyalty to their platoon; they refused because they feared for their lives in giving up. True, but not the whole truth at all.

Americans and British gave themselves up as prisoners in less desperate circumstances than the Germans. They were more confident of victory than the Germans. The penalties were less for surrenderers. Moreover, the American believed that much rested upon his individual fate; at the same time, he had a larger belief in his own value as a person. Furthermore, a matter both important and little understood - for it seemed so odd - was the fact that experience in combat improves one's judgement about when surrender is a necessary condition to survival. The experienced German soldier realized better than the inexperienced American when his situation had become hopeless, and, since the normal inclination when endangered is to be pessimistic, the American soldier would surrender under conditions when the German soldier would not, even when, objectively viewed, the German was receiving much more murderous shelling, air attack, and small arms fire.

Amidst the continual blasting of the cannon, in this desolate landscape, party to the falling dead and anguished wounded, there was a considerable dialogue going on between the German common soldier and the little propaganda group inside the cave, representing the Allied troops. Troops knew this and, although the fearfully rigid soldier would almost invariably react spitefully to saying any word to the enemy, he soon wanted to carry on discussions and became eager to hear what his representatives were telling the other side, and why weren't we telling them that they had better surrender right away or else we'd massacre them, something they, of all people, did not really believed could be done. They were in despair. They wanted to give voice. The propagandists gave voice. There were developed several potent and tested messages, based upon careful analysis of expertly conducted interviews of the enemy. I came to memorizing them.

You could call them the Product Line. There was the "One Minute that may save your life." It was generally useful, to remind the enemy of the possibility of his giving up and of how to do it. There was the official, formal-looking and dead-serious surrender pass, the *laissez-passer,* the *Passierschein*. "No soldier should be without one," was the motto. They were copiously distributed. More and more enemy kept a copy tucked inside a boot, under a canteen, or in a pocket; it was a misdemeanor to possess one. It was designed to lend courage in the event of surrender, when a man is completely at the mercy of his captors. The weekly *Frontpost* was welcome among the Germans for its timeliness, calm, and reliability.

A translation of this was afforded the Allied troops as well; translations of all messages to the enemy were given to the artillerymen doing the firing. *Frontpost* was a world round-up that was every bit as honest, though self-serving, and competently chosen and presented as, say, the typical American network television news half a century later.

Besides these general products were the special items. When the 5th Austrian Mountain Division or the Herman Goering Division entered the Front, each was given a message of greetings, which played upon terrors past, present, and future, adding, as always, you are welcome to come over any time. All Austrian units received copies of the declaration of the Chiefs of State promising to restore the independence of their country. Again, a particularly fruitful set of interrogations resulted in a firing to a battalion, entitled: *"Wo bleibt Hauptmann Eberle?"* Eberle, the unit commander, had been hanging around the rear, and the leaflet reported a number of troubles in the battalion, but "Where is Captain Eberle?" He would have been kidded by his fellow officers afterwards. It helped to humanize the Allies as enemy and impress the Germans at how much was known about their behavior. The "Shingle" leaflet that I described above was another kind of special operation. Working at top speed, which I, liking races of all kinds, arranged and clocked in the case of Hauptmann Eberle, the Team could gather intelligence, draft a text, print it, pack it into shells, deliver it to a battery and fire it quickly. The several shells burst in small puffs of sooty smoke, letting their silvery cloud of leaflets float down upon Captain Eberle's men within ten hours.

The half-dozen officers discussed and argued and reached agreement on the principles of propaganda to be employed against the German troops over the long winter of Cassino. What had best be said to the enemy! Their principles, tested from day to day, came to form the doctrines that were authoritatively handed down to the several armies in the great campaigns of France later in the year. For better or worse. As we shall see.

One day near the middle of February, the combat propaganda officers were called together by Lt. Col. Weaver who explained that Fifth Army HQ had finally determined to bomb the Monastery, to wipe it off the face of the map, with a great air and artillery bombardment. Afterwards, the infantry would attack and capture Monastery Hill. The officers were impressed. Who would not have wanted to see this bottleneck at Cassino blown open.

They did have doubts. I, for one, disbelieved the intelligence that was supposed to lay behind this decision. So far as the bombing was concerned, I did not know enough about the limitations of air bombardment to dispute whether a bombing, if heavy enough, must really wipe out the usefulness of the Abbey to the enemy. Yet the prospect occured that troops can fight from behind rubble as well as or better than they can out of windows. I had not seen any action from the windows, for that matter, nor was there any consensus of the divisional intelligence officers on this account. I had argued, both on aesthetic grounds and on military grounds, but mildly and circumspectly, with artillery officers who wanted to open fire on the Abbey. Nor had Herz brought back from the interrogation of German prisoners any evidence that other German troops were fighting from or were even present, resting or observing, in the Abbey; yet Herz was known to get amazing confessions from his prisoners; furthermore, I talked to the military interrogators regularly; no word from them, either.

My advice was not being asked at this point. I was expected to help prepare a leaflet to be fired into the Abbey, telling the Italian civilians hiding there to get out lest they be gravely endangered by an impending action. No help was to be promised them in fleeing; no instructions were to be given; the Germans were not to be accused outright of occupying the premises; no indication of the nature of the threatened action was to be given. The leaflet was drafted in English. A deliberately vague wording was managed: the Germans had known how to use the Monastery.

Italian Friends
WATCH OUT!
We have until now been especially careful to avoid shelling the Monte Cassino monastery. The Germans have known

> *how to benefit from this. But now the fighting has swept closer and closer to its sacred precincts. The time has come when we must train our guns on the monastery itself.*
>
> *We give you warning so that you may save yourselves. We warn you urgently: Leave the monastery. Leave it at once. Respect this warning. It is for your benefit.*
>
> THE FIFTH ARMY

Neither the Army Group Commander, General Alexander, nor the Fifth Army Commander, General Clark, dared sign the message. The Chief of Staff, General Gruenther, approved the text. Italians at Army HQ worked on its translation. Tom Crowell printed it. I supervised its packing into shells, and consulted with Division G-3 about which battery was to fire the twenty-five rounds. I pulled the loaded trailer to the firing site, where the shells were unloaded.

It was 13:00 hours of the day before the bombing. I had gone as far forward as necessary - it was probably well beyond a rifle shot; there were eminences from which to observe the Monastery grounds and windows, all of them - and I waited. Below and behind me, to my right, I could view an American infantry company in reserve. A number of men came out of their holes to get at the hot food that a crew had brought up to serve. Enemy artillery shells came flying at them and they dove hastily back into their holes, their lunch interrupted. Not far from them and slightly above were elements of another company; these men witnessed the scene and laughed, pointing.

I turned to the Abbey. Massive, impressive, calm, silent, many windows broken, here and there a piece chipped off its facade by an artillery shell fired "accidentally-on-purpose," claiming that the round had fallen short, or been defective, or that a wrong setting was used. At the designated time, the artillery pieces fired their thousands of leaflets upon the lower face of the Abbey. I observed that most fell short of the windows or drifted beyond reach. Then I saw leaflets fluttering down, several unmistakably wafting into the windows of the bottom story. The message must not only get inside but it must go to where the people were sheltering. Other leaflets were observed to fall upon the grounds to the west side of the great building. I descended to the rocks next to which I had parked my jeep, and drove back to camp. The leaflets got in, I reported, we could call HQ and tell them.

At the outposts of the Allied side of the Abbey, a kilometer from the gates, sentinels had been warned to watch out for escaping civilians, perhaps a great many of them. In fact, none appeared. Night fell. Still no refugees. Dawn. The period of warning had passed. Once more I climbed a height facing the abbey, not so close this time, Mt. Trocchio. I - there were others there as well - waited for the planes to come. They did. Almost precisely at 09:30. From over the Apennines came the bombers, wave upon wave, suffering no flak, no enemy fighters. Passing over the Monastery each Flying Fortress released its three tons of high explosives. This went on for some time, to dump their thousand tons. Some fell far off target (to where, I would learn, Indian and New Zealand troops were struck as they waited to attack. American vehicles were hit three miles away. About 17 miles away, at Presenzano, 16 bombs exploded around the advanced camp of General Mark Clark, working at his desk.)

I went down the hill now and worked my way East to where any survivors might show up. There emerged a few Italian civilians, women, children, older men. "Is this all of you?" I asked. "They are all dead," they said, "all dead." "Didn't you get our warning," I asked a woman who appeared to be fairly composed. "Yes, and we tried to get out..."

But it may be best here to extract from my report of March 5 to "D Section," Naples, through regular Fifth Army channels, the section that deals with the bombardment. The document, as can be seen, is carefully drawn; for I am treading on dangerous ground; the Abbey Affair is being suppressed. It will continue to be censored for a long time. On March 9, in answer to an inquiry from the British Foreign Office, General Wilson, the Mediterranean

Commander, submits evidence and claims that the Abbey has been part of the Germans' main line of defense. By then, every concerned officer on the ground at Cassino and Naples knew that the Germans had respected the Abbey to the best of their ability, and in fact, that they benefitted from letting it stand unoccupied, for there was little to be gained by firing from exposed windows.

REPORT ON THE ABBEY AFFAIR:

Dates: Weeks previous to February 15, the Abbey was under observation. Our men stopped several hundred yards from it under machine-gun fire, about a week previous. There were widespread reports of German use and occupation. These reports so lacked confirmation that on February 13, the Command was still not sure and draft of leaflet was so worded.

*Types of [*here scratched out in original: *rumors] reports: Flashing of glasses seen; Mg fire reported received; Germans seen running about.* [Here, in the original, I have scratched out, probably as provocative, the words, *Mere dogmatic supposition:*] *SP gunfire reported. Received Italian reports that it was fortified by the Germans. The Germans were at least using the shelter of its walls. At least 16 shell holes existed in the Abbey previous to all-out assault. Civilians in Abbey variously estimated at 1,000 - 3,000. January* [Note: February] *13, in the evening, Mr. Clark got call from II Corps to draft leaflet. It was approved same evening by the C.S. (Chief of Staff), translated into Italian and fired next day at 13:00. Morning of February 15, all-out assault began.*

Inside story of Abbey: First man to cross the lines appeared about 0200 hours on February 16, a group of about 8 at 12:00 at the CIC, two miles from Cassino. He was about thirty, wounded in the head and somewhat bruised. He said among other things: The Germans closed the gates after the leaflet was received, just as they had been doing all along. This was due, I think, as much to stupidity on the part of the German guard as to any other command. He said the leaflet was "Scheiss." Even on the day after the bombing the guard kept the gate locked. For two weeks the Germans had been outside the gates. There was not a single German in any part of the Abbey. There was no OP, no SP gun, no MG. Once two Germans and an interpreter, probably German, came to the Abbey grounds and spoke with the priests, who totalled six in all. The Italians went for 17 days with hardly any food. Water was hard to get since any one who wandered out came under Allied fire. There were some dead and wounded before the big bombings. A German Red Cross man came in to perform an amputation. There was no medicine at all in the Monastery, except for a little ointment. The civilians were allowed access to the whole Abbey, save a section which was near our forward lines on the slope, down to the town. The reason given for this is that the Americans would see the figures and think them German. This would bring on the destruction of the place.

The warning was known to every single person, through at least two leaflets which were blown into the Abbey. This was fortunate since no one wandered out at all and the leaflets were dropped over the Abbey and not into it. The people only half-believed it. There, several voices were heard, - one which thought it was phony. (For example, it said that the leaflet was not signed by anyone.); one, that it was not meant to be carried out; another that they would be safe despite the bombardment which was not expected to be so heavy; and finally the voice of those who would have liked to get out but realized the terrible danger involved for anyone who stepped outside. The German soldier(s?) outside told them to stay. The bombings began next morning to the consternation of all.

The bombings killed, wounded many. There were many who were in the upper reaches of the Abbey and did not get down to the cellars in time. When afterwards, they started to run from the Abbey in panic, the Allied artillery-observers mistook them for Germans and ordered them fired upon by air-burst shrapnel. In the night of the 15th, some got away; the morning afterwards, the Germans opened the gates. On the afternoon of the 16th, there were successive air assaults again. Artillery fire on the Abbey was continuous.

One woman, a land-owner, who spoke intelligently and restrainedly, whose husband had been killed next to her, said she passed some German soldiers on the way through the lines. The terrific blasting of our artillery and air force was felt in the area around the Abbey, and she remembered one German soldier clinging in a shell *crater, sobbing convulsively. Despite her own terror, she cracked at him: "Why don't you stop crying and come with me, if you feel that way about it?"*

The interrogation of the others that escaped failed to reveal striking new facts. It was not possible from these people to tell how close to the Abbey German positions actually were. The number of dead and wounded cannot be ascertained. Most of the refugees seem to have escaped into the German lines.

My report did survive. It was read and forwarded, "D Section" to both Army Headquarters, 15th Army Group and ultimately to London and Washington. And it ended up in secret archives until an official British inquiry quoted it in 1949. The evidence in its favor has been mounting steadily - from the friars, the Church records, German witnesses, a scholar. In 1969, a United States Government document will get around to admitting that the Germans were not in the Abbey.

There was no access to the Abbey except from the German lines. No one had thought to seek an armistice to collect the wounded and dead. No one had thought to have ambulances and litters and first-aid personnel ready. The Germans would have given some help but they were desperately busy. Allied artillery had begun an intensive bombardment immediately. To the joy of the gunners, every cannon was unleashed. They were psychologically massacring the Abbey. The Allied troops waiting to attack had been pulled back because of the great expanse of the bombing, yet were ordered to attack as soon as the bombing ceased.

The Indian Division was unready to attack; conditions were such even before the bombing that it could not get ready, General Freyberg was told; but the Air Force could not be asked to do this every day, you know, so the attack must go forward, ready or not. By the time the Indians had crawled back up to the original jump-off line, the rubble had created an entirely new configuration of stone and debris, cut new paths, and given the Germans time to bring up reserves and ready themselves for the inevitable assault. The attack was a ghastly failure. And now there was no reason to observe the sanctity of the Abbey; the Germans dug themselves in securely. Their defensive positions were stronger than ever.

It did appear that General Clark had opposed the attack, whether for fear of the repercussions from American Catholic quarters or because he sensed the illusions of the intelligence reports. Those who backed the attack included Air Force General Ira Eaker, 15th Army Group Commander Alexander, and the New Zealand General Freyberg, Corps Commander, whose 4th Indian Division troops were to attack after the bombing. The Division General of the Indians, Francis Tuker, who had been opposed to a frontal assault on Cassino and considered only the heaviest imaginable bombing would be effective, had come down with an arthritic attack and was hospitalized while the final decisions were taken.

The Germans got around to disseminating a leaflet among their enemies weeks later, declaring that "all decent people in the world were set aghast by the news that one of the most venerable monuments of Christian culture, the Abbey of Cassino, has been destroyed by British and American bombers." It denounced "the colossal lie" of German use of the Monastery. "And What Have You Gained?" shouted its headline. "By thus violating this sanctuary of Christianity, your bombers have given us every right to incorporate the remnants of the Monastery in our system of defenses. The ruins have been turned by our men into a formidable fortress which has defied all your efforts during the past weeks and caused you an untold number of dead and maimed." Thus has your shameless crime boomeranged, it concluded.

It was not to be the last disastrous air attack that cursed the battlefields of Cassino. When all other tactics had failed, and exactly a month later, on March 15, a huge air armada attacked the town of Cassino, hurling down 1200 tons of bombs in the single assault. I was again there. As awful a sight as anything else was the flight that I observed coming in from the Southeast and, not waiting to reach Cassino, but coming upon the town of Venafro, there released its bombs upon French and American troops and the civil population. The towns must have looked alike to the flight leader; but, too, he had read his maps badly and had not been briefed well, nor watched the flights ahead of him and the smoke of their bombings. Hundreds must have been dying in the bursts before my eyes, I thought. Had such an accident happened to American, or even British, troops, rather than to French troops in one case, to Indian troops in another, and twice to Italian civilians, more criticism would have fallen upon the generals from home, despite the heavy censorship. Now once again the debris suited the defenders nicely, the attackers had had to withdraw and then return, and once more they were mowed down, and must retreat. Thus phases three and four ended in fresh disasters for the Allies.

After the destruction of the Abbey, the American newspapers were quick to justify the Army's action. The *New York Times* carried a five-column headline: *"U.S. Blasts Nazis in Mt. Cassino Abbey!"*, then a three-column picture headed *"Historic Abbey Turned by Nazis into Fortress Before Their Rout!"*, and several captions above the story itself: *"200 Germans Flee," "226 Bombers Alternate with Artillery to Rout Enemy!", "Monastery is Wrecked!"* The news report was credited to C. L. Sulzberger, who was at the Cassino Front representing the *Times;* I encountered him only once, and, after a few words of casual conversation, deemed him a conceited and unpleasant fellow.

The same correspondent had been headlined on his January 29 despatch provocatively: "Clark Order prohibits 5th Army from Attacking Church Property! Courtesy to Vatican Handicaps Advance as Enemy is Said to Use Religious Sites for Artillery Observation!", and writes that "many lives may be lost" in consequence. (The use of the word 'courtesy' in this context was probably as poisonous a thrust as General Clark ever received.)

The presence of a great many civilians and monks was known to Army headquarters and hardly a secret, but their fate was buried like many of the civilians themselves. Indeed, the Officer briefing the heavy bomber crews prior to the action exhorted the crews to recall how the enemy had used mosques and churches in Africa to protect their skins, and told them that the Abbey was alive with German troops and that no civilians were inside the place. Some 144 Flying Fortresses were involved, these from Foggia. Another 22 medium bombers came in from Sardinia later, and there occured still another bombing of the Abbey ruins the next day by 59 fighter-bombers. The briefing officer for this last occasion told his crews that the substructure of the ruined Abbey was still alive with German troops. In all, some 500 tons of bombs were dropped upon the magnificent structure, the heaviest bombardment ever to occur of a single point target. The official Army Air Force Diary concluded: "This medieval fortress has been gutted and now lies in ruins. It is difficult to see how any of the occupants of the building could have survived the weighty attack." The Air Force generals were delighted to display their capabilities.

President Franklin D. Roosevelt called a press conference the same afternoon as the bombing to say that he had read accounts of it in the afternoon newspapers and that these had shown how the Abbey was being used by the Germans: "It was a German strongpoint - they had artillery and everything up there in the Abbey."

Not one German soldier was killed in the bombings. A couple of hundreds of Italian men, women and children were ripped apart, blasted to death, crushed, the rest miraculously escaped, many with wounds. The monks, save for one who chose to abandon himself to the destruction, were preserved. All of these had weathered the devastation. There was a strictly military lesson here, on the coordination of bombing and ground operations, on the proper weighing of intelligence, on the control of riotous rumor, on the limits of bombing even of the heaviest kind, all considerations of morality aside; but the Air Force refused to acknowledge the facts, much less reconsider some of its tactics and procedures.

Moreover, it was not as if this kind of bombing came free of cost. The Mediterranean Allied Air Force, with its aircrafts to the number of 4000, was composed of 315,000 men who used equipment and supplies extravagantly, as much all told as the whole of the Fifth Army. They were not employed 100% in support of the Cassino campaign, true enough; a larger part of their effort went directly to bomb targets in Germany and occasionally to the Balkans and Central Europe.

Could one argue that this immense Army of the Air, on the occasions of its two attacks upon Cassino, was, in net terms, fighting on the side of the Germans? In each case, the net casualties were friendly soldiers (never mind the friendly civilians), the huge costs of the operations were Allied, the military damages were to the tactical advantage of the enemy, and the destruction of art and culture was a propaganda victory for the enemy and was to the detriment of mankind. So the answer must be affirmative.

Could one also argue that the Monastery and all the lost lives might have been preserved and saved? Certain German officers had taken upon themselves the salvation of the Monastery. They befriended the priests and did not wish death upon the civilians inside. They were even trying to keep up a three-hundred meter neutral unmilitarized area around the Abbey walls (violated by their troops to some extent, using a cave for refuge, for example, and placing a couple of cannons there for a time; but, recall that the Abbey itself was pockmarked by Allied shelling). They arranged for the art treasures of the Naples museum and the Abbey itself to be transported to safety. All of this was known to the Pope at the Vatican. There were also means of making the facts known to the Allied Command through diplomatic agencies in the Vatican and even in Washington.

It would have been simple and not even exceptional for a Commission of Church, Allied, and German representatives to enter the Monastery under a truce and reside there for the duration of the battle, assuring both sides that the Monastery is not being used to military advantage. Here the Pope erred. He should have contacted both sides and proposed the arrangement. Both would probably have accepted. Only the great fool General Freyberg might have obstructed the idea. Perhaps nothing would placate the many soldiers and their journalist mouthpieces, however, except an effort at destroying the Abbey. Still, once more, my answer is affirmative.

I was not of an infantry battalion, hence my own chances of survival were excellent, and you can expect to have me with you for a while longer. Never did I intimate in my letters home any doubt of this, and was often gabbling about the great future She and I and now all Three would have together. Early in my stint, on a call at the 34th Division, the Artillery Officer asked me how I got there. "I went up to St. Pietro, and turned off where those three tanks of ours are burned out, and cut back down." "That road is under fire; why don't you take the lower road? Why take chances?" The

Major's concern was touching. "I will." But I didn't. The lower road was rough, as well as long. Nothing happened, of course; the chances were against it. I figured it out as I drove around. In a single day-long infantry attack, anywhere from 10% to 60% casualties would occur (before the troops would, if they could, break and withdraw). On my milk route it would take me all year to accumulate a considerable chance of getting hurt. Occasionally you could see incoming bursts ahead or behind. Almost all of it was counter-fire to the sides here and there where the enemy believed he could hit a battery or group of men. Actually, if you wanted to estimate the number of troops engaged in combat, even over a whole war as for an engagement, you needed only double the number of casualties. For if you come near to getting hit, you'll get hit sooner or later.

"Am I rash?" I never thought so of myself. "Am I brave?" Whatever that means: the word is obsolete. Not likely. "Do I believe, as someone asserts, that it can't happen to me?" Not at all; on the contrary, I carried at all times a conviction that I was likely to catch it. Why was I comfortable under long-lasting, fairly risky conditions? Perhaps there was a sort of nihilistic sense of freedom and also a possessiveness, that you have something that is precious and that almost no one else wants (except the poor guys who were laying around out there and must stay where they were come what may.)

Could it also have been that my preoccupation part of each day with personal life and a love five thousand miles away could act as an antidote to the fear of death, preventing me from developing such an obsession? In the four months on the Cassino Front, I have written 131 pages in 46 letters to my wife and received even more in return. I have been enabled to follow from one day to the next the growth of our infant, *viz.,* on March 3, received the middle of March:

> *Darling - another letter from you today dated the 20th, a record day it seems for literary output (unless you have the dates mixed). Gosh, it seems we're or rather, you, are still no closer to Cassino than when it was written. It must be maddening. As you say, even the papers here*

forget about Cassino for a while. Its importance is minimized or, in the case of my favorite rag, the Sun, completely pushed off the pages by the damnest other events. Like today, an ill-tempered librarian was killed by an even more ill-tempered Negro in the National Cathedral in Washington. That's the one up Wisconsin Ave. that Mrs Singleton was the pillar of. God, you'd think that the millennium had come from the headlines in the Sun.

At Kathy's present rate of growth, or rather, her prenatal rate (fects, I'm telling you, fects) she would reach the size of the sun at maturity. She gets fatter and I get thinner. It's positively obscene. Actually, I weigh 124 with funny shoes on, but I'd like to weigh more, just out of perversity. Correct, her hair is brown and fuzzy, her complexion flawless and tan. She really has beautiful skin. I could simper and say I use Ivory and thereby win a big cash prize but to tell you the truth, I never use water on her face at all, not since she had a rash about a month ago. I douse her with olive oil; gnashing my teeth all the while since it tastes a lot better in salad than on her, and as a result, she always has a faint aura about her, like zucchini. I wonder if you would be able to appreciate all the miracles about her - things that seem so miraculous to me. Possibly not, but then, when we have another child, you'll think a lot of things are wonderful that I'll be completely blasé about. For instance, there is the primary miracle, which fortunately for my peace of mind no longer appears as such, that she's able to live the night without my standing by with pulmotor and pediatrician. Apparently - I've discussed this with Mir and another gal -- every new mother feels that way the first week she's alone with the baby. I don't know what peculiar psychology it is that makes the mother think the child will stop breathing the minute the lights are out. But, to quote our famous friend Mr. Marquand, there it is. Then there is the miracle of the cereal. Leave us face it (remind me to send you that song, same title) - even the hungriest little gal, and ours is, resists taking things off a spoon at some time or another. As a result, I still have cereal on my shin bones from this morning. And tonight's feeding is on a blanket, the floor, the baby's nightshirt and my forearms. She still gets some of it down her. That's the miracle. And then there are the assorted miracles of the smile, the laugh, the coo, the boisterous laugh and the general ability to stay awake alone for long periods of time without crying. She really is a non-crying baby, though when she does get sore, like today when she was hungry and I gave her a bath first, she gets purple and her eyes get wet and red from crying. But as soon as I immerse her in the little tub, her expression changes through apprehensiveness finally to a big smile. She likes the water. Then when I take her out and start to dry her she yells again. You bet I'm a little heroine, with bottles exploding to the right and left of me...

Thus does the theotropy of life defeat the entropy of war.

Perhaps my reading led to the same end, that of keeping me part of the world that existed beyond cannon-shot. I did a lot of reading, principally in contemporary novels of the better sort and high-level treatises on the war and foreign affairs. Perhaps I realized more than the others how the chances of disaster diminish as one is taken out of the firing line of advance and retreat, away from the grips of a machine-gun, away from the handles of a stretcher. I was not only relatively relaxed, but despite everything felt that the Front would crack and the Germans would retreat.

Even when the Campaign ended, I hardly appreciated how terrible it had been; nor will I for a long time; nor will the rest of the World ever come to realize that it was worse than the Normandy landings, worse than the Break-out in Northern France, worse than the Battle of the Bulge - more agonizing for all concerned, and with more casualties. That its fearsome rates may even have been worse overall than those of the trench warfare in World War I.

Considering only the American case, proportionate to the number of men engaged, United States troops at Cassino and its 'left flank' engagements at Anzio suffered many more casualties over a seven month period than would be endured by American troops in ten years of war in Vietnam.

Over 400,000 casualties will have been suffered by the struggling armies during the Cassino Campaign. Two-thirds of the men of the contending battalions will have been eliminated by death, wounds, imprisonment, or disease. Six times as many Allied troops as Germans will lose their lives. I felt the folly of the campaign but was too young to understand the weaknesses of my generals and to criticize them confidently. Nor was I well enough informed about the true state of affairs; actually no one, not even some one of these generals, was sufficiently informed.

I did believe this: after the inexcusable failure of my generals at Anzio, the best way to break the stalemate was across the western coastal plain and hills, letting Cassino be isolated; for the Germans, although they could defend themselves there forever, could not break forth from there with sufficient force to cut and strangle the Fifth Army from the flank. I did not know then that General Alphonse Juin had this plan in mind and would execute it.

Thus came the last phase, a French attack through the mountains near the Tyrennian Sea and a Polish attack upon the Abbey's eminence from the East. The Poles, recklessly brave, suffered casualties beyond belief. Only this last French attack could be called truly successful. Some would award General Juin and his two French-North African Divisions top prize for performance and effectiveness, from April through May.

But the "victory" at Cassino - never mind who was left in command of the field, which was determined by the production quotas achieved by Detroit as against the Ruhr - could also be assigned to the First Parachute Division of the German Army, granted that they were entrenched in a practically impregnable bastion. Outnumbered by the attacking enemy two-to-one, five-to-one, more. No air force cover. Probably no group in history has received a greater enemy barrage of fire - ten, fifty, tons of high explosive per man? Casualties at sixty percent and more. Inflicted four times, perhaps ten times its casualties upon the enemy. Used all of its weapons ingeniously. Built bunkers and surrounding defenses indefatigably. Repelled several major attacks. Counterattacked continually. Few were captured. When captured, they divulged little information. The units disengaged in the end reluctantly, when the Army's flank was being turned on the West and they were repeatedly ordered out by the Army Commanders. Their high morale stemmed from their *esprit de corps,* their training, their belief in miraculous "secret weapons" to come. They were dedicated to Adolf Hitler.

The better they were as soldiers, the more of Our Boys they killed. Furthermore, the longer they resisted, the more time they afforded to Himmler, Borman, Ley and the SS butchering battalions of Germans and East Europeans to kill innocent and harmless men, women and children. To their valorous delaying actions, prompted ultimately by heinous ideals, is owed the death not only of thousands of Allied soldiers but also of as many actual and potential teachers, scholars, writers, artists, scientists, and highly qualified citizens of Europe as they themselves numbered, some 20,000. These were the months, and year, during which two millions persons were murdered by the German authorities.

Still, so mad and absurd is the Inner World of Values, if the First Para Div were the German's weakest division, and its soldiers were uniquely less loyal to Der Führer - in short, ideally my kind, our kind, of German - both friend and foe would ignore them or treat their history contemptuously. So it goes.

The First Parachute Division and three other first class divisions had been negligently permitted to escape from Sicily where they could have been battered from a distance by artillery, naval guns and aircraft. The costly, grueling man-killing campaigns of Italy might have been unnecessary. Hitler was criticized for having fought for Italy; but the Allies' most experienced troops were fighting here instead of on the French invasion front.

I wouldn't be around Cassino much longer, though. My half-millionth of the Allied flesh and blood was not much needed: with or without me the carnage went on. I was not enthused over my part of the war here any more, doing what another guy could do as well, all was dulling clockwork, while in Naples friends in British Intelligence were beckoning. I let them know: promptly the "D-Section" people in Naples put in a call for me, and a gobbledygook 5A HQ AG TO of April 3 sent me off. It was extraordinary; they still numbered no Americans among them, not a military officer; they had seen to this somehow; they had among them only the famous American violinist, Albert Spalding. I was their lusty, ironic, laughing companion of yore, spouting episodically the radical epistemology and sociology of the University of Chicago, knowing something of British history, and could be as insulting of the English as they of the Americans. And so it happened.

I left the Front depressed and strangely nostalgic. I loved the faces and voices that had surrounded me. I would miss the tired slovenly figures along the paths, in the tents, sprawled among ruins, who between wanting to know nothing and forced into knowing nothing, did know practically nothing, but would say something to be helpful and would even speak up, muttering phrases on occasion.

I wrote of Sgt. Harrari who could beat three chess players while blindfolded. Of an officer reciting insulting jokes about the President and Eleanor Roosevelt at a battalion mess I happened into down the line. Too, of a visiting OSS Captain, a Kansas editor and Chicago graduate, who was amazed by the sight of Britishers playing soccer within cannon range. And of Brownie Roberts who came in one night, having spent a while in a hole while shells were sporadically descending, to say that two G.I.'s playing dice on a sunken path near him wouldn't stop for anything, until exploding shell-fragments hit the crap-shooter in both of his waving arms.

> *...I feel,* [he writes] *as tired these days as I've felt anytime until now. The full impact of this creeping, petty pace comes down on us here. The illusive town of Cassino stretches prettily out before us but mocks any advance. How many times have I seen it there, languid in the morning mist or crystal-clear in the bright afternoon, its windows sharp checkers of black, or dissolving and dying into the dusk, spitting out flashes like blood. So near and yet so far, so quiet and yet so menacing, dead but full of the vermin of mines and machine guns close-in. When there is a lull in the fire, there is such peace that at times I feel like driving straight down Highway #6 into the town. A couple of visiting firemen almost did by mistake. And there is or was the Abbey that I learned to like very much, standing as it did so majestically above the town, untouched by the fury of cannonading around it. Its change was ghastly, like the beautiful girl from Shangri La who turned repulsive before our very eyes upon leaving the sacred protection of the valley. The Abbey now looks like any one of the gutted, aged castles that crown many an Italian mountain. People at home can forget Cassino for a week at a time, but every minute we must hark to it. That's why the War seems to move so slowly to us.*

It was more than a month later, early April, that I departed. The Italian campaign was still going poorly. The Second Front was nowhere in sight; hopefully it was near in time but that was a well-kept secret. Luckily for the Allies, the Soviet armies were absorbing the energies of over 90% of all the German armed forces of the land and air. On the eve of parting from the Cassino front to join "D Section" in Naples, I wrote to Her: "The Russian news is the hand of the only clock that brings me nearer to you."

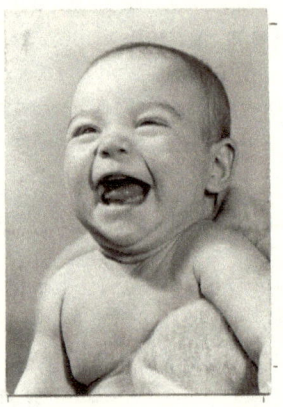

The first picture of Kathy

A French medic drew the picture and entitled it "Waiting for the Nurses," before a party that the Fifth Army Combat Propaganda organized in their cella at Varino. The blown-away wall permits this view of the interior. There can be recognized from l. to r. Nat Getlin, "visiting fireman," then Business Manager of the *New York Post;* Jim Clark, publisher, uniformed OWI officer and my close friend: "Tiny," a huge New Zealand captain nest to a diminutive New Zealand colonel... Below, the nurses have arrived...

Chapter Eleven

NAPLES, SARDINIA, ANZIO

EVERYONE who could quit Algiers for Naples now did so. Witness one familiar face encountered beneath the charming Galleria, the nicely thinned-out, debonair Major Rathbun of the First Mobile Radio Broadcasting Company. Hearty greetings, and *"molto piacere"* to a pretty girl hanging on his arm. The Major was there with the "advance party" of the leisurely outfit. He could sing, you may recall. He was indeed singing. He disclosed that he had been admitted to the eminent ranks of the San Carlo Opera Company of Naples. He was mightily proud. War? What war?

"You must come and hear me sing, Al."

"I sure will, but excuse me, *scusi,* I must find my jeep."

I had left my jeep down the street for a few minutes. That was the limit of endurance for your property on a Neapolitan street. It didn't matter that I had chained its front axle to a post with a great padlock; chain-cutters prowled the streets. The unchained jeep would swiftly be stolen and driven to one of the innumerable companies at the Front; and which commanding officer or motor pool officer had ever objected to the sudden appearance in his motor pool of a jeep? If the jeep's body could not be removed, the same could not be said of tires, wheels, horn, distributor cap, spark-plugs, windshield wipers, and locked welded boxes - to begin with, the gas would be siphoned out.

The Neapolitan thieves were on the loose, and intent upon honoring their mondial reputation. The Allied troops were close on their heels - as competitors. The traffic of Naples was still military.

Naples, Sardinia, Anzio

The troops came in on leave, jumped off the trucks and spread about. The difference between Germans and Americans was this: the Germans would come to town, drink something and walk along the street in a group, arm in arm, singing; the Americans, as soon as they arrived, split up, and went off searching for girls somewhere. These were the profound observations of an Italian intellectual, one of two dozen who worked for "D Section" and shared its board.

The port was booming; the materiel of war and the troops poured out of the ships. The warehouses were filling with supplies and the racketeers were conniving to get at them. Since practically the whole population needed food, notions, clothing, and medical supplies, and everything was destined to be given away anyhow, whether to the troops or the civilians, the black market could be regarded as an alternative distribution route enriching to some modest degree a few unworthy souls.

Corporal Laudando was affected when discovering the poverty of the neighborhood he was born in before being carried as a toddler to America, and procured for the people there foodstuffs in some quantity; he had the CIC and MP's hot on his trail, and appealed to me to help him out of his jam. He got cool sympathy and a referral to Major Greenlees, now Commander of "D Section," a man of so many principles, half of them aberrant, that he could afford to forego one or another of them from time to time. "After all, the wheat flour in question has gone to women and children who are quite hungry, one must admit, don't you think so, Sergeant?" Thus Greenlees to the M.P. investigating. "Waaal... maybe." "Surely. Let me be responsible. I shall straighten matters out." And so the problem was solved. There may have been added an intimation that the man was soon to be sent to the Front; there was punishment for you!

I was allotted a magnificent room atop the Palazzo Caracciolo that "D Section" had taken to itself in the old heart of the City. The rest of PWB was housed Hollywood-style in a modern hotel that was reached by a twenty-minute drive through the tunnel that took the seaside drive to the north and Pozzuoli; it stood on a cliff looking out to sea. The personnel commuted to an office building in the City whence they sought to control and direct the communications and media of Co-belligerent Italy. I had it so much better, being independent of transport, near to the incredible fish and produce markets, a step from the old port, assailed by the noises and smells alternately so charming and odious. When I stepped out of my room in the morning, scaring up flights of pigeons, it was onto a large roof garden, blooming with great plants. I could see much of Naples and beyond; Mt. Vesuvius, still erupting, eluded me. Friends had gone up and returned from the lava fields, astonished as much by the villagers sitting upon their stoops praying that God might bring it to a halt as by the red hot wall descending upon them.

The large number of Italian personnel put a strain on the rations and fresh food was costly, so that the portions at Palazzo Caracciolo soon diminished and I was found complaining that I was still hungry after meals, a gripe that Greenlees, who outweighed me by fifteen stone, and was a gourmet, took to heart. "They have so little to eat at home," he apologized, but pointed out that there seemed to be no limit to the number of agents, secretaries, reporters, archivists, painters, broke nobles, politicians, and military visitors at the ever-enlarging table, now in two sittings. And who knows, I added, haranguing Robbie and Greenlees and Hadfield and the Howard brothers, how much food is leaving by the kitchen's back door; there was no limit to leftovers. And when it came to the cats and dogs of Naples, would we go on to feed them as well? They agreed. They loved me and besides, I was their only American officer, their ultimate argument when demonstrating that their effort was truly Allied. Yet I felt slightly embarrassed when my word was indeed heeded: a bit like I felt in Syracuse when I slammed shut the door against the crowd that was bursting into the printshop during the air raid, or when stuffing myself from cans of rations set out on the hood of my jeep, when there gathered around a little crowd, of kids, too, hungry perhaps, though they never asked for anything, almost never.

John Reyner, just in from England as a top administrator, gave me graciously a chance at an outing and dinner, insisting that I take a couple of visiting American Generals and a nicely made-up American WAC officer on a tour of Sorrento or someplace akin.

Having protested my ignorance of Sorrento or restaurants to no avail, I found myself reluctantly in the command car directing the chauffeur along the beautiful hillside roads of the peninsula. We stopped at a picturesque restaurant, where I overly engaged the attentions of the WAC, rather to the irritation of the Generals, who had probably not counted upon me at table, or paying for my lunch, or my entertaining their good-looking companion. (But, after all, I was no tour guide, and I ranked with the WAC officer certainly, and they invited me, so what could they say?). The adventure was a bore, though; the Generals didn't know how to behave in the grand manner, less so than the lowliest echelon of "D Section." During the meal, a small boy sneaked up to the table, snatched a couple of buns and raced off. The generals stared for a moment blankly, then turned back to themselves.

Generally, I was dismayed and disgusted by social conditions in Naples and inclined to blame the Neapolitans. The city was too large and condensed, overflowing with the unemployed who seemed to have thronged it from the beginning of all time. It was dirty, noisy, full of shysters and thieves. The soldiers brought in their own forms of thievery. Sometimes I wished some kind of stern communism upon them all, not outright Stalinism, although at the time I knew only of a fraction of the horrors that Stalin's cruelty and paranoia had visited upon the Soviet people and its neighbors, and of course nothing of what was to come. Nor was I even a socialist. But I saw nothing but misery and disorder in the present and projected future of the City. (Strangely, I did not even think to compare the place with American cities such as my own Chicago which had already arrived at, and were well on their way of rapidly descending to a level far below that of Naples in many respects, without any of the redeeming aspects of its hospitality, its style and beauty, or its *joie de vivre*.)

I refused to confront my own generosity, whose material modesty came from my material poverty. Literally, I had "fuck-all to give." I was writing to my wife about this time:

> *Don't say another word about the insurance. It was done almost a month ago. And I maintain firmly that my admittedly mild*

> *argument had nothing whatsoever to do with that old plaint of 'everything of yours isn't mine.' Of course everything I have is yours. Christ, all I have at this minute that isn't in your possession is four dollars and thirty-nine cents, some chocolate and cigars, and a couple of bags of Army junk that I wish were yours too. I might mention my body, which I would also offer up most eagerly...*

I prefered to think of myself as hard-hearted. I tried to be tough, wishing to discipline the Neapolitans, the troops, etc., but in actual encounters I was not so mean. Not even in speech.

Still I certainly wrote and spoke angrily against the *lumpenproletariat* of Napoli. The horde of thieves. The poor common bony shabby mass. The ragamuffins all about. (Yet I admired and was affected by the rough-humored, tender horseplay of soldiers and street urchins, mocking, swearing, cursing fiercely, throwing things at each other, laughing, exchanging food and things, "Hey, Joe, wanna meet my sister?")

The Neapolitans would not admit that the accusations against them could be valid. They were unashamedly and hopelessly manipulative, demanding, rhetorical, irrelevant, unimpressed by any conquerors or liberators. To a man they would agree with St. Thomas Aquinas (rather a close neighbor of theirs, 600 years earlier) that you were entitled to steal food when hungry. Furthermore, they knew, but it was also incontrovertible, that they were warm-hearted, hospitable, clever and affectionate, by comparison with most of the world's people. Were such qualities to count for nothing?

I might have spent my time simply meeting characters and personages. Colonel Professor T.V. Smith, transferred from Sicily, whose scratches from his critical nails were quickly healing, was now applying his arts to Napoli. The father of Gertie Goldsmith, my high school and college friend, had come to town to purge and reorganize the social services, even as Gertie was a fleeting reference in the letters of Jill from Chicago. He had been for many years occupied with the Jewish charities of America; he would do about as much as any man to organize help for the poor and disorganized here. It was of the spookiness of historical cycles that

I should visit Goldsmith in the company of Edmund Howard whose ancestor pioneered charitable organizations in Britain. Charity is so special and rare as to appear genetic, a family strain or a Jewish instinct. So I thought, if I didn't say so.

Captain Professor Leland de Vinney, a stolid, orderly, uninspired and uninspiring sociologist who taught me Sociology at the University, put in an appearance with Assistants named Strang and Sheffield: they were studying the morale of the American soldiers; they were working for Professor Samuel Stouffer, Jill's mentor in statistical sociology, who was directing research for the Morale Division of the Army and was last heard of, if you will recall, excusing his inability to co-opt me for his services.

I could unload myself upon the impassive De Vinney: There were three universes of morale, the morale of the winner, of the doubtful, and of the loser. Morale changed with the echelons, from home to the frontline spearhead. Morale was multiple in the same person. Morale was the willingness and determination to carry on a fight in the belief that one was right and rightfully directed. The Germans had the capability to possess morale. The British, and to a greater extent the Americans, and even more the French, and to a still greater extent the Italians, had less of the capability. They were not capable of being such true believers. Hence, I tended to think, morale was amoral, a trait on which you scored high or low even before you enter the situation where your morale was to be judged. Then there could be a certain variability of your morale under the changing circumstances of this situation, such as a conflict setting, a war, a battle, suffering, winning or losing. Just as some people were resistant to a disease that felled others, so the morale of some was more or less impermeable to the indulgences and deprivations visited upon them. De Vinney listened quietly; it was doubtful that he understood. Stouffer had provided the questions; it was for De Vinney to fill in the blanks. He and his team were interrogating a large number of wounded soldiers.

The Italian liberal and radical leaders were close to my British friends. The foremost Italian philosopher, Benedetto Croce, was in touch with them from Sorrento, and we visited him; his publisher was La Terza, in Bari, whom Greenlees had immediately locked into when he liberated the City. Tarchiani and Carlo Sforza, with his son Sforzino Sforza, regarded the "D" group as sympathizers. So did the supreme Italian Communist politician, Palmiro Togliatti; I didn't know what Greenlees was up to there and when a private dinner at the Palazzo is being set up with Togliatti as honored guest, I thought that I ought be invited. "By all means," said Greenlees, "do come." Togliatti seemed to be just about what he would appear to be for the rest of his life as leader of the largest Communist Party outside of the Soviet Union, affable, reasonable, intelligent, alert, unthreatening, an incongruous partner of Josef Stalin, incomprehensibly forever in his good graces.

I had devised a plan that had the approval of Greenlees and of the others, to go to Sardinia and organize political intelligence all over the place, meanwhile peering about, here and there. Sardinia had been occupied by a couple of British torpedo boats in September, a week after the Germans withdrew. There had been almost no political information coming out of it. You may not hear from me for a little while, I wrote Jill, my signal that she has now learned, that I was off to an unsettled situation. My orders, which I wrote myself and which Greenlees signed, gave me leeway to do just about anything I could get away with, and far more than I could possibly achieve. I was to send in a weekly Report, by secret cable if needs be; I was authorized transportation to visit the whole of the Island; to arrange to get regular reports from agents at all principal centers, paying them 5000 lira per month, less if part-time or members of the Committees of Anti-Fascist Concentration; to see to it that copies of all political pamphlets and regular press issues were channeled to "D Section," Naples, and to set up well-located receptors for all of our 'bumpf.'

I wanted to go by boat so I visited the Headquarters of the Italian Navy, and asked to be placed upon the first ship leaving for Sardinia. Soon I find myself aboard an Italian cruiser. There was almost nothing to fear by sea or by air; the only potential enemy threat was from the Italian North and Southern France and little had been signaled from those quarters; the Luftwaffe had more valuable naval targets at Anzio. Soon I landed in Sardinia, which was run by the Italian government, occupied by Italian troops and used in scattered localities for guiding and landing Allied aircraft.

I checked in on the local Psychological Warfare representative, Major Siepman, and met an American civilian in uniform who was running the radio station, Guido d'Agostino, a writer. The senior American nabob officer must be informed of my presence, I hear, and this turned out to be a Colonel Doyle who was of the Air Force and who had set himself up at the most impressive building in Cagliari. When I opened the massive door to his office, I was amazed to see this figure seated in the center of a kind of ballroom at a massive desk. I didn't want to offend him by a salute; they didn't salute any more in the Air Force, did they?

Oh, yes they did - when they wanted to. This hulk had probably been slumping there in that enormous gilded chair imagining himself as the Duce and wondering why he was not commanding legions of troops and planes. So when I managed the some fifty meters of approach and did not salute, but introduced myself in a civilian-like manner, the Colonel refused to acknowledge me until I returned to the entrance to the chamber and approached him again, this time in a proper military fashion with a correct salute. I, astounded, did as ordered and came back, to give and receive the Colonel's salute. I was so full of rage, however, that I could only speak in mutterings and hisses from behind clenched teeth, and had to repeat myself because the Colonel could not understand me. Which I did, still hissing, but more clearly. The Colonel looked at the piece of paper containing the Special Orders, and handed it back. He had nothing particular to say nor did I want to listen. He had had his chance to receive me on friendly terms, and wanted to pull his rank. So he got the treatment that his rank required and nothing more. He could sink back into his silent stupidity. I snapped him as smart a salute as he had ever before received - and which would be interpreted as a gesture of contempt by some - swiveled about-face, and clomped off, British style.

I was entitled to a jeep and driver and got them. I looked up my new bearded acquaintance, Guido, who seemed to know everything happening on the Island. Siepman was just a nice chap in the uniform of a British Major, he said. Guido filled me in profusely, took me to the military club, showed me the sights, and told me about an Italian parachute division, intact, in bivouac not far away. The idea of fresh cannon-fodder occurred to me and I asked Guido to take me to visit the outfit. It was agreed.

I then bumped into a couple of acquaintances from the Columbia University Law School, guys I had known in 1940. They were Naval officers now and their gunboat sat in the harbor of Cagliari. It was exceedingly mysterious how such people were able find themselves. They moved among hundreds of thousands of uniformed men, here, there, and everywhere; then, with a frequency that could not have been random, like homing pigeons or penguins finding their families, they came upon one another and recognized their kinship. It was a kind of "Old Boy" network, but it wasn't fully that, because the network was defunct as such; they were not looking for each other in particular.

Next afternoon, I went with Guido to the large encampment, full of alert young soldiers. This was the famous Folgore Division, sister of the Nembo Division that had fought and finally surrendered in Tunis. Therefore, one of two parachute divisions of the Italian Army. Here, intact. Unsurrendered, except by protocol. We went to the Headquarters barrack, met the top officers, were invited to dinner and to a show that night, and taken on a tour of the camp. I was secretly excited. I watched everything closely. Everywhere there appeared to be a high morale, coming from the type of elite unit, persisting despite being on the losing end of the War, despite the division's being forgotten by the outer world.

The dinner was excellent, and after dinner a musical comedy was put on by soldiers of the division, men playing the parts of women, just as they did in Blackfriars at the University of Chicago, riotously funny, well rehearsed, as one can imagine, given the ample time at their disposal. Meanwhile, I had been asking a hundred questions on the morale of the unit, attitudes toward Mussolini, the King, the Americans, the British, the Germans. I had begun to feel that I may have made a great discovery: here was a division of troops, well trained, already under arms, knowledgeable about all that concerned the German enemy, that could, reequipped with American arms, be put almost immediately into the line in Italy.

Early in the morning I composed a report to "D Section"

Naples, Sardinia, Anzio

recommending it be forwarded for the consideration of the Commanding General of the Fifteenth Army Group in Italy. The Division, I declared, had all the earmarks of good unit morale. On the general level, their attitudes were favorable to us. They were monarchists at the high officer level, but this should not be confused with Fascist. They were also nationalist, which should not be confused with Fascism, either. The Division was ready to fight for the liberation of Italy, and it numbered about fifteen thousand men and officers with basic equipment. (This was not all inference, for I had spoken directly to the Commander and Chief of Staff, to other officers, to several men, alone and in groups; I worked fast and knew how to phrase a good question; this was one thing I had been trained for, after all, at University.)

The failure to put a great many Italian troops into the line in Italy in the middle and later stages of the Cassino and North Italian campaigns was a costly error, ascribable to the incompetency of the Allied Generals and the fearful, weak Italian Government that the Allies had installed. Speaking not so much of the British, which by this time was taking more of its cues from the USA than it was giving back, but of the Americans, our generals thought of war and planned the War - though there were limits to fighting it so - in non-human terms: so many men, so many planes, so many tanks, so many boats, so many bullets and rations. Anything special, different, or protruding, including outstanding, they were at a loss to handle. An instance of the opposite kind of risk, rashness instead of caution, was sending the Polish Corps into a blunt frontal attack at Cassino. The Allied Command, not realizing the heroic psychology and towering morale of the Polish Corps, or, worse, failing to see its dreadful possible consequences, did not restrain the Corps and was willing to let the Poles be practically annihilated in successive engagements. For that matter, this was the same kind of mistake that Navy Admirals and Marine Generals were making with their splendid divisions in the atolls and islands of the Pacific Theater.

Then I pouched the report and headed North for Sassari. Sardinia was Sicily without people, without the major riches of the Sicilian plain, without Mt. Etna, without the profound high culture, without the large intellectual and artistic class, without the industries. But it had less of the *lumpenproletariat*, less of the crime, less deviousness of mind, it had more straightforwardness, beautiful simplicity, uniformity of conduct, and a more than respectable level of artistic creativity. It revealed to me planned mining towns of a pleasing modernity not to be found in that empire of mining, the United States. When I arrived at Sassari, I found a small city that compared favorably with any in the United States for order, beauty, serenity, modernity, architecture, and setting. There it was, at his California ranch-style house, that I found Mario Berlinguer, chief of the Republican Party, an anti-Fascist who had had to stay home and managed to do so without being drawn out to be murdered, or losing face, or being imprisoned. We talked for a long time, I told him of conditions in Italy from the Allied point of view, Berlinguer telling me in turn what he had in mind for the future of the country.

I bade him goodbye and good luck, returned to my hotel, and typed out a report urging that Berlinguer be brought back, if he would come, and placed into the Italian Cabinet immediately. I then headed back south, my self-imposed missions finished. On the way I spotted a radio tower for aircraft guidance. I drove up the mountain, curious to meet these isolates. They were happy to have me for dinner, talking the while about their poker game that was coming up. Every night they started up their electric generator and played poker into the night, and that was about all they did with their time.

I tried to refuse, pleading that I had only several dollars to lose, and it would not be fair of me to play, but they insisted desperately. To my dismay, I began to win, I raked in more and more money, I drew one good hand after another. I topped a hundred dollars and would soon begin to break them. They were sweating. I was afraid of leaving them with no money at all until the paymaster next arrived. So, as in a nightmare, I tried to lose, without insulting them or myself. Finally the chance arrives. I have a good hand. The three others have decent hands. Fine. I can bid high. They will hang in. They do. I note that at least one of them must have a very hot hand. I double into it; the others double as well. I redouble. Two stick.One redoubles. That's it. I lay down. I lose. I am happy. Over half my money is gone. They are happy. We finish our drinks and close down the memorable evening.

Next day in Cagliari I bought the two hand-carved cigar boxes I had wanted for my wife's letters, and located a plane headed for Palermo. The night was celebrated with my friends there, the next day I was back in Naples, exactly three weeks from my date of departure.

First person I bumped into was Charlton of the Eighth Army, so we cheered our comings and goings, this time Charlton was off to London, for good. We tossed off a few bad Stregas, and began to talk about Charl's book in its new version. Charl went to fetch his manuscript. We took it to the Royal Navy Club bar where we drank merrily to the brave new world. We ate a meal then and there with two bottles of vino. We separated, for me to find ice and for Charl to get the whiskey he drew from the Naafi stores for the trip to London. That was the last of Charlton's Anglo-pink face, alcoholically refulgent, bobbing above the crowd. He never resurfaced.

So I went to visit Joe Ferla in the hospital. He was flat on his back still. He'd had the War. He was going back home to Massachusetts. "See you back home, Joe." What else?

I unwrapped a large Sardinian cheese and we gathered for a homecoming at the Palazzo: Robbie, Greenlees, Vernon, the Howards, and Albert Spalding, who had given up his violin concerts to become a propagandist, just as he had been under La Guardia in World War I. He was heading something called *"Italia Combatte,"* a radio station and leaflet disseminating organization for Italian partisans of the North. He told a story of performing in Berlin in 1936 and attending a party with Ambassador Dodd following the concert, where Frank, the Nazi Governor of Poland was present. Frank was a lover of the arts, like Goering. Felix Mendelssohn had been the latest target of anti-Semitic epuration in Germany: his statue had been torn down that very day. Frank asked Spalding's opinion of Mendelssohn's Concerto and Spalding acclaimed it as one of Germany's mightiest musical works, to the embarrassment of Frank and his guests. "He's a bad type," said Spalding, meaning sewer scum.

I could hardly stay away from the combat propaganda teams, so drove up to visit Jim Clark, Tom Crowell, Herz, a newcomer called Duke Ellington and the Fifth Army Team, and thereafter the Eighth Army Team, where Beauclerk and Foster hung out. The Duke got drunk daily, he didn't have enough to do; he was a cheerful soul, round-faced, balding, blonde, heavybodied, liberal, witty, and so easy-going; I studied him, wondering whether Duke was going to be the true American character of the future, the Californian, and how America was going to run the world with lovable characters like him all over the place.

I, you see, was not liberal in a number of regards; I incorporated a sense of national destiny, and I was always on the look-out for the instruments of that world-unifying mission of the USA. I was thinking, probably as a result of too much self-propaganda and Washington directives, that the Soviets were going to be partners in this enterprise, junior partners to be sure, because they lacked the technology to support the future world and the experience to govern it, which were concentrated in the Western countries and America. I wanted to Americanize the world.

The front was boiling up continuously around Cassino with terrible losses and small gain. It was the last month of the struggle. The 15th Army Group was throwing, against the Germans' mortars and machine guns, French troops, Australians, Indians, Poles, Italians, New Zealanders, anybody who came to hand, as well as the depleted American and British Forces, which had been diminishing from casualties from deployment at Anzio, or by removal and shipment to England for transhipment to the invasion forces readying for assault upon the West Wall.

While I was visiting Fifth Army Headquarters, the Polish Corps liaison officer introduced himself and congratulated me on the Folgore Report from Sardinia; it had evidently reached its target, the Army Command; you are right, he said, especially in your analysis of the distinction between fascist and nationalist attitudes, and how the nationalism factor would make the Italians reliable in the line. At this point I should have pushed in to see the Chief of Staff or an Assistant, but I did not think to do so; the Army does not encourage an Officer or Enlisted Man to go over anyone's head to make suggestions; I was already unusually bold for a twenty-four-year-old Lieutenant, witness the Report itself, but here I let the intelligence work weakly its own way up. I was surprised at how far the idea had gone.

Finally, with pressures from four directions and the Vatican pleading against turning Rome into a Montecassino, the German positions began to crack around Cassino, in the mountains, along the Sea and at the Anzio beachhead. I puttered around for a week longer in Naples. I finished reading Dos Passos' *USA: Trilogy,* Borgese's *Common Cause,* and several other books and wrote a couple of reports. I wrote letters, too. Why should I have been so critical of Dos Passos, who had tried to write realistically and sincerely about World War I and American Society? I said that the Author provided goodness in his characters but destroyed their environment such that they must fail, and he could do so because in retrospect, the country had failed its people.

> *In other words, the thoughts he reads into a character's mind in an early stage of their life (including the tone of his literary treatment which is more important than the direct thoughts themselves) are the thoughts of an old and frustrated personality, shamed, beaten, and resentful. We can look back at our past, and pick out things we are ashamed of now, of incidents that were silly, of attitudes that were stupid. But their meaning and associations at that time were altogether different, and if a picture of the psychological state at that particular time is desirable, the cynical increments of time shouldn't be added.*

Ironically, these remarks must apply to me, the writer, now, as well as to Dos Passos, for here I am, adding the lugubrious nostalgia and hyper-criticality accumulated over six decades to Our Boy and the forces affecting him then.

I contemplated "D Section" and asked what they were achieving. I expected too much, of course; I asked whether they were significantly helping the generals to win the war and I exaggerated what they were not doing and what they might have been doing. Top generals and politicians almost always have their minds made up along several leading lines - as with Churchill's obsession with attacking Hitler's "Fortress Europe" from the South and his fondness for Italian culture, or Adolf Hitler's obstinacy when a withdrawal was called for, or General Ira Eaker's belief in precision bombing and victory through air power, or General Clark's insistence that Rome can be taken by any means so long as he takes it first. In the end these were non-rational feelings coloring all directives and suggesting subordinate forms of behavior: "'Oh, Shit,' said the King, and ten million subjects squatted," as my school-chum R. Elberton Smith used to say.

As I viewed it, "D Section" was a fine case of muddling through; totally uninstructed and unrehearsed, but effective. It was hardly credible: despite all the different jobs I had done and all of the communal living, not once had anybody said: "Now here is what 'D Section' does, Alfred," nor had anyone had the temerity to propose that we hold program-planning conferences or engage in any of the dozen different procedures that were elsewhere employed and recommended in the new science of public administration and business management in America. A spy observing what I and the others did might correctly have surmised that "D Section" provided liaison with political factions and lent them active support where suggested by top policy. An army, whether liberating or occupying, must deal with the many conflicts and political needs of the region. Its officers, not party to the obsessions of the top, need a continuous flow of balancing information, to keep their mental equilibrium, to feel that they are moving properly, even though in the dark, to feel real and alive in the middle of large events; they could not be let to feel that their machine was driving like a great power drill into a mountain tunnel.

Further there was little way of their knowing the effects of an action in their totality by military intelligence alone. The waves of a military event go out in ever-widening circles and splash here and there against obstacles, or for that matter assist in the launching of boats into favorable winds under fresh crews. My reports were filled with snippets: an Austrian POW, back from convalescent leave, said: the Austrians are cracking up; a partisan passing through the lines said a good-sized gang of them was holed up near Lago Trasimeno; a letter of a dead German mentioned a riot in Modena against the Fascist conscription drive; an Italian civilian said that two downed British airmen were hiding in a sculpture studio at Pietrasanta; the Badoglio Government was detested in Bologna, where Communist activity and organization were strong. Put it all together, it spelled, it may have spelled, it may have hinted at - well something, a something that might have been useful in detail and in the broad.

I wrote to Jill more grandly now that I was reading reports from everywhere. The German soldiers in Russia use two acronyms, I quote her from a DNB despatch: 'Kik' and 'Kak', *"Kamerad im Kessel,"* meaning "Comrade encircled" and *"Kamerad aus dem Kessel,"* meaning "Comrade out of encirclement." Funny, tragic. "Today it is Kik, tomorrow hopefully Kak," they say.

I commented on the world scene. I was beginning to sense important developments in Palestine. I was irritated by an article in an April 3 issue of *Time* Magazine that came to hand. (It and others were being sold now in Naples.) It was *"the story of the oilmen's opposition to the trans-Asia-Mediterranean pipe-line. It is so obviously a case of a few men racketeering against our interests and the people. If they get out, the Russians and the British will do exactly what they would have done."* The other gripe was the bumbling over Palestinian independence.

> *I am more than ever convinced that an independent Palestinian state would be a good thing. For the United States, in that area, a friendly advanced state would be helpful (since we aren't especially interested in empire there, but others are). For a most sweeping settlement of the Jewish problem which is as simple as it is misunderstood (I am not ideologically a Zionist). For the development of that area, which would help the benighted and misguided Arabs. While I'm warmed up on the subject, you might send a check for ten dollars or so to that committee for a free Palestine."* (May 8)

I have not been saying enough of the Home Front. You must realize by now, should you not have known before, that half the Army lives half its life mentally voyaging four thousand miles away. Utterly foreign to American military experience was the Army without home ties. Think of it: they would seem to be zombies. I was writing now to Jill that her letters were "the nuclear element in my life," and they certainly became more so as they enlarged in number and regularity to describe the Home Front and life with an infant.

She sent pictures of herself and Kathy (though a great beauty, she always showed to disadvantage in pictures, but not her baby!):

> *I showed the pictures to three neurotic and unattractive English girls at lunch today and they said you are both beautiful. The poor things are in Italy for a rest cure I guess... Granted they do succeed in doing very necessary typing and one of them, Rowina Vining, a little, dumpy Irish girl, is very intelligent. Unfortunately every woman I see actually makes me more angry that she isn't you.*

I had also, however, to answer her inquiry about the problems of sexual abstinence during our prolonged period of separation, an inquiry prompted no doubt by a justifiably incomplete belief in my continence.

> *Now to answer the sixty-four dollar question. Do I find it difficult to get along without a woman, specifically you? Well, taking the query component by component, every letter I send you is an affirmative answer to the `specifically you' part. As for getting along without woman simply, there is a natural safety valve the male fortunately possesses when the biological accretion gets pressing. It's annoying but effective, even though it disturbs one's sleep. So that's the answer to your inquisition, there are day-dreams, some glimpses of women (there's a universal appeal about a flash of legs and swirling skirt), letters from the woman, pictures of Her and pictures of others, night dreams and nocturnal emissions that I mentioned above. You can well say that these are all frustrating nasty bits of life. But I am not defending them. They are typical of most men in the Army, and some think of them less and some more. And so strange a thing is the human mind, its habits, fancies, failure to distinguish between reality and fiction, indistinguishability between actual experience and sensual experience, its unconscious adaptation to sensual famine by creating the food for its own appetite, and especially in the sexual, so indisputably*

> mental is the sexual experience, that actually life is tolerable and doesn't become divided into blacks and whites on the basis of when one was getting it and when one was not. And then, of course, the more active one is, the more work he does, the less he is physically uncomfortable.

Fine words, fine ideas, but not the whole truth. I have already shown my sexual dormancy for what it was: a lazing tomcat that could suddenly spring alive.

Ian Greenlees was dining in a fancy night club. Robbie went along. Also I. A notorious Italian playboy, charming and suave, was at table, his relationship to Ian quite mysterious. But then too, an incredibly beautiful woman accompanied him. My buddies were not interested in women for their bodies. I was. After several glasses of wine, I was getting ready to climb over the table upon her. Pasta, quail, more wines, flambeaus. Greenlees, I beseech, *sotto voce:* who is Toni, who is Gloria, how are they related, she is smiling engagingly at me, what shall I do?

Greenlees merely chortles and gestures magnanimously, no problem, I'm sure... I turned to Robbie: Robbie, she is amazingly beautiful, don't you think? How would Robbie know: the lovelier, the worse, so far as he is concerned. I went to the toilet, stumbling over my third leg. Greenlees is murmuring to Toni, always murmuring he was, whether secretive or in anger or commanding, but when informing or discussing rationally he spoke in a normal louder voice - Greenlees and the playboy burst out laughing.

They all laughed, the girl smiled, and I grinned, too, because I could see that everyone was enjoying the proverbial spectacle of the deprived soldier with a few drinks under his belt. Amazingly, they all turned to me, urging me on, saying, why not? Why not? Gloria, the principal, after all, was herself laughing and obviously interested.

The party could not break up soon enough for me, and I ended up in her apartment in the center of Naples, in her bed - either Toni was supporting my evening, or she was, or she was an heiress or a war widow or a super-courtesan. Whatever she may have been otherwise, in the here and now she was the most deliciously curvaceous of any woman I would ever have occasion to envelop.

With all I have drunk and my sexual intensity, I am lucky to come off, and again in the dawn, and am too fast and don't play around enough. I probably would have deserved to be kicked out of bed, but there must have been something to the lithe body, the Americano, the stereotypical young officer, that even got to a sophisticated woman, to a sensitive woman, which perhaps Gloria was not quite.

Gloria was a pretty sight in the sobriety of morning, too, I was glad to discover. I dropped in on her once more; she swished around smooth and curved like a seal; I brought her a carton of her favorite Chesterfields and a PX eau de cologne. Withal that she was cast in the ultra-feminine ideal and was a decent, gentle person too, I was not enthralled and anyway must get along. The Front was cracking and it was time to write some special orders to get me up and into Rome. *"Arrivederci, cara Gloria!"*

On the Eighteenth May, the Abbey fell to the Poles. On May 23, I was back in the field with, this time, a remarkable driver, Alfredo Segre, a corporal in the Army Engineers, who had been a translator for the General heading a regiment of engineers. Someone had pried him loose on the plea of an emergency, and he must return soon enough. He was an author of novels and a political publicist, an American now, a refugee from Fascism, whether because of communism, socialism, Jewishness, or general opposition to the regime, I did not know nor asked. He has knocked around, a solid type, well-built, not talkative, ruddy-faced. (Much later, his book would come to hand, *Mahogany,* a powerful novel of Central Africa.)

We proceeded into the newly liberated area of Gaeta, a fine Bay that perhaps should have been a debarkation point in the very beginning of the Italian campaign. Elements of the Fifth Army Team were there. Men came running in as I arrived, a mine had exploded beneath an American soldier who, with several others, had been bathing in the sea; our men had pulled him out. They should get a medal for heroism, Lieutenant; put them in for a medal.

I did think that they were brave and deserving of a medal, although I never thought about medals and had no idea of how they were given out. But I never got around to filling out whatever papers were involved. I had to get going. Although I did not stress the issue, because it would only stir up indignation, I wondered mildly, deliberating, at how lucky they had been not to be blown up themselves, rushing in like that to drag out the crippled soldier. What would the medics do, creep into the waves with a stretcher? Medics had the highest casualty rate behind riflemen and Lieutenants. They died on these occasions, rather frequently in fact. Corpses could be booby-trapped, too. What is foolhardiness? Should it be discounted or discouraged? It's a riddle; what's the answer? Lacking a firm answer, I let the matter slip out of mind; so it was not just a matter of filling out papers.

Pushing ahead, Segre and I drove through the collapsing Tyrrhenian Coastal Front. The Americans had taken to the Coastal roads with ponderous armor. The French Expeditionary Force, which accomplished the breakthrough, was sent into the mountainous area between the coastal roads and infamous Highway #6, so long blocked at Cassino. The "French" troops were mostly French-led Moroccans and Algerians, and a rough lot they were. The French had not been long in Italy and felt little sympathy for the Italians, a feeling that conveyed itself readily to their colonials, who anyhow regarded looting, rape, and the killing of unfriendlies (whether in uniform or civilian) as combat pay.

We steered our jeep into the hills on a detour. (The country was the same that you penetrate by a broad smooth Autostrada today.) It had suddenly grown quiet, only a few heavy vehicles, with no firing to be heard. We moved slowly, passing among swarthy, helmeted, long-gowned *goumiers,* often indistinguishable from the soil and stone when resting. We saw a line of women at one village, then another at the next. Some were weeping. They hardly appeared liberated. Was food so short here? I wondered. Actually, they were in line for medical examination. They had been raped. They needed treatment. Some wanted testimony, also, that their virginity had been violated - for when they would marry.

I was incensed, Segre even more so. Segre urged me to do something! I thought I knew what to do. Get a report into "D" Section - to Ian Greenlees, Edmund and Hubert Howard, Albert Spalding and the others. They would stick it properly into the

Generals' hierarchy - Alexander, Clark, Juin, who would not wish the Nazi and Fascist propagandists of Rome and the North to play the story, nor the Home Front press.

More immediately, I sighted a couple of French officers at their command post, a café table amidst bombing debris, and decided to speak to them. So that I might speak bluntly, I sent Segre off in the jeep to scout the village above, and joined the Frenchmen. Your attack was *splendide,* I tell them, *vraiment brave,* and so it was: unlike any of the Allies except the Poles, the French knew the meaning of *"toujours l'attaque."* Too bad they had not spearheaded the Cassino operation from the beginning.

They spoke of Paris before the War, and I spoke of women - then, naturally, of these poor women being raped by their "goumes." They apologize: "We know... But things are improving. We just shot two of our men ..."

Segre returned, his face swollen with suppressed excitement. He could hardly wait to get me away before exclaiming: "There is a couple from Rome in hiding, the farmers told me, in a shack up there. They are writers." He thought he knew who they were. "Their name sounded like 'Moravia.'" The name meant nothing to me; Segre was a little disappointed.

"Let's go, then," I said. We drove up a steep path, in and out of woods, and must stop short of the hut indicated by a farm woman and climb by foot. The woman ran ahead yelling excitedly. We were, of course, armed to the teeth, and the pounding on the door and the sight of us might have been distressing. *"Siamo Americani,"* said Segre, and a most complicated expression overcame the faces of the couple inside, incredulity, relief, wonder, and still, some fear, because the *Americani* were the ones who had just destroyed the magnificent Abbey of Montecassino and were laying waste much of the country by land, sea and air.

I looked first more at the woman than at the man. She was Elsa Morante, all right - so she informed us - wearing a shapeless dress and old shoes; her hair was a curly light-brown, uncombed, with intimations of grey, though she looked young. She had a smooth round sweet face, a soft buxom figure. Now that she smiled, with even teeth that were parted in the middle, what she conveyed was a mild and generous soul.

Alberto Moravia, her husband, who was answering Segre's questions, was a head taller than she, well put together, save for a gimpy leg, he was a bit slumped of shoulder, and of a somewhat satanic countenance, that refused to transform itself pleasantly. His lips were tight, his jaw clenched, his attitude grim. When he smiled, he might be sincere, but you would never be sure. He appeared to be retaining secrets. Intelligent from all appearances, he either could not or would not express all he knew or felt. Just now, he had every reason to feel anxious and fearful, but now and ever after he seemed to be expecting the worst, and to be suspicious of good fortune.

I handed him a cigarette and seated him down. Segre interrogated him further. Segre's own feelings had been declared on the way up. At least some of them. He wondered whether Moravia had not been collaborating with the Fascists: how else could he have spent the war years in comfort? Moravia, partly Jewish by origin, had always rejected identification as a Jew, which was his own business, to my way of thinking, but the Nazi lexicon had finally caught up with him. True, now, he might fall victim to the Neo-Fascists and Gestapo, but, before then, whose friend was he? The question was whether a person, particularly an intellectual, should be adjudged guilty for having subsisted under a totalitarian regime relatively undisturbed. Segre adduced no hard evidence. Nothing Moravia answered or said - nor certainly his gentle moon-faced Sicilian - could be fashioned into a condemnation.

Segre had only been with me for a couple of days and nights, but this was already a lot of togetherness, under the circumstances - worth a month of café encounters. Much had been spoken and noticed. I gathered that Segre would have liked to arrest Moravia and finally even have him tried in court on the title of his first novel, *The Indifferent,* and on the basis of his several other works, too, that spoke against the Fascists only in ways that even ordinary Italians could employ, according to Segre, with words that only in retrospect and among the unknowledgeable or forgiving could be considered anti-Fascist. Segre, that is, presented himself as a committed guy, whereas Moravia did not. And, Segre asked, where were the denunciations of Nazism and racism during the increasingly terrible years from 1932 to 1944, twelve years of silence?

Moravia had never been politically committed and could not put on a big act for our benefit. Segre wished for more but would have settled on punishing him for indifference alone. To their credit, Morante and Moravia did not defend profusely their thoughts or conduct; they did not plead a case; nor for that matter were they being accused.

The situation descended to this: They could stay hidden where they were and risk murder and rape, and French or American gunfire and strafing, or even a German counter-attack, bringing with it the Gestapo and, worse, the desperate Neo-Fascists, killers who find informants everywhere. But, if all went well, when Rome fell, they could manage the journey home. Or, perhaps with help, they could move with greater safety behind the American lines, and scrounge around as best they could until Rome was freed.

I broached still another option; I could deliver them to "D Section" at the Palazzo Caracciolo in Naples, where, if they proved themselves useful, they might go to work for the Allied cause. I had little doubt that this would be possible. I did not want to hurt the feelings of Segre, who was right in his own way, if inordinately exigent, and who, although the truer hero, would soon be back dogging it for some Engineer General.

I had in mind a plan that required trusting Segre. For myself, I was intent upon getting to Rome. But I could and did write a letter to Major Greenlees, explaining my action, to be delivered by Segre upon arrival, along with the report on the case of the raped women and other notes. I gave the Moravias, too, a letter, signed by myself, cavalierly authorizing them, in the name of the Commanding Officer of Intelligence, G2, Fifth Army (American), and of Operations (G3), Eighth Army (British), to travel by military conveyance from the battle zone to Headquarters, "D Section," AFHQ, Naples. I figured that this trick, logically defensible were I to be called on the carpet about it, was needed, lest otherwise the trio might be arrested en route and disappear from sight; moreover, the jeep with them, would be returned, if at all, as a wreck.

Moravia jotted a message for his relatives in my ragged little notebook, finding space amidst a welter of notations dealing with my prior mission to Sardinia: "At Via Donizetti 6, our relatives, the Pincherle-Moravia's live (telephone 80592). Please, if possible, inform them that they are well, they will return as soon as permitted and they beg them to keep an eye on our house and to keep it ready for our return." This would be Via Sgambati 9.

We drove over to Highway 7, where the American II Corps was thrusting Northwards. There I turned them South, wished them well, and got out. I caught a ride up and into the Anzio beachhead, which had finally burst open along this road the day before. I located the cave where several members of the Combat Propaganda Team had been holed up, following the unhappy blasting of the across-the-line crew by German artillery and machine-gun fire. They were eating rotten food, but deep in the cave Sergeant Harrari was playing fine music on some patched-up equipment. Our own Duke Ellington was there, along with several others. The food was bad. Shells had been arriving now and then near the mouth of the cave.

The Germans were covering their retreat from Cassino. The Front was degenerating, but as usual the Germans knew just the right tactics for pulling out their troops before the clumsy and un avid allied troops could catch them in a trap. Here was where the French troops should have been used. The French were more daring than any of the others and were very ready to attack and pursue. But this was a bureaucratic army. The French were pushed out of the way. You have to follow orders. Now here, you move up, now there, you move up, no, wait, not too far, and so on. It's a hell of a way to fight a war, I thought, but then I was not leading the attack. Nevertheless, Allied troops were moving massively up Highway #6. There was little fear of air attack.

The Germans were first thought to be defending Rome, then it became apparent that they would do civilization the favor of not fighting through the City. They did allow themselves the right to retreat through it, and the SS and the Neofascists committed some barbarities before fleeing. Yet the absence of an enemy did not faze the Allies in entering and establishing a passel of offices.

Mark Clark need not have marched through Rome. He was

intent upon it, though. He was especially eager to do so quickly, because he knew a secret: that world headlines and radios on June 6, just two days off, would scream, "Landings in France!" It was a costly useless unmilitary gimmick, another victory handed the Germans who escaped around Rome and out of Rome, half-heartedly pursued, actually crossing a couple of Tiber bridges farther North that the innumerable Allied planes had not hit, and uniting thus their dispersed Armies.

As for the Liberation of Rome, it was a great party which I desired as badly as my vainglorious General. Since I had little idea then of the General's tactics, I could not be blamed; in fact, I had a real job to do in Rome: "D Section" and all of that.

The night before the Liberation of Rome found me in a field outside the city with two men. No one had gotten in yet, but the rumor was that American troops will snatch the honor, General Clark being so insistent upon it. You sensed that there were great armies breathing somewhere nearby, but just where we were it was fairly quiet. It was remarkable how you could step aside from the Allies' 4000 aircraft, 1900 tanks, 10,000 cannon, 20,000 trucks, 23 divisions, 67,000 riflemen of 182 battalions, a total of 675,000 men grousing about the center of Italy. Not to mention their scanty match, the German forces, fielding one-tenth the number of tanks, aircraft, cannon, one-twentieth the ammunition, one-twentieth the trucks, one-third the riflemen, one-third the soldiers, practically all of these passing around and through Rome at the moment. It all had been a bloody battle for the small units, at the fifty fiery points of contact of the past ten days, where half of those engaged had become casualties. This has been the "real" war.

Another set of casualties had randomly befallen, Germans mostly, from long-range artillery and dive-bombers. The Allied forces, so huge and potentially mobile, were tripping over themselves, while the Germans were plodding up the roads ahead by whatever means could be found, under constant aircraft attack. There seemed to be no way the jammed-up British could catch up with them. Or the French, who had been side-tracked. Or the Americans, who were enticed into the Liberation of Rome at the price of letting the enemy disengage and escape.

Naples, Sardinia, Anzio 299

There are two main roads and several minor ones. They all lead to Rome, of course. I choose Highway #7. Darkness. Rumor had it that a German rearguard with Panzers and *Panzerfausts* and *Nebelwerfers* and *Schmauzers* was blocking the road ahead. Unlikely... Still, who would want to get into Rome in the middle of night? Nothing would be open. I found a small stone cabin littered with electrical junk and we occupy it, possibly for sleeping, anyhow for refuge in the event of bombing or a smashing runover by one of the friendly tanks or half-tracks lumbering about.

The night continued quiet. Then voices. I heard voices in what sounded like German. I called halt in three languages, moving my position with each translation, then fired a couple of shots unenthusiastically in their general direction. Amicide, enemy... who knows. A plane came over and dropped a couple of bombs at a safe distance. Amicidal? Or enemy? Hell will freeze over before the "Stars and Stripes" or "Union Jack" mention that U.S. P-40's have just knocked out a hundred Americans of that Third Division Column at Valmonte; or the "cooperative effort" by German and American artillery to decimate yet another U.S. infantry battalion; or the repeated strafing of the First Armored Division by friendlies; or the U.S. strafing of the French at the very gates of Rome.

A figure, American by silhouette, moved over from the road. "What the fuck you shooting at, you want to catch enemy fire?" Argument ensued. Enemy was looking to escape, not fight! Civilians... they didn't count much. (There is a contradiction in Tactical Doctrine: you find the enemy by making him open fire and then call down your pieces upon him; but, don't give your position away. The answer: fire, then move; nice trick if you can manage it; apropos, don't step on a mine. Corollary: if you don't open fire, you are useless. Fact is, a lot of soldiers are continuously useless unless forced to fire.) Anyhow, there was no room at the inn for this dark character; let him fuck off into the night; he didn't, though; he curled up nearby. I and my two men lay in the hut. Then I moved out to several yards away from the hut and slept better; I didn't want to be grenaded through the window of this nutshell.

At dawn we climbed into our jeep and joined the stream of vehicles that was converging from all directions to enter the city.

The Romans were up, dressed in their finest, and out on the street, a million of them. The streets became crowded. Dusty cloth, canvas, metal were polished by the pressing people. They climbed up on the vehicles shouting and cheering. Kids rode cannon barrels. Out of the crowd, a young woman and her friends fixed themselves upon me. This will be Bianca Moffa, a slant-eyed, dark-haired Neapolitan beauty, with the figure of a Minoan bull-dancer. A blonde slender man was with her, he will be her husband, Paolo. Someone else, too, Bruno Leonardi. *"Su!"* I call to them, with an inviting smile, and they climb into the back and upon the hood. They directed me to their elegant, modern apartment building. The archetypical scenario: all the insignia of the Liberation surrounded me, human and material. The dream of the soldier: to capture and be captivated by the Eternal City.

A very cold bath in a very Sardinian stream. 1944.

With village elders in Ozieri, Sardinia

CHAPTER TWELVE

THE LIBERATION OF ROME

THE hurry-scurry and tiffs among the Generals to get into Rome and be photographed was *opera buffa*. Several were nearly killed, whether by enemy or friendly fire. A small special force under General Frederick, who should not have been there, was clearing a bridge of mines. Approached from the other side by a small force under General Kendall of the 88th Division - he shouldn't have been there either - the two forces shot at each other and men were killed and wounded, including Frederick, before the amicide was stopped. Not until the afternoon of June 5 did all hostile obstruction and sniping quit. By then, the City was infiltrated by a score of processions, one from every lane of entry, whence flowing out into every street. Wave upon wave of trucks and guns washed through. Fifty thousand soldiers marched at route step, dragging their feet, pausing, gawking, camping, eating, drinking, dispersing. There was no looting. Onto the streets poured many thousands of young Italians who had been hiding from the Neo-Fascist and German conscription gangs.

These were glorious hours, the greatest triumph of Allied arms in the West, the moments when the ordinary soldier could grasp what he might be fighting for, beautiful cities wrested from a cruel foe, innocent girls in clean dresses, imposing boulevards and vast cafés, churches so grand, with Christs and Marys so sublime, that the hill-billy Baptist might begin to doubt that God was a bedouin. Rome was taken in a glorious spirit. Because everything was in such good order, the soldiers behaved themselves. Because so little had been destroyed, they destroyed nothing. Because the people needed less food, they received more. The soldiers were so happy to find so wonderful a city that they believed the people must be admirable, even virtuous; hence they deserved better than those others they had seen on the way up the Boot of Italy whose ruins, rags, hunger, shivering, opportunism, and depression proved their unworthiness.

For days celebration continued. Once more the population went on promenade. Genuine partisans and freebooters tramped the streets in search of Fascists. There was sorrow and rage to support them: in the last weeks there had been roundups of Jews and murders of anti-Fascists. My jeep was blocked by a cluster of people, who had in hand a man they shouted was a dirty Fascist. They would have liked him to be killed on the spot. I glanced the man up and down. Could be. I could not stop to handle him. "Hey, soldier," I said to a loitering G.I. "Go with these people to the nearest M.P. post or police station and turn him in." The soldier said: "Yes, Sir!" but who knows: he was probably A.W.O.L. from his unit.

A large number of Allied soldiers were gadding about the City. I reckon that the Fifth Army must have lost at least temporarily a division of troops just by passing through Rome. Rome had been promptly declared off-limits to the troops but there could be no stemming of this initial tide of the awe stricken and hilarious. Repeatedly I was accosted by a soldier with: "Sir, can you tell me where my outfit is?" "What is your outfit?" "The First Armored." "They're all gone North, I think, I don't know, try the M.P.'s." Not likely. His conscience appeased for another day, the soldier wandered off.

Meanwhile the battle had moved North. Thanks to the vainglorious Clark and all those taking cues from him, including the French, the two German armies that should have been isolated and destroyed, fled up the Tiber Valley until they found an undestroyed crossing and joined forces. The line would not settle down until the Germans ceased their retreat short of Florence and built a defense across the peninsula.

Bianca Moffa put me up in a kind of sun-room. From there I went out upon the street, helped the others find a billet by the newspaper plant of *Il Messagero,* and discovered the staff of *Stars and Stripes* already inside readying their first Rome edition. There was little for me to do; I loitered outside thinking where next to stick my nose; a blonde girl, she was of course beautiful, stood nearby looking calmly at the comings and goings. *"Buon giorno"* and all of that - her name was Clara Unghy, she lived next door, *"Grazie, non fumo,"* but, yes, she would like to have lunch with me tomorrow, meeting me here, she knew where we might eat well, she was calm and unpretentious, with not a flicker of flirtation, plainly dressed. By the next day I had a hotel room, the lunch was excellent, the siesta was put to good purpose: we were lovers; I counted her in on things, I knew where I could find her.

Bianca introduced me all around, to Giovanni Makaus, for instance, with whom I became friends. He was an Italian naval commander, now wearing civilian clothes, who was in hiding in Rome and worked for Italian Intelligence. Bianca would like me to be her acknowledged lover, but there were Clara and Paolo - would it have been proper? I moved out of Bianca's nook but not from her circle. Nearly every evening there was some party with her friends.

PWB Naples had come up in force - day by day trucks arrived. John Reynor was in charge of operations; Lt. Col. Culligan was military head. I found it no problem to be under two bosses, especially since neither gave me any orders and I stayed in "D Section," for the time being. I lamented the loss of my jeep, which had been turned in to the motor pool by general order. I went onto the street and seized a halted car, signed for the owner a slip of paper telling him that he could apply for compensation at some future date. It was one way of getting transport, and also a form of looting. I had my eyes set upon a full garage of cars, in fact, and envisioned my comrades driving about town in style, but when I showed up to make the final arrangement for requisitioning the lot, a blustering Air Corps Lieutenant had preceded me and waved convincing hunting licenses in my face, so I slunk off humiliated.

I lent my seized car to Gianni Makaus who drove it to Ostia near where he had concealed his uniform and valuables when the Germans took over and he had gone underground; his watch and most of the other stuff was retrieved. He also brought back with him a batch of fresh sole, the most delicious fish that I, quite deprived of seafood, could ever have tasted. But the car I had seized was stolen by persons unknown, probably by its owner. I wondered whether the man would ultimately be compensated for the car on the basis of his piece of paper, while having the car as well. Now I had to use cabs or the motor pool of the newly established HQ of PWB, a handsome modern office building next to the hotel where the personnel lived and ate.

Soon, however, I rented an apartment with a garden, not far away. Rome was still a manageable city. One could walk from one end to the other in the course of the morning. As soon as I moved in, I threw a party for the old gang, combined a little differently into a new gang: Brown Roberts (he never did leave the theater), Rowina Vining, the clever Irish girl who carried on now as a kind of office manager for "D Section," Fred Annunziata, an Office of War Information radio engineer, Jack Collins from Manhattan and Seattle who had worked for the Associated Press, Gianni Makaus, Lt. Gasperini of the Italian artillery that was now attached to the Eighth Army, *et al.,* not to mention the aforesaid beautiful Hungarian, and more and more people, visitors from the Army Teams, and the Bianca set. It was really too much for me; I am not a socialite. At one gathering, somebody it might have been myself - tipsily tipped a gas lamp and set fire to the place. We put it out in short order, but the apartment would never be the same, thankfully.

Clara escorted me to a great Mass at St. Peter's Cathedral. Trucks from a hundred Army units pushed into the square. Never had such a sea of khaki swept over the flagstones and in through the grand doors. The Pope officiated. The crowd stood reverently still for the Alta Maggiore, one hour at least, a platoon of officiating priests, music, hymns, bells swirling their sounds through the air swallowing all human breath, so loud as to be tasted. Clara knew the Mass, the ritual, when to kneel, when to cross oneself, when to repeat the Latin and Greek. I merely imitated some of what she did. It may have been the first full Mass of my life. She looked so serene and lovely in profile; it made me fond of her; I hoped that she would not be praying for me to fall in love with her, to have my love for life.

When asked, she said she was a ballerina. She could have been:

her legs were sturdy; she walked well; she did not flinch at people, peek, engage in useless gestures. Anyhow, what else could a girl of twenty-three years in Rome in 1944 say that she was: it was either that or a student. Perhaps she could say that she worked in the movies, which at the moment were shut down. She lived with her mother in a small flat next to the Piazza Messagero. Her father was a Hungarian army officer last seen heading with the Fascists for the Russian Front and extinction. Clara had a beauty that only Hungarians, or so it has seemed to me at times, possess, a blondness without pink, suffused overall, brown eyes, a skin white and firm. She was quiet, even-tempered, honest, un-demanding, just the kind of person you would want to have around if life were hectic, you were cagey about flamboyant Italian women, you had important privileges to dispense, and you hoped to move on one of these days to points north, like Berlin, for instance.

She was not of the swinging set, too poor, too unconnected (Moffa directed films, Gasperini's mother was a countess and gave a nice tea party to us all -, Bianca's father was the petroleum distributer for Standard Oil in Naples, there was the daughter of Eli Culbertson, the great bridge expert who wrote, as I well knew, a good book on world government, and so on). But she carried herself perfectly and was well-liked by women who in a way envied her and might have disparaged her, and by men who might have chosen not to respect her.

As usual, I did damned little for her - and she probably needed a lot - except to introduce her as the occasion demanded, have her for meals whenever possible, take her to view a church - or did she take me? - walk about with her in the evenings, and provide a sexual partner who may or may not have been premier in her experience but probably was - at least she acted as if that had been the case. Somehow all the propaganda, circulating in both male and female circles, that a man must continually show his affections by gifts in order to please a woman, had not captured me. Perhaps the propaganda was false. The subject is fascinating. Perhaps what counted most was that I did not indulge myself materially. Not being greedy, I did not attract greed.

I would have been quite drowned in the almost purely Italian milieu if it had not been for occasional visitors haunting me from yesteryear. George Peck came to town and was my guest. Last seen at Pacific Palisades in California, with his wife Christine Palmer, at the home of my friends Giuseppe and Elizabeth Mann Borgese. (I happened to be finishing Giuseppe's latest book on the war and the peace to follow, *Common Cause;* I have just received a letter from him as well.)

George was apparently sane but quite mad. His wife Christine was as good a proof as you'd want of his inner psyche; she was a dramatic actress and had been a wheel of the University of Chicago's sophisticated student carriage set. She took George just where he wanted to go, light years away from *Peck and Peck, Clothiers.*

Now George recounted to me a horrendous story about a mutual friend from the University of Chicago, Dieter Dux, who, largely because his father was a German in high office, and because his mother, an American, had some peculiar notions and a high social standing, was suspected by the pro-Allied group at the University of being pro-German; George said that Dieter escaped army duty, fled to Mexico and was last seen in Berlin. I registered the story, could not help but recount it to Jill in a letter about George's visit, angrily denounced Dieter, who was my friend, but fortunately heard contradictory news of Dieter soon and wrote back home quickly, this time denouncing George. So the slander did not reach far.

"D Section" sent me over to handle the Press at the inauguration of the new Italian Government on June 9. Badoglio had resigned and Ivanoe Bonomi, who had been once Premier before Mussolini seized power, became once again Prime Minister. He was a nonentity. The strongest member of the new Cabinet was Alcide De Gasperi. There was a hullabaloo at the ceremony, photographers, Ministers, reporters. De Gasperi spoke out in exasperation: "What's going on? This is too much! Begin the meeting!" I tried to get the cameramen in and out. *"Patienza!"* I exclaimed to De Gasperi and everyone else within earshot. It was a cliché dear to Italian speech, used for all occasions. Coming from a young American officer, it made De Gasperi laugh. It eased the tension. The scene quieted. The First Democratic Government of

Italy at Rome since the Fascist Revolution could begin.

John Reynor, now heading up the "propaganda ministry" of the Allies, had acquired Stephen Pallos, an Anglo-Hungarian film director, who was to be in charge of the Italian film industry. Pallos and I got along well; the job needed a military man; so John asked me whether I would like a transfer over to films. It sounded good, and I set up shop with Steve: "I vorked with Villie Vyler." He looked like a crook. Didn't appear to be doing anything. Still, he was cheerful, voluble. There's never a dull moment with Hungarians.

I became an attractive nuisance. At once beset by Italian film producers and directors for licenses to produce films. Nobody had a notion of relating to the Greatest War in the History of the World. They trotted me around to enjoy excellent meals. They sent to me starlets to offer themselves as assistants, secretaries or whatever, despatched to help the war effort by Direttore Greco or some other such ex-*Cinecittà* nabob or would be such. I asked one of them, sitting demurely before me: "You were sent by Signor Greco to be my friend and help him get a license for a film, *nevvero?*" She smiles winningly and says: *"Sì, è vero. Però..."*

Bianca and Paolo Moffa laughed at my stories. Paolo was a little to the side of the mad scramble, never asked for anything, had done documentaries for the Vatican. I did not succumb to Bianca's lures; nor was she bashful to employ them; she had the black slanting Neapolitan eyes that must come from the neolithic Mediterraneans. Or maybe a recent Circassian, as simple as that. I wrote Jill on her behalf: Dear Jill, I have this friend, see, who would love and embellish a good pair of American shoes and here is her footprint, and Jill should know that I would never send her a request for a gift for a lover of mine; still, somehow, the package of shoes for Bianca never arrived.

Better than many another happening, Elsa Morante eventually appeared at my office, courtesy of "D Section," and, with her, Alberto, grim as before, and I asked her, "Will you work with me on films?" to which she responded, "On what films?" "Oh, I don't know... A film on partisans!" And Elsa consented. We enjoyed several pleasant gatherings in those halcyon days of the Liberation.

The Liberation of Rome

On Bastille Day, more from coincidence than out of regard for the French Revolution, I went to a large party with Alberto and Elsa at the home of the Painter Severini's daughter. Capogrosso was there, with other *pezzi grossi*. The Moravias had taken up again their former lives in Roma but with the new strong connection with the outside world through "D Section." They were, as I had expected that they would when I sent them South, doing some work for the Allies. Alberto was, of course, typically ungrateful: he must have been quite spoiled by over-indulgence and inner rage accompanying his childhood infantile paralysis.

A Director of well-known films arrived and Steve and I talked with him. He wanted desperately to begin work on a film. Look, he said to us, if you think that I am a Fascist, why would I risk my life in crossing the lines to put myself in your hands? I never said, I told him, that opportunists lack courage. He got angry. But what could I do? It was not a matter of killing. Some things were.

Professor Hartshorne arrived. He was in OSS, though he didn't say so, and got attached to PWB headquarters. I am naturally drawn to professors. An informant told me, Hartshorne was dealing with some of the worst Fascists. Confirmation extended from another source. Watch out, I told Hartshorne, I have bad news on this, or that guy. Hartshorne resented the information. Sometime later (I could wait for six months of the story to tell you this, but I want to show right now my perspicacity) I heard that Hartshorne died, mysteriously murdered. I was in no position to follow up the report. I was far away.

What we needed, I said to Steve Pallos, as shifty-eyed, physically unimpressive, over-verbal, and unconvincing a chap as ever you might encounter on the side streets of Istanbul - but all ears, so you can sense his intelligence - was a film to help the war effort, on the activities of the partisans in Italy. Great, said Steve, and off we go signing up people for a film on partisans.

Not content with a lovely fictional set-up amidst the rapidly coagulating bloody Hollywood atmosphere, it occurred to me that we must have fresh live footage on partisan activities on the other side of the Front. "D Section," to which I regularly referred, though I was no longer a member, collected a continuous stream of reports of resistance activities in the North, of trains derailed, power plants destroyed, electric lines cut, enemy soldiers killed, industrial sabotage, and so on; indeed we were the best informed people in Italy about Italian affairs in German-occupied Italy. On June 19, General Kesselring, Commander of German forces in Italy, had issued to his officers a license to murder:

> *The partisan situation in the Italian theater...constitutes a serious danger to the fighting troops and their supply lines as well as to the war industry and economic potential. The fight against the partisans must be carried on with all the means at our disposal and with the utmost severity.*
>
> *I will protect any commander who exceeds our usual restraint in the choice of severity of the methods he adopts against partisans...*

In consequence and for example, when partisans kill two German soldiers at the quaint village of Civitella della Chiana, in the province of Arezzo, SS troops appeared by surprise on June 29 and massacred all male inhabitants, 244 of them, and dynamited the houses. (A surviving infant will become many years later my son-in-law. His father and his grandfather were killed that day.)

I talked privately to Gianni about the film about partisans. Might you undertake to go with a camera across the lines and take some pictures of partisan action, and bring them back? One explosion, even if you have to blow up an appropriate target yourself, would make a film persuasive. Gianni unhesitatingly agreed. He himself might be able to commit the authentic act that would be the subject of the filming.

I had discovered a partner for him, a partisan, a red-faced Milanese engineer, Pietro Boni, who had just crossed the lines. It was typical: the man who had just done the heroic deed was the one who was turned around to do it again. Still, Gianni had his companion vetted by Italian Intelligence. He was probably a Communist. No problem. Togliatti had told the Communists to collaborate, not to destroy the existing coalition government.

I arranged a couple of days of training in the use of the camera equipment that I had bought for us on the open market. I went to

John Reynor for clearance and funds. How much do you need? About $2500.00 in old lira. O.K. He trusted me. One wondered whether he knew the odds. Fine. "I also need a car to take them up to the Front Line." O.K. I got a car alright. It was a new English jeep, right-hand drive. I was afraid to look its lamps in the eye, for fear its axles might buckle. Its metal had been stretched to the thinness of paper before fashioning it into a vehicle. It had a two-wheel drive. Its tires were as delicate as Cinderella's slippers.

The Northern Front was fluid. Fermo and Perdaso fell to the Eighth Army on 20 June. Foligno was liberated on 16 July. Ancona with its seaport and communications was taken by the Poles in a three-day battle between 17 and 19 July. Somewhere in-between Ancona and Lake Trasimeno ran the Central Front, over which I intended to pass the two men, then wish them well. Before the three of us left, John's last words were: "Alfred, you will not, I trust, be gone for long. Not over the lines, mind you."

Morning became evening and we were following first one and then another of the poor roads that paralleled the Front, going beyond Lago Trasimeno, heading East. The last outpost of which we inquired said they did not know, and could not locate on the map where the enemy might be. That was not unexpected. No two Fronts are ever the same. Soldiers may lay in swarms at one point, as thick as bedbugs, while the enemies may be separated beyond mortar fire distance at some other point - as in this case. We were on the main ridge of the Apennines, the forest was dense, the underbrush heavy. It was a hell of a place to let off two men on foot with equipment, men not trained as forest rangers either. Men who would be shot if taken, or equally easily shot by friendly soldiers.

We camped for the night on a hillside, with a wood and brook below. The slope resembled more the Sierra Nevadas of California than fabled rustic Italy. There was the usual little stone cabin, without windows, with a crooked door. I looked in. We can stay here, I said, but I don't want to sleep inside. We will, they said, it's better than out in the cold. I thought, well, let them sleep inside, I can be of help out here if any strangers happen by, and I don't like filth, and probably bugs. I was nonetheless in poor shape. The grippe that had seized me that morning had progressed into a feverish influenza. At least I would be able to breathe and cough and thrash about outdoors.

The night passed. My flu had worsened. My comrades emerged, Gianni eaten up by insects. On our way once more. I explained now the problems as I saw them of getting past the lines in this area. Too, that I had found out the OSS had no agents hereabouts who might help. That we should continue driving until we reached the coast where I had heard that OSS had a band working into both Italy and Yugoslavia.

The roads were bad. I hit a pothole and the car made an appalling noise, then began to thump every now and then as if to say, from here on we are going at my speed not yours.

We descended to the sea below Ancona, which was falling to the Poles. There we located the OSS agents. They had boats operating, one that same night. They would take Gianni and Pietro by sea to enemy-held territory, and put them ashore where they would hopefully find their way through enemy territory and ultimately join up with a band of partisans. Good-bye. Good luck. *Ciao. Buon fortuna.*

Slowly, painfully, sick and dog-tired, I proceeded on the way to Rome. The car was in a poor state, worse than myself. How I hated it! And I could find no motor pool to fix it. Junk it, I was told! I still got it across the mountains into the city. All in all, some 600 miles, with 8 hours sleep in all. Ergo I slept. I arose. I decided to put in a show at my office.

Reynor wanted to see me, when, and if, I returned. "How did it go?" "O.K., I suppose. We'll see." He said: "Alfred, there is an important business coming up, and it may be the sort of thing you like."

Every bell rang in me! I knew what was coming. They are asking us for somebody like you, said John in substance. It is up to you. If you want to go, you can go.

I will go, no doubt. Goodbye, John, let me know! Goodbye, Steve! Smiles. Goodbye, "D Section," heartfelt fare-thee-wells and see-you-agains. I didn't fully appreciate how final was this parting from dear friends. Elsa Morante was still in my office when I left,

The Liberation of Rome

holding the line for integrity, I am inclined to say, though she may have been too shy. I had seen already so much mal-administration in my brief career that I wished to regain the life of chaos where no apology was needed. It was easier and more outgoing, and therefore more fun.

Good-by Clara, gentle smiles, gentle hugs, I took her home in my car, left with her whatever little was of use from my month-old residence, saw her last beneath the large sign of *Il Messagero*. I owned somebody's fine shot-gun, in a barracks bag full of the kind of possessions I had gathered over time with some discrimination, and I left this all with the supply officer, whence it will be forever gone.

On July 27 I wrote Jill to hint that a new invasion would soon be underway and that I would be leaving these parts. At the moment I was encamped South of Naples. I had lots of time to deliver myself of pronunciamentos on higher education, among other things. Hutchins, I said, wanted to teach people to think first and foremost and that was the basis of education. But see what had happened. A foremost thinker of my close acquaintance, Mortimer Adler, had gone all-out for the good war and victory. Hutchins himself had remained restrained, skeptical, almost isolationist, the mark of Goethe heavy upon his forehead. And Milton Mayer, his disciple of the Great Books, had become a conscientious objector and a pacifist.

I went on to tell her that her former boss at *Coronet-Esquire Magazine,* Oscar Dystal, had shown up and partaken of my board. I had also met Major Rathbun and gone to the Naples Opera with him. A youngster (probably of my own age, twenty-four, though you'd never know it) had arrived, classified 4-F (physically disqualified for military service), and asked all kinds of questions about what war was really like, and when pressed about why he didn't join the Army, said, and he truly meant the old cliché, "give me a gun, I'm ready to fight anytime," and they all laughed at this.

Hank Miller and Jay Toberty, Illinoisans, have come, I have seen them, I have seen them! There were times in Naples when I felt that I was in Chicago, on campus, or at City Hall, or must be at the Neapolitan-Sicilian neighborhood of the West Side where the wine gurgles red out of a barrel and the air is hanging heavy on Dago

Rope.

There would be no "D Section" in the campaign to come. "D Section" would remain in Italy. Almost no Brits were called for in the invasion of Provence. It would be American and French. However Captain Foster hitched on. He was Artillery, not Intelligence. The old group will always be part of me. They had marked my attitudes toward war, a way of receiving its experience, not self-pitying, but strongly ironic, as something expectable and contemptible. I had shared their respect for wit and humor, and for the comfortable life; they had been raised as *bon vivants,* educated to the tastes of the highest class in a society of strongly divided social classes.

They had had little awareness of a movement called Social Science and regarded it as a tolerable aberration of mine, a habit of mind, an eccentricity with which they, such eccentrics, could sympathize. Their respect for me, which with Robertson and Greenlees expanded into an avuncular affection and indulgence, given our large age differences, was for qualities that were American but which were unexpected and indeed would not be highly regarded in the American Army, of intellectualism, of regard for the arts and a quick adaptation to the art of living. With them, I became more human, broader, more tolerant, more skeptical, strangely more frank, less aggressive among acquaintances. I came to regard war as less of a monopoly of the bomb and bayonet. Perhaps this was actually a better way to win wars; it was certainly a way of enduring them.

They had given me a new attitude toward Europe. The American, whatever his origins, tended to regard Europe all the way from Cork, Ireland, to Omsk, Russia, and from Trondheim to Sicily, reproachfully and contemptuously. Their folk had had to leave Europe (and the same would apply for Africa) and they were unconsciously resentful at having been removed, rejected, and at the same time, most having left under their own will, they now felt superior to the oppressors and fools that had remained behind. I did not hear General George Patton's speech to the American troops on the eve of their landing in Sicily, where he reminded those of German and Italian descent, a large proportion of his force, how their forefathers had chosen a superior kind of life and possessed a superior virtue and spirit; I had not heard it because I was with the British Eighth Army; its reading came later. The speech received much criticism as representing prejudice and arrogance; Lieutenant De Grazia, when he read it, thought that it was well-suited to the occasion.

But this typically American attitude that I had possessed was heavily overwritten by the attitude of the small group of British with whom I had campaigned. They led me to an attitude toward Europe which was more affectionate, hardly superior, and enveloped happily in the process of cultural exchange on a fully personal as well as general political level.

When I arrived at my camp one night - when I chose, that is, not to stay out at the Pozzuoli PWB Hotel - I found that I had been assigned a French roommate, who was enormously excited at thoughts of returning to *La Patrie*. We drank toasts to his homecoming - my homecoming, too, for didn't Jefferson say that every American had two countries, his own and France? - the land of Lafayette, of the *Rive Gauche,* too. I felt towards him like my Dad, who would never go to bed until everyone in the family had gotten home and he could then lock the door. To usher everyone home free. It was the *noblesse oblige* of my Twentieth Century America.

I was optimistic. Optimism must have been deeply imprinted upon the Chicago Babe from infancy. I should now know better. I write to Jill - we have the proof of this in black on white - that all the moves of war , no matter how costly, are just sloppy chess, where the players exhaust all of their pieces and finally one player will end the game with a checkmate. Yet I arose from the writing table and my first thought was, let's get about winning this damned war! So it was time to take up one's pack and climb up the gangplank.

I bore an illicit extra bag with me, containing a cotton khaki uniform, a novel of Turgenev, extra cigarettes and soap and chocolates and whiskey. I thought, I shall never see half of my possessions and half of my friends again. At least I shall have these creature comforts. If I could get it all ashore, all to the good, if not, the sailors or the sea will have it - a whisper of *Kismet.*

Clara by a Roman fountain...

Chapter Thirteen

THE PROVENCE CAMPAIGN

THE assault ship was British, and the cabin, which contained bunks, gear and tea mugs, lodged for the nonce three officers. Captain Foster of His Majesty's "Lancaster Foot" still looked like an old hound dog, although his winter of dysentery along the Rapido River had long past. The third man was a stranger, a lieutenant of the Third American Infantry Division on his first voyage into the unknown. Then there was Lt. Alfred de Grazia, AUS, apparently in fine fettle, splashing himself sloppily from the two pots of hot bath water brought him by an Indian steward. That's the British: blah food but good personal service.

The sea breeze cooled the sense of mid-August. I dressed comfortably in the cotton uniform I had brought along in violation of orders. I had collected a lot of cigarettes, four cartons more than prescribed, and brought them along, too. A list of what must and might be carried had been issued from on high; all else was to be left behind. No gas mask: "That's something, Foster, what?" I would have in any event mailed off the thick pack of letters from home. I had stuffed them into the wooden cigar boxes I had acquired in Sardinia. Several I kept to represent my beloved until the next mail should arrive, if ever. I wondered whether I should have brought along the lovely 12-gauge shotgun I had confiscated but had left behind for an illusory safe-keeping. I hefted everything I had to carry, including my tommy-gun and 45-calibre sidearm, plus a German Walther 38-cal automatic, each with its special heavy packets of ammunition, jumped up and down a few times and folded in a couple of more cotton things and several indestructible English chocolate bars; hot woolens made my tender skin itch. I figured that if things got tough, I could dump the extras, but, if not, they could boost life's pleasure-pain ratio.

Calm seas, with many streams from many ships of different forms: I studied them through my binoculars and wished I might see them from the air. Hardly any friendly planes in the sky: they were probably routed off the flanks to preserve them from Friendly Fire. No signs of an enemy at sea or in the air. Two years earlier a quarter of the Allied Fleet would have been blown from the water. Now we sailed through the Straits of Bonifacio between Sardinia and Corsica, where once we would have been clobbered from both sides.

Word passed that we had been joined by an equally large fleet from Africa. I was not sure where we'd go ashore; it would be near a resort village called St. Tropez. It didn't matter much. So long as it was not heavily defended. It will be largely a matter of luck, as in Normandy, one beach blasted, another abandoned quickly.

The lounge was crowded with officers all day and night, smoky, blacked out. I had finished the Turgenev novel in my bunk. I wrote a long letter to my wife on deck. It carried slight overtones of a finale, appropriate to the circumstances. I played chess with Captain Foster, my old friend. I had just come to know my Team commander, a Major Erik Roos. Roos was a blonde civil engineer in his thirties with an unbecoming, down-turned mouth. I was to be his Executive Officer; we had only a half-dozen going in on the first wave, but a hundred more men and thirty vehicles would arrive to join us over the next two weeks - if all went well. Then more later.

This was Roos' first experience of close-in warfare. Nor had he education or experience in propaganda or public opinion or psychology. Nor of Germany; he had worked once in the Middle East; he spoke Danish. He had been sent up from Africa for the expedition; Mike Bessie, an American civilian who had been a book editor, a dark skinny little guy, pleasant enough, together with a British counterpart, had chosen Roos from the PWB pool, and put him in charge of the operation. The team had not trained at Naples; Roos hardly spoke at all, and could hardly impart such knowledge as he conceivably possessed. There was no use asking him about anything. What is more shocking, or should be, was that the I and the Captain were neither surprised nor indignant. Being badly commanded was ordinary in the US army, whether infantry or intelligence, and you might as well throw in the British Army on the balance.

The night of the Fourteenth of August, 1944, before landing, the saloon was jammed with officers. Foster and I were hunched over our tiny chessboard room, breathing befouled air, concentrating fiercely, for we were well-matched, both poor players. All of a sudden the ship's guns blasted into action and as by a word of command, the officers stampeded from the lounge. Two chess players lifted their heads and slowly returned from the game to awareness. We looked about the empty room. We had lost our moment to panic. An ineffectual air raid apparently - lucky if nobody was clipped by Friendly Flack while out on deck. Since there was nowhere else to go, the officers straggled back in abashedly.

We were up at dawn; amidst heavy firing, we were served breakfast. We clutched our packs and guns and went out on deck where the early light had the shore well in sight, no batteries firing from it, a calm surf, a fine prospect. Puffs of smoke appeared where the shore was being struck by naval gunfire. The landings began at eight o'clock, the first assault boats motoring in without immediate opposition, striking no mines. My group watched for a signal to disembark from our loading master, the particular one who had us on his list. The sun was well out before we jumped into the landing craft and went ashore. We trotted up the beach, over rocks, through brush, always following a path marked by the sappers, hastening because of the lines of men converging upon our path from the beach. After a mile or so, the line became a fan as the soldiers went off into their own units at their assembly points.

Since my mission was not to seize terrain from the enemy, I lead the group in search of a billet. No civilians were to be seen; they were off the roads, hiding back of the coast in the hills. We found a partially destroyed villa. A cursory inspection detected no booby traps: "Remember Catania," I thought. We took it over. The furnishings were largely gone. The water and light did not function. The garden was overgrown. We could have done better, but a colonel might have come along and turned us out of a luxury dwelling at this point, or a whole company might have descended upon us. We no sooner settled in than our two jeeps and drivers arrived. Several slept in, several outside.

There was no telling if the enemy was still about, they may have assembled to attack the beachhead from somewhere out yonder. I took a jeep and went in search of an operations intelligence officer, some S2 of a task force or battalion, who may have heard some news from the flanks and ahead. There was little for us to do, we discovered. The Germans were retiring generally and were not waiting for messages inviting their surrender or exhorting retreat. There were reconnaissance units out searching for them, picking up contact, cornering them. I picked up souvenirs that the Germans have left behind, a fur-lined pack from the Russian campaigns, a flat canteen that I considered superior in design to my rounded one. They had left in a hurry, probably as soon as the first shells from the boats began to come in.

The conquerors were eating K-rations, with some C-rations thrown in. There was little food to be seized or scrounged. General Washington's surprise crossing of the Delaware River at Trenton found Hessian tables laden with a Christmas banquet. Here, five generations later, everybody ate badly. It would take a while for the better grade of ration to come ashore, and I would be gone by then. I walked Foster down to the beach road and said good-bye; the Lancastrian hitch-hiked on an armored weapons carrier; he was going to work the Eastern end of the Front, over by Italy.

The night was not too noisy: the artillery had already moved beyond its position and the enemy had withdrawn his pieces. Not the distant sounds, but the passing vehicles and men going this way and that, to and from the beaches, disturbed your sleep. Major Roos awakened me. "I hear noises from the garden, go see if it's the enemy," he ordered. No use arguing: I put on my boots and took a walk outside, saw nothing and pissed in the starlight. "Nothing to worry about, Major, maybe some of our men looking for a place to sleep."

The next day I took off by myself to drum up trade and to make observations. The pattern for future activity was set. Roos was a homebody. He liked to be by himself in a corner. I did not think much about the reasons for this, not yet. I was making myself at home in France and keeping up with the front, which presented an intriguing panorama, kaleidoscopic, because it changed so much with every shake of the hour-glass. I was looking for a place to plunge in and do a job. "Make yourself useful," was my mission.

Overnight the situation had radicalized, no thanks to me. We were now as deep into France as Naples is from Salerno, Messina from Syracuse. In the beginning, there were these four to six great convoys converging off Corsica, one from the heel of Italy at Taranto, another south of Naples (that was me and company) and the Salerno area (so therefore really two), then a couple out of Africa, and some boats and a large airborne armada from Corsica. They landed in five main bodies, Alpha in two branches, on the peninsula of Saint-Tropez, my own being closest to town; and then all along the Coast. On Alpha's right flank were Delta, Camel (split into three) and Rosie, close to Cannes. On the left flank, Romeo went ashore at Cap Nègre. Airborne troops dropped near them by Saint-Tropez and inland, at Le Muy. The Twelfth Tactical Air Force was operating out of Corsica and Sardinia; some flights were running out of Foggia, a long ways off. For lack of target, our planes were not much in evidence along the beaches of Alpha. Franco-American Special Forces tackled some coast artillery positions only to find that they were dummy emplacements. So much for the perspicacity of aerial observation prior to the invasion.

Confronting the Seventh Army with its several divisions and task forces, American and French, was the Nineteenth German Army, a shapeless conglomerate which had a number of elements stretched out between Toulouse in the West and the Italian frontier in the East. The Allied Forces advancing into France from the West had emerged from the Normandy beachheads and were engorging large sectors to the East; they did not threaten in the next several weeks to sweep East across France, for they were driving northeast in a giant envelopment strategy, designed to liberate Paris, crush the main German armies in France and drive toward the industrial

Ruhr. For the time being and in the minds of its soldiers, the Seventh United States Army was fighting its own isolated war.

The Germans knew we were coming. The 19th German Army Group of Southern France was headquartered at the marvelous medieval Papal city of Avignon, up the Rhone River from Marseilles. There, General Wiese, Commanding, had been told on August 11 that an armada was heading in his general direction and that it might strike the Italian Coast around Genoa or the Riviera-to-Toulon area. He received gratefully an order that transferred the 11th Armored Division over to him from the Toulouse region. His other troops included seven divisions of infantry, most of which were under strength; one was made up largely of disemployed Luftwaffe personnel. Since a large number of units had been engaged in coastal defense, they had to spike and abandon their cannon, leaving the troops merely with small arms. The Germans had far too much territory to cover and could not resist strongly at any point, not in the beginning.

Formally, at first, they did not appear determined upon the logical tactic, which would have been to get out of southern France as quickly and neatly as possible, suffering only the losses demanded to prevent their total capitulation. This tactic called for a quick retreat North, where they might join their retreating comrades from the West to set up a line of resistance across France, anchored upon Lyon. Some troops, at least a division of them, could escape easily into Italy, closing the mountain hatches behind them. But the Führer hated retreats and would not approve of an immediate turning of tail.

The whole movement from Southwestern France should have been initiated even before the landings. A week and more was lost, enough of a delay to make a fully successful retreat and defense impossible. When the orders did go out, they were reasonable enough: The Nineteenth Army would converge from all sides upon the Rhone Valley. It would then proceed up the Valley. It would pause on the way to Lyon at seven phases of resistance, starting with a line at the Durance River. The Order of August 18 commanded a general withdrawal, to begin on the evening of the 21st of August, with one division covering their Riviera flank, and a second the Eastern Alpine foothills. Their right flank (facing to the Mediterranean Sea) would be pulled in and assist in the defense of Marseilles and Toulon, where some help could be expected from French Vichy forces. The 11th Panzer Division would protect the reassembly and withdrawal.

But it took the 11th Panzer a week to get to the Rhone and cross it. I could watch its progress on the G-2 maps that I studied when I visited Advance Headquarters of the Seventh Army. The 11PD had to suffer continual air attacks. Many a repair job was necessitated by the wear and tear of the trip, too. It would have taken them longer and cost them more if the Twelfth Tactical Air Force had been able to destroy all bridges in the Division's path. It tried but failed. Too, a strong uprising of the French resistance might have interposed delays; it did not occur.

Various hearty messages had been beamed out to the French resistance fighters, and they were encouraged to harass the German columns. French units of the underground did spring into action. Much of the effort went into subjugating Vichy police and troop units and chasing down individuals. Still one must wonder whether the *résistants* or partisans or *maquisards* did not serve to galvanize the Germans into hurrying up their assembly, into pulling themselves together. An unforeseen disadvantage, unspoken, unmentioned, unconsidered even by G-2 and G-3 analysts, Counterintelligence, OSS squads, and combat propagandists, who were so enthused over helping the partisans, unforeseen even by Our Hero, was this: that the Germans as individuals become terrified at falling into the hands of armed partisans, so that the large number of desertions and straggling that one might expect from demoralized, too young and too old, under-equipped and under-fed soldiers scattered over a large area and now thrown together, ill-controlled by the SS military police, beset by the Americans, simply did not ensue. They preferred to take their chances on the long haul to the *Heimat,* even if they had to walk and be shot at by enemy planes and artillery along the way. The strong German "togetherness" trait, raised to a peak in its armed forces, was now reinforced by the fear of being killed if they turned themselves in or let themselves be captured by anyone save an American soldier. Even then, of course, the fear of being butchered remained, but it was less. An obstacle in psychological operations against the Germans was that they would like to surrender only in a group, but, once in a group, they acquired a high morale against surrender.

In July, heeding the call to arms from London, a large group of French *maquisards* took up positions in the Vercors region, South of Grenoble, intending to fortify a redoubt and hold it against the Germans until ultimately contacted by friendly forces. It was not to be. A German parachute battalion was dropped and, with the local German troops, disabled the uprising and killed 2000 French. Of this incident, I will be writing to my wife:

> *They marched from one village to another, burning them to the ground and massacring the inhabitants, men, women and children. They raped and looted in that strange, twisted German conviction that orderly and complete brutality is a part of permanent government. The empty houses, walls that point with jagged, black fingers at the blue sky and green mountains, and rows of graves are all that is left. Many of the young men were hiding in the mountains at the time and they are some of the people who have to say what to do with the Germans.*

The Vercors area lies between two of the four major routes from the East to the Rhone that the German 11PD and the American 36 ID and Task Force Butler would be fighting over. If the uprising had been delayed for a month, the resistants would have been better supplied and reinforced, and in turn have encouraged the American troops to stronger efforts to cut off the Germans in retreat.

In August, the civil population of Charol, on the Front of the River Roublion, did rise up against a column of Armored Engineers of the 11th Panzer Division and inflict serious losses upon them. In this case they were cheered by having already made contact with the Americans moving down from the Route Napoleon.

Besides their sporadic independent operations, the partisans supplied many recruits to the two French divisions of what now became Army B under French General de Lattre de Tassigny; the budding Army was at first attached to the American Seventh Army, to whose Headquarters - the G-2 section, under Colonel Quinn and his Assistant, Colonel Parry - I, from Psychological Operations reported. The French, apart from commando units, landed after the Americans, and were hastening toward Toulon and Marseilles, the large port cities to the west; nearly all sea-going traffic would be directed to them as soon as possible. The French troops were the colonial divisions, Moroccan and Algerian, our friends from Italy, with numbers of Europeans among them and leading them.

I understood that I could have little control in respect to the French people. They had long expected liberation. The Vichy supporters and militia had run away; rarely, they sniped or defended some strongpoint briefly until killed. Everybody else was more than cooperative. Whatever problems and opportunities they might present in the way of communications and propaganda were to be handled by the French themselves. Exceptionally, George Rehm of my team has now landed and went East to the Cote d'Azur to start up a newspaper.

A mixed lot of French patriots, partisans, ex-officials and military officers began a cantankerous caterwauling over public policies and media controls that would never end. Half their time was taken up with explaining who they were to each other and why they should be in charge of this or that installation and policy.

The Americans from the Army Headquarters on down were singularly unconcerned about who was running this part of France, now that they had liberated it. I, for instance, realized that I would have a hard time taking over the Marseilles and Toulon media, even had I the personnel to go in, arrest, purge, appoint new staff, program the outlets and commence emissions. The task might have been delegated to the French command explicitly, with some representation of the Americans for surveillance, counsel and material help. Information control was quite unplanned.

The front and the occupied territory were expanding crazily. The French troops settled around the two cities for ten days of siege. The three American divisions were among the best, perhaps better than any that had landed in the North of France for they had engaged in one or more amphibious invasions and were loaded with the experiences of Italy: the Third headed up the Rhone Valley; the 45th moved up through the Luberon to Apt and beyond; the 36th went up the Route Napoleon toward Grenoble. Then there was a task force that closed to the Italian border, and another that was formed of various units, given the name of Task Force Butler after its Commander, and sent up the Route Napoleon alongside the 36th Division specially to intercept the German retreat up the Rhone.

Matters were going poorly for the Germans, but General Wiese knew just what to do. He had been deprived of the division that he thought would resist on his left flank, at the Riviera. He found that the second division that he had in that area was being poked to bits, what with being spread out all the way from Italy in a crescent around the coastal mountains and the foothills of the Alps, the Basses-Alpes. And he saw that the 36th Division was marching - nay, driving - at a bewildering pace up the Route Napoleon. So he ordered the 11th Panzer Division, even while maintaining its front to the South against the Third and Forty-fifth American Divisions, to send four Battle groups to cork up the four river valleys that lead toward the Rhone and through which Task Force Butler must push, if it will emerge upon the Rhone and cut off the line of retreat of the 19th Army.

The principal site to be controlled was the town of Montelimar, where hills on the East and West narrowed the Rhone Valley and provided commanding heights. Through Montelimar, which was located on the East Bank of the Rhone, ran the main railroad line from Southern to Northern France, and the Main Highway #7 that ran from the South and East to Lyons. An important, if secondary, North-South highway #86 ran along the West bank of the Rhone. Heavy German traffic to the North started up immediately along all three routes, and American planes were busily engaged in its destruction. The shoulders of the routes were soon looking messy.

Only one week after landing, after poking around Draguignan and Gap, I was cruising into the beautiful mountain city of Grenoble, its buildings undestroyed, its people joyful, the French resistants very much in evidence. How many miles from the sea had I come? Three hundred, more or less, plus two hundred zigging and zagging. The Americans were overwhelmed by the hospitality of the town; it was a little Rome. I traded cigarettes for perfume to send home. My soldiers had already arranged a party for the night of the liberation with a gang from the University. The evening held great promise.

However, no sooner did I arrive and hear these glad tidings, than I learned, too, that Major Roos was urgently concerned to find me. The Major was swollen with an important mission. There had come a request from Corps headquarters for help: What kind? I don't know. When? Now, right away. Where? Find the Corps. Where is it? I don't know. It's getting dark. Roos tightened his lips, their sour curl was gone: look, orders are orders, this is an order! I looked hard at the guy. He was crazy. He could not discuss a problem. He had never been out in the dark.

Still, despite the almost hopeless nature of the mission, I was pleased to hear from Corps, that they believed something was urgently needed. Of course, the matter was up to the Propaganda Team to decide; it knew better than Corps whether it could be done or not; the sad fact was that no one in the Army from General Patch down knew anything about this kind of military action and therefore, unless it was to be so stupid as to be criminal, a perceived action needed to be framed as a request, not an order. As an order, as Major Roos would have it, this was absurd, yet I did not regard the idea as ridiculous in itself. Moreover, I was the only one in the Army who could undertake the peculiar mission. Lt. Johnny Anspacher had arrived, but he was a novice.

It was uniquely mine, this kind of work. I drove about in complete darkness over quite unknown roads, through uncertain lines of enemy and friends (who could not be relied upon to recognize you), trailing behind me a load of messages for the enemy, having in mind finding a corps headquarters that had been on the move, who would tell me where some divisional artillery might be located, and what the problem was, for the purpose then of proceeding to find a battery of artillery that was set up and targeted to do the job. It would not do, for instance, to shoot the stuff at the 11th Panzer, which had high morale, was standing and holding, and was concentrated in small groups; the cannon had to be pointed at the retreating enemy mass.

So I drove along. I have hardly ever asked myself whether the

Enemy would kill me if they caught me. Nor did I ever wonder whether bashfulness of some of my company back in Algiers to move up to the Front were due to such reflecting; I considered them as mere ordinary goldbricks. Mine was a straight military task, one might argue, but the SS police had peculiar notions of what constituted the military; in Russia they (and the whole Wehrmacht, in fact), were under orders, obeyed with alacrity, to kill (or starve to death) any political personnel they came across, any communist party workers, as well as the usual legions of Jews, Gypsies, partisans, and others who simply weren't lucky enough to get out of their way. I knew enough of this to be warned, but somehow, though I always thought I might be killed, I never thought I'd be captured. Strange, since I worked so closely to enemy prisoners of war.

At any rate, I was enough of a soldier, or a simpleton, or rash enough, to try to carry out the Corps idea. If someone out there was intelligent enough to think of what should be done in this case, I was going to try to help him, instead of driving off around the bend of the road and going to sleep for the night. I thought of Old Hank, the locomotive engineer in the folk song, who leapt from his engine as it headed toward the broken bridge, singing:

> *Oh I may have shirked my duty,*
> *but I've got a sweet patooty,*
> *who would rather have me home,*
> *than dead.*

I often thought of old songs and old jazz while driving, but not of the popular hits. I headed West across the mountains. I did find Advance Corps HQ. I discovered what the problem was: The main task of the Seventh Army was to capture or destroy the Nineteenth German Army, amounting to about 150,000 men. An excellent chance to do just this was electrifying the summer air of the Command Post of Corps. They knew as well as the Enemy that, with the 36th Division well above and in control of the Route Napoleon, the whole lot of Germans must pass up through the Rhone Valley. The Americans were trying to shove motorized infantry, armor and artillery through the narrow hilly roads that lead out, like rungs of a ladder, from the North-South Route Napoleon that they controlled to positions where they could command by fire and capture by assault the North-South roads of the other leg of the ladder, especially where one of the rungs reached the beautiful little city of Montelimar. There, hills on both sides fashion a gap lending itself to closure. If the Americans could plug the gap, 150,000 Germans would be out of the War, casualties if they tried to get through, prisoners if they didn't. Task Force Butler and the 36th Division, in part, were moving speedily, or with painful slowness, depending upon how you saw it, to shut off the escape routes. Their orders were clear and concise; no commanders could have orders more telegraphic.

On the 21st, at a Seventh Army briefing, Task Force Butler was commanded to turn West off the Route Napoleon and seize the heights Northeast of Montelimar; following this up, VI Corps ordered a full Infantry Regiment of 36th Division and most of the 36th's two battalions of 155 millimeter heavy guns to reinforce TF Butler: blocking the Valley of the Rhone was their primary mission!

Still, all was not going well. Clausewitz says *(On War)* that the principles are simple, but the details are difficult. General Lucian Truscott, commanding Corps, did not seem to have much confidence in his 36th Division or in Task Force Butler, which was, after all, mostly a chip off the old 36th block. The General was issuing commands on the Battalion level! For instance, on August 22, he is ordering the 36th Division Commander to get the 977th and 141th Artillery Battalions into positions in which they can fire on Montelimar and the roads to the South of it. At some point, some bright junior officer on the Commanding General's Staff must have remembered the Italian experience and said: "What we need is some surrender leaflets dropped on the roads so we can get more Krauts to surrender. Where do we get hold of some of that shit?"

Four hours later I showed up pulling a load of the shit in a trailer. At this point it was the "shit of Divine Uranus," gold, the signature of Eisenhower on the insignia of SHAEF. The Germans were promised heaven if they surrendered, that is, safety, food, and ultimate return home. The packs of paper were gift-wrapped in glowing bronze shell cases with explosive heads and fuses with timers set for air-bursting at 1000 yards or whatever the artillery observer gave as the grid of the road where these Germans were trudging stolidly along, just now under cover of a night that they wish would last as long as the years of darkness covering the Jews in Exodus from Egypt, whose descendants even at this moment were being rounded up and killed by the masters of these same cattle tramping dustily up the three roads of the Rhone Valley.

The few rounds of shells I carried should have been many more, so that every artillery battery of the Seventh Army wherever it was would have a hundred - a score on hand, the rest allocated to it at the ammunition dump. The propaganda shortage was not nearly the main shortage, which was of trucks and truckers. Anticipating fierce combat in breaking out from the beaches, the Allied logisticians had provided a great deal of ammunition at the expense of trucks to haul it. In one of the letters to Jill, it is written: *"we are moving too fast for anything, including the human frame. The group that are really winning this campaign are the truck drivers, white and colored. They are worked beyond all reasonable standard of endurance..."* I specified gas and rations as being short, but strangely the very surplus of ammunition on the shores meant a shortage of shells at the front, for lack of the trucks to get them there. In one place, a 36th Division battery ceased to fire upon the retreating Germans and was useless against counterattack because it lacked ammunition. Perhaps after the Italian campaigns, where ammunition seemed in infinite supply, the Americans were firing hastily and wastefully.

If all had been well prepared, the retreating Germans, including those elements that turned to counterattack in order to protect the withdrawal, would have been treated to thousands of several different leaflets along the right of way dropped by air and shot from cannon; they would have heard loudspeakers advising them to surrender. These capabilities would have been present had the propaganda command been fully experienced and seriously planning, instead of quarreling and quibbling, in Algiers and Naples.

Too, combat unit officers and their generals (gung-ho, to show that they are *mensch*) are usually thinking in terms of explosives. Or yet, inasmuch as many infantrymen would rather not personally

The Provence Campaign

blast their fellow-men, and considering the limited number of assignments a combat commander can shift them to - for assisting the small true "killer-group" - a detail of one or several men could be formed in a company to specialize in capture. They would be trained when in reserve and on the job.

I knew better than anybody what made an enemy surrender. The soldier who is close to surrendering because of hostile fire or injury or demoralization faces a terrifying decision. He is threatened with death on the spot by his next in command, or after arrest and trial by his own commanders, and he is likely to be shot as he tries to give up, whether by accident from the enemy who shoots on sight without understanding his intention to give up, or by an enemy who would rather kill than capture, especially if given an easy target and a crowded agenda. In a way, deserting or surrendering is like dying, or, even more, like suicide. Hence the enemy has to know how to surrender as well as being convinced to surrender, and friendly troops have to know how to accept a surrender. So these leaflets I was carrying bore not only solemn assurances of decent treatment, under the signature of the highest Allied authority and were stamped with iconography of authority, but also described on their reverse side the technique of surrendering, including the use of a white rag and of the proper words, along with the removal of the helmet, and so on. Part of my job was to insinuate as casually as possible to my fellow-soldiers how to go about picking up prisoners: surely the veterans knew how, but the replacements, usually a third of the Army in battle, were most nervous in going about the business.

There are always doubts about one's mission, beyond the ordinary doubts trying to crowd into the mind, if one is special and an innovator. What made me move through these strange mountains and dark roads was a conviction not so much that I could save enemy lives (for there was a lot of opposition to saving enemy lives) but that I could take a number of the enemy out of action, and even if I got rid of one enemy soldier - never mind that I might catch a hundred of them - I would justify my bit of this immense war in terms of what many years later came to be called "costs-benefits analysis," and "more bang for the buck." I was one of a million

Americans, British and other troops who had managed to land upon the continental shores in Italy and France, and as of this point in time all together they had managed to dispose of 400,000 of the enemy, within the year following the invasion of Sicily and the Italian surrender; that would be an average of 0.4 per man. Actually, with the Luftwaffe counting for very little all of this time, Allied troops in France, subject to the risks - small or large - of combat, numbered perhaps 300,000 divisional personnel plus 50,000 in air crews. That is, the truer average in combat would be one-to-one. Whatever the ratio, I felt that I had already far exceeded it.

It was hard to measure who disposed of whom, of course: few men recognized directly whom they were killing or even if they were killing anyone. Was I engaged in killing or not killing when my own infantrymen shot enemy soldiers led to attempt surrender, or when my leaflets were used to entice Germans out of their holes in order to strike them with an airburst of shrapnel? This would occur sometimes even though I might advise against such tactics, which were generally forbidden, when an incident would arise, and even though the Geneva Conventions bound the warring armies to take prisoners and treat them decently, and even though expediency reinforced mercy; for the enemy would cease to place any faith whatsoever in the American propaganda, denying what it said on all subjects, aside from when and how to surrender, and, furthermore, the enemy would fight to the end, with devastating results.

I drove into the falling night, to when two tiny slits of light became my guides to the road ahead, following the Route Napoleon down to Die. The hundreds of tracked vehicles, trucks and cannon moving on it were grinding up the pavement of the narrow highway. I took the right-hand fork when I reached Die, and the road became less and less travelled as it approached the area of Montelimar. I asked of several murky figures and knew I had not arrived. At last I came upon an outpost, manned by a major with a 50-caliber machine gun. We exchanged greetings.

The Major waited, wide-awake, impatient, for the light of dawn. He could then resume his slaughter. He had a piece of the road in his sights. He knew that hundreds of Germans were even now, especially now, pushing along the road. Come dawn, he would repeat his act of the evening before. He sees a column of Germans straggle into range and he opens fire, killing and wounding a number. He is protected by the forest; he moves his weapon then, before a panzer self-propelled cannon can draw a bead on him or an enemy party can get by his soldiers who are covering him. It was actually a machine gunner's job that he was doing and I was a little surprised at it. Either he was a dedicated killer or he had to do it himself in order to get the job done. Officers in the American army frequently do the work of their enlisted men, not only because of the tradition of equality, and because they are more skilled, but also because in situations of danger their morale is higher than that of the men. In any given platoon, company, regiment, division, army, only a small minority do the effective work. It doesn't matter whether one is speaking of killing or of paper-work. But isn't it the same in all groups?

I felt sorry for the exhausted Germans plodding along, under the hammering of the heavy lead slugs of this beefy exultant type, as if they were pigs moving down the corridor of an abattoir. But it is the way in which most of the death and maiming of war occurs. Soldiers are caught in a barrage and killed and maimed. They are helplessly trapped and destroyed. Their boat sinks and they are drowned. Most of the rotten glorification of war is based upon the obscenely false idea of chivalrous men facing one another with similar weapons and expecting a decision that will be based upon courage and skill at arms. That this was all false, I had long known; it was the fallacy of the ass of Fred Faas. Fred still couldn't sit down without a twinge. Even if war were as it was faked to be, it would still be as morally wrong to kill under idealized tournament conditions as to kill with the typical treacherous advantages of real battle situations.

Moral or immoral, I liked to think of myself as a warrior, however, and therefore admitted to the need and occasional usefulness of battle under such circumstances. Too, I would have behaved like the Major. Indeed, I wondered whether I should stay for the duck-shoot. But time was passing, no second heavy machine gun was handy, and the Major appeared in no mood to share his luck. The Major, whose face was obscured by the darkness, did allow some idea of where the nearest artillery piece was located, by recalling its muzzle flash. I circled around and found it.

The gunners were mostly glad to have a human contact and were willing to fire the leaflet shells at dawn. Yes, they would get several shells to their sister howitzers as well. They had been pulled out of Cassino for the Provence operation; they had had experience with propaganda operations. They liked the thought of talking to the Germans, so to speak. My jeep drove bumping onto the gun site and they unloaded the shells.

Then I steered off into the damp gloom, with a twinge of mourning and nostalgia in parting from the little squad tending its piece, isolated in the dark green forest, so tiny a part of the worldwide scene of war, their serious small voices receding into the blackness. This small feeling impinging upon comraderie, repeated hundreds of times, this too is a cause for the recurrence of war. It covers senseless warfare with a balm and bandage of brotherly love. Absurd, yes; true, yes. "I should have stayed for the action," I thought, as I crawled up the road like a snail. But they had a forward observer who should be able to tell them if the firing worked. It would have been better to drive in the daytime, too. Or would it?

What happens in the end? During the eight days of the Montelimar Battle, the cannon of the Seventh Army units of the East, not counting the Third Division and Forty-fifth Division who came firing up the roads from the South, shoot off 7000 rounds a day upon the Germans along the Rhone Valley roads and at the units of the 11PD defending them. My 35 rounds of leaflets in the battle of Montelimar amounted to 1/1500th of the 54,000 rounds that were fired by the cannons of the 36th Division and Task Force Butler and I was 1/60,000th of the total manpower engaged (counting the aviation troops) or 1/30,000 of just the American combat troops alone. To the artillery fire must be added the small arms ammunition, the machine guns, the mortars, the automatic rifles, rifles and handguns (practically none), but emphatically the bombings and firings of the Twelfth Tactical Air Force that rattled off an abundance of machine gun ammunition and at the same time dropped 851 tons of bombs upon communication facilities and 953 tons on troops.

Notwithstanding, three bridges over the Rhone were partially maintained until the last Germans had escaped to the North. At times, wreckage rather than artillery and small arms fire blocked the route of the escaping Germans. And of the advancing Americans of the Third Division! For the Germans blew up on the road whatever could not carry them farther. Viewing the approach of the Americans to the South of Montelimar, the German rearguard on August 29 barred their route by an assemblage in three files of the wrecks of 500 trucks and cars, and of metal junk galore.

The 11th Panzer Division did its job well. Despite a flash flood that made the Drome River almost impassable for a day, and despite repeated, if half-hearted attacks, from the hilly flanks to the East, by the much better armed and more numerous American forces, they were able to withdraw without surrendering a single unit as such, and furthermore, before they pulled out their own last element, had protected the withdrawal of most of the rag-tag Nineteenth Army, perhaps as many as two-thirds of the total, the remaining third having fallen into the hands of the Americans and French.

There were some bitter complaints from German infantry commanders whose troops had legged it for seven hundred kilometers from the coastal defenses to the final line established across Northern France. They felt that they had been contemptuously abandoned by the 11th Panzer Division. But on the whole the Germans could claim victorious retreat.

And the Americans might have asked themselves, once more, why they did not pursue the enemy vigorously, why they retreated from the high ground that they had first taken in several places over the Rhone Valley, why they had tended to let air power and artillery take on the total job while the infantry stood by like lazy male lions waiting for an easy kill.

I got back to Grenoble. The party of the students and my team was enjoyable, said Anspacher; Roos did not attend. *Tant pis.* I got some sleep. I was roused up by Captain Galitzine (Prince Yurka Galitzine, had czardom not perished) of British Intelligence, who had joined the team. I was his friend from Italy, the favorite

American of "D Section," and Yurka said: I have just been to a trial of some Vichy militiamen, they didn't get much of a trial, they're just young kids. The *maquisards* have them in hand. They're going to shoot them. This morning! Galitzine was disturbed, almost as if the Royal Family of the Czar was being gunned down. Well, I said, the least we can do is go take a look.

The event is pure Hollywood. But all too real! It takes place in a grand square with a convenient great wall that will catch the most errant bullet from a firing squad. A large patriotic crowd has assembled, buzzing with excitement. The lorries drive up with the condemned. They are ordered to stand against the wall. They are indeed young; what could these teen-agers have known about what they were doing, what they stood for; were they being executed for being of the militia that had as a corporate group committed so many crimes, or for being criminal as individuals? If the latter, then individual trials and varying sentences might have been called for. So they represent the militia and the deeds and the principles of the Pétain government and as such they would die. A couple of them are smiling, others put on a brave face, one is crying.

An American soldier, a red Indian, is staggering drunk and is impressed by the dense crowd to the point where he thinks he must keep it in order during the ceremonies. So he moves about shouting commands, which the crowd takes in good humor, since he makes no effort to force their compliance. To me, when he encounters us, and quite ignoring Captain Galitzine's more resplendent outfit, he casts a stiff salute, and, with grave concern and respect says: "Lieutenant, Sir, you have to be careful here, now, but don't you worry, I'll keep them under control."

The shots ring out, the men slump drearily to the ground. The officer in charge gives a couple of them the *coup de grâce* with his hand-gun. The crowd disperses. I leave Yurka, walk thoughtfully and somberly about, then go find someone with a large bottle of Chanel #5 perfume to exchange for one of the cartons of the cigarettes that I had carried ashore. It is for Jill.

The troops were moving north and northeast, away from Provence. Tentacles moved West to contact the Americans of Patton's Third Army. I headed back South to check the situation of

Toulon and Marseilles. The cities were still under siege, heavily penetrated. The French divisions were converging upon them in several columns from several points. They could not hold out much longer. Scattered resistance. I write to Jill about a French intelligence officer I transported with me, and of another action:

> *Lt.Samarselli didn't sleep all last night. It is his first night in France in three years and he was too excited to sleep. The French are that way now, not too excited not to fight, but almost. The other day I was with a French battery that was set up near Toulon. We had just captured the ground they were emplaced on, and there was a full scale celebration going on in the middle of the battle. There were several farm houses and the families and soldiers were eating in shifts at a great table outside under a tree. The wine was drunk as fast as it hit the table and the rations were spread all over the place, with bowls of fresh tomatoes and fried potatoes here and there. With one hand they were fighting the war and with the other they were celebrating the liberation of France. The cannon were set up hardly ten yards away and went booming off over the heads of the celebrants all the time. The captain of the battery would snatch himself a glass of wine and a handful of* pommes frites *and dash over to his CP a few yards away to give the order to fire. This kept up for hours, well into the darkness. The guns kept hammering away at the bedeviled Germans who were fruitlessly counterattacking, old diners would get up and fresh ones would take their place. The black-as-tar Senegalese sweated, swung their trucks around, and fed up the ammunition, grinning broadly and almost dancing while they worked, in their enthusiastic excitement. A forest fire on a nearby hill lit up the sky as it darkened and the volleys of the howitzers flashed brighter and brighter. The vineyards were coated with dust, many of the grapes crushed under the great wheels and trampling feet. But no one cared -- they were French feet and French wheels. The French were liberating themselves.*

Then I turned my wheels toward Marseilles and took up a main road into the city. Halfway in I noticed some skirmishing ahead. I parked behind a wall and ventured along the street. Snipers - some guys never give up - especially when they are convinced, with some reason, that they will be killed; this is better; you die in a duel; like I say, it's more of the ideal war. I espied a bookstore. It was open. I entered and browsed. I came upon a book that I had never heard of, in my own field, *Théorie des Opinions Publiques,* by a scholar I had never heard of, named Jean Stoetzel; it was published in Paris only the year before, employed American sources profusely, almost as if there were no chasm of war splitting the scholarly world. It handled the material with a competent theoretical system, too, and I recognized promptly that it was superior to any American work in this regard. I paid for it with Allied francs that the proprietor accepted with pleasure.

The firing had stopped. I weaved my jeep through the debris of the Old Harbor. Most places that were not damaged were open for business. A barber shop, what a luxury! I got a haircut, shampoo and shave. No charge, said the Proprietor. You are the first American to arrive. I walked about the breakwater, it was quiet out there, the sea was calm and dark blue. A pretty flame-headed freckled girl, full-bodied in a tight white dress, was also walking about, and responded smiling to my greeting. She was a nurse and was from Corsica. I talked with her for a while as I peered through my binoculars at the half-demolished old city. I felt I must move on, take her name, should I ever be back, and drive North. I never returned.

I was eager for the mobile presses and loud speakers of the combat propaganda unit to arrive. There might be opportunities at any moment to catch up with a group of Germans and persuade them, if they will not surrender, to resist less and to hit the road to the *Heimat.* The cheery Old New York blarney face of Tom Crowell did not poke out of a truck window until September 9, by which time the Montelimar bottle has emptied itself of Germans. It was early, but not early enough.

The French army was dressed American, equipped American, and has acquired some American habits, which very often were nothing but practices that the American army learned from the French from 1776 to 1918. Until now it had been mostly Muslim in the ranks but increasing numbers of continental French were being enlisted, especially from the forces of the resistance. Their leadership was first class down to the sous-officiers and their morale was excellent, being especially obvious and noteworthy and commendable on the assault when most troops wanted to drag their feet, naturally. They would incorporate all types of people and their ranks swelled.

Seventh Army Headquarters let the French HQ attach a small platoon of men and two officers to the American Combat Propaganda Team and I had the responsibility for employing them. The two officers were Jacques Pregre and Jacques Villanave. The enlisted men worked under Corporal Francois Bernard, who hailed from Paris and handled the boys well. They were supplied by the American company, were under its orders, but let alone to do their job. Principally they drove around gathering political intelligence and using a loud speaker truck to inform and control the population. Their connection for liaison was the French Army B G-2 section and principally André Malraux, who had recently joined up following upon a brief experience in the Resistance.

One morning a month later, I was eating breakfast at the small field desk I carried with me, when I heard a shot and the thud of a falling body. I sprang out of the room into the hallway and found Corporal Bernard prone gushing blood from the neck. "Who did it," I shout, "grab the son of a bitch!" I imagined a fight and shooting. Top Sgt. Annunziata followed behind me, muttering disgustedly, "for Christ's sake, take it easy." I lifted Bernard, stuffing a first aid pad someone had handed me into the wound, calling out to get a stretcher and a half-ton truck, and gagged on my breakfast of greasy fried bacon and powdered eggs now acting up worse than usual. Enter others, Pvt. Cook in hand, a befuddled look upon his usually silly mug. It was accidental. Cook was unloading his 45-cal. automatic after coming off guard duty and accidentally pulled the trigger, exploding a bullet that pierced one wall, struck the Corporal, and buried itself in the wall above where I was sitting.

We rushed him to the field hospital, but his spinal cord and brain are ripped up, and in a few minutes he expires. The several soldiers huddle a few feet away. I assume that he is Catholic, recall vaguely the sign of the cross, and mumble a few words of improvised prayer; some proper words should go with him, I believe, and an officer should administer last rites. The Americans were humiliated that one of their number should commit the accident, rather than the less skilled French.

A couple of days later Johnny Anspacher wanted to know whether I was going to the funeral - the Corporal's Mother would be there, crossing France through the newly connected Allied armies. I was surprised; I thought all the dead were promptly laid into a hole and covered with dirt, given a GI cross plus identification for possible reburial. I had no heart for it and asked Johnny to cover for me while I took off for the woods; she believed her son killed in action; so he was, like many another case of amicide.

I was furious with Cook, an amiable sociopathic fool, and I brought the case to the Army Provost Marshal who fixed the charge as "negligent discharge of firearms" and sent it back for company level trial and punishment. That's not much. They decided to let it go. The idiot was liked by his comrades.

For many weeks, the reduction of the German resistance in the Belfort Gap and Alsace was a problem of the French troops. I, who had considered the French masters of the sharp, savage relentless attack, now could wonder. Were they reluctant to shoot up France? Were they not so dashing when the composition of their infantry had fewer of the sacrificial Africans? Were they learning American habits? Did they long to stay alive for the Victory celebration, now near at hand? Were they preoccupied with quarreling amongst themselves about who was guilty for the Fall of France, who was author of the resurgence of France, who would control France now?

The Combat Propaganda Team did its bit to help the French army in their efforts to break through the Belfort Gap, the most difficult part of the operation, extending into winter, skirting Switzerland, and cutting through the Vosges Mountains into Alsace, where the German army began to resist the Allied advance more stubbornly. A number of them were trapped with their backs to Switzerland and the Swiss did not want to take them. A special leaflet operation was prepared for them, with the usual accent on how to surrender.

The procedure here, now that the First French Army had been created, under the general supervision of U.S. Seventh Army and ultimately Sixth Army Group, was for somebody to get the idea of the need (which occurred through the two Jacques being in liaison with the French forces at the Gap), and hustling the need to the Team; the Team had the means of drawing up the propaganda message, printing it in large numbers rapidly, and loading it into shells for the French forces' American howitzers - then finally, of supervising the cannon firing.

The operation was deemed a success and the two Jacques, who were looking for an American medal, no doubt, arranged with the First French Army (Army B's new name) to give a couple of Croix de Guerre's to Roos and to me. Months later, special orders of the French Army were supposed to have contained the commendations, and, when informed by the two Jacques that such was the case, Major Roos promptly pinned the medal on himself, urging me to do likewise, which I did, but with a lingering suspicion that was never set to rest, that some kind of a deal had been cut to which I would not want to be party.

The French divisions were also experiencing a new foe, an anti-communist army composed of Cossacks, deserters, traitors, and ideological opponents of the Soviet Stalinist regime. They were softer targets and there was no problem getting intelligence material from the first prisoners and the media translated into Russian and printed in the Cyrillic alphabet to fire upon them and distribute by patrol. The Soviet defectors when they were reached were told that they would not be turned over to the mercies of the Soviet Government, which the French, more casual than the Americans, let themselves say.

Actually Roosevelt and Churchill had acceded to Stalin's demand that all Soviet Citizens except some thousands of Armenians be returned to the USSR following the surrender of Germany. But the French enlisted some of the fresh prisoners here; they were treated as French soldiers.

Patrols who scouted out and tested the enemy positions were good media for distributing propaganda. They left their literature and the enemy patrol would find it. However, a returning enemy patrol was not likely to admit that it had been collecting enemy propaganda. American soldiers, protected, you might say, by the First Amendment, save German leaflets as they would postage stamps. One series, which my fellows called the "Sam Series," caricatured a Jewish war profiteer named Sam who was having enjoyable rendezvous with "Bob's girl friend" while poor Bob was slogging away in the mud. They were distributed by plane and patrol or left behind when retreating from a position.

With perhaps too ready a contempt for the enemy's rhetoric, and too much confidence in the proper attitudes of our troops, the Team dismissed their effect. Never were the troops, in all the action from Africa to Germany, warned against harkening to Nazi propaganda: it was just as well. The Germans, by contrast, had strict rules for dealing with enemy arguments and punishing their circulation in any form; there was no sign that the *landser* resented such suppression; given everything else in the way of constraint, this was small enough; from a command standpoint, the censorship was effective because it kept discussion of the tabooed subjects of losing the War, desertion and *Gefangenschaft* to a minimum.

The fall weather joined the Seventh Army's northward drives. I bivouacked my company far enough back to light fires. It was only September 8 when I wrote Jill, apparently from the Belfort area:

> *Now that we are in the mountains a good deal, I shall certainly be precipitated into the chills, for the coming of fall is obvious. It is already field jacket time and the nights are two-blankets cold. The rains have been coming in spurts and I have been good and wet a couple of times already. A week or so may tell whether we will spend any more winters in a campaign or whether we shall be at least warmly billeted for the duration overseas. The country is very beautiful... There are magnificent slopes everywhere, the kind that run throughout Northern Italy, Switzerland, and Austria, too. At the present, the mountains and valleys are green and brown, and the clouds are blue and grey. There are mists and clouds that sweep in and out of the gaps, now filming the sun, now letting it through to make the green of the fields brilliant. There are many forests of small pine and tree-shaded highways that curve smoothly around the sides of the mountain. The*

people are all working. There is very little damage and they are very optimistic about the country's future. The Germans were generally disliked though they behaved better in most of the country than they behaved in any other part of Europe...

Then I added: *"There are strange and ghastly exceptions,"* and described the Vercors massacres.

There was little to fear from German aircraft. The fires were needed not only for warmth but for cooking. The Americans waited too long to take the needed steps; now the swift advances of Patton's Third "Panzer" Army on their left flank have been halted by a shortage of gasoline. Some is flown in, but substantial amounts must come in from the western and southern ports, and from adjoining armies. I was scandalized to hear what had happened. How could our leaders have waited so long before cutting back on the distribution of gas and the unloading of less useful supplies? Sometimes I wondered whether the generals, indeed the top echelons of the total war machine, unless they were special types like Patton, temperamentally and rationally did not want to end their experience of war. On the one hand, as at Verdun, Stalingrad, and, yes, Cassino, the generals will throw their human material into the slaughter compulsively and obsessively. Like crazy poker-faced gamblers they will up the ante. The justification is the enemy's doing the same; generals tend to act like their counterpart foes.

At other times, they will withhold contact, wait for more than enough of everything to engage, and indulge all kinds of wasteful practices in a world where logistics should be, if not the dictator of action, the most respected of counselors. I engaged in useless speculation of how all units should be ordered to reduce their gasoline consumption by half, and to cut back on all fresh and heavy rations. Further, they should have been forbidden any movement unessential to battle. No unit headquarters should have been moved until further notice, only its advance HQ. I wondered whether there were enough horses and mules left to pull wagons of fuel up forward. I remembered, at Cassino in the winter, the startling sight of Italian pack trains of mules laboring up and down the mountainsides; nobody would ever have thought that the

American army would once again be back to mules. I fretted over our losing days, weeks, even months, in ending the war, by letting the German armies get to the Rhine without close pursuit all the way. The gasoline shortage was the main cause.

Actually, you may add this to the failure of the Seventh Army to close the trap upon the 19th German Army at Montelimar and have most of the explanation of why the war lasted into 1945 at great cost all around, at the cost of losing a voice in the immediate settlement of a government upon Poland, Hungary, and East Germany, at the cost of a million and more Jewish and other prisoners' lives in the death camps. But no one, repeat, no one was saying these things within the broad scope and confidential mass of information and intelligence pouring into the bivouac of the Combat Propaganda Company from the radio systems of the world, the army intelligence sources, and the populations, prisoners, refugees whom the friendly troops were overtaking. The War in the Pacific aside, a large issue can be raised over the total conduct of the war on the part of the top leaders and their subordinates, whenever these latter were given the right to make strategic decisions. It was not a job for me; I was powerless even to obtain the captaincy that had been recommended a year earlier by Colonel Hall, Chief of Military Personnel back at AFHQ in Algiers.

Anyhow I was much less critical of the great strategy - unconditional surrender, Yalta, the aerial bombings of cities, the points of invasion, the handling of the Nazi mass murders and dislocations, and even of unimaginative propaganda policies than I would give you to believe here. I had to be, or I would not have endured so far so good.

The issue is still troubling, whether the top Allied Command, including the heads of state, was not immersed in a logistical mass, a bureaucratic system, flapping to the surface for air on occasion to ejaculate decisions before subsiding. Before and after the war, the top command was immune to fundamental political criticism, as if their method of conducting warfare were not political. This is choice idiocy. Yet not even Jewish leaders perceived keenly that the delays in bringing the war to an end, which contributed so greatly to the total distress and slaughter, were inordinate and avoidable.

It is highly doubtful that I had made a proper correlation of events, or knew of the half of them; the same might be said of my comrades, several of them Jews with access to all that I might know. With respect to the genocide of the Jews, the twisted Nazi logic and the events that were determined by it went generally as follows:

1. The job of extirpation of the German and Austrian Jews was nearly completed and remnants had been moved East as the attack on the Soviet Union was launched in June of 1941. Many thousands had saved themselves by flight abroad. The euthanasia campaign against the mentally ill and the old and disabled was carried out on Germans in Germany actively in 1941. Many Jews were being rounded up in France and elsewhere. The Big Rationalization that married Genocide to Total War was not quite born. Total War, including the redeployment, resettling, and moving of hordes of people was in itself a favorite and early Nazi concept. Not yet Total Murder.

I knew this and had assimilated its meaning. That is why I was so anti-Nazi and pro-War. I had been well-grounded in the origins of Nazism and chauvinistic fascism in its several forms; my professors and fellow-students at the University of Chicago had seen to this. I had spoken at length to German and Austrian refugees. I knew nearly as much as any well-informed and anxious Jew, and much more than the average politician and citizen or general officer.

2. By the Fall of the first year of the German offensive against the Soviet Union all of the genocidal elements of the Nazi vision and apparatus were coming together and becoming dominant politically and militarily. In the Fall of 1941 and the year 1942, immense massacres were conducted by the SS forces; they had the extensive help of native anti-semites in Poland, Lithuania, Yugoslavia, Latvia, the Ukraine and other conquered Soviet regions, anti-"Jew-Bolsheviks", impressed laborers and prisoners, and often even the German Army. Soviet prisoners were frequently butchered or put into camps and starved. Over half a million of the more than one million Soviet prisoners of the first campaigns died within a year. That the Nazis, with popular German support, waged Total War in fact, and against whole peoples physically, was known to me and my circle of friends and in the civilian and Army milieus where

I found myself during this year, the year which saw terrible warfare in Eastern Europe and the beginning of the equally Total War of the Pacific with Japan. At the end of 1942, the British Government, speaking through Anthony Eden, began finally to describe and denounce publicly the accelerating destruction visited by the Nazis upon the Jewish people. It was tardy. Worse, almost no change in policies, nor speed-up in the War, occurred.

    3. From 1942 through 1944, massacres by the hundreds occurred throughout Eastern Europe except Hungary and Rumania. In Yugoslavia, fanatic Croatian Catholics, the Ustachis, given an independent State, brutally disposed of over half a million Serbians, including all Jews who could be found. Camps were constructed to hold Jews and others. Great numbers of deaths by starvation and disease occurred. The brutality, rape, torture and hardships affecting 50,000,000 of those alive and those to die go beyond the record for any other historical epoch. The black-uniformed Nazis and those they set loose had the equivalent effect of the Black Death of the plagues that killed a third of Europe in the Fourteenth Century; they were worse by being flesh and blood, wolves of fellow humans.

Did I learn of all this? No, only part of it. The media were full of "real war" between uniformed combatants, and had no major interest in following the "human rights violations" intensely and continually. East European ethnic exterminations were remote from everyday life in the army camps throughout the States, and displaced by the widespread attention lent to the Pacific War against Japan.

    4. The middle of 1944 witnessed landings in Normandy, Russian victories, the German officers' July 20 attempt to kill Hitler, the defection of Rumania, and abundant absolute evidence of the approaching extermination of Jews when the SS heavily pressured the Hungarians to round up half a million of them. Then on July 24, 1944 the Majdanek Concentration Camp was liberated before the SS could remove all prisoners and raze it as they had intended to do. (They exhibited a consistent pattern of attempts to hide genocidal operations up to the very end.)

Between August 1944 and January 1945, the population of

German work camps and extermination camps rose by 200,000 to over 700,000, despite high death rates. Millions of foreign workers were in Germany, living miserably and under threat of extermination.

The Seventh Army Combat Propaganda Team knew little of the vast cauldron of torture and death that Germany, and Central and Eastern Europe had become. They only knew that it was very bad.

By a strange contradiction and irony, this unit that could have been used to advise the Seventh Army on morale was used strictly against the enemy. Its officers, unlike the Army command, did not believe that American soldiers got their morale from Red Cross doughnut stands by the roadside and Betty Grable movies. Nor, and here is a misfortune, it did not believe that morale came from ideal convictions concerning the War and the Nazi horrors far away. It is hard to believe that this very team, or, better yet, something that should have been coming out of the Army Morale Division, that was mainly justifying soldiers' fears by careful research and putting on vaudeville to divert them, could not have mounted a propaganda campaign among the troops with just enough effect to have cut off the Germans at Montelimar and gotten the Army to all points of the Upper Rhine by October.

The idea that American troops would have been insulted by, degraded by, dictated to by propaganda ("information"), or that the job was well left to a jolly troop newspaper like the *Stars and Stripes*, may be emphatically denied. American troops, more than the German troops, needed continuous "education" and encouragement to do their job. The achievement of high morale was not a function of newspaper reporters asking soldiers questions designed to expose how tough their personal conditions were and how pitiable.

I could be scored high in knowledge and indignation, high in wish to "do something about it all," but was as powerless as any general officer or U.S. Senator to push against the inertia of the system that had grown up for winning the War. So I lived an ordinary soldier's life for the most part, as I tell it here, with much more personal freedom and awareness of what was happening; there was no stimulation of the morale factor among the American troops, and only had such been called for would I have been spurred into greater action. I was always wary of being characterized as a trouble-maker, although that is what I wanted to be and sometimes was.

5. Between January of 1945 and the capture of Berlin four months later, 200,000 camp inmates were brought within the borders of the Reich. Most of these were killed or died. They were brought in a) to hide them, b) to keep them hostage and ransom them, c) to kill them, and d) to use them as workers. The Nazi mind was seeking desperately a way to escape or, barring that, a way to bring down the world with their own destruction. The Nazis' early terrorist slogan turned upon the Nazi mind: "Better a terrible end than an endless terror!"

As the Seventh and Third Armies joined in a solid front moving North across France, and only a pocket of resistance remained in Southern Alsace after the liberation of Strasbourg (I had already entered Alsace in September), Nazi killings were at peak and a million people were being driven into Germany. At least 150,000 lives a month would be saved for every month by which the War might be shortened. Were the War to end before the end of the year 1944, as many as a million souls would be saved. Not included would be the saved lives, otherwise to be lost, from among the friendly and hostile armies engaged, including the American armies in Europe and the Pacific, the hundreds of thousands of civilian lives saved (from aerial bombing, as well as on the ground, as in the bombings, largely useless, that devastated Berlin and Dresden). The atomic bomb might not have been rushed to completion or might not have been dropped.

Could so much of the disaster that actually occurred really be traced back and laid to the frequently uninspired and incompetent political and military leadership of the Allies? There was some indication that such was the case in this soldier's taste of war that trailed back to the initial landings in Africa and included delays all along the line in the timing of invasions and the giving of battle. And perhaps even back to the delay in inducting me into the Armed Forces, the transfers about, the largely useless training that I shared with twelve million other soldiers.

There were numerous psychological facets to this hippopotamatic military behavior. To complicate problems at the top, to give excuses, too, for all manner of timidity and delay and logistical excess were a cavernous and maddening echo of the egalitarian slogan: "Not one of our boys shall be sacrificed unnecessarily." The British recalled the Somme and Verdun, the Americans: Mom. An obsessive inflation of the word "unnecessary" led often to inactivity and indecisiveness.

The thoughts, no less than the feet, of a soldier often stink, so one could imagine two additional reasons for the generals and politicians of the West not to exert themselves over reports of the destruction of Jewry in the East. Jews had disappeared from the West of Europe, hence no vivid emergency was close at hand; the Nazis had thoughtfully murdered their Western victims in walking columns, trains, and gas ovens elsewhere. Moreover, importantly, Western high conservatives, industrialists, and military officers consciously and unconsciously identified Jews with Bolshevism just as did the Nazis, and were therefore turned off by the news and mental pictures that arose from it.

Can even also this be possible: that they had to have reasons to be conducting this World War that were quite sufficient in themselves? That is, they would prefer not to introduce the problem of a lot of strange Jews being driven into camps and killed. The more the Jews who were murdered, one ought to reason, the more the Allied elite could and should in all conscience justify the War. But, not wishing to justify a War to save the Jews, they would suppress considerations and evidence of a veritable holocaust.

Moreover, psychologically, they would avoid taking any steps to establish its occurrence, extent, and significance. Thereupon they could rest upon their strongly preferred rationale for the War: Nazi aims to conquer the World, attacks on kindred democracies, and aggressive attacks by the Axis powers against the United States of America. All of these things I remarked upon from the beginning of the War to the End. My data bank was enriched, also, when I came to be invited by a grateful Army Orientation Officer to stop off whenever I could and talk to combat troops in reserve or in rest camp, crouched on their cannon and carriers or sprawled on the floors in a half-ruined factory, where I could sense how tenuous was the men's commitment to the Great War as the focus of life's ideals. To venture that they were at war to protect anyone from extermination but Themselves, construed personally, and suspiciously, would have been foolhardy. It would also be deluding oneself to think that their experience of war had enhanced their taste for it.

To all of this, as I confessed, I had my back half-turned. I knew more than I needed to know and infinitely more than I had the power to act upon. I could even sympathize with a helpless *Landser* prisoner, who claimed to know nothing of large affairs, who was loyal to Der Führer, and who interpreted the crashing down of his moral and physical world as no more than the maddening din of American artillery bursts.

The 'Gutenberg Special,' a captured German truck
which Tom Crowell transformed into a mobile printing plant (below, a
view from above, uncovered)

EINE MINUTE
die Dir das Leben retten kann.

Lies die folgenden 6 Punkte gründlich und aufmerksam! Sie können für Dich den Unterschied zwischen Tod und Leben bedeuten.

1. Tapferkeit allein kann in diesen Materialschlachten den Mangel an Panzern, Flugzeugen und Artillerie nicht wettmachen.
2. Mit dem Zusammenbruch im Westen, Norden und Südosten ist die Entscheidung gefallen: Deutschland hat den Krieg verloren.
3. Du stehst keinen Barbaren gegenüber, die am Töten etwa Vergnügen finden, sondern Soldaten, die Dein Leben schonen wollen.
4. Wir können aber nur diejenigen schonen, die uns nicht durch nutzlosen Widerstand zwingen, unsere Waffen gegen sie einzusetzen.
5. Es liegt an Dir, uns durch Hochheben der Hände, Schwenken eines Taschentuchs, usw. deutlich Deine Absicht zu verstehen zu geben.
6. Kriegsgefangene werden fair und anständig behandelt, ohne Schikane - wie es Soldaten gebührt, die tapfer gekämpft haben.

Die Entscheidung musst Du selber treffen. Solltest Du aber in eine verzweifelte Lage geraten, so erwäge, was Du gelesen hast.

Was ist zu tun?

Einzelübergabe: Kleine Gruppen von nicht über 8 Mann ergeben sich indem sie Waffen, Helm und Koppel ablegen, die Hände hochheben und entweder ein Taschentuch oder ein Flugblatt schwenken. Sind alliierte Soldaten in unmittelbarer Nähe, so sind diese anzurufen. Passierscheine, wenngleich nützlich, sind nicht unbedingt erforderlich. Sammelplätze für Kriegsgefangene befinden sich entlang der Haupt- und Durchgangsstrassen.

Gruppenübergabe: Sofern die Übergabe in kleinen Gruppen erfolgt, gelten dieselben Bestimmungen wie oben. Für grössere Einheiten ist laut Haager Konvention vorgesehen, dass Offiziere ihre Mannschaft unter dem Zeichen der weissen Fahne an den nächsten alliierten Offizier (wenn möglich, ebenbürtigen Ranges) übergeben. Sind Besprechungen erforderlich, so können bevollmächtigte Parlamentäre sich mit dem nächstgelegenen alliierten Gefechtsstand in persönliche Verbindung setzen.

Behandlung von Kriegsgefangenen

1. Anständige Behandlung. Auf Grund der Genfer Konvention werdet Ihr wie Soldaten behandelt.
2. Gute Verpflegung. Ihr erhaltet dieselbe Kost wie wir, das bestverpflegte Heer der Welt.
3. Lazarettbehandlung. Eure Verwundeten und Kranken werden genau so behandelt wie die unseren.
4. Schreibgelegenheit. Ihr könnt je Mann 4 Karten und 4 Briefe per Monat nach Hause schreiben.
5. Rückkehr. Nach Kriegsende werdet Ihr so bald wie möglich nach Hause zurückgeschickt.

ZEIGE DIESES FLUGBLATT BEI DER GEFANGENNAHME VOR.

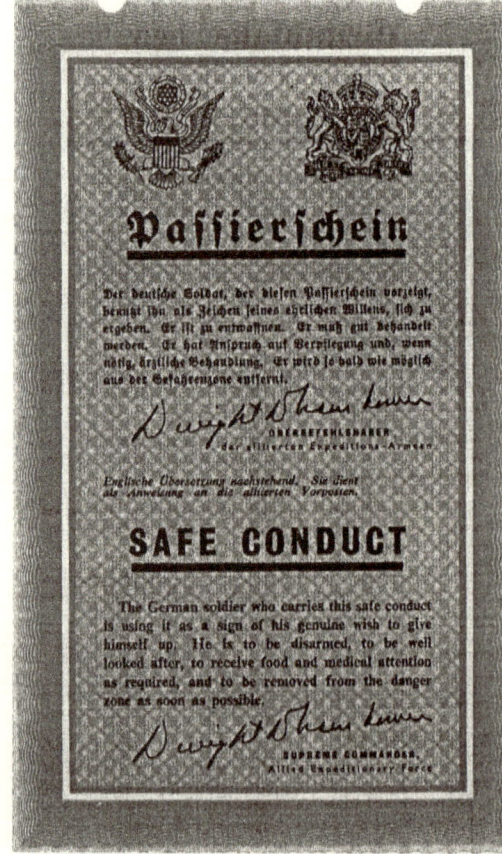

TRANSLATION OF ZG 73 K

ONE MINUTE
which may save your life.

Read the following 6 points carefully and thoroughly. They may mean to you the difference between life and death.

1. Courage alone, in these battles of materiel, cannot make up for deficiencies in tanks, planes and artillery.

2. With the collapse in the West, North and Southeast the decision has been reached: Germany has lost the war.

3. You are not facing barbarians who kill for the joy of killing, but you are facing soldiers who would spare your life.

4. But we can only spare those who do not force us, by senseless resistance, to use our weapons against them.

5. It is up to you to let us know your intention clearly, by raising the hands, waving a handkerchief, etc.

6. Prisoners-of-war are treated fairly and decently, without harshness—as becomes enemies who have fought bravely.

The decision is in your hands. However, if you should find yourself in a tough spot, remember what you have read.

TRANSLATION OF ZG 73 K

What is to be done?

Individual Surrender : Small groups of not more than 5 men surrender by putting away weapons, helmet and belt, raising their hands and waving either a handkerchief or a leaflet. If Allied soldiers are in the immediate vicinity, they are to be called. Safe conducts, although helpful, are not absolutely essential. Collection points for prisoners-of-war are located along the main highways and thoroughfares.

Group Surrender : As long as units surrender in small groups, the same applies as above. For larger units it is provided under the Hague Convention that officers surrender their men under the sign of the white flag, to the nearest Allied officer (if possible, of equal rank). If parlays are required, accredited parlamentaires may take up personal contact with the nearest Allied command post.

Treatment of prisoners-of-war

1. **Decent treatment.** According to the Geneva Convention, you are treated like soldiers.
2. **Good food.** You receive the same nourishment as we, the best-fed army in the world.
3. **Hospital care.** Your wounded and sick are treated just like our own.
4. **Mail connection.** You can write 4 post cards and 4 letters home per man per month.
5. **Return home.** After the war you are returned home as soon as possible.

WHEN TAKEN PRISONER, SHOW THIS LEAFLET TO YOUR CAPTORS.

ZG 73 K

Chapter Fourteen

ALSACE AND LORRAINE

THE campaign to reconquer Northern France may have paused on that fine autumn day when Pvt. George Glade and I had dropped off some artillery shells designated for a special target, and were picking our way from the gun site in our jeep along a forest path, pulling an empty trailer, crunching the leaves beneath our wheels, and in this forest came upon a field of mushrooms, enormous, like elephant ears, freshly sprung-up. I laughed at Glade who had never tasted a mushroom. I was not sure of the species, whether it was poisonous, but loaded the trailer with them, brim-full, a hundred pounds perhaps, covering them with a tarpaulin, thinking the while of the Dad back home who might be just now with the daybreak pacing some greensward of Chicago hunting the mushroom.

We drove back to camp and went among the villagers, asking whether these were good. "The best!" they exclaimed. Some of the troops were uneasy; it was like offering them snails; an American officer is expected to be a very ordinary person with ordinary tastes. Let them learn! So the gourmets among the troop feasted upon them and I gave a vast quantity to the villagers who had their most memorable treat in a long time!

Yet depression fell upon the Company's mood as Autumn advanced into Winter. The slowdown was gradual. I was almost like the normal human response to the seasonal withering of the world, but it arose from a higher level of wholesale despondency. By September 15 practically all of France except Alsace and Lorraine had been freed; three months later, in mid-December, a pocket of Germans still held out around Colmar and Mulhouse in Southern

Alsace. Northern Lorraine - where the Combat Propaganda Team bivouacked - was still in enemy hands. The moment when victory could have been grasped passed unbeknownst at some point.

Where was my outfit then? No one recalled. Epinal, perhaps, a modest city already foggy in the gloaming of fall. It was even before this point, however, that I had been disgusted with the order to cut back on gasoline consumption, because it was so obviously a tactic, yes, a logistical tactic of war, that should have been in force from the first inkling that the Germans would break and close up to the North. Now it was too late to push on through, not really, but, given the deficient energy of Allied movements generally, a gas shortage could conveniently be claimed. For lack of gasoline and all that subtends from it, Eisenhower brought Patton's Army to a halt on September 22.

I claimed not to understand the delays, but of course could not ask penetrating questions. The Rhine was to be grasped and held along its length, from Holland to Switzerland, why? Where were the countless engineer battalions each of which could build a bridge? Could not at least one Cassino-type, or Hamburg-like, bombardment by aircraft be directed at a beach-head across the Rhine and maintained until there would be a sterile zone of several kilometers upon which a large air-drop and infantry crossing could be established? Yes, this can be tried, but later. After all, there was a horde of enemy to be defeated and pushed back before the several points on the Rhine could be reached where, according to theory, proper crossings ought be made.

Who decided that there should be another six innings of war to liberate France, overwhelm Germany, and organize the occupation? Though my indignation might subside, I was continuously irritated at the growing inaction. It was as if this dinosaur, heedless of its purpose and quite brainless, swelled itself up to a glossy weighty mass of millions of men and machines, stretching like a mighty monster from the flower beds of Holland to the meadows of the Alps and slumped into its winter hibernation. I myself was not at all ready to doze off. Nor were the Soviets; they were going hell's bells in deepening winter.

Words were found to explain why the front lines were hardening together with the frosts on the ground. I examined my own G3 and G2 overlays that contained less and less of fresh movement, more and more of unit numbers and names. Logistics were the greedy preoccupation of the Seventh Army. The same with the other great armies of the Western Front. They were less agitated by the slowdown than by rapid advances; shouldn't it be the other way around? One should be grim on the attack, anxious upon a halting.

"What is happening?" I asked the Maps Clerk at Army Headquarters, and also Colonel Parry, my calm and methodical boss at Army HQ. I hardly ever exchanged a word with Colonel Quinn, Army G-2, who occupied another tent or room, the ultimate commander of the G-2 zoo, which consisted of CIC, OSS, POW Interrogation, Signals Codes, enemy documents analysis, operations intelligence, and censorship, besides Combat Propaganda.

I spent more time with Major Ogden who numbered among his other duties the censorship of my mail (that revealed hardly a sign of intervention, however, so cautious was I), and must have known me better than anybody but never mentioned what of my words he had read. Ogden sat on his camp stool by his folding table, in the collapsible tent of Colonel Parry, round-faced, pleasant, a westerner, from Utah, probably a Mormon, quiet-talking, twinkly blue-eyed, uncritical or at least suppressed, glad to oblige, but I had so little to ask for. Except the big question: why are we here and not there? To which they could respond less imaginatively than myself. The complacency was such that I half-believed the strategy of consolidation and found myself writing to my wife that the War was taking longer in order to gather all forces together before attacking, a strategy sure to save many lives...

The Chiefs of G-2, of Artillery, and the others let the propaganda Team alone, exceptionally, happily. The Team reported in writing each week on operations, daily on personnel; also, I conveyed orally stories of interest - that there were pleased German customers for their propaganda leaflets, or some bit of news about local French politics, or a prisoner's interview protocol that was remarkably informative from a political standpoint. Then some small talk. Mess Sergeant Williams meanwhile picked up rations at the Army HQ Ration Dump. Sergeant Roger Villeneuve, Company Clerk, or PFC

Connie Wilson, his assistant, picked up the mail. I formed my opinion of what if anything was happening along the Western Front, and of the seemingly ever-active Eastern Front.

I had lost interest in the Italian Front. I had exchanged a letter with Clara, had heard from John Reynor that Gianni's mission across the line failed, nothing from "D Section." But then, soldiers do not write horizontally, they write vertically, to home. I heard what I wanted to hear from visitors of the Mediterranean Theater; there were enough of them. There was no front in the Pacific Theater for the Yanks to speak of, just a lot of islands and at the moment the great air-sea battles. I barely noticed the miserable actions taking place on the Burmese-Indian frontier and inside China.

I listened to the sounds of the Great Beast of the West slipping sighing into the rut, and heard respectfully its explanations for the slowdown, which might as well have been growls, grunts and squeaks. "Pausing to regroup and reorganize." "The Germans are bringing in troops from the East (an inexhaustible source of troops, to read the G2 reports)." "The Germans are setting up new divisions from the last of their manpower," and presumably we were waiting for them to do so - to commit new divisions against us? "They cannot last much longer under the immense air bombardments; Hamburg is a ruin." "We have to rebuild the harbors." "Our armored spearheads are short of gas and ammunition." "Our supply lines are too long." "Difficult terrain is being encountered in the Ardennes forests, the Vosges mountains, and the great barrier of the River Rhine." "The enemy resistance is stiffening as they prepare to defend the territory of the Homeland for the first time." No one would dare mention it publicly, but with the end in sight and the Soviet forces making excellent progress, why not leave it up to them to defeat the Reich? Sit back and wait for the vaunted Soviet Winter Offensive. (Never mind the vaunted Allied Winter Offensive.)

Once the great drive had slowed, it became self-slowing; thousands, myriads, a million men began to think, "Well, how lucky that I have come this far intact; I'm going to let the others push a little; I'm not going to press matters if SHAEF is not pressing." It was true, SHAEF was all too ready to enjoy the feeling of a steady ride for a few months. If Patton had been in charge instead of Eisenhower and Bradley - would the mighty monster have been spurred to continue its rampage? Probably so, I believed. However, since feelings against Patton were strong, and my own General Patch was well-liked, I could make only the mildest of insinuations.

So SHAEF was snug and the troops were making themselves more comfortable. The propaganda trade was booming, because all of the Allied artillery was at the Front, more was arriving all the time, and more and more of the enemy units were being identified for mental massage. It was obvious to me that my Army was continually being reinforced. As I have said, new unit designations appeared on the G3 overlays daily. I passed them on the road, or met them. I spoke to the men when they were locked in a jam or at a tent where the Red Cross was giving out coffee and doughnuts, silly people, as if the troops were starving refugees. It was about the only way a dog-face could exchange a few words with an American broad; the French colonial troops forthrightly brought along their whores.

Meanwhile, back in Chicago, the infant proceeded regardless. Her mother heralds that a tooth has appeared:

> *She bit me today and for the first time drew blood, and I looked in her mouth, and there was a little edge of white peeping up, as crooked as can be. I am putting nickels in an empty milk carton, starting tomorrow, to pay for the braces she will undoubtedly wear ten years hence, even as her mother did, otherwise known as the Blight of 86th St. in the old days.*
>
> *Jane Hess and I spent a pleasant day. I met her down at the bank building where I was distributing leaflets and she helped and then we went home for lunch. Kathy was the best publicity the Democrats could possibly get, because of the sign on her buggy (My Momma is going to vote for Roosevelt) and the way she stood up in her buggy and yelled for an hour straight. I don't mean crying either. She just hollers out of sheer exuberance, a kind of protracted "Hi!". Anyway, Jane and I sat around and talked all afternoon. John is in Holland with a tank company and she's naturally pretty edgy about*

it, although she doesn't say it or dramatize her woe as much as little Liz Evers, who surprisingly enough has proved to be the most desperate of all the war wives I know, from point of view of feeling terrible consistently. I think that is because she has been the most sheltered of the girls I know, a veritable tender little flower compared to such worldly hussies as Jane or J. Kelly or I. Despite the swankness and apparent sophistication of being brought up on the continent, I don't think anything beats a good public high and co-ed college social life, with access to a big city, for hardening one's intellectual and moral arteries, so to speak. And a little of that toughness helps. Anyway, Jane left and then I went to Laura Bergquist's for dinner, where I had a terrible argument with Jane Cates, another war wife except her husband isn't overseas where he pines to be. He was being trained to be a member of a French interrogating team at Ritchie before he got re-assigned to the infantry, the reason being that (she says) Eisenhower doesn't want any more specialists. I said, that's perfectly reasonable, if you spend a lot of money and time and good red blood getting a man to the front he should be a fighting man also. But no she said any old dope can be an infantryman, etc. etc. Well, you get the drift. I'll have you know I spoke with great authority about t.o.s combat teams, etc. etc., of which I know absolutely nothing. But I am your wife and somehow the glory seeps through, lighting up my red (says the laundryman) hair like a halo, making me unpopular as hell with my friends.

Practically at the same time, though, I was telling her that I wished I were in the Navy.

> *It has cleared up today after raining all yesterday and this morning. There is enough work to keep one busy and enough to do with one's leisure time, but everything is petty, inconceivably so when one thinks how large this war will look in history. But it's as important as the little figures who participate in it are unimportant. That's the fate of modern man - to do things bigger & better yet to decrease his own stature by the same stroke.*
>
> *This country is pretty dull, too. Nothing so grand to liberate as Rome or Paris or lovely mountains - just ugly products of the*

machine civilization and some ragged old farms that never had a chance under any economy, free or otherwise.

In the next war, perish the very thought a thousand times, I'm going to join the navy. They really never suffer a war. Imagine a warm shower, a shot of whiskey and a good clean bed always on hand. A ship's laundry, easy chairs, etc. ad infinitum. The poor damned infantry. I don't think anyone can know what a war is who hasn't spent some time in an army on the ground, from headquarters down. Anything else is a picnic. No wonder that armies have always been the sources of new ideas, contagions of all sorts, mental as well as physical. I'm sure I've learned a great deal more about everything than if I had been in the navy. But I'm tired of wandering through the circles of purgatory. Every new idea hurts - as some pragmatist pointed out some time ago - I'm tired of hurting - and having the GI's too, without proper toilet facilities. Several of us have a mild dysentery at the moment and I think you can imagine how miserable it is to get up in the middle of a freezing night to use a stinking damp latrine a hundred muddy yards away. No fine ship's drainage system, no clean food & dining room. There is absolutely no comparison, nor with civilian life either, God bless it.

The new American troops had not had much training; or some vital functions were absent from their training. They were not very good: what in the hell had they been doing all this time? They were no match for even the bad divisions of the enemy, not yet at least, but there were a lot of them and they were physically in good shape; they probably believed that they would never get up front in time to see combat; now they were hoping that the tempo of war would slow down until they felt ready to die.

The proportion of small-armored soldiers, those who take most of the casualties, actually was diminishing in proportion to the total men in uniform. The American Army was over-specialized and over-manned. With headquarters the size of thinned-out divisions. Every little inspiration of a Washington Congressman found someone detailed to look after it, like a medal for Joe Glotzi from the 6th Congressional District - the officers can parcel out mutually their own medals. Grave-digging companies leaning on their shovels. Visitors by the thousands eating off the rationed board. There were millions of people under arms or working upon the war or living in the romance of others at war, who found war comfortable, were at minimal risk, and did not want it to end. On paper and in fact, millions of uniformed men in the various theaters of operations were permitted to make the same demands on the Army that a combat unit makes while in combat, more or less, which was owing to a great pretense, a myth, bucked up by the Press, Congress, and the Home Front.

My Team kept getting new personnel and many visitors (official and unofficial, with and without orders), yet it had almost no losses by enemy action, disease, accidents, and home leave. ("Home leave" did not exist; only First Sergeant Annunziata got it, but it was really because he was wounded and mentally becoming quite irascible.) Here comes Lt. Chester Oseieki. A cheerful sort, lean, chummy, affable, untrained by any visible standard for anything except perhaps in basic infantry processes. Who knows where he came from? Perhaps as Major Roos sits in his corner sucking his bottle, he thinks of sending pleas for reinforcements to the rear echelons.

The Team had a fantastic Table of Organization. This TO, made in Washington and Algiers, called for the most complicated, specialized, over-equipped aggregate of supernumeraries in the whole Army, not excluding the Supreme Headquarters, Allied Expeditionary Forces (SHAEF). Fortunately only half the requests were shoved upon the Team. I, while still a lieutenant, was filling a Lieutenant-Colonel's slot. The Commanding Officer of the Company was supposed to be a Chicken Colonel. Actually since I was doing Roos' job for him, I was an Acting Colonel; lest you scoff at this, consult the proverb that says the First Sergeant runs the Battery, that's four levels below the Captain, who is supposed to be managing the Battery.

Tom Crowell liked the phrase: *"C'est la fucking guerre!"* and said it whenever some unexpected nuisance occurred, daily that is. It had become a theme of the American troops. "Our mission is to take Hill 231." "We have to be out of here and at Betzelheim with our guns lined up by 1430 hours." "This has got to be printed and fired before 1900 hours tomorrow." The higher the level of command, the more godlike and imbecilic the order. This was supposed to display firmness and clarity. Its impossibility was buried in Caesarean myth: *Veni, vedi, vici.* "Seize all enemy positions to the Rhine!" "Clear the Colmar Pocket of the enemy!" "What? When? Unbelievable!" "Yes. *C'est la fucking guerre!*"

Lt. Oseieki was supposed to be a liaison officer for leaflet operations, and therefore I handed him over to Johnny Anspacher, not without misgivings. Like Roos himself, the officer was supernumerary, so far as I was concerned. I'd rather have returned him to base for credit, for he engaged in conduct which I distrusted: he started cultivating buddies among the enlisted men. What was he going to do for these guys? - feed their egos and that was it, but they had just about the best egos around unless, like Connie Wilson and Lennie Cook, something happened to them in infancy and they were psychically crippled. His conduct seems good, democratic, egalitarian, friendly, considerate - but I recognized in it dangers of incompetency, inferiority complex, inability to command, and a few other salient defects of an officer. Living close, talking much, a group becomes a democracy and overrules command; decisions require some isolation for planning, sanctions, self-defense, and evaluation.

But how could you resist such a sweet guy? However, he took a driver, got in a jeep to call on a French division, the roads were slippery, he drove too fast (this after I told him, just a few days before, Steve, you drive recklessly, watch out!), and he skidded off the mountain road, breaking his arms and legs and throwing his driver for a loop (he had insisted upon driving). I was so angry I would not visit him in the hospital, leaving the decent gesture to Lt. Anspacher. I never saw him again; that was the end of his war.

I did not see much of the French Army, not even their propaganda detachment, but dealt with them through Lieutenants Jacques Pregre and Jacques Villanave, and their mixed aggregation, French *pieds noirs,* Algerian, Tunisian, Spanish, Moroccan, Corsican and Continental French, all under my command. Back of these stood a mistily forming political and propaganda intelligence section of the First French Army, minus the American know-how, technical apparatus and organization for direct delivery of messages to the

Germans. They were in the midst of the struggle to determine what role the communist, military, and liberal Resistance shall play in the new order of affairs. They were bent upon the uncovering and punishment of collaborators among the French; the political mess of the next generation could begin. At least, they relieved the Americans of the task of sorting out the pro-Nazi French.

An Algiers acquaintance, the nearest to a professional soldier-propagandist among us, had been sent in from Algiers, Captain Fernand Auberjonois. However, the leader of the group was Quick-Colonel André Malraux. I did not get to meet him, but had read parts of his book, *Man's Hope,* and knew him to be an outstanding writer. Malraux was obviously up to something more than defeating the Germans. He would have been welcome to come visit the Americans; he might have learned a few tricks; but he didn't come. I would have liked to talk about literature and philosophy with him: Malraux and Arthur Koestler and Ignazio Silone had much to tell me; I felt the romance of their struggles - personal, party, national, worldwide in scope - carried on in the bowels of revolutions. But a combination of pride and principles kept me from approaching Malraux. And as for the rest of the tribe they had little to say. Except but it is too early to hear the beginnings of a love story - except for Simone Thomas.

But, wait, stay, I must pause! For here comes an unnecessary whole level of command! It is called the Sixth Army Group. General Devers bosses it. It sets up by the beautiful spas of Vittel, and receives copies of the Seventh Army Team reports and sends visitors to the Team. It speaks to them formally from on high through "Psychological Warfare Section," G-2, Sixth Army Group. Nice guys: a Major Shields shows up, cheerful, happy to be where he is and to know of the fine combat aggregation which the theory of military hierarchy lets him believe to be his command responsibility. Jim Clark, tiring now after being around so long and of a certain age, ineffable still, goes to join him there, so they work up a cozy group, and they stare right through Roos, who stares through everybody anyhow, which is important, for I get no backlash at speaking on behalf of the Seventh Army Team; they tolerate Roos as the Army suffers its myriad incompetents until they have done most of their damage, and then are gotten rid of too late, like Colonel Hazeltine of the U.S. Cavalry, who, it will be recalled, was summarily removed from his post as Chief of Psychological Warfare in the Mediterranean Theater as a Christmas present to all the year before.

Roos was to stay some months longer but his *modus vivendi* with me developed nicely and before the winter set in he was drinking quietly in his successive rooms (I always gave him the best spot to lay his head), while Wallenberg and Crowell and I and Headquarters Sergeant Roger Villaneuve and the First Sergeant and the others carried on effectively. When First Sergeant Mike Annunziata's wounds and memories got to his head and he became too surly despite his beautiful Michelangelo face, he was wafted homewards, and First Sergeant Taubert came in out of nowhere. He was good, he handled Roos well, respectfully. He was Danish-American, too, like Roos, a big swarthy version, as Roos was a middle-sized platinum blonde.

The feeling against the Commander was general. I and the other officers did not go about singing his praises, nor were some of the other ranks reticent in criticizing. It may have originated with Clark or Shields at the Sixth Army Group, or perhaps in anonymous letters from the Team, that a Colonel from the Inspector General's Office of the Army should show up one day in the Village of Herimenil. He circulates, interviewing soldiers and officers about their Company and especially their Commander. I realize that the critical interview is to be with myself. What am I to do? Worse than anything the Army hates disloyalty. Moreover, it smacks of insubordination. Criticism is *prima facie* proof of insubordination and disloyalty. Criticism from the second in command is almost always fatal - to the Second in Command.

I said that there were no serious problems with the Company, that the Major was a heavy drinker but generally kept to himself and is certainly no mad bull. There was nothing good to say about him, however. I would have liked to recommend getting rid of him, but the least that would happen was that the Army would get rid of both of us. Anyhow, that was the way I figured it. Perhaps I was mistaken. The Inspector General departed. There was no further word about the matter.

And here come even more visitors. As in Africa, in Sicily, in Italy, so in France and then in Germany. The Team is an attractive outfit. They are in close touch with the Front and at the same time not as misanthropic and exposed to mishaps as the infantry. They eat well, mostly with the same rations as the infantry, but better prepared and with more skillful scrounging in outside markets. They have mobility and know everything that is going on, from the German side, the American side, locally, along the Front and from the enemy and Soviet radio and press. Earl Pittman and his assistant are manning the radio monitoring truck continuously. Tom Crowell's printing trucks are converting electric power into word-power with interminable click-clacking. Harold Adams has no business as a civilian taking on the over-the-lines amplifiers and the half-track armored reconnaissance vehicle that is used to get the equipment forward and to protect the orators, and to get them in and out expeditiously. He is a sweet guy. I feel sorry when I learn that his wife has decided to divorce him. Harold is seriously downcast; he is now drinking and talking incessantly.

Our frontline one kilowatt radio broadcasting station was not functioning here. It was working far back near the Riviera, with Captain Hoagie and his crew. It never had fulfilled its promise of a station that could be heard by the nearby enemy across the lines. It was best used for newly occupied areas where the radio broadcasting facilities had been damaged or were non-existent, or were dependent upon a station still in enemy hands. It depended, too, upon a stable front situation; it was not as simple to move around as a tow truck. But it was a cute technology. Like the other equipment, the fast little printing presses. Too, the mobile hear-all monitor van.

Also the half-track amplifiers, for it must be said that this armored vehicle was useful for approaching the point of broadcast to the enemy, but then it had to be hidden and the amplifiers toted up to the auditory location, and there abandoned until the operation was over, because it was usually subjected to small-arms and cannon fire. A cheap small amplifier would have been just as effective; no matter if it had to be abandoned. It would cost only as much as a few cannon shells. But it should have been stocked in some quantity, like the shells, say at least a score per army. And divisions should have been encouraged to employ them on their own initiative, by means of recordings and even broadcasts live by German-speaking Americans, who were always to be found.

In addition, there was Fred Faas, the photographer, who showed up on November 5 and was harbored. Then a Britisher was assigned for a while, Lt. Crossman, whose big brother was an acquaintance from Africa now with SHAEF, Dick Crossman. (We knew even then that he was destined for high office in some future Labour Party Government and he had picked up the name "Doublecrossman" already, thanks to his many enemies in politics and military affairs - the English public school boys like to coin these naughty nicknames for each other.) Sociability, news, nothing much else. They carried away ideas, stories, scuttlebutt from the scene of action.

Lt. Col. Culligan came in, he who had been top military administrator in Rome after the Liberation and was now with the Sixth Army Group HQ. Culligan had been an entrepreneur; he still owned a company that he described to curious me. The company matched quickly people from all around the country and of every skill with emergency jobs - a guy who can work a telegraph while holding his breath under water is needed for testing an underseas installation, that sort of thing - a glorified operation later represented more mundanely by the Kelly Girl, or by what are called "head-hunters."

Captain Galitzine, handsome and humane, somehow detached himself and even got back to England to get married, but then returned like an eel to the Sargasso Sea, very much alive and smiling. He had smashing pictures of the High Society wedding and articles from the Press.

Captain Beaudry of the Canadian Army was another free spirit, and he, too, became loosely assigned, perhaps because he was an uncommon Francophone in a largely Anglophone volunteer army. No one would think of asking anything of him but a favor, which he was delighted to render. Next to the drunk hung on with Captain Charlton in Naples, my worst binge occurred the night Beaudry took me to a French outfit with which he had connected near Epinal; it had a great chef and good wine; we made the most of it, and afterwards talked and drank till dawn back at my bivouac. Beaudry was reporting to someone, somewhere, I forgot, *in vino amnesia*. Beaudry was a dare-devil and I pulled out of a couple of my proposed expeditions, pleading larger responsibilities. Beaudry described a little hotel in Paris and Julie, a French girl so beautiful that I had to write home promptly in order to dispel the notion of the trip for the moment. I was sorely tempted.

Then I did go to Paris with Beaudry for two days - hardly time to say hello all around. Julie was there at Madame Heller's little hotel, but a) wasn't all that beautiful, b) was either menstruating or sick. So back I went - remarkable how little I allowed myself in the way of leave - especially when you think of how easily I got it: it was not really called leave - I wrote a pass, ordering myself to talk to this one or that one, to pick up this or that piece of equipment or set of reports, to deliver something or the other, all destined to end the war sooner - I asked Roos to sign it, put various stamps on it for Seventh Army Headquarters over at Headquarters itself, and now it looked almost as impressive as the aforementioned *Passierschein* leaflet that was disseminated among the German troops in large numbers, that one that guarantees them safe conduct through the lines and decent treatment - nothing so nice as Paris, of course.

I had visited Herz, though, and whoever else was around; the liberation flush was almost gone. I was embarrassed and annoyed by the large banner flung across the Champs Elysee, exclaiming in huge letters: "Hart, Schaffner and Marx Employees of Paris Welcome Their Liberators!" (which Army Historian S.L.A. Marshall, writing about Liberation Day much later on, relishes to say was shot down by a French gunner the next day; either Marshall is mistaken or it was re-erected.)

Once again I would catch the Paris itch, in the wintertime, and would go with Tom Crowell and Earl Pittman, staying at Madame Heller's hotel again, where we put on a big drunk with three prostitutes, waving goodbye to them from across the subway platforms as dawn struck La Madeleine. A couple of days later Tom as downcast; he has caught the clap. We exchanged a few sour jokes. Fortunately modern medicine, penicillin and all of that, ridded him of the gonorrhea promptly; in respect to Madame Heller, it must be said that Tom had refused the escort of a plain-looking woman, insisting upon the better-looking one, who had been noticeably reluctant to go along; as he recovered, he lectured about beauty being only skin-deep.

The people of Alsace and Lorraine regarded the Americans as liberators, and, on the whole preferred the French to the Germans, especially so long as the French were democratic and on the winning side; they had had enough of the Nazi Party, disastrous War, and appeals to their Germanic origins. Heeding their town crier, the villagers turned out in goodly numbers for a dance with the Americans; the mothers watched with keen interest; the local men appeared indifferent but steadily drank down the three barrels of beer the Yanks had bought ($10 for one barrel came indirectly from my Chicago Addison Street neighborhood association); the boards resounded with cheerful, heavy-footed jumping. At first it was *jazz Américain,* but then an authentic accordionist appeared and the polkas and waltzes blare out through the Company loudspeakers. Hardly a sexual orgy. But the cowsheds shivered their timbers.

Private Cook - the same of the fatal shooting - had his own private stock. She was a pretty girl whom I had glimpsed a couple of times; I heard that she had followed one of the soldiers up from Lyon. Private Cook disappeared with a two-ton truck one afternoon and a blizzard came raging in. We worried. No truck, no Cook. A vehicle and two men were sent to the rescue in another truck. All returned well. Cook was stuck in the drifts.

I was angry: the killing was still in my mind, and the truck could have been cannibalized, and the rescue truck had been endangered. I determined that there was to be a Court Martial: Cook had gone too far. He was given a fair trial, and the maximum punishment of thirty days confinement in a Company cell by a unanimous panel of two officers and an enlisted man. This meant finding a private unpleasant space for him now, and for when we moved. He was kept in a stairwell most of the time. He was brought his meals. The men could visit him. He had no duties. He emerged from confinement smiling and good-natured, as ever, always ready to help when called upon. "Sir," said one of my most affectionate soldiers, a private from Boston, "I thought you were a great guy, but I have to tell you that I am very disappointed in you and have changed my mind about you." "Sorry to hear that," said I.

The complications of the romance had not finished. Second Lieutenant Hardbill approached me. "Sir, I would like the permission of the Commanding Officer in order to get married." So the Army rules state. But who would be prepared for the stunning news? "Married?" I exclaimed, "but how? Where would you find a girl?" I looked incredulously at the small erect North Carolinian, handsome, always serious, his chin and cheek traversed by a slash scar. "I have known her for a while." Her name? "Lucille." The same Lucille who - the same Lucille? "Yes Sir." "But you know, Hardbill, that she has been around the company, has had relations with Private Cook and, well, you know." "Yes, sir, I know." "Well..., if you love her, I shouldn't want to stand in your way. Good luck." "Thank you." "Don't mention it... Why don't you take three days leave and maybe George can go along as a driver to watch the car." I told Major Roos about it. "Disgusting, don't you think?" Roos said, curling his lip, but he signed the permission.

How soldiers manage to fall in love and keep up an affair - when the front is stable - well, yes - but when the front is fluid - will always be a ticklish mystery. It can happen anywhere. Wasn't it thus that Moses wandering in exile beat up a ruffian, helped a girl to draw water from a well, and married her in short order? Even in a small Company, secrets are born, and they are kept by their little networks. What seems to be important often is not whether others know the secret, but whether a certain person or group - the Commander, the officers, the First Sergeant, the Orderly, the Technician Second Class named Joe, does not learn it.

Generally the American soldiers spoke and probably thought the less of sexuality the longer they were in action. The response of the soldiers to the seductive flirtations and dancing in the occasional movies that came in and were shown were more subdued than they were in the Stateside camps. There occurred a letdown in sexuality. A small group were pledged to women back home and kept the faith, others didn't feel the urge, some were afraid of the troubles and disease and ugliness of the situations in prospect. I took it for granted that a normal proportion of the soldiers and officers masturbated but was incurious about it, and never came upon instances; the Company usually occupied a large space and the men were spread out and had their own recesses of privacy. There was an actual diminution of testicular activity, also.

I did not come upon overt homosexuality, but only a warmth bordering upon it, as the strong devoted affection Sergeant Villaneuve, the Chief Clerk, displayed quietly toward Private Connie Wilson, his assistant. Not even an emulation of the traits usually assigned to gay types, such as Major Greenlees would uninhibitedly display, and what the British usually condone, would make Americans angry. A libidinal, unexpressed, and unexercised homosexuality emerged from the shared dangerous and deprived associations among the men; this would vary with the expectation of immediate danger and was therefore found much more among the risking-killing units than the safer ones. Direct combat brings the soldiers to embrace one another psychologically, profoundly, to become attached by the fear-fight, masochistic-sadistic aggression against the enemy. Combat makes blood-brothers of them, in more ways than one.

Martin Herz, oldest friend of the global horror show, returned to visit once, twice, thrice, lean, black-haired, hawk-nosed, soft brown eyes turned fierce, speaking crisply but dispassionately like a Prussian staff officer. He came to sniff the Front and refresh himself from his labors at SHEAF where he was now chief leaflet writer and soon became a Major. His operation there had become gigantic. A full bomber squadron operating out of England had been assigned to leaflet operations. More of the same: one did not know why they didn't go in for noisemakers, shriekers, boomers, or more exotic forms of printed material. One might as well take the occasion to scare the next generation of Germans to death; but, by now, most children had been evacuated to the countryside, as was known from prisoner interrogations. Too many of the casualties of the bombers were impressed friendly foreign workers, afterwards to be counted not at all, or as German-inflicted (which, indirectly, they were).

Martin was more technocratic about the whole business than I. He was doing a job for which he was well-suited and was well-recognized, promoted and decorated; he lived in a fine hotel in Paris with private bath, with complete laundry and other services furnished, excellent board, and a bar at prices far less than he could afford. He was unmarried. Indeed the only reason you could see for his not wanting the war to go on and on was his basically responsible and generous spirit and knowing that better things were beckoning; he hated war in principle, and detested human stupidity, which manifests itself so openly and completely in war; he hated the Nazis but felt an almost maternal affection for the ordinary German soldier, of whom he had seen many, worn-out and docile as newly taken prisoners of war usually were. He genuinely wanted them to get back home along with all the other soldiers, too. So he worked very hard, at least three times as hard as he might have gotten away with.

He was happier than I when I was at last promoted to Captain. "Congratulations on th' promotion," he wrote, apologetically, "somewhat belated, to be sure, but nonetheless sincere," and blamed the Algiers mafiosi for delaying the orders. But now I was twice promoted to Captain. What happened was that Colonel Quinn, Seventh Army G-2, decided that the promotion process had dragged on too long, and short-cut the Algiers Headquarters that was formally my parent organization. He put me up through Seventh Army HQ and the matter was promptly attended to. But meanwhile Algiers had gotten around to promoting me too, and these orders worked their way up through Sixth Army Group. So I found myself with two sets of promotion orders, and should there and then have coined another identity and sent myself home on leave while remaining ostensibly in the theater of operations. I was advised by G-2 that unfortunately two Captaincies did not add up to one Majority and to adopt as my date of promotion the earlier of the two, November 17.

I had become stony hard on the "German problem." When Martin Herz arrived one day, only to leave the next day at dawn, we talked until two in the morning, according to one of my letters, "about what to do with the Germans."

> *It will be immensely difficult. I can't see our several nations agreeing together on social planning on a scale they have individually been incapable of doing in their own countries. If we don't even teach American children American government and democracy properly, it is difficult to see how we can teach the children and adults of Germany the immutable principles of democracy. Anyone knows that historical examples are very weak in teaching people democracy and yet we are determined not to treat the Germans as democratic equals. One way out might be to abandon all pretext of being severe with them and forget about the war. That is not only impossibly impractical but also serves as a confession to the Germans of our own weakness and their own justified conduct under Hitler. The other extreme of a brutal oppression over a period of years is likewise impossible, because it is a vicious circle and requires constantly increasing stringent disciplining. I am myself in favor of executing offhand all of the Gestapo, the SS, the Parachute Corps, the General Staff and the State hierarchy, despite the fact that five or ten per cent may be "innocent." But there is your root and there is your example. Then, despite the fact that everyone shares a little guilt, treat the rest of the population as in a certain sense victims and as being capable of creating a democracy with our help, abandoning all severely repressive measures.*

Herz would not accept the plan, but he had none of his own, and, after returning to Paris and thinking it over for a while, he wrote to me that he agreed with it. Since I repeated this idea time after time in correspondence and conversation, I must have developed confidence and assurance with it. Something approaching it actually occurred, except, as will be recalled, the punitive actions taken were transformed into the forms of trial and punishment under international law in an attempt to make law. (This is not to object to the making of such law, but to recall, also, that the American Government under Truman then embarked upon a program of crystallizing "sovereignty" of national states: sovereign states and a world law are a contradiction.)

The would-be executioner of a quarter-million Nazi bastards did not sleep much on the same night because *"the landlady's little girl has a little black kitten which is put out at night and which cries loudly."*

> *Last night I took her in, but she clamored just as loudly in my room and wouldn't let us talk in peace. I thought she might be hungry and started to look through my musette bag for some crumbs when I found myself face to face with a little mouse with large eyes and a long tail. He hopped nimbly under the bed leaving a partially chewed up Hershey bar, one that you had sent me and which I was conserving and the nibbled portion of which I turned over to the kitten who devoured it and went to sleep by the stove. She was all right until about six in this morning, when she climbed up the bed and started stomping on me, so I threw her out.*

With Herz gone, I talked to Lt. Hans Wallenberg. We two should have been closer; we were, in fact, together almost daily, but Hans was not witty, nor imaginative, he was very Prussian-like indeed, a small dumpy man with a deep bark. Businesslike, serious, he regarded me as cavalier, even reproached me once for spending too much time with Tom Crowell, the low-brow cheerful printer. Hans lived in a dingy room a couple of doors down the one street of the Lorraine Village where we bivouacked. He caught the flu and I visited him, taking him an article just received, written by my brother Sebastian on the propaganda values buried (but discoverable) in Shostakovich's "Leningrad Symphony."

I cogitated aloud before my friend, with ideas that would have been useless to offer to Tom Crowell, or anybody else in the Company, for that matter. That great artists needed to communicate with the masses when great events were at hand; that the objective analyst could not be creative. I felt that Hans was not the most creative of propagandists, no Goebbels he, the Nazi being a genius of the highest order, none the less for being diabolic.

I saw in music a form of expression whose symbols and devices could be shown readily to diverge from or coincide with the understanding and sympathy of the auditors, but where greatness in modern times more than ever could not be achieved because of the huge gap between the artist and the common man. I would have liked to admire James Joyce highly, to take an instance from literature, but could not because Joyce spoke to a very few people, which disqualified him from greatness to my mind. I really believed then that others, and perhaps even myself, could bridge this gap, could be both profoundly expressive and at the same time popular. This was a myth, a dream, really, because I would have been scarcely able to name truly great artists who were popular, or great scientists, analysts, that is, who were popular, never mind whether they were good men.

Both I and Hans read as much as anyone else in the Company. My latest favorite has been Sassoon's *Memoirs of an Infantry Officer:* "I find it the finest book I've ever read on war on the level it's pitched at. It's much better than Remarque *[All Quiet on the Western Front]*, for example." Hans was reading the letters of Frederick the Great and quoted from them, showing them to me; how apparent in them was the deep-rooted German sense of duty. There would even be startling parallels to Hitler's own situation a few weeks later to be found in Frederick's thoughts at a particularly rough time in his career, when about to give up to the coalition of nations fighting him, but hanging on, and suddenly finding reprieve with the death of the Russian Empress.

Dr. Joseph Goebbels adverted exactly to that very same drama that struck Wallenberg and which he had related to me. The very last days of *The Reich* had arrived. Hitler moved about the rooms of his bunker, demented, deteriorating physically, demanding the impossible of everyone, accusing all of cowardice, incompetence, and treason. Goebbels, who had been told by astrologers to expect a last-moment reversal of fortune, was reading Carlyle's biography of Frederick the Great. He phoned Hitler, exclaiming excitedly: "My Führer, I am reading how the Emperor Frederick seemed to be losing everything, and was determined upon suicide, when just on the brink, by a great stroke of luck, the Russian Empress died, and Prussia lived, and now - get this, My Führer, President Roosevelt has just died, and we shall win!"

Wallenberg and I, and, too, Herz, Mann, Habe, Langendorf, and those who came to visit, were continually struggling for a logical, just, practical policy toward the Germans. There was a lot of cursing and railing at the foe from the Army and the home press and population: these men were more knowing and experienced and thoughtful - you might think that we would have reached a consensus. We did not. The arguments drifted off into drunkenness, our work at hand, departures, trivia.

I, beholden to my educational masters at the University, tried to be as precise as possible. How to separate the population from the elite; how to re-educate them. Yet who were we to re-educate one of the most educated people in the world? Well, they had terrible flaws: what were they, where lodged in their minds and their society? It was an impossible problem and yet there must be a policy and the young officers, operational, at the nodes of action, had as much to say as anybody, and what the generals said, and what Churchill and Roosevelt and the oppressed peoples said, was to some degree what these young men said, because they were opinion leaders, and also they had some control over the apparatus of propaganda, the press, radio and film, and the selection of the crucial second-level liberators and occupiers.

They talked unceasingly of the key ideas, argued them, these men in the age group between 24 and 34, in the grades from Sergeant to Major. The issues were unconditional surrender; war criminals; reparations; the new constitution of Germany; the treatment of collaborators in the rest of Europe - the Fascists of Italy and everywhere, the Pétainists, the millions of crushed souls and wicked ones and turn-coats; the support of Governments in Exile of Eastern Europe that had fled West and their reconciliation with the Communist Governments installed by the advancing Soviet forces. My ideas took shape on each of these points, as the troops suffered the worst winter in memory of Alsace and Lorraine.

Corrupted by the anticipated and actual work of the military censor, and deprived of reference to intimate affairs that I would not let myself confess, great letters were not to be expected, but I persisted in writing at a gallop. Not so Jill. And fortunately hers were not censored. There were a great many of them, sent at the rate of three a week, averaging over five hundred words, arriving less regularly, sometimes several at once, sometimes not at all for two weeks. I saved them all and explained to her:

> *I've studied and sorted your letters I've received since being in France and they make quite a book. Do my letters amount to so much too? They must, I guess. I must have said 'I love you' a thousand times, still it's no more than the number of kisses you used to get in a single day, or will get. And the thousandth one didn't seem repetitive at all.*

All our epistolary jabber swelled into a substantial outflow. The whole body of letters, extending for more than three years of military separation, all told, would ultimately approach a million words.

I had other correspondents, parents, brothers - the two young ones growing up and readying themselves for military service by means of unashamed loafing, my older brother already in the Office of Strategic Services - Bill Steinbrecher, kept out of uniform by medical disability, Mike Holmes, out of Eton, now an Ensign in the Royal Navy and anticipating convoy duty, Bill Evers, hoping to translate his new Captaincy into a Company Command in the next Pacific island romp, and my former professors, Earl Johnson, L.D. White, Harold Gosnell, together with a score of others. I was far and away the luckiest man at mail-call.

My letters to Jill unconsciously followed a formula. They told of the outstanding non-censorable events of battle and campaigning and the men around me; they recited the foodstuffs of the day; they reported other personal communications; they commented on the world scene, especially the general strategy of the War; they reviewed briefly the books and articles I had been reading; they described the weather; they professed my love and intense desire to return home. I declaimed viciously against the liberties that civilians enjoyed, mindless of the need for civil rights; perhaps I would have shut down the nation into a prison for the duration; soldiers cannot be trusted with liberty, especially in wartime. The more obvious the fact that the War was being won mainly by the civilian workers and abstaining civil population, the more I snarled at them, calling them "spoiled children;" *"While I must struggle for a crumb of freedom, they want icing on their cake."* (I was commenting on labor unrest, complaints against travel restrictions, and the like). My letters almost always notified her which of her letters had been received.

The Presidential elections got an early vote out of me by absentee ballot. It was scarcely an informed vote, except for the top of the ballot, where I choose Roosevelt over Dewey. I violated the secrecy of the ballot for Jill,

> *I shall undoubtedly vote in a half-informed fashion, and against the candidates you've gotten laboriously to know. What can I do? I can't wait now for you to answer this letter with a filled-out sample ballot. Therefore I must take the fateful step without your helping hand. Since you are my only darling wife, I'll tell all. I have just scratched the ballot for our true and good F.D.Roosevelt, and nice, conscientious Truman, for Lucas* [for U.S.Senator] *because he still votes right and Lyons is no good at all, for Courtney* [for Governor] *because Green has been a drab failure, for Hunter, Barrett, Vicars, Merritt and Johnson because without his own party in office the governor can't do a thing, and inactivity and internal squabbling is worse than a Republican slate any time. I know nothing about the candidates for Clerk of the Supreme Court* [of Illinois] *save that the office shouldn't be elective, but Cassie gets my vote to keep perhaps a little more the Supreme Court from paying too much attention to nefarious interests antagonistic to mob rule. The University Trustees are Republican for my money to keep the party in power from having an opening wedge into the educational system. Emily* [Douglas] *gets my vote senz' altro. Govier and Rowan also tally with me. After that, everything becomes dark. Berman gets three from me* [Illinois has a unique partial proportional representation by allowing voters to lump their vote in selecting among several candidates for a State Legislature's Assembly District] *(Lee is a jerk), and all the rest are Republican save Szumnarski. Do you still love me and are we pals?*

As the Front stabilized and the propaganda shells fired unceasingly, I borrowed from the main Army ammunition dump a crew of three men and brought them to live with my own men under Sergeant Becker, in a kind of cave. For them it was a holiday from the wretched discipline of the battalion; their rations improved; they set their own routines. I wrote of them:

> *Yesterday I spent an interesting, otherwise unoccupied hour at our ammo dump conversing with Sgt. Galloway, one of the widely divergent souls I have assigned to me. He is, as Jim (Clark) suggested when he saw him while accompanying me on an inspection, a `colored gentleman.' That is, he is smooth and has "been around." He lived strangely enough only about a mile from us in Chicago, just the other side of Washington Park. We had an interesting talk about the neighborhood, mostly just repeating the names of streets and other mundane items which become important to the exile. He used to be a cook on a Pullman, which fixes very well his wide experience and savoir faire. Among other things, we got around to talking about politics. He is a Roosevelt man and said that most of the Pullman workers were also. The most intriguing idea for me came when in a discussion of how the colored people, according to a story he told, voted Republican whenever anyone mentioned Lincoln. He then went on to say that he heard someone say sometime that Lincoln only freed the slaves in order to win the war. Now, the significance in my mind is that he, and men like him, independent, proud, and competent workers, unconsciously and consciously dislike the idea of crediting Lincoln with freeing the slaves, because it presumes that they were an inert mass and that some omnipotent white man waved his wand and they were free. Galloway thought that, though he was cautious in expressing the idea, the negroes would have been freed by the forces of history apart from the desires of any white benevolence societies or philanthropists. The principle behind his attitude I find very striking, and I am now almost convinced that the whole propaganda of the Lincoln myth is a bad thing for the negro and among the more intelligent of them is actually a subtle insult.*

As it happened, I had worked up a study of the life of Lincoln shortly before entering the Army; the thesis figured well enough. When Thanksgiving Day arrived, I consulted with my soldiers and we invited the group to join the whole Company for the day of feasting. For the moment, it may have constituted the only racially integrated unit in the Seventh Army.

At a point in the festivities, I had a word aside with my racist barometer, unreconstructed Southerner Pfc Connie Wilson, who in a surprising moment of enlightenment said: "I think it's a good idea, Sir, to have niggrahs over to eat with us." Than as an afterthought: "You know, Sir, I have come around to thinking that the niggrahs are all right. I have changed my mind." I was pleased; I had made a convert. But Connie was hesitating and then explained his further brainstorm: "It's the Jews, Sir, I know now, they are the problem." Here! In such a company as ours, how could it be? I was mentally flattened one more time by the intricate, patterned messiness of the human mind and soul. Sweet, neat, dutiful Connie the Clerk: he was prejudiced against every possible subject, French, Italians - especially Sicilians, the worst of them, he could be overheard to argue when drunk, that would include his own beloved Captain, stretching the point a little. He dared not spill out his hatred for all Yankees as such.

Enlisted men were allowed to choose, if they wished, which of their officers would censor their mail. Most did not bother to do so and I ended up censoring some of their mail and dumping the rest upon Lt. Anspacher. It was a dull job. The lives of the soldiers were richer than was apparent in their letters, which were almost always brief, unadorned, laconic messages. In 820 days I did not read a beautiful full letter. I could only commend an occasional phrase; a rare outcropping of lines of profound love or yearning or suffering or despair. Some expressed themselves well orally. They could sing a popular tune with clever or moving lines. Scribbling original messages conveying true feelings and their environment was beyond them, even on politics. Elections, Dewey or Roosevelt - hardly a word in the letters, little enough arguing otherwise.

Captain Alfred de Grazia felt also that he must end the year 1944 with a reckoning. I therefore elaborated a message to all of the Seventh Army Artillery Personnel concerning propaganda operations. Not every 24-year old is permitted to address an Army like General George Washington, but strange powers dropped upon youthful soldiers in World War II, and it goes to show that I didn't spend all of my time scrounging for food and drink and writing home. (George Washington, incidentally, delivered himself of a voluminous personal correspondence while conducting the Revolutionary forces in the War of Independence.) So, hang on as long as you wish:

> *Subject: Artillery leaflet Operations against the Enemy*
> *To: All Artillery Personnel*
>
> *1.* General. *This memorandum is published for the information of all artillery personnel and especially for those artillery units which have not been fully informed on the subject of propaganda by leaflet shells before assuming their posts of combat.* [These new outfits are arriving continuously and no one thought to train them in all the time they were hanging around in the States and Britain.] *The purpose of American leaflet propaganda is to diminish the will of the enemy to resist our forces...etc., etc.*
>
> *The number of 105mm smoke shells, base-ejecting -- R1QLA - which are converted each week and fired as leaflet shells has averaged 1000 for the Seventh Army. Though calculations of the results of the various types of shell on the enemy are impossible to make exactly, it is expected that they do their proportionate share of damaging the enemy's resistance. The number of shells used.. depends upon 1) the total supply of ammunition, 2) the availability of transport priorities, 3) the total number of enemy troops facing our troops, 4) the availability of good targets.., 5) the number of firing batteries.. in position, 6) the vulnerability of the enemy to propaganda at the particular time...* [I cite, as an example, that a large number of troops may be in range who are demoralized and easy victims of propaganda but our advance may be too rapid for artillery to be drawn up in firing position before the situation dissolves - but all of this rests anyhow on the efficient organization of the total system to begin with. I go on to describe the general and the special types of leaflet, the fancy "Surrender Pass" designed to bolster the psychology of any surrender tendency and the leaflet poignantly directed at a special injustice or misery of a targeted unit.]
>
> *2.* Initial Arrangements *for Fire.* [Here a

tedious iteration of the hierarchy underlying the operation occurs.] *Leaflet shells are fired by army order, corps order or divisional order. They are also fired by verbal arrangement with PWB ... etc, etc.* [Counting the hierarchies and the exceptions to using the hierarchy under different conditions - when speed is sought, when phones are down, when somebody gets a good idea (but he had better be sure of it!), there must be fifty sets of circumstances and methods of triggering the descent of a shower of paper upon the hapless enemy. It is all part of the eternal struggle in the army between centralization and extreme decentralization down to the mouth of the cannon.]

3. Firing. *A Provisional Firing Table follows:* [Here I go into the appropriate settings and the numbers of leaflets that are set to spew forth at the proper height above the enemy. The Table will never be but provisional, still I would not dare call it less than that. There should be an experimental battery in Fort Sill, Oklahoma, firing test rounds.]

4. *Reports of Firing.* [I have prepared a form to be filled out upon firing, and sent in to me, recording any unusual events and also the circumstances of the enemy before the event.] *Leaflet shell fire may be observed in the same manner as high explosive, especially air-burst, and smoke shells... With a light breeze, if the leaflets leave the shell at the height of 300 to 400 feet, the area covered by the leaflets is approximately 150 yards in diameter, below the point of burst. With a cross-wind from 12 to 15 miles per hour, the leaflets reach the ground approximately 500 yards from a point below the burst. The area of coverage does not vary appreciably with the velocity of the wind.* [I should have offered a prize to the best cannoneers; ordinary firing does not take into account such winds; the weapon should be aimed 500 yards short of the target and 180 degrees against the wind direction.]... *Once grounded the leaflet may be read easily* [despite crinkling or wetness]. *The most economical terrain for leaflet coverage is flat wooded country. Targets in mountains are most difficult to reach, and in open, bare country, the leaflets blow along the ground*

from the point of impact.
    5. Results. [I end with an exhortation to the troops: granting that the contents of the messages are all-important and will have some effects, which I describe, the diligence, cooperation, and skills of the artillerymen are vital to the accomplishment of the mission.]

With that, I sign off, "By Order of the Commanding Officer, Captain Alfred de Grazia, CAC, AUS", hoping for the best. The problems are many, and subjects of written complaints, reports, and expostulations over field telephones, in themselves the generators of numerous misunderstandings, even misfirings. Trucks cannot find the propaganda shell dump, or they arrive there without knowing what they came to get. When nothing can be done, as when a tank runs over 50 packs of explosive powder, or a leaflet intended for the Second Mountain Division is shot at the SS, there is the customary cursing, black humor, alcohol, and a turning to other tasks and pleasures.

I had arranged for record keeping beginning in early October for the first time - an historic First! - and therefore we know that by December 10, 20 leaflets had been produced and fired all or in part. Each shell case was stenciled with the title of its contents, the converted shell, its metal base screwed back tight, double-tested. It was rare that a base piece and the paper wads ejected in a muzzle-blast, which was dangerous (hopefully, over the enemy, the pieces would clobber somebody). The shell fuses were not completely reliable, at the longer ranges especially. Artillery units sometimes failed to pick up their allocations. Sometimes they fired excessively, at other times under-firing out of fear or uncertainty or ignorance. (An enemy divisional front would typically require 100 shells, and about 250 propaganda shells would communicate with them in the course of a week.) An unfortunate general condition prevailed: when psychological conditions for firing were best, targeting conditions were worst.

The editorial policies that the Team settled upon were initiated mostly on the Italian Front and fully developed in France, so that there was nothing at all new when finally, as the War was nearing its end, on February 7, 1945, Commanding General Robert McClure of the Supreme Command, PWD, SHAEF, issued general orders to follow certain policies. I summarize them:

> *No direct appeals for desertion. Carry always some reference to decent treatment as prisoners. Don't say prisoners are sent overseas. Say prisoners will be repatriated "as soon as possible after the war." Suppress all names or indicators of deserters. Use only the fancy "official" surrender pass or safe conduct guarantee. Do not disparage the enemy to his face. Do not boast of our valor. Reiteration is no fault; don't strain for variety. Do not answer German propaganda directly. Stay off of larger political agitation. Tie in news of operations consistent with the news as announced by SHAEF. Tell no untruths (except in the rare special black operations where the identity of some party of the enemy is pretended).*

All of this had for a year and more been part of our operational code in the Eighth, Fifth and Seventh Armies. Consider, if you will, for a moment: the *Frontpost* newsletter had been fired regularly all this time at the enemy; it was factually accurate, unemotional, unabusive; it was more accurate and objective than most American and other Allied newspapers and magazines sold and read by the civilian millions of the homelands. The soldier propagandists felt that they could not afford to lie; the journalists around the world and their editors at home felt that they could not afford to tell the truth. Even when we were winning!

But isn't that a sign of a well-working Army: when the Commanders issue orders that are already in effect? Just as I wrote my wife proudly that I spent only an hour and a half per day administering the Company; a man would be an incompetent meddler to put in a long day at it. I would not argue that I might have been a better Commander if I had reached out to do certain new things, which I had mentioned and would continue to bring up - things that hardly any officer went around to doing, it is only fair to say, like running a book club, or insisting that everyone be trained to do the jobs of several others, in case of need, or daily equipment inspection, or instituting voluntary services for needy civilians, or arranging visits to historic sites, or getting men to write home more often. Come to think of it, much of this was being done in one way or another. Lieutenant Johnny Anspacher had a decent knack for it.

The Germans were doing very little frontline propaganda. Captured directives, however, showed that the flood of Allied propaganda annoyed the leadership all the way up to the Command and General Staff, and field commanders were urged to prohibit any circulation of the leaflets and to devote resources to replying in kind. They relied upon rockets, patrols, left-behinds, reconnaissance plane drops, and civilian carriers to distribute an undistinguished set of messages. Antisemitism was a persistent theme, also slackers on the Home Front. Nor did the theme of useless sacrifice of troops by dumb leaders escape their attention. "Where is my Daddy this Christmas?" asks a rocket fired leaflet of its Third Division targets. The 45th Division gets one reciting its losses from Sicily onwards, assuring them of their good chance to die in the mud for the warmongers and profiteers who contrived to stay home, and ending in a clever P.O.W. appeal: "Your buddies are glad to be out of the mud. They are sure to return home safe and sound. You still have a long way to go. Keep alive if you can. For remember, YOU ARE STILL WANTED... FOR JAPAN!" (Query: wasn't this admitting that Germany would surrender?) They did a lot of humble boasting: "You are not finding the German soldier such an easy foe to overcome, are you?" And "What is the German soldier doing? HE FIGHTS LIKE A LION FOR EVERY YARD OF GROUND!" (This was too much! The surviving *landser* was painfully cynical: he called the Iron Cross the "Frozen-meat cross," a phrase from Russia.) Letters from Americans in Prisoner-of-War camps were reproduced, also sad letters removed from the pockets of dead men.

"Do they have an effect on our troops?" I was occasionally asked, never with fear or concern, generally with the attitude that the Germans were wasting their time. Sure, I said: there is always somebody around who can be discouraged by a sympathetic communication to the point of giving up earlier than necessary. "Winning can cause more damage to combativeness than losing." The idea was not too difficult for combat soldiers to comprehend.

The idea needed to go unexpressed, however, and tabooed back of the lines. Although quite a few Americans were taken prisoner, the universal vocalized supposition was that they surrendered to save their lives - which covered an extended gamut of judgements.

The Germans rigged up balloons made of oiled paper, 11 meters in diameter, which, when inflated with about 22 cubic meters of hydrogen gas could lift up and carry over into French-held territory, much of it Alsatian, about 40 pounds of leaflets. The leaflets were in bundles; no mechanisms were used to bring the balloons down to earth or to scatter them about. They depended entirely upon vagrant breezes for their direction and traverse. Conceivably they landed when the gas was leaked out, or when shot down by an agent who then circulated the leaflets, or more likely by an Allied soldier. They were couched in English and French, not in German, though doubtless the people who would be most inclined to obey instructions and further the adventure would be German-speaking Alsatians of the more rural type.

On November 23, after having reached the Rhine first of all at Rosenau, the French made a dash for Strasbourg and liberated it. Everyone was pleased. I went to have a look. The city had emerged well, stately, well-preserved, its fat buildings ready for Peace. Delighted with the sight of the French troops exhibiting their wonted verve, did a bit of shopping, *pâté de foie gras,* the best in the world, of course, cans of it, fresh, too; the cans were gifts for Ann and Paul Oppenheim in San Francisco, no one would better appreciate them. On the way back home - home is where the cows moo and the chickens run along the streets -I took a shower at a G.I. roadside facility, and handed around the *pâté* for the cocktail hour.

As I said, the Front stagnated. Should I now say: "What is war Really like?" Is this the time to tell it? But I have already done so and of course have still more to say, because everyone except the rational people on both sides, numbering a baker's dozen, were sure that it must last much longer and if they believed so, it became a self-fulfilling prophecy, and it did last longer than it should have. To repeat, for most of those who are likely to be killed, wounded, captured, War is usually a going and coming and sitting, then abrupt deadly events ordered by leaders, friend or foe, spiced besides times by murderous skirmishing, stepping on or running upon a land mine, catching a few surprise shells or an aircraft incursion, or an individual or collective accident - the literal meaning of "casualty" is "mishap or accident" - including especially one's own planes, shells, mortars, small arms. Time elapsed here among the grave risks is short, a few minutes, an hour; a bombardment for days is rare. The greatest number of casualties are brought on by forces and people one doesn't see. Rarely according to plan. Often in consequence of being forced against one's will. A large number of deaths are legal and illegal murders - the difference being that the legal deals with helpless, fleeing, unaware enemies, the illegal with men disposed of while trying to surrender or in custody. Battle and war are aimed at profiting from the greatest advantage, imposing the greatest inequalities, the unfairest tricks. It has only a little to do with hunting and almost nothing to do with competitive sports. It is fear and sadism, and these are hidden in the countless cases surrounding the "legitimate" casualties of war and overlain by thick layers of myth and amnesia. But why go on? You know it all.

When the Seventh Army artillery got within range, a 155 mm cannon was driven up to fire leaflets upon Karlsruhe, across the Rhine and miles away. See here, it proclaimed, the heart of the Reich is in reach of our cannon; stop your foolish resistance. It was a little premature, four months early, like the leaflet that announced to the enemy that their troops at Cassino would be trapped via the Allied landings at Anzio. Still, it felt good.

But now there was Hitler's Ardennes Offensive to contend with, beginning on December 16. I drove back to Army HQ at Saverne every day to follow the news carefully on the Army HQ map. I refused to believe it could be as serious as it was taken to be - here again was that conflict of feelings: when thousands of men are falling, the very fact of casualties stamps events as monumental; never mind that there is no ultimate sense to the enemy's strategy. I was confident from the beginning that Hitler had thrown all he had into this crazy attack that could not last long. The enemy was attacking forces several times its size. If the Allies had been less complacent and unexpectant, and more aggressive, the German attack could hardly even have been launched. Where will it break down? Eisenhower cast division upon division into the fray. True, in woods and hills and sleet, air power dwindles to little effect. Also, Allied communications were a mess; divisions were overcrowding and stumbling about while isolated units, as large as a division in the case of the 101st Airborne, could become isolated.

Let the enemy in, this undergrade strategist thinks, and then they cannot get out, what with all the forces that the Allies can bring to bear upon Northern and Southern flanks. Indeed, Montgomery was told to hold up everything else and dig into the Northern flank of the enemy. Patton's Third Army was ordered to attack the Bulge from the Southeast. The Seventh Army was told to lengthen its lines to cover Patton's rear and flank. It did so. I moved my Company to a new village by the German border in Lorraine. Snow was deep over everything. The village was deathly still. Christmas came and all seemed well. At the dump the soldiers set up a small Christmas tree, decorated it with insignia, tinsel, bits of glass, and they grouped with me when I came, to photograph ourselves around the bar and tree, a family portrait.

The week was dismal but the Germans were retreating out of the Ardennes Bulge, not by any means trapped. Closer to home, G-2 warned that an attack against the Seventh Army was being prepared. Another absurdity: why would Hitler have destroyed his few resources in attack, knowing that every time he reinforced and attacked in the West, or even resisted more stubbornly, the Soviet troops sped up on the road to Berlin? I and my cohorts could not send this in a message to the Germans, because of our top leaders' promises to the Russians; but the Nazi leaders, and the Wehrmacht Generals: must they not see the plain truth and want to save something of their country?

There were steps the Team could have taken. They - Wallenberg was the key player here - could have despatched a message to the German troops huddling for the foolish attack: "See here. We know that you are trying to get ready to attack us. We are ready. What are you waiting for? Whatever your personal qualities, this is madness. The odds against you are enormous. Hold off. Take it easy. Survive." As I said, there wasn't the imagination for this kind of propaganda. Instead, I became involved in two typically play-safe ploys. The first was a leaflet printed and distributed to American soldiers, not German, with a headline "...if you should be captured" and telling them that, with the Luftwaffe reconnaissance gone, the enemy had to extract intelligence from prisoners, and you know a lot that he wants to get out of you, so "in case you're that unfortunate" to be captured, remember that he can get nothing from you but your name, rank and serial number. Practically a license to surrender readily. This was the brain-child of G-2 Counter-intelligence.

A second request came out of G-2 for a leaflet to be fired into enemy territory, civilian as well as military, warning them to give no information to the enemy - this in case the enemy returned - lest they be considered as spies later on and dealt with accordingly. I reacted negatively to the proposal: if people were to be informers, they would be now alerted to the need for keeping their activities secret. The project was dropped.

The New Year stomped in for the Team on white snow by black night, with a feast and boisterous inebriety. Like the Hessians at Trenton we were. Thick snowflakes were piling upon the village and its host of vehicles. I, well-oiled, tucked myself into my bedding roll. The deadly nonsense of the Ardennes attack - the very idea of crashing through the Allied lines to the sea, the exaggerated accounts of Nazi successes, and the inevitable collapsing of the Bulge - made it all the more ludicrous that the depleted foe should launch itself upon the well-led, well-supplied, confident American Seventh Army. But it did. In the first hours of the Year 1945.

Christmas '44 in
an Alsace schoolhouse

Wallenberg demons trate
the classic ballet to
Villanave & Prepre

Hans Wallenberg created the important postwar German daily 'Neue Zeitung' and was a founder of the *Springer Verlag*.

Chapter Fifteen

THE BATTLE OF GERMANY

MORE snow was falling and the wind was rising. The fire in my hut burned warmly and I was sleeping soundly upon the toasts to the New Year. At four o'clock the guard appeared with Sgt. Villeneuve to awaken me. G-2 Army had messaged an order to move back somewhere, but fast; the German attack has begun. (Of course the enemy will gain some ground; how much, nobody knows.) I call the First Sergeant to reveille the troop. Pitch dark, luminous snow, faintest of lights. As I wade through the snow to find Major Roos, I snap words into several doors. Roos is up watching the office junk being collected. I will lead the convoy, the Major cover the rear.

Trudging back, I pass soldiers emerging like maggots out of black holes in the snow. Muttering, grunts, packs being tossed thudding, a couple of men sucking up coffee from a still warm tin of the night before as they dismantle the kitchen. The first motor revs up loud against the stillness of the village. I dump my stuff in my jeep. Corporal Scott drives it to the edge of the village and begins to wave the vehicles into line. Not lights, but sounds; one after another, now several at a time, the motors sputter and catch, spewing filth from their exhausts onto the perfectly pure snow.

Sgt. Villeneuve had gone to tell the *Maire* (until lately *Bürgermeister*), that the troops were leaving.. *pourquoi...?* orders.. to where?.. I don't know.. But the Mayor and the people - they were awake, hardly moving - they knew. They were staying. The Americans were going. Would the village see Germans again now? Would it be destroyed?

Who would be denouncing whom? The soldiers were sorry to depart, and gave their brief friends candy and cigarettes, what else did they have? A few francs, the new Allied franc, to be hidden until the next liberation.

I walked up and down the forming line with a "Let's go," here, a "Come on, now," there and a "Morning," and "How ya doing?" everywhere. Tom Crowell's big trucks are the last onto the road, shambling out of the drifts with some urging. I love Tom, whose mood was always just right, whose crew was so dependable. It was guys like Tom who made war tolerable. The vehicles were bumper to bumper so as to see one another by their tiny slitted eyes. A damaged truck was hitched to a prime mover. Double check the line, Sergeant: see whether we're leaving some drunk or anything behind. There was no roll-call; every man was connected with another man or several men or a vehicle; so no one could be left behind; and of course here no one would want to hang back. I wondered who might have been out on a mission; whoever it was would not have a home to come back to; he may find the enemy in charge of things. I pondered sending George Glade on his heavy black motorcycle to the ammo dump to warn the men there. They were back a-ways. I could send George when we knew where we would be.

Finally, I mounted my jeep, knowing that any lingering vehicles - and these there will always be - would fall in frantically as they heard the line beginning to move. My map lay unfolded upon my lap in the open jeep; it caught large flakes of snow that flickered in the glow of my flashlight. I didn't know where I would be taking the troop; Advanced Army Headquarters would be moving somewhere at the same time; I understood that I should bivouac somewhere in Southern Lorraine, near a village called Hérimenil. Good of G-2 to remember to tell us to get out! I pumped my gloved fist in the air and the column staggered out into the country. I felt slightly ashamed at abandoning the village. I felt exultant, too, at the flare-up of battle; the German attack was foredoomed, I knew, but there would be thousands of personal and collective accidents and tragedies now and millions more to come before the end, all to no avail, craziness. Thanks to Hitler, Goebbels, Himmler,

Ley, the Generals, the SS, and the millions of collaborators and minions who did their every last bit as commanded. At this moment somewhere behind me were lines of German troops advancing in the blizzard, who were miserably thankful that the murkiness would not let them be targeted by artillery and aircraft.

I couldn't see much of anything; but then who could? Certainly no enemy planes, if they could afford such in support of an attack anymore. What was not white was black, but even the black atmosphere was becoming whitish, long before dawn. Already the word had been signalled along the line and other outfits were feeding onto the roads. There were problems: To go in the right direction. To avoid taking roads that dead-end into meadows. Also to keep to the road when circling around tanks and trucks that are stalled. I didn't want to lose my trucks either, which would happen if some column cuts in or one of my own slides off the road and the others stop to get it back on. Too, recall the land mines: only a fraction of them had been removed. Stay to the beaten path; path? - the snow filled in tracks as soon as they were laid. Traffic got heavier, got slower. It merely crept. Plainly we were caught in a general retreat. The blizzard flourished with the dawn. Cold in the open jeep, I wrapped myself in my every covering. I uncorked a bottle of schnapps, swigged it and handed it to Scott. I took out the salami that had cost my mother countless food stamps and been mailed to me from Chicago two months ago. Slash off a piece. Munching on it, I cut a chunk for Scott, and guzzled more of the booze. Very slowly, we edged up to an absolutely congested crossroads. Four, or is it six, columns, tanks, trucks, half-tracks, jeeps jostling for position, snorting, jostling for advantage. Alone there, directing traffic, was a short stocky MP in a greatcoat, with his helmet down to his sweater-collar, his gloves flapping, baton hardly visible, boots shuffling in the freezing muck.

My jeep nosed up to the intersection. I got out of the jeep, walked up to the MP to say something about the weather and ask permission to turn the column upon a road half-right. The Private looked up at me, a gentle, patient face, swarthy, hook-nosed, its black lashes laced with ice. It was Fred Pera from the University of Chicago. Hadn't seen him in five years. "Hello, Fred, what the hell you doing here, brushing up on Nietzsche?" (Philosophy was his subject.) The Private's thin lips smiled. We couldn't shake hands, we just clap awkwardly at each other and exchange a few words. Want some schnapps? No, thanks. Go ahead, he said in his mild, musical voice, you can go now. I waved my arms and gave my people the pumping 'let's go' signal. It was daylight, after all, it was nine o'clock, but opaque white because of the blizzard. The convoy steered my way and files off to the West, solemn, hooded, like a funeral cortege.

No one else had occupied the village of Hérimenil, so we billeted ourselves on the population, Crowell with a couple of his men and I billeted in a large loft over a barn, quite livable - it had been the master bedroom, in fact. Below, next to the stable, the family dwelled; their cows smelled sweet and warm. The soldiers set up their own army stoves. Crowell brew coffee. The pot would sit there fragrant from now until this town, too, was to be abandoned. A calf was born below us one morning early and I stopped on my way out to watch the throes; mama finally reached around, licked it all over and it slowly pulled itself together and got to its feet, needing a few more swipes of the tongue to show its big beautiful eyes. Comforting. And we kill them by the thousands and eat them. Oh, well. What can you do? Out into the snow drifts of day. I write Jill about it:

> *I assisted in the birth of a calf in the barn below this morning. That is, I stood by and admired the smoothness of the proceedings. The cow was down in labor, amongst a lot of other cows in a dirty drafty barn. And while Barbary ducks and chicken*[s] *trooped backwards and forwards, she dropped a fine bull calf. Once the head came out, the rest occurred in a minute. The sac was broken and he lay there sputtering and blinking. The farmer's wife and the little boy were also there watching. The old man was visiting at one of the neighbors and arrived after the whole thing was over. The little boy enjoyed it a lot and let out a shout of glee when the calf started to move, almost running over it with the runners of his sled which he was dragging behind him. The only human touch needed was a bowl of salt sprinkled on the calf's glistening body, partly as an antiseptic, I*

suppose, and partly to give the mother added incentive to lick him. At any rate, she lost no time and a few minutes later, he was stumbling around, brushed well and dried. Tomorrow he'll be running around and nursing with great lust.

The human animal goes quickly from the brute to the sublime:

I've just finished reading Cakes and Ale *by Somerset Maugham which, if you have not read it, is just as well. He is smooth but knocks himself out thinking of dull things to say, a not uncommon faculty amongst modern writers. In one of those very old* New Republic's, *I read a review of a three-volume work on Greek "culture."* [This must have been the translation of Werner Jeager's great work on *Paidaia,* the ancient Greeks' ideas about culture and education.] *It is no doubt most interesting and deep, but sometimes I wonder whether the time spent excavating ancient ideas might not more profitably be spent on exploring modern society, if the problems are approached in the same spirit of scholarship and not as a journalistic exposé. The classics have been a more unfruitful drain on the store of human genius than the priesthood and they have produced nothing that will serve to explain society properly. Only great minds can play chess with Greek ideas and what is left for the masses - nothing, only their prejudices and glimmerings. Sociological data can be assimilable by masses of people, however, and that is another point in favor of sociological education in a democracy. You know, of course, that I am not talking about what you were handed as "sociology" at Smith College, or even what is taught at the U.of C., but of* [a] *body of data and generalization I am convinced lie before us to dig up. Education on classic Greek culture has always been aristocratic education. Interest in sociology has developed with interest in the common people. The world has always been divided into "us" and the fuzzie-wuzzies. Each "us" group has studied the Greek classics and loved them principally because they were so remote and couldn't possibly have come from "fuzzie-wuzzies." There is no doubt that ninety per cent of American Christians would be shocked into heathenism if they could know at first hand the dirty physical circumstances under which Christ was born - the lack of plumbing, the unbathed people, the cold, the smells and the violence of it. It's just as well. We haven't yet any preparation for reconciling them to it and they would only be unhappier.*

The Germans of General Blaskowitz, led by the XIII SS Corps, penetrated ten miles through the Saverne Gap and were stopped; his XC Corps cracked the American lines at Bitche, and the Americans began to withdraw to a pre-determined position next day. Now it was proposed to abandon Strasbourg because our lines were too long. My Team and I hate the very idea. Strasbourg is practically the heart of Europe, for Europeans of culture an amiable marriage of what is good between Paris and Berlin. The orders were handed down, to evacuate - it's what the technical manuals of strategy seemed to dictate. Even so, it seemed absurd. The Team sent its amplifying equipment into the streets of Strasbourg telling the people to evacuate the City if they had anything to fear from a return of the enemy. An ignominious mission. From street upon street families began to move out by truck, cart, bicycle, motorcycles and on foot. De Gaulle was furious, the Team learned from its French Army contacts. The French Army, to hear our contacts talk, was on the verge of telling General Patch to go to hell, and move in to replace the Americans. It would have been little less than a mutiny. I would have agreed with them; certainly I would have done my best to justify them. De Gaulle finally prevailed with Churchill and the White House. General Devers had to reverse himself and order the City held at all costs. My trucks were delighted to return along the roads leading out of the city telling the people on the move that the City would be defended and that they should return. All of them were happy, and practically all turned back.

The German attack made some progress. Without being informed we would have been lucky to get away with our skins. A couple of battalions were trapped and lost. Some of the new infantry regiments took a beating. Unit affiliations and commands were shifted around like shuffling card decks. I was bewildered. Was this something new? It had gone on and would go on for the rest of the war, I believed. Somebody upstairs looked at his maps and reports and decided the 398th Infantry battalion ought to be with the 46th division while the 14th special Recce Force Baker should be broken up into three components and sent to relieve the 14th, 779th and 33rd at Grundheim, Gonifsheim, and Weldburg. (I should quote from records instead of using these fictitious names.) In fact most of what was considered news was just this shifting of units around. I wondered how unit loyalty could be built, and experienced collaboration can take place.

What were the Germans up to? They had had almost no effect in relieving the pressure to wipe out the Ardennes bulge, though they had created a Bitche Bulge and it took quite a long time for the Seventh Army at its leisure to move in upon this. Once the main line of resistance hardened, the propaganda to the Germans increased, with several themes: "what's the use, you are not supermen but are being asked to do the impossible, you know now what you are up against, you never had enough backing for an attack," etc. Consideration was given other themes but in the face of obvious contrary directives, they could not be used: "Surrender to us rather than to the Soviet Communists!" "Home-coming or Siberia Forever?!" "We observe all treaty obligations for fair and decent treatment of prisoners and civilians, unlike the Bolshevists." They would have been highly effective. But without the personal O.K. of the messages by Joseph Stalin himself, they would be also very divisive and prejudicial to post-war cooperation with the Soviet Union. (Or so it seemed to the psychological warriors then.)

The themes listed above that were actually used were for a stable front; strangely, propaganda against attacking and advancing troops was not prepared or even considered. There had never been such. One would excuse this by saying that there never had been a use for it, but here was a case and the Ardennes attack had been another. Aside from the confusion of being under attack, and apart from the feeling of shame for considering that we might be retreating, there was the belief that the enemy was immune to propaganda when on the offensive, which in turn came from the improper notion that the effects of propaganda were limited to cases of crushed morale. Actually the theory of propaganda holds that everyone is vulnerable under all conditions to symbolic manipulation. Here this most experienced of outfits had not, although given adequate notice of an impending attack, prepared messages to be left behind by the thousands in all the positions that were being evacuated. What to tell them: Go slow, everything else is collapsing, your family needs you, you are facing unlimited artillery and mortar fire, panzer divisions just waiting to suck you in, land mines and booby traps by the thousands, we have been prepared (citing early HQ warnings), with the front loosening up take the occasion to turn yourself in (German prisoners are being kept now in and near Germany): such arguments would have been effective and saved lives and brought in prisoners.

The Americans were not as smart as they pretended to be, and no one higher up had had any experience or paid any attention to such matters. No one and not ourselves certainly were asking penetrating questions. There was little concern for recovering immediately the lost ground. The Germans were over-extended, under-equipped, under-manned, and could go nowhere, but pretended to be holding their insignificant gains. At Army Headquarters, the Joke made the rounds that "The Bitche Bulge has become the Patch Pocket." The German Home authorities are desperate *"Sieg oder Sibirien!"* they paint on the walls. The Death Camps were going full blast, hundreds of thousands of people were being put to death, but my company did not know this. Death was raining from the skies upon German cities, also. The Russians were encircling and capturing more and more prisoners, and these had a shorter life span on the average of, say, twenty years, after surrender. My life was not uncomfortable even in the middle of the winter and at the front. Or had my standards been properly lowered by the military life? I had the fine rubber felt-lined boots that my toes swam around in. The food was getting better as the supplies piled up excessively.

Sex, too, peeked into one's life. Lt. Wallenberg casually mentioned to the Captain that his landlady, a stocky hearty woman - is he in with her, no beauty she, but then no beauty he? - had a sister whom I didn't know and she wanted to make love to me. Was she pretty? Well, not bad. Where do I meet her? At my landlady's. When? When you wish. Two days later. She walked down the narrow steps from the second floor. She was a peasant-plain, perfectly built, tight-bodied woman, several little lines encroaching upon her un-creamed face, a thin-lipped tense smile: appearing to say, here I am, I offer nothing except I want you to make love to me. But a second visit was expected. Not at all, say I. (I made up my mind fast, and with my mind, my extremities.) Oh, but she must excuse herself. Her small son just broke his arm, and she cannot be wanton under the circumstances. They made another engagement. In the little room upstairs. She was stiff-backed. I was hasty. Perhaps she was happy. Perhaps she wanted a clever, pretty baby. When we said good-bye, it was not to meet again. The troop moved on, and I did not feel like returning the compliment.

The mails speeded up. On February 12, I received a letter written only eight days before in Chicago. I commented on Yalta. It sounded OK, I said. For all I might tell, FDR was in good health and anyhow had a couple of good men around him, and seemed to have driven a hard bargain, and the liberties of Eastern Europe would indeed be guaranteed, and all the world will be united thereafter, for they agreed, too, that there will be in San Francisco a United Nations Conference to set the stage for the new democratic world order.

On February 17 I had an unhappy dream to relate about my childhood home on Hill Street: I could not locate it. The dream was contradicted by a later dream in which I happily brought home to Hill Street a company of men, and when they were settled in I await Jill's arrival as well. On February 13, I described the frustration of putting through a phone call on an operation. On February 20, I was telling how badly I missed my beloved, and on the 27th composed a poem on the subject, and on March 17 recited a bad dream about losing her. I told about bed check and guard duty, and sharing the village with an infantry battalion. And one time, a story of my landlady:

> *My Darling,*
>
> *It's a very quiet afternoon and I don't know what to make of it. The weather is dirty, chilly winds and rain, the remnants of the great snows still here and there, or wherever the careless boot treads -*

then the helmet rolls down the street and one is gazing with a certain lack of calm at the glowering sky. The arctic shoe-pacs are all rubber and slippery as the devil. I just had one of those rigorous, humorous arguments with the Madame downstairs that the Latins get so much fun out of. She was berating me because I wouldn't give them a couple of gallons of gas to make an essential trip to some town. It seems that the Germans stole all the work-horses in these parts before retreating, and now the government is giving a horse sale at this town. Several of the farmers want to go together to replenish the livestock herd. They have a car but no gas. But we are forbidden to give gas out under any circumstances to civilians. They are supposed to have an allotment which is probably sufficient to get the sous-préfet around in his car but no more. I fully sympathize with the vital need for work horses, but gasoline is something that is dangerous in more ways than one. There is so much stealing of it going on, and just a lot of mistaken generosity on the part of soldiers who bleed for the obvious justice of so many cases. However, I can give them a lift in a vehicle going that way and may do so. Of course, the lady told numerous incidents in which soldiers sold or gave away gas and that makes it harder on anyone who wants to preserve a semblance of honesty. I solved that particular rhetorical dilemma by telling her to find some such soldier and get it from him.

The simple things really count in this war. It is won less by romantic strategy than by gasoline, guts, and organization. Our army ought to be trained better on the conservation of gasoline and materiel than it is. If Gen. Patton's Army hadn't cooked on gas in Normandy they might have gone farther into Germany. Of course, no one ever thought they'd have to get there so fast. We had the same trouble.

Back to my landlady, I told her I was going away for a couple of days and gave her my field jacket to wash. Then she gave me a piece of pie and I came over to write this letter.

The weather is ugly and bitter, working conditions abominable. I feel fine. It's about midnight, I've removed my mud-caked boots, gulped a good strong shot of whiskey and am about to turn in. But, as always when I have any reason to be happy in the slightest, I think of you and feel I must tell in a few lines anyway how much I love you and feel happy thinking of you too. Despite a number of things popping up even at this hour I think I ought to be able to sleep the night through. The only thing that may get me up is a report on one of our soldiers who was stricken with some sort of heart attack and was carried off in an ambulance. I tired myself both mentally and physically today, the latter by the simple method of driving over 200 kilometers in a jeep over some of the most horrible roads ever rutted about by the machines of man. What bomb & shell craters hadn't done, ice, thaw and traffic accomplished. One time we got stuck for a half an hour or more in knee-deep mud. Finally a prime mover was enlisted to pull us out, happy day. I thought we might have to spend the night there. The only nice thing was the weather, and from our mud-bound roost we could see lots of sleek planes dashing hither and yon.

This was February 19, three years after I walked over to join the Army in Chicago; my spirits should long ago have been crushed; but I carried on in my world of epistolation - how sad the person who cannot put pencil to paper when all else is miserable.

Did I ever finish telling you about my last trip to Paris? The play I saw with Martin was composed of episodes in the life of Molière, who, apparently, was a bad lover and like most comedians (so the saying goes) quite a tragic character - you know "On with the show" and all that sort of hogwash. We walked over a good part of the city afterwards, trying to find a bar open but without success. I find that Martin leads a very dull, busy life there and it's mainly his fault. He hardly seems to go anywhere. Many other officers do worse. They stick together & waste away their time at the bar of their hotel or play cards or go out with Wacs. It's a rare one that gets into Parisian life to any extent. One of that type is old Earl Pittman who used to be with us in the Seventh Army & is now very comfortably set up in the big city. He has a half French, half Indochinese girl as a mistress. She speaks English well and that is fortunate for Earl is unilingual. He is also an incredible wolf - very sultry looking for a blonde. Since he hails from Chicago, you'll probably have the opportunity of judging for yourself some day.

Here is that bad dream that was mentioned above:

MARCH 17, 1945

Darling Jill,

I am still shuddering from the effects of a dream about you. We seem to have one great trait in common, that our dreams about each other have a large element of at least partial frustration in them with a resulting overwhelming sadness and perhaps a saving sunniness when we awake to find the dull reality much preferable to the depressing sleep. I dreamt I had come home or at least was somewhere over there and was walking down the street, not thinking of meeting you at all, when, all of a sudden, I looked across the street and my heart almost tied itself into a sheepshank. For there you were, very tailored and shapely. I ran over and swept you into my arms. You were as happy as I was. Then a cloud came over you and you let me understand that this was the End, and then, much to my dismay, you disappeared. I searched frantically for you and finally found you in the company of some detestable boys and girls in the room of some house. I was told by the girls that you felt something had occurred which would make our relationship impossible -- this only a few minutes after a two-year separation. I felt very badly but got you out into the street again in order to get to the bottom of it all. At this point, you changed into a man and apparently I changed into you, because the man was now the person who was explaining why he was incapable of carrying on the affair -- but was half hoping that you would not believe him. He seemed to have various effects of wounds which he thought might be difficult for you to accept in the Brave New World. The final issue was undecided when I awakened. I'm not at all sure of the meaning of this dream or whether it has any sense. I believe that the principal fear of losing you to some unaccountable reason held me unconsciously long ago, in our pre-marital state. I loved you much more than I cared to admit even to myself. I think the war and separation elements are not too significant in the interpretation. They perhaps only increase the insecurity which fosters the dream. Nor does the change in identification mean much, except that I am you and you are me. The main thing seems to be that there exists always this great love which I certainly can never abandon, neither to the obstacles of my dreams or of my real life, and which makes me unhappy only when I'm afraid that I'm losing it. And yet our characters are such that we have these nightmares that show the other person slipping away, and are never so sure of ourselves that we have only pleasant dreams à la fairy tales, without fear, since we have not only our difficult characters but our even more difficult environments of war, work, and society to face and conquer. That we sometimes lose in our dreams is not surprising. That we invariably win in real life is astounding. I never feel the slightest doubt when I sleep next to you, with my arm around you.

But now back to the War - as if these dreams, by the hundreds and on both sides of the Ocean, were not some of the most poignant bits of the grand fracas.

My support of the Free French for years and my backing of De Gaulle's stubbornness against the evacuation did not prevent a growing disaffection with the General:

I was happy to note in recent French newspaper dispatches considerable disapproval of De Gaulle's actions in international affairs. For example, Franc Tireur *wrote: "We should prefer our country to brandish the torch of international democracy rather than to accept the leadership of the small powers as if out of spite at not being a Great Power." Again, "Why oppose the secret diplomacy of the Big Three with a still more secret French diplomacy? Why, in general, give the world the impression that France's foreign policy varies from one day to the next according to mortifying setback, a missed rendez-vous, or an unfortunate phrase?" And* Combat *writes: "We have no desire to play the oracle at a time when a policy inspired by the obvious French concern for security appears to have received a severe setback. We shall only repeat, however, what we have often said already, namely that it is vain to look for power when we have no force at our disposal and that the only realism which we could afford corresponded to the deep feeling of peoples and that by expressing this we should have achieved real greatness". Thus, a great many French realize that the old French diplomacy of sécurité failed miserably before and it is a mistake for France to try it again.*

The French were to annoy me greatly. We were all rather crazy, I thought but the French even more so. I perceived as early as January that they had won the war in their own minds and couldn't wait to get rid of their Allies (something that was not realized until De Gaulle quit NATO and sent a few more insulting gestures our way). But they were terribly dependent. The Americans gave them everything they had including the reason why they could possess a fighting spirit. The Yanks rationalized the whole war for them. I began to see how De Gaulle would lead France, on the path of its historical perennial delusions. (I knew all this but was far from revising my romantic notions about the French. It would take me many years before I could utter a new attitude and see the French for what they are and no more than that, and capable of no more, but I am the same way for my own America. Indeed I expect and will expect too much from humanity for a long time to come.) How could the French, not to mention the Germans, deny the stupendous American power? (I could not know what the Soviet Army with its immense artillery assemblages and fleets of tanks must have looked like just then as they were moving up to the last great battles in the East; I would have thought them propaganda, just as the Germans up to this very moment had insisted on the evanescence of the American hordes.)

I heard that my brother had lined up a teaching appointment at the University of Chicago. I was glad. Maybe Sebastian could safely resign even before the war ended because he was a civilian with OSS and had a wife and child. I didn't understand how he managed to escape; maybe they exempted teachers of certain subjects like communications, if they taught soldier specialists in training at the University.

On March 1 I was talking of doldrums. I traveled around but not so much, for it was a dull country. I had plenty of help in operations and people who liked to drive; I visited Army HQ, also 6 AG, and wrote more letters and read more books. It took me only an hour a day to manage all my company administrative functions, another hour for operations against the enemy, so I went back and forth to HQ, hold discussions with Wallenberg and a couple of others, and planned special meals. For all of this, I appeared to deserve something, so the Seventh Army decorated me with the Bronze Star Medal; for close support of combat operations, the formula was worded.

Lt. Manning, one of my officers, stepped on a mine, got it in hands and legs, luckily not in the balls, which was the first thing one thought of; but he was crippled for life. I sneaked a bottle of Martell Cognac, the best, in to him at the hospital. We had no other casualties in this period. Casualties generally were few and almost entirely of the infantry, for the Germans were going out of planes and artillery and their supply. They were not coming in waving leaflets, they preferred to wave a white cloth and have the leaflet in their pocket.

The German prisoner of war talked volubly, answered questions readily, was surprised at the educated, perfectly fluent, but differently uniformed sergeant or officer who was interrogating him. But no one had gotten this idea of a sophisticated empirical morale test to apply to a unit. If someone had delegated me to the job, I would have made some progress in its invention. Herz, Habe, Wallenberg, Langendorf, they were probably the best German morale specialists in the U.S. Army, but not theoretical methodologists, nor had anyone ever suggested to them nor they to themselves that there could be a science of morale measurement that they might develop on the spot. (Fifty years later, there still was no development to register here; although the related sociology and psychology had advanced somewhat and in detail, the application to military conditions had not been made.)

Thus, if the average, quartiles, medians, and extremes of time of soldiers in a platoon and company were known, the resulting figures would help determine the breaking point. But numerous other factors counted. Next to Der Führer, the loss of the experienced platoon sergeant was the most severe blow. He had held together the old and new men; he represented the tradition of the company and thence the army. The latest and present moment and predictable front experiences, geographical composition, experience of battle, food, supplies, ammunition, higher echelon leadership, background noise (home news, rumors, pressure along front) - these and other elements entered the picture.

The German soldiers were in a worse way than the Americans facing them, from every standpoint, though, after a certain point is passed, comparisons are less meaningful, because when you feel rotten you feel rotten, and that's it. Look at the seventeen German soldiers taken captive by the Americans in the general area of the Bitche salient between the 13th and 15th of January, and then interviewed by Technician Third Class Irwin Y. Straus, who wrote up a thorough account of them.

By occupation, they had been a textile mill worker, lathe hand, airplane mechanic, mason, merchant, hotel cook, rotogravure printer (he was full of technical advice), a railroad surveyor (so was he), a coal miner, a baker, a fur tanner, a cutlery worker, and a professional soldier. They came from four different units, five, if only the one man could have remembered his own unit, which he did not. On the average they had been committed to action in this sector of the American Seventh Army for five weeks. Two of them were deserters, one a passive deserter, three were captured on patrol, five were picked up while guarding wounded comrades, four were surrounded with their unit on a hill they were supposed to defend - "to the end" and "at all costs" were the usual words - and surrendered with 23 others when apparently surrounded on three sides.

Several deserters, not interrogated, were led by a former Dachau concentration camp inmate, named Wessel, an anti-Nazi, who had been tortured and forced to work on war materiel, and finally was released only to be sent to the front. They had been told they would be holding a bunker in the rear of the Siegfried Line, but "smelled a rat" when they found themselves exposed to American fire; they volunteered for patrol, hid their weapons and managed to turn themselves over to American soldiers. The second deserter, Kutzki, said, "I'm no Nazi, I want to be a free man, everybody wants to live, after all... It was quite simple, old man, I was on guard during the night, so I beat it, and reached your lines in the morning." He had heard of reprisals against families of deserters and other shirkers, but had no family, both parents being dead, the father from a bombing.

Sergeant Stengelhofen had been pulled out of a non-com school, where they were told that new doctrine called for Officers to stick with their troops up front, then, after Phillipsburg was lost and the Germans counterattacked, First Lieutenant Berg had been nowhere to be seen. That pissed him off. When there had been no intelligence reports and no orders, and his squad leader had gone over the hill, he just stuck in his hole with a comrade and waited for capture. Corporal Eberhard had bad feet but had finally been drafted; he fell behind his unit marching near Stollingen and after wandering for three hours encountered an American patrol to whom he surrendered. Two medics stayed with two wounded men to care for them and two corporals, both in their late thirties, did the same with others when their company was relieved.

Sergeant Schlagowski, a veteran of Poland, Leningrad, and Southern France, said it was he who gave the order to the platoon on the hill to surrender, but so too said the other two non-coms of the group who were interrogated. Lieutenant Pottmann and his squad ran into an American patrol and, in the fire-fight that ensued, took one dead and two wounded before calling it quits as hopeless.

Of the seventeen, four said they were Nazis, seven felt hopeless but had belonged to one or another Nazi group, two said they were anti-Nazis, the others claimed to be apolitical. Practically all had fear of reprisals being taken against their families, withholding of mail, rations, living allowances and even imprisonment. Six had been forced to sign acknowledgments of the reprisals-system when they were brought up to the front. Several urged T3 Straus to tell his commanders that they must inform the Germans how to surrender without implying dereliction of duty. It was agreed that guarding a wounded comrade was the best means. (American propaganda was careful always to pretend that a German soldier would be taken prisoner under dire circumstances, yet the very fact of the propaganda itself denied that "dire" would always be dire enough for the Nazi police system.)

Seven prisoners had seen American leaflets, remembering most forcibly the colorful and signed-by-Eisenhower Surrender Pass. Others had been told of the leaflets by their comrades. A couple had read with approval *Frontpost* or an equivalent. Significantly, Wessel, the anti-Nazi, had seen six kinds of leaflets and identified four: "He who seeks shall find." It was hard to get hold of the leaflets when locked into a bunker by orders and enemy fire. Powerful Allied radio broadcasts, American jazz, mail from German PW's in the States, American prisoners of war working (voluntarily, it was presumed) among Germans, and civilians of towns that had fallen to the Americans and been recaptured: these all were positive propaganda for the Americans, one or more of the PW's said.

Bad news for the Americans obtained in the interrogations: despite all bombings, the railroad lines still operated with remarkable efficiency: three days and two nights from Vienna to the Western Front for the unit of one of the men; impressed worker gangs of Poles and Russians kept up the lines. Moreover, a new item of hardware was in readiness, an anti-tank weapon, "Puppchen;" it will replace the excellent old *Panzerfaust* and send a projectile accurately to 400 yards and effectively to 750 yards; it could penetrate ten inches of steel armor; it was aimed optically with automatic adjustments.

The men's clothing was inadequate and in poor condition; their promised winter blankets, boots, and clothing had never arrived. Wessel also said that his company counted now 56 to 58 men, had lost 8 dead, 10 wounded, and 30 by sickness (mostly diarrhoea); talk of surrendering was becoming open; they were last located at Pfaelzerhuette. From one or another PW came items of potential use, of a well-decorated First Lieutenant, Giemann, who wore the Golden Badge of the Nazi Party, of another officer who was the son of a regional minister, and so on. The ex-Dachau inmate provided a roster of eight names from Dachau of Germans committing murder and other atrocities against the prisoners.

Soon now, most soldiers seeking to desert would try to disappear into Germany, even though they knew that, if caught, they would be executed or put in a batch for the Soviet Front. They didn't ask themselves whether they would win the war, they knew better, but asked how to get home and what was the news from home; they felt as safe as the home folks with the air bombings and drastic shortages. Most of the children were in the countryside, it seemed.

The enemy formed strong small group bonds as they had always, but now it was practically the only one, and it cemented fast, because they had either had much war experience or they were very young, or old and docile. Casualties didn't affect them as much as they disturbed the Americans, who were less used to them. By this time they had suffered, proportionate to numbers engaged, ten times as many dead, wounded and captured as the Allied troops, not from the western combat but from the Soviet Front, and men who have known death and wounds and terror repeatedly are better masters of their fears and that is all-important at the front. (In the so-designated Rhineland Campaign, 8 February to 21 March 1945, that brought the Allied from the German borders up to the Rhine River, only 1,330 Americans were killed. 53,000 German prisoners were taken. The Wehrmacht suffered at least twice as many dead and wounded in the same period. It was a worse period on the Eastern Front, where German and Soviet casualties were very high. The killings of civilians of several nationalities, including Jews, were at a peak, as were their sufferings from invasion, rapine, bombings and displacements.)

Facing the German borders, General Eisenhower commanded 71 fully manned and equipped divisions and all the logistical and special troop support that was needed for them. His airplanes were myriad. By contrast, the Provence campaign from St.Tropez to Alsace took the same period of time, suffered the same casualties, captured the same number of prisoners, inflicted the same casualties on the enemy and conquered as much territory: the Seventh Army, too, disembarked to begin with rather than fighting from immense bases and numbered only 10% of the soldiers that served in the Allied armies of the Rhineland campaign. Obviously, the absurdly weak German Nineteenth Army of Provence and Eastern France had been stronger than what faced the Allies inside Germany.

The Allied commanders refused to believe in the German weakness. Their intelligence sections went on finding the enemy in force everywhere. The War was winding down rapidly, but they insisted upon foreseeing new large battles ahead. Only sporadic resistance was being encountered, yet the despatches were using the language of large-scale engagements, viz., to parody a typical bulletin, "The 1012 Inf.of the 217 Division met with stiff opposition in crossing the Main River and was forced to turn South, there to await reinforcements from 141st Combat Engineers."

In hopes of getting across the Rhine at the earliest moment, I found myself cruising in Third Army Territory. The Third Army was a shiny one, as it had been in Sicily; Patton liked spit and polish. Anti-Pattonites, of whom there were many, ridiculed this facade. I agreed with General Patton, however, up to a point, and regretted the bespattered, banged-up condition of my jeep; I was shaven and clean, though, my guns were burnished, I was ready to confront any superior inquiries as to the reasons for my presence. But, as had happened often before and under stranger circumstances, nobody asked questions. In fact, they were glad to see a vehicle with "foreign" markings. It was like seeing a stranger in Podunk, Iowa.

I had not given up the concept of morale, but it had changed its shape in my mind. It had been two years since I had had any faith in coffee and doughnuts, if ever I had any. More seriously, I began to doubt that faith in one's country and in one's form of government mattered a damn. The Home Front began to dwindle in perspective and grew hazy. Religious faith did not dawn upon me nor did it seem to seize anyone in the Company, nor did the Germans talk about the comforts of religion or practice noticeably a religion except National Socialism which, too, is less and less alive to them. In all the hundreds of letters that I sent and received, no talk of religion consoled us, though the baby was baptized at the nearby Roman Catholic Church after months of hesitation and indifference. I felt that if Jill and my Mother decided to have her baptized, that was O.K. with me. At the Front, God is not conspicuous by His presence. I had not tried to recall a prayer since I watched the French Corporal die, and before then since putting myself to sleep in the first days of the Sicilian landings. When I remembered the hokum, blarney, media splashing of God in the face of the war mobilization on the Home Front - "God is My Co-Pilot," "Praise the Lord and Pass the Ammunition," I felt disgusted.

So far as I could see, and in every army, and on every side, and in the units from the infantry platoon to the Army Group Headquarters and SHAEF itself, the war was irreligious. God was completely wanting, and perhaps that was just as He would have it.

The letters to soldiers from home would say from time to time, depending upon the family, "God bless you, son!" and "We pray for you at Church every Sunday, John." There was no standard of the Cross leading the battle nor was the Cross anywhere to be seen, except occasionally as an amulet, and of course every man's dog-tag had an indication of his sectarian attachment, should he or his family have one. Wallenberg told me he was a Catholic, though he came from a Jewish family, but that was more for information rather than to indicate that I should bury him beneath a cross if he caught death.

Like the Germans and all other nationalities, the Americans waged battle because they happened to be there by reason of a host of varying circumstances and from having nowhere else to go at the moment and from having a feeling of being wanted by a few men around them, and of wanting them. The military was a profoundly homosexual experience as it moved closer and closer to battle and death, even as overt homosexual conduct was carefully avoided and penalized. Remember the last words of Admiral Nelson as he lay dying upon his Flagship following the tremendous victory at Trafalgar. But read the *Iliad,* too. Or Plutarch. It was not much of a puzzle save that myth, wish, prejudice, ignorance made it so: Faced with prospect of death or wounds, the soldier felt that he wanted to die right there in that group and among those men who felt the same way as he did and therefore would mourn him properly, although he would commonly not admit that he wanted to die and may claim vociferously that he would do anything not to die.

It did not take many whining bullets and screaming and booming shells to give the front line troops an obsession with what they were doing and a conviction that events elsewhere were irrelevant, and that, starting with the regimental staff, the whole string and network of organizations going back to the civil population could not be trusted and was against him. What he possessed was a negative value of great preciosity, the equality or near-equality of risk-taking of everyone around him, and it gave him a feeling of kinship sufficient to dampen differences of background and attitudes.

This was the way I sensed the men's feelings, whatever the Army, whether American, British, Italian, French, German, Austrian, Canadian, Indian, Polish, New Zealand, Australian, Algerian, Moroccan, the Jewish Brigade, the German Cossack Division, these being those I had watched in action up to this point, not too close to the crunch of action too often, else I would not have survived to be telling of them. There was no explaining otherwise than in the mutual affection of their fellows the near hopeless bravery and staunchness of the Polish Corps in their assault upon Cassino, as they went about losing half their force owing to the idiotic strategy of the Allied Commanders, and this mutual love came from the loss of country, family, property, almost everything they had once cherished, and being victims of not one but two most brutal occupying forces. I would look at them, look at them, look at them. Men on their way to death or to be maimed or to at best suffer a hell for a while.

There came a time when the number of replacements broke through the remaining cords of morale. A more careful and informed study might devise a formula for this occurrence, but too many unknowable factors were involved to know much more than that the breaking point occurred around and about some kind of situation, with certain types of events and behavior. A large volume of authentic information about the people of a unit existed, but the fluidity and fog of war destroyed its most meaningful unit statistics.

I was writing on Feb 19 about a drive to Paris and made a prophecy for "ten years from now," to wit:

> *On the return trip we stopped underway for lunch, and a woman in a café heated our water and C-rations for us. The incident is worthy of comment because she didn't want to take any money. She acted almost as if we had liberated France. You see, darling, the honeymoon is over on the liberation. Ten years from now the French will have liberated themselves. We were very angry today when a small news item reported De Gaulle to have refused to meet FDR outside of France somewhere. What used to be pardonable pride is now only disgusting arrogance, disgusting because it is so ill-founded and short-sighted. The British & ourselves have given them most of their modest reasons for self-aggrandizement. It is disconcerting & disillusioning to*

keep giving to people who keep nipping at your hand, but I suppose it will be worthwhile if they once become contented & turn to purring. No one should be so naive in politics as to expect gratitude from favors rendered. A tougher attitude on our part might be more impressive. We ought to insist on credit where credit is due.

So much for the French at this moment for we were about to leap into Germany, yet it would not be long before my most important Frenchman of the war showed up, or, one should say, Frenchwoman.

The Casablanca and Moscow Conferences of the year before had announced the policy of demanding the unconditional surrender of the Axis enemies. The doctrine had seemed somewhat abstract at the time, especially since most people didn't feel that it meant much regarding Italy. But now, as the European War was going into a post-climactic stage (though it never did appear to have a climax, on the Western and Italian Fronts, being inclined one way from the start) the doctrine of unconditional surrender aroused more concern among the troops. A letter of a February meeting with soldiers illuminates the point:

My conscience forbad my reneging on a request that I give some spare time to a couple of rifle battalions that someone thought were in need of education; and I was with them part of yesterday. It was no doubt interesting but fatiguing. For example, a couple of companies were crowded into a big, dark hayloft, and I had to stand up and talk them down. One common worry the men have is about the matter of unconditional surrender. A lot of them think that may be making the Germans fight harder. I don't believe it does and make a point of telling them so. Some of them felt that we ought to trick Germany into surrendering and then beat her down, as Germany did with the Czechs. Another company was very much interested in the Crimea Conference. Generally the men agree with its decisions so far as they understand them. I was asked to return, and if I am in those parts the middle of next week and nothing has happened meanwhile, I may do so. Too bad I dislike public speaking; that sort of thing is perfect training for a stump orator: never prepared, conditions always foul, difficult and unknown audiences. You are my perfect audience, toi seule.

It was a difficult doctrine. The Team discussed it many a time. It conveyed a notion that all German leaders were guilty of aggression and war crimes, perhaps a proper attitude for the victors to possess, but received by the German elite as a blanket condemnation (however deserved) to be resisted at all costs therefore. On the tactical side, the doctrine made the enemy fight harder against the Allies, at least, because it gave him no better future, whatever his conduct. I was reminded of what I knew anyhow, of the powerlessness of prisoners of war. The feelings against "a separate deal" and "a break in the ranks of the Allies" were justified to hold the Alliance of East and West together, especially since the Big Three did in fact agree to agree after the War, to the point of setting up a permanent United Nations Organization. However, Stalin, despite every assurance and various proofs of concord from his Allies, would not believe in Allied intentions and in any event was compelled by his paranoia and the logic of totalitarian communism to stretch all agreements to the limits of mutual confidence, lying when convenient. For instance he told General Eisenhower, in reply to a direct personal inquiry, that he would not launch his last great attack upon Berlin until May, and in fact speeded up the attack into April.

SHAEF, under no obligation to refrain from an assault upon Berlin, and actually prepared for the final dash, held back, over the strong objections of Churchill and Montgomery, not to mention many Allied generals and soldiers, because Eisenhower hoped thereby to save many casualties. He realized, too, that the Western Allies would have to give up all the territory gained between Berlin and the Elbe River. Such was the grand directive for the partition of Germany into occupation zones, as contracted for at Yalta. Since the Soviets were to take over this territory, let them fight to win it.

Neither I, nor my soldiers, - practically nobody on the ground - knew of the partition plan. Perversely, a careless Britisher had let the partition map fall into the hands of the Germans; the few top generals who learned of it could do little to turn it to advantage, but perhaps resisted a little harder to surrender, believing a terrible fate would be visited upon eastern regions under the Soviet regime. Possibly Stalin's distrust and haste, conveyed to his chief generals, cost an extra 100,000 Soviet casualties. On the other hand, the month gained by the Soviet sacrifices saved that many and more deaths among the remaining Jews and condemned groups, concentration camp inmates, Allied prisoners of war, slave workers from several countries, and German civilians, all of whom were suffering murder, bombings, and severe attrition from other causes.

Whatever the ramified effects, foreseen and (mostly) unforeseen, the doctrine of unconditional surrender was a myth when postulated, and carried on as a myth working upon a kaleidoscopic reality. My fellows always knew that the Russians would treat the defeated enemy in ways significantly different than would the Western Allies. The Western troops had not suffered enough, despite the revelations of what had happened to the Jews and Eastern Europeans, to exact cruel revenge. Most of them had not seen bloody battle; nor had most of the large bureaucracy of officers now readying themselves to govern the Reich.

Twice during 1944 the British and American psychological warfare central staffs attempted to persuade President Roosevelt through his staff to moderate the harsh policy. They were rejected. The policy did not, however, prevent the propagandists in the field from promising the enemy decent treatment if they would give up as individuals. The famous SHAEF surrender pass had been next to every German soldier's boot since Cassino. Leaflets and radio messages spoke to German civilians in "helpful" tones, urging them, for instance, to save their families by leaving the cities.

When, on July 20, a top-level conspiracy against Hitler nearly succeeded and was then crushed, there might have been some point to praising the martyrs and encouraging new efforts of the same kind, instead of giving up the military leadership as hopeless. Nor was there any gesture toward forming and assisting a German Government in Exile, granted the troublesome efforts to agree upon and sustain such groups from other countries. The effect, sad to say, was to impress ever forcibly upon the German people that Hitler and the Nazis were their one and only genuine legitimate government. Every last German had to feel that he or she must go down with the ship. Unconditional surrender as a concept was nebulous, abstract, impossible, paranoid, against all reason: as such, it worked rather better than one might imagine. And, had it truly reassured Stalin and his coterie that wartime and post-war cooperation were valid prospects, it would have been worth its cost.

I remembered after my lectures two questions, especially: "Why not give Germany to the Jews and get out?" To which I responded there would have been hardly enough German Jews to begin with for running Germany, and most of these were now dead. (The query revealed, of course, a twisted anti-semitic logic. And was hard to deal with.) The other was "Shouldn't we keep on going, otherwise the Russians would take over Europe." To which I replied, nothing is sure, but you have to trust the company on your flank; we needed to build up mutual trust, else we'll go on fighting forever. And the Russians had done most of the fighting and taken most of the losses, and you can forget about just going in there and pushing them around.

There came the break-out on the West. I experienced it personally as happening on the day after I received the cheerful letter from Bill Evers that made me nostalgic and sad; my old Columbia roommate was with the Marines en route to Iwo Jima. I write to Jill:

> *The day has been beautiful, a day when one wants everything to stop and bask. I got a letter from Bill Evers dated Feb.15, which is somewhat ominous, since he is with the 3rd Div., and that was just before Iwo. I hope it was a light wound - that's about the way I feel on his chances. I know what the CO of a rifle company has on his hands and though it's fun while it lasts, it has no pretensions of being lasting.*

And I commented on the fact that two other officers in Bill's Battalion are apparently acquaintances from the University, Lieutenants Reid and Ray Ickes. The date I wrote is March 19; Bill was already dead, killed on February 26. Only now, as I wrote, was the news being transmitted to Elizabeth. Dearest Liz wrote to Dearest Jill, Godmother of her baby Louise, on March 20 upon receiving the report, Dearest Jill wrote to Al Dearest the same day, and Al Dearest, copy of the letter from Dearest Liz in hand, replied to Dearest Jill and addressed to Dear Liz his word of sorrow and condolences.

> Dearest Jill,
>
> I'm sorry I didn't get around to writing you yesterday, but I've been on the go almost constantly. The first mail from you in several days reached me this evening. I can't say that the news contained therein made me feel less tired. There is such a thing, I suppose, as bracing oneself against the possibility of a dear friend's death, but there is no escaping the incredibility and melancholia of it. I had to read your lines several times before actually fully believing that the words meant Bill was dead, that he wouldn't be around for this or for that, that he had slipped his groove in life and had gone wandering off somewhere. And every time a good man dies, it seems impossible that he can be replaced, personally or socially, that our lives must be less full forever thereafter and that our world must be in straits more dire. The traits he possessed and the type he represented are in many men, for no man is unique in his ideals, and will weave their way into our lives in sublimation and surrogation. Therefore it is true and it is not true. I feel you should not commit yourself to a philosophy of pessimism if he shall have died "in vain". All death is in vain. And wouldn't we be presumptuous to believe that the many millions of dead in history may have been in vain but that here in our year of the Lord, 1945, we shall so manipulate destiny that our cherished friends shall not have died in vain. A man is no more to be mourned because he died in a lost cause. Nor is evil any different when one has not lost some friend to it. Some may claim that to involve oneself is the real mistake, that the struggle is to be avoided, granted the foregoing once one has entered the arena. Even if one accepts the allure of this proposition, however, it has its practical difficulties. The age is particularly severe on innocent bystanders. Life is a continual frustration and fright. Better a decent gamble, accompanied by self-respect and a zest for life.
>
> Apart from these thoughts, there are sentiments I can't

express. Bill would never express them about me, and I won't express them about him. I will write Elizabeth tomorrow.

I learned much later through Ray Ickes that Bill had just leapt ashore and was moving up the beach when a Japanese bullet struck him dead. It would take another volume to tell how this bullet changed peoples' lives. And another fifty million volumes for all the other shot and shell that killed and ruined. Where does one stop? Why does one begin?

In Chicago: Kathy and Jill

CHAPTER SIXTEEN

THE DISSOLVING REICH

LURCHING over a ribbon of timbers that is lapped by the Saar River, I intruded upon the Third Reich. The Army is on the march again; Jill gets the news from me with the Spring Equinox of 1945, to wit:

> *We are, of course, in Germany now and we feel fine about that. The civilians are surprised they aren't being killed off and are still half-convinced they will be sent to Siberia. Some of them ought to be, I'm sure. Their standard of living, save where the AAF struck, is higher than anywhere else, but the AAF struck everywhere in the cities & many towns. It is so obvious to all the soldiers that the Germans had no reason to start a war.*

The very next day comes the comment:

> *The Nazi flag at the moment is any sort of white cloth. Sheets and pillow cases wave in the conquerors of the Third Reich. Hitler is unpopular among many civilians now that they are completely crushed. It took all this to make them change their minds. There isn't much difficulty getting things done by the civilians. They will do anything they're told. Unfortunately we don't tell them nearly enough. There just isn't enough that the American Army needs. I imagine the Russians must be doing a much more thorough job of gathering in German local resources. A considerable number of people try to be friendly but so far without any success. The American soldiers are*

> almost unanimous in their support of non-fraternization regulations, even though they are very difficult for the individual to observe. Things that one does most naturally if he has been taught good manners are forbidden. So most offenses against the regulation will be through lack of self-control rather than deliberate non-participation in the spirit of them.

I find myself in a jeep driving through the destroyed town of Kaiserslautern turning to look at a young German girl, apparently oblivious of the invaders, sweeping with deliberate movements the stone steps of a totally blasted house. Yes, the house is gone, only the steps are left, but she has to sweep them! What is she sweeping up, I wonder, and ponder too the German mentality; but I think, when you can't think of anything else to do, why not grab a broom and start sweeping? Actually ain't that like the Old Army of the USA, an hour before Retreat sounds. "Arms length! Pick up Butts. Route Step! Forward, March!" Or it may be that her sweeping is a pretext to find out what the invaders are like.

In search of targets of opportunity, I turn southward toward the Rhine River roads. Scott and I sleep in the open with the jeep against a wall at their back and an artillery blast hole in front; it is a habit I have developed. As night falls, we can see upstream the enormous fires of the city of Mannheim, set ablaze by the bombers. "God, Captain," says Scott, "it looks like a Hollywood Movie!" It does, and I reflect upon how in these days the media studios set up the scene for man and nature to imitate. Although there is not much information on what lies ahead, I guess that we can drive a long stretch along the West Rhine road and perhaps find some engineers throwing a bridge across. Soon we come to where Ludwigshaven begins to stretch out on the other side of the River.

On our own side we encounter an American outpost. Apparently it had advanced from the South. We pull up a few yards from a couple of riflemen, and somebody I cannot see yells, "Hey, get that jeep out of there, we're catching fire." So I jump off, send it off to hide and skulk over to the river edge. There a rifleman tell me anxiously, Sir, there is somebody sneaking in and out of the warehouse across and he looks like a civilian but maybe he is observing fire. Should I shoot him? I catch the scene and the man in my binoculars. A doubtful case. Might be some old coot scavenging. I query myself: Should I take the rifle from his reluctant hands and fire at the man, or should I say, yes, and give him the imprimatur of authority to take a life or, even better from his point of view, an Order to shoot, or should I tell him to do what he thinks best under the circumstances. Surely he must have someone in command, who might even resent a seeming interference. I tell him to do what he thinks best, adding, prejudicially, you have to protect your own people, remember that too. And I leave. Silly, ain't I? Given the unspeakably murderous war, the life of this geezer is a trivium. Yet shooting a person is by all canons of morality a decision of utmost gravity. So much for that. Then, too, consider this: as insufferably elaborate as all this reasoning is, might not there be another level of even more private reasoning, or, at least, motivation: that I both did and didn't want to kill the man and rationalized myself out of the dilemma without permitting myself to believe that I did not want to kill.

I wonder, too, whether the civilized letters of my wife and the talk and photos of my daughter are not keeping me from the fierceness that should long ago have captured me. I still think of myself often as a civilian. When my wife disposes of most of my clothes by gift and garbage, I evince surprise and mock indignation - or might I not be really feeling hurt: it is a kind of death, isn't it?

> *Thanks, my Love, for the synopsis of my sartorium. It's nice to know amidst all of this that I am a man possessed of three suits, even though only one is any good at all. Sometimes you are too unromantic. Suppose I like to see an old familiar shirt. What then? Won't you let me? You ought to abet anything that makes one's memory more exact. All I could remember before was a vague, dark closet with some of my clothing in it.*

> "They really were bad
> So don't be mad."
> Who said they were good?
> So long as they stood
> My own unkhakilike array

> In disarranged peace
> Of inferior fleece
> Woman, spare that shirt!
> If you want something to hurt
> Try selling all those shoes*
> That a beggar'd refuse.
> (*Including those moccasins)

So I do live part of the time in Chicago, and wonder about a described delay in Kathy's approach to speaking. She says only "mama", "bah," and "yeah" and she is already 15 months old!

> *Do you think Kathy's speechlessness may be partly a result of your own intelligence. She probably doesn't feel it worthwhile learning the proper symbols so long as you seem to know exactly what she wants anyway. Like the butler we had once in Catania. It wasn't necessary to know a word of Italian, because before you could open your mouth he anticipated what you were going to ask for.*

I even concern myself with my taxes! That makes me feel like a civilian.

> *I know even less about taxes than you. I assume your missing paying them means*
> *1) that your income alone wasn't enough to pay a tax.*
> *or 2) I don't have to worry, being a soldier just now.*
> *or 3) that your not filing your own return means that ultimately we can file a joint return for that period.*
> *(a) If (3) then: Do we lose or gain by the delay?*
> *or 4) We shall be behind the bars jointly.*
> *Search me, too, but I'd like to know. Incidentally, would you please let me know where you are keeping all our bonds, even if the rest of your financial system defies specification? Sometimes I would as lief bite your ear as kiss you.*

I revert to the War, reporting that the invasion across the Rhine now is spectacular:

> *I wish that everyone at home could stand along one of these roads and watch the American army move by. It is the gigantic spectacle of history, American to the core and absolutely awesome, unending, stretching on all the roads to the horizon, columns of the most mechanized force of all time, little tanks and big ones, ducks, six by sixes, darting jeeps, huge steel monsters that carry tanks or pull long artillery pieces with flashing lights and shrieking sirens, machines that take up two lanes in a roaring, blinding cloud of dust and that sometimes pull off the corners of buildings where the street is too narrow. No one walks. There is not a single horse. And the whole swiftly moving mass of metal is directed nonchalantly and gracefully by the GI's in the seats and the MP's on the roads with a flick of the wrist. We haven't given to this war our last gasping effort, but what we have given is like the slap of a bear's paw to the biting ant, iron blood worth more than the blood of millions of men towards winning the war, that in addition to the human effort, and our human lives. The weather has been fine for this war of movement.*

Where is the Front? What is a Front? It is occasionally what is commonly imagined or played in films: a constant inferno surrounding bunkers or tunnels or holes into which men have dived. However, whatever and wherever it is, it must support the variable possibility that "all hell will break loose." The Front is wherever two patrols clash or where time after time violent exchanges occur, as at Cassino, where a belt of a quarter of a mile along the Rapido River was bloodied repeatedly. The Front is extended sometimes by "carpet bombing," as at the Abbey and Town of Montecassino, or upon the Second SS Panzer Division as it moved up to counterattack at Mortain against the Americans who were breaking out of Normandy. There we consider up to a couple of round miles as the Front. The Front is also where first friendly, then enemy, forces occupy or pass through an area, occasionally meeting. It is a moving border between retreating and pursuing forces, too, who may be in contact or running battle, or may be out of contact.

The Dissolving Reich

The Front is also wherever artillery can reach, up to several miles, up to thousands of miles by missiles nowadays, but, fifty years ago, only several miles. There is the Front of bombing aircraft, which could reach the line of troops, if such exists, or in any event long distances beyond the men on the ground, as in the costly battles over England and Germany. The Front can be a large region practically devoid of troops, into which anyone might penetrate for days without hostile encounter. Then the Sea Front needs to be defined in terms of the bases available to the opposing forces and the likelihood of encounter on the high seas; the Front is a troopship being observed by an enemy submarine. The "Home Front" can be more than a rousing slogan; it can be disorderly, plagued by police and riotous troops, by resistance groups, and a target for airplane attack or missiles. Often, when not in combat, German and Allied troops were gratified to be whiling away time far from the Home Front.

So, when you reach the nut of the matter, the Front is a quantitative concept: a more than "X" probability that in "Y" time a given space "Z" will become the aforesaid "inferno." Given this concept, you can calculate or guess at the chances of a given space becoming a Front, today, tomorrow or in ten years.

And, of course, while I am at it, I might add that each Front has its Maps, to which you become addicted insofar as you are confined to one or another Front and have to find your way solo around in it. You can imagine that in a Space War, the relevant map may be the Earth as seen from Space. More realistically, it may be the interior plan of a town hall in Belfort. Map-reading of all sorts up to global dimensions took up its hundreds of hours of the Soldier's time from Tennessee to Munich. I was embraced daily by the folds of World maps, Theater maps, Army Group maps, Corps maps, Division maps, Regimental maps, Battalion area maps, Company maps, Artillery maps, Platoon maps, Squad maps, and personal maps, the kind that is being drawn to show or be shown a nearby location not on any map - where the command post is, where the entrance to the ammo dump is, where civilians are hiding, where the enemy fire is coming from. I never lacked maps of various kinds, as I never lacked a flashlight and a tin cup.

Ironically, the more detailed and closer to your spot the coverage of the map, the more unlikely that you can depend upon it for what you are after, because the stuff you are interested in, that was there before, has often been blown away explosively and the people in whom you are interested are doing their best not to be where your map says they are. And a lot of nasty human and mechanical surprises are lying in wait, unmapped. In this real sense, from one moment to the next, the Front changes.

Ironically, soldiers who were supposed to guide other people as well as themselves were, as often as not, lost. Since everyone wanted to hide, and at the same time be in touch with others, a nice contradiction blossomed. This accounted not only for their being lost and unfindable, but also for their committing amicide all too frequently. Thus, coming upon friendlies unexpectedly is a likely way to die, yet if you announce yourself too visibly and audibly you are likely to get both yourself and them in trouble, and rile them up, as happened in the incident above at the River's edge. As the risk rises at a given spot, the danger thereabouts to anyone not of the immediate squad goes up also. Further, though the risk may not rise, the perceived risk - panic, that is - grows: raw troops slaughter themselves and their own, as the ack-acks off the Gela beaches in Sicily did to their airborne buddies.

The need for sensitive troop training regarding topography, demography, ekistics and cultures had always been, was, and still is, poignant and unsatisfied. I never heard of combat troops being taught, whether by lecture, print, film, or action scenarios, the physical contours of the settlements where they might well be dying within minutes or hours of arrival. The Arab, the Algerian, the Italian, French and German cultures and provincial sub-cultures, had their peculiar architecture, living habits, and neighborhood construction, their special by-ways, interiors, staircases, windows and shutters, cellars, barns and lofts. The North African desert was only halfway like the Mohave Desert. The French villages were not at all like the American: most Americans didn't know how to open and close a shutter. One warns here not only of delays, blunders, and deadly ignorance, but of the anxiety of ignorance added to the panic-potential always present in the soldier's breast. The next generation coined the term for this - "culture-shock" - but it was for tourists and immigrants.

Now begins my tour of the countryside and of Ludwigshaven, Mannheim, Heidelberg, Darmstadt, Stuttgart, and forty other cities and towns of the Rhineland and Bavaria, Munich, yes Dachau. In Darmstadt I am handed a fluegelhorn by a soldier, who has picked it up as combat pay in a burned out fire station and who admires my playing "Danny Boy," "Return to Sorrento," and "Stardust" upon it. It has sticky valves and a tiny mouthpiece.

In Heidelberg I burst in with my three soldiers upon a university building that is sheltering displaced persons - the pathetic D.P.'s - and a few students. A distinguished-looking Polish army officer has assumed command, and at first denies me admittance and warns against bringing in a company of troops. He says an American officer from Military Government has placed him in charge. I am not to be put off, so the Pole pleads on behalf of his charges. I am touched with this and pull out some of my rations and schnapps. The Pole does likewise. A large party ensues, going far into the night, with the inevitable accordion playing Polish mazurkas and I blowing my fluegelhorn for all it is worth, and dancers tromping and stomping all about. They all collapse toward morning and as early as I can manage, I rouse my comrades to get out and on our way.

Heidelberg is practically undamaged, therefore crowded, beautiful, very few uniforms in evidence. I am happy about its preservation and consider again, as I gaze at the unsightly bands of freed slave workers, the German civilians, all guilty in some sense of outraging *die ganz Welt* that they expected to take over: what is the price of people relative to the price of culture, the Cassino dilemma, which proved to be a false dilemma at Cassino, where both art and people were destroyed to no avail? What is human life worth in terms of art? There is no avoiding the problem. Every time a shell smashes into a house, a poor woman's shack, a rich bourgeois' stately townhouse, the artifacts of man spiral like horrible genies out of the smoke, and the people scream and crumple in the dust. Is there a chart to be drawn, where people - ranging in value from the soldier who must be killed (beautiful and talented a young specimen as he may be) through the ignorant ugly and useless up to the divine humans, the best, the kindest, the world citizens - are given a score; and, then, a chart of the relative value of the cultural and natural beauties being destroyed - ranging from the Cathedral of Nuremberg to a rusty scupper and bird nest in a spruce tree. What Mastermind of ethics and aesthetics is to be charged with assigning the charted values, what Genial Survey-master with the inventorying of the human and natural units, what Mathematics Wizard with the instantaneous calculation of individual and collective sums before a cannon blasts off or a bomb-bay opens. God, of course, but God is so obviously away attending to other matters, without leaving instructions, compelling you to exclaim, "My God!" as you see the steeple fall, and "Oh, God!" as the shrapnel comes to grips with your groin.

At this point in time, Jill, across the ocean, decides that she and her baby will go West to stay with her brother for a while. A quarter of the country is traveling West, another is travelling East: she harries me with the details of readying for the trip and finding transportation. I respond in a surly mood:

> *Dearest Jill,*
> *As if I didn't have enough to worry about moving myself and the whole ensemble, you present me with a completely nerve-chilling serial on your own movements, Kathy's, two suitcases & the dangling diaper bag. You ask "Can you stand the suspense?" I answer, "Not very well". It's getting me down. I wish to hell I get a letter telling me once and for all that you have arrived in SF. I think that* only *would make me happy. If, after everything, you didn't go I might be still more enraged! I was glad to know, at any rate, that you and Kathy are feeling well again. I have been bad about writing letters lately, but c'est la guerre. Nothing is describable at all well. As you say, leisure is a condition of art.*

Jill has arrived in San Francisco, not without having received his misgivings. I can picture traveling in the turmoil of the war, even without the enemy bombing as here. It is a difficult trip on a crowded train, carrying a baby, two grips and a diaper bag. But there are plenty of jolly sailors around to help her, and she has the earmarks of a faraway soldier's lament, so she gets priority over old ladies, disabled veterans and what not. America is hell bent to mobilize and doing a great job of it, to a degree that neither the Germans nor Japanese have achieved.

She goes riding, is surprised by some Boy Scouts, the horse shies and she is thrown upon her shoulder. A bad fracture, a severe concussion, worse than anything I have received from my old war. So it goes. I write her more dreams of love. I tell her that I am driven to contemplate volunteering in an infantry division being prepared for the invasion of Japan, which will have a month's leave in the States on the way there, or so they say. All believe that it will take millions of men for the landings and conquest of Japan, given the resistance put up at Iwo Jima and Okinawa.

I tell of weapons confiscation and souvenir collecting combined.

> *Jill, my Love,*
>
> *As the stereotyped telegram goes, "You are more than ever in my thoughts lately," because I have been seeing your family name plastered all over the place on road signs. That makes me feel very much at home. I only wish you were so near. I haven't yet been to Oppenheim to tell you what it looks like, but the chances are that even though it is a rear area already, I will pass through it some day. I see that Lauterbach is also in our hands and may do the same there. Any more geographical locations in your family? I picked up a souvenir dagger for you yesterday and will send it on in due time. I have another which I will send to Ed and then I will look for one for Vic. Is everybody happy? Your dagger I got from a surreptitious character who sidled up to me and handed me two of them which I threw into my jeep. They are afraid to be caught with weapons. One guy gave Fred Faas a handful of Lugers and rifles in Heidelberg. Fred really should have nabbed the guy to see whether he knew where some members of the* Volksturm *or* Wehrmacht *were hiding out in civvies, but he was in a hurry. The trouble is that everybody is in a hurry. There isn't time for anything. I would like to find the guy who had my rooms in this place before me. He is still in the neighborhood since I kicked him out and he can't go far. I had no time to search the place, but had to get*

> *out on the road again. When I returned, I found his personal documents torn up and put in the stove, but unburned. He was an SA in 1932 and 1933 and a regular since then. There will be more time later, however. I am sure that there will be enough Germans too for a lot of housecleaning of their own, once they are organized and permitted to operate.*

Secretary of the Treasury Morgenthau ventured a scheme at one stage of the hostilities that would prevent future German aggression by suppressing its industrialization. I and most others thought this daffy; a machine-less German was an oxymoron. But I say, ironically:

> *About the bombings, there is hardly any urban life of any consequence any more. I think Morgenthau's plan is practical if only because the stage he wants the Germans to arrive at, i.e. an agricultural nation, is practically achieved already. No superlatives can describe the completeness of the bombing. Many of the people left in the cities are mental cases or perhaps it is that only queer people can remain under the conditions. Pray, sister, that this is the last war. I am also convinced more than ever that there is nothing like a good isolated farm, providing the tactical situation doesn't come your way. Incidentally, all our spare time at this place we're in now is occupied with removing the after-effects of its habitation by a German demolition team. They left odd little knick-knacks of mines, TNT, and booby traps in all the corners. None of them were set for us, however (he said, tapping gently on wood), because they had to leave in a great hurry. Still it was with some bemusement that we stood back and watched the German occupants do a preliminary cleaning of the basement before getting out.*
> *Das ist alles. Always your pal & lover,*
>
> *Al*

And more of the humane gestures of life at war:

> *Darling Jill,*
> *Just to make a full envelope, I'm sending you a V-mail from*

the New Yorker *cartoonist in reply to my request for the conditions under which I might have the original. You may remember it. A frowsy woman is drinking breakfast coffee, reading a V-mail, and says to her mother, "Of all the dismal, god-forsaken places to spend Christmas -- Palestine!" The other note is thanks for a collection of chocolate and cigarettes we took in the company for a hospital, badly equipped and most dreary, which was just liberated. Most of the occupants were old PW's. ("Mon capitaine et cher camarade, Au nom de tous nos petit Français et alliés malades, je tiens a vous accuser réception de votre colis. Le geste est joli et il est émouvant...") A third thing I want to enclose but which turned out to be too thick was a letter I just got from Hank Dannenberg. He has been in a morass of tough luck for the last couple of months. He exhausted his money paying for treatment of his father-in-law who has been very ill. Millie had a surprise operation for a tumor in the uterus. Then she had a nervous breakdown. Then they doubled the rent on his garage after a lot of controversy. His balance has been bad since his ear operation and he had a bad fall as a result. He claims my letter cheered him up. I don't see how it could do anything else under the circumstances. Unless you object and I think you won't mind, though I can't reach your pearly ear at the moment, I believe I'll send him a loan of $100 from my cash on hand. I know he'll appreciate it physically and morally. I sure hope he gets out from under. He has lots of ability & energy but he is really plagued by tough breaks. Look at me being sorry for a civilian.*

My incredulity at German greed is manifest again:

The weather here lately has been cool but bright. At the moment, supper is over and my field desk is receiving the only warmth it ever gets from the setting sun. Otherwise, it is cold in here and I'm glad I don't have to spend too much time indoors. My favorite sport is speeding along superhighways these days. They certainly have a magnificent road system here. How abysmally stupid the Germans were to have started this war. They had more than any other European nation I know of the material goods. If they could have had

> *a developmental socialism instead of their criminal, atavistic, militaristic, tribal socialism, they would lead the world by example today instead of being the dirt trampled by the feet of millions of men. Now that our time is drawing near an end over here, we are noticing with increasing enthusiasm our great victories in the Orient. I feel that the two wars (geographically speaking) will not finish very far apart. Our cleanup job is much greater here, and the basic war potential of Germany has been much greater than that of Japan can possibly be.*
>
> *The German population continues to get rebuffs from the soldiers in its attempts to be friendly. In individual cases, the policy is untenable, but time & investigation will bring out those cases. The desire to make friends with the troops is a very natural one, to have friendly conquerors if one must have conquerors. Already I've had the cousin in Milwaukee gag pulled on me. That's in the same class with those people who are now conveniently pulling a Jewish grandfather out of the bag in asking for privileges. Granted the degree of personal responsibility for any form of government is small, but it shouldn't be encouraged to be small, and therefore a theory of personal responsibility for the group (a "myth" after Sorel, if you prefer) is needed, except in cases where individuals have actually worked vigorously & consistently against the criminal government. One may say, now, that Italy, Petain France and Franco Spain are of the same category of evil & aggressive governments & their peoples ought equally to be judged guilty with their countries, but I think the difference lies, unfortunately for the Germans, in the teutonic traits of duty-culture, thoroughness, and organization. Taken together with the evil direction, they add up to the greater crime. By their incapacities, these others escape the final penalty. I might add, in the case of Spain especially & with much truth about France, that their peoples put up a noble struggle. The Spanish have atoned already.*

In a later letter I will be saying:

> *The Germans have no conscience about having fought this war, as far as I can make out. They are only sorry that they didn't win. They are already insisting on rights to which they have no pardonable access. And, willy-nilly, we are their liberators, for the*

> *most severe measures which we can deal out to them now are nothing compared to the punishment we gave them while we were conquering them. The only thing worse than the Nazi Party, total war, and the AAF would actually be what Hitler promised them, the burning of all their villages, the raping of their women, and the dispatch of a good part of the population to Siberia -- "Sieg oder Sibirien" as it is scrawled on the walls. But, granting that is mostly impossible, what can you do with a people like that? Their ostensible qualities of cleanliness, orderliness, thriftiness, and modernity baffle, as well they might, most people who seek for something tangible to reform in the enemy. It is much easier to wash a boy's face than to develop his character. And civilization for most people (i.e. what we are fighting for) is the opposite from wearing a loin cloth and sporting a spear. That is bad enough, but even for those people who know better, the problem of what to do with and how to handle the reformation of a nation is perhaps beyond their powers. That is one reason for not feeling too badly about some regrettable policies which may ensue. We have no right to criticize many nations and all their millions of people for not performing a clean operation which we ourselves can hardly or not at all do as an intellectual operation.*

In Darmstadt, where I had set up the company on the grounds of a red brick factory, I confiscate a well-cared-for Opel automobile and drive it around for a while. Better still, we acquire free a magnificent convertible Mercedes, such as only top Nazis used, polish its black body, oil its seats and assign it to Tom Crowell, theoretically a civilian, and not quite subject to military orders; should some general take a liking to it, he can try refusing and at worst be thrown out by the General's aides. He take his three visitors for a grand drive.

There had been in the hard past winter these three guys from the infantry replacement depot who were assigned to the Team. I couldn't understand why Roos had put in for them. They were not needed. They were strong, handsome boys, of the same background as Tom Crowell, and he took a liking to them. Then came the big battles and the retreat. The Army sent out a squeeze order, taxing each outfit to replace casualties of the German offensive. Tom spoke to me on their behalf. They're good soldiers. Can't you keep them? Fine, then send back who? The other guys - public opinion, yes, why not? - wouldn't like it, even if I sent back Cook, the notorious fuck-up Private Cook. Back to the reppel-deppel they went. They hit it lucky, maybe it was the reputation of the Team that did it and my recommendation, for they weren't sent into the killing slots. The three came back now to visit Tom. I am glad they harbored no ill feelings toward me, and that they have survived without harm.

My taste for parties whetted in Heidelberg, I encouraged the bruiting about of the conception of a big party in conjunction with the girls of various nationalities who had been slave-workers in a nearby factory. I had passed by a group of them and, pausing, had noticed in particular one beautiful brunette specimen, French from the Belgian border, straight out of an academic salon painting of the Nineteenth Century. I had her in mind for the party and more, and when the music (naturally the Team had the best amplifiers and records in Europe) and dancing (at which we were poorer than the average unit, the infantry being the best dancers) were in full swing, I sidled in upon the floor and, half-coaxing, half-compelling, absconded with her around the corner of the factory yard and up a staircase into my private room, where, again, without her saying much one way or another (for she generally was observed to say very little), whether "no" or "yes" was undefinable, but my lust was quite clear and pressing, until she felt that she might as well lend herself to importunity.

Perhaps I was half-drunk, else I should (or so it would seem in retrospect) I should have made more of the occasion, for she was truly a superb creature; yet, for that matter, so should she have; but perhaps there was nothing deeper in her than appearances, nor in me than swinishness - or lusty sex, if you will - or did I awe her, and if so was she pleased or made helpless to do what she would not really have wanted to do, and what, then, is the meaning of rape, and the line between rape and seduction in 1945, for if you are not scintillatingly definite about it, you ought be let into an interminable discourse that could begin with this particular situation alone, complicated not only by the many circumstances that complicate and befoul such judgements, but too by the laws of war and the compulsions of the war zone - and need I warn you of the intricate vagaries of Americana where "no" and "not now" were not ordinarily deemed to mean such, rather thought to be normal responses of women who were aiming at guaranteeing their reputations thereafter as normally abstemious sexually and "hard to get." I leave you merely with these paltry considerations in mind, for to carry on my story I must go on to report, that I may or may not also have implanted a hostage upon the French Republic, given the lack of precautions we took, and that I returned her, unruffled, Jeanine was her name, unobtrusively and courteously, to the festivities, from which I soon disappeared, and I heard the trucks with their gay enough loads take off down the road to the ladies' dormitory, with Jeanine in one of the cabs, her prestige enhanced withal, whatever your opinion or mine of the proceedings.

It is April (I should have piled the lusts of Spring upon my apologia, were I not preoccupied with probing into conduct unbecoming an officer and a gentleman). The Seventh Army HQ has in mind heading through Southern Germany. I ready two vehicles to leave the company at Darmstadt and cruise the area of the fast-disappearing Front. Before I depart, Lt. Jacques Pregre enters, neat, his fat jowls closely shaved, his brown eyes snapping, his cigarette dangling. Let's move to Ulm, say I, come along. No, says the Lieutenant, the French First Army has just taken it. How can they, exclaim I, it was already liberated by the Seventh Army! It makes no difference, Pregre calmly pronounces. Napoleon scored a great victory in battle at Ulm. *Entendu!* The French must now take the city again; it is their historical mission.

I, marveling without grieving, go cruising without him and in good time come upon a castle southeast of Augsburg. As imposing as Wuthering Heights, had you seen the movie. (I didn't think that way, for everything that would have let me play Hollywood to a Fare-thee-well was scratched and discolored by my limbic homesickness.) It was so fancy, so groomed of roof and garden. Untouched by war to outward appearances. Quiet. Inside, a subdued splendor in the best of taste, fifteenth to nineteenth century all-inclusive, time spiraling gently among innumerable artistries. A proper group of aristocratic Germans living as if on a long week-end.

They appear to be lolling about as I enter, as if they were expecting me for tea. The Lady of the Castle lean, tall, elegant, cordial, superficially fearless. Alongside her an old man who could have been anyone, if not a Chief of Staff retired, at least a Captain of Industry: he was leaving the reception up to her; he might be asked difficult questions. A Hungarian count, who could not keep quiet: he played about her flanks like a cavalryman, which he probably was. Complete with the beautiful castle maiden; I looked her up and down; they should have hid her away; how could they know I was bent upon non-fraternizing, even as I said, when I heard her speak English, "How nice, you can teach me German," and looked keenly at the old lady to catch the flash of alarm traverse her face. Meanwhile my men have been surveying the grounds. French slave workers, Captain, fifty of them! Inform them that of course they are free to go or not as they please, and send the wagon tomorrow morning for rations. Find some place in the slave quarters for the family tomorrow. Sleep, sleep, the day has been long. Where to sleep, but in the room of the Hungarian count, who has already shown it politely. Its centerpiece is a smallish grand bed of the Sixteenth Century, canopied in silks, embroidered with dumpish nude maidens of the age floating about, seeming on the verge of precipitating themselves upon the occupant of the bed, tonight I myself.

The Count is informed and crestfallen, no cordial tale-swapping comrade-in-arms this lad. In the morning, the soldiers excitedly report a treasure discovered in the great cellars, silverplate, gilt-framed marvelous paintings, you have to see it, Captain! What is wrong with me? I say, I know what it is, the main thing now, before this place is overrun, is to report it to the Cultural Preservation Team of the Army so they can take it over and maintain guard. So far as we are concerned, men, we're moving on, except you Discoverers; you stay until the Culture guys arrive and return then to Darmstadt; we can't hold a place like this. Some General and his Staff are going to pull their rank on us. Adieu, beautiful castle, castle maiden, mama aristocrat. What was it she said while offering the hospitality of the manse: "I know *Der Führer*. He is very nice. I am certain that if you were to meet him, you would find yourself much in agreement."

The ranging party crosses the valley and comes upon a warehouse of finely bound copies of Hitler's *Mein Kampf* intended for *Bürgermeisters* to give to newly married couples. The thought of each little couple of newlyweds, beset by all the problems of a likely living hell, receiving this as their wedding gift drives the American soldiers into a fit of laughter. Still, it is a genuine token of the bizarre social order that the Germans have accepted without the faintest revolt. As soon as I return to camp, I call in Lt. Little, who has recently joined the Team, and ask him to go burn the books. Lt. Little protests the order. He argues that it is morally outrageous to burn books, no matter what kind of books they are. That's what the Nazis did. That's what we are fighting against. I am probably one of the few officers in the American Army who would not now be kicking him in the ass. Instead, I express myself as agreeing in principle, but tell him that countless millions of copies still circulate, and unless Lt. Little will burn them, they will have to be handed out forever at weddings, or as souvenirs, or in schoolrooms or in stores, and there won't be much room for other books. Books are trashed, Lieutenant, if there is no market for them. Keep a copy for yourself; I am. And I did and so did the Lieutenant. But it was a matter of religion for the Lieutenant, and others had to set the match to the heap.

Lt. Little is a very ethical person generally. One morning, he turns himself in for failing to have awakened during the night for guard duty; I soothe him and order him to serve as Officer of the Guard for two straight weeks in consequence. He protests, asserting that he had, after all, been honest in turning himself in. I know, reply I, and I respect you for it, but the offense still demands its penalty.

I go out cruising again with my artillery old-timers Charley Wagner and Corporal Stubbs, together with now-Captain Villanave, and Blackie driving in the command car, and spot several Germans cutting across a field. I mutter to Blackie, stop quick, let's get' em, drop off the right side, and level my automatic rifle at the group yelling "Halt!" They do. "Hands *auf!*" They do. *"Kommt hier!" "Langsam."* I have them draped over the hood like dead prey, order the truck to start up and carry them that way as far as a blasted house on the road ahead. They turn out to be SS, which makes me think of shooting them, but I am afraid that I will be court-martialed if there are witnesses. Also they deserve to be interrogated, if only to see whether they are among the majority now being pressed into SS uniform. I am relaxing upstairs, smoking a cigarette and thinking over the issue, when Villanave comes rushing up excitedly; "Stop Sergeant Wagner, *Mon Capitaine!* He is beating the prisoners!" I wonder what the hell he is so excited about, and walk down the stairs, "What's up, Sergeant?" "That young punk had a gun concealed on him, Sir." Good reason, I feel; I am wondering about Villanave, who looks cold with his thin mustache, beady black eyes; how can he be kind-hearted; he was Alsatian, joined the Resistance, when?..a sympathizer, a neutral, a pacifist, what? I finally give the prisoners over to Corporal Stubbs to drive them to the PW compound, offhandedly adding, "I don't care if they ever arrive safely." Stubbs gives me a quick alert glance to catch some meaning in the words. They do arrive.

The cruising continues. Investigate a farmhouse. Discover a young man, not really trying to hide, claims to be Jewish. He wears clothes that fit him, no weapon or uniform to be found. Marvelous if true. Ironic, if not true. The householders look like decent folk as they plead his case. It has been known to happen. Let him go. Why? Because maybe he was actually Jewish: Germans are not so unanimously Nazi as people think. If he wasn't, maybe for the rest of his life he could contemplate his good fortune at being considered a Jew.

I lead my party out to the jeep. A bullet whistles past my right ear. I wheel around to the left. Connie Wilson is staring at me horrified, paling. Blackie has nearly blown my brains out uncocking his weapon. (About now, on April 6, off Okinawa, seven U.S. ships are damaged by "friendly fire" during a Kamikaze attack.) I put him on two weeks of extra guard duty and sentence him to lessons in handling weapons. I register Connie's look forever: he doesn't want me to die. I recall it when a promotion opens up and several close good men put up their comrade, a fine soldier, for T3. I refused to pass over Connie. They couldn't understand him. You know, Captain, he has said some bad things about you. I know, said I, but here's the way I see it. He does his work well. He is off his rocker. He is full of prejudices. Still, he has been overseas more than two years, he has a wife and child at home. It would kill him if I put him down on this one.

The next country villa they come upon looks prosperous. Search reveals nothing suspicious, nothing of interest. Leaving, I note a space without a corresponding door. Break it open, men; the Germans stand there in dismay. Inside, a great cache of liquor - cognacs, wines, the best of brands. Everyone regards liquor as legitimate plunder, whatever you can eat and drink and employ to survive at the best level of the aboriginees. German loot becomes American loot. The truck is loaded up, enough to last out the war if it is measured out appropriately and imbibed normally and the war ends soon. Each officer is issued several bottles of hard liquor and one of champagne and wine. Each enlisted man of the Team gets half a case of excellent wine. Not quite equal, but it all equalled out in the process of consumption. And "the Army is not in the business of setting up communism," as I once told my men when I was altering in favor of the officers an arrangement of quarters, fixed by the first men into them. (The beneficiary was Major Roos, so I was obviously acting on principle.) "Except," I stressed, "for the sick and disabled."

There is anxiety over the possibility of last ditch resistance to be undertaken by the Nazis in the Bavarian Alps. Hitler's mountain residence at Berchtesgaden would serve as the Headquarters for an *Alpenfestung* of vast extent. The fear of another Cassino may be haunting Intelligence. An expectation prospers in the Seventh Army, at SHAEF, at home and abroad, that the Nazis will fanatically retreat into the Bavarian fastnesses, and there in the mountains, where they are believed to have constructed impenetrable defenses, will hold out for a long while. Even as the Soviets closed in on Berlin, the whereabouts of Hitler were unknown. They would remain so until the German radio itself announced his death. Meanwhile, the Allies were expecting to hear at any time that he would address the world from his "Alpine Fortress."

This was one of the great myths of the War, and one day would hardly be understood, and passed over in embarrassment, although it was not only passed along as gossip but related in one report after another to be a most realistic scenario of *Götterdammerung*. Interestingly, for those who would pursue manias, madnesses, myths, rumors, psychopathology, and the science of intelligence as practiced, the Germans seem to have played no more than a bit part in the enactment of this phantasmagoria. Typically, the very absence of news from within the area of this mighty *Redoubt* lent credence to the idea of a defensive system so well organized and guarded by a great many special forces that information could not be expected to leak out. A veritable "Black Hole" it was, sucking in rather than giving out intelligence and materiel.

A map of some thousand square miles of terrain showing supply dumps and artillery positions occupied wall-space at Eisenhower's Headquarters. Misinformation came from every usual source, intelligence operatives in Switzerland, the War Department, OSS, and, to the discomfiture of Captain Alfred de Grazia, his respected G-2 Chiefs of the Seventh Army, who, on March 25, imagined "an elite force, predominantly SS and mountain troops, of between 200,000 and 300,000 men," and reported the continuous arrival of supplies in the Redoubt area, including new types of artillery and a put-it-together-yourself Messerschmitt aircraft factory. There are indications that a belief in the Redoubt had some influence in the decision to hold the Seventh Army on its Southeastern course, therefore thinning the main spearheads of advance farther North, therefore helping to rationalize the decision of Eisenhower to hold the Allied forces at the line of the Elbe River, where the Soviet troops would be awaited.

As for me, I could boast (not that I did) that I had ceased to consider seriously the story by March and by May was prepared to traverse the Redoubt by jeep. Which I did, as will be told.

On April 12 the morning news is that FDR has suffered a massive cerebral hemorrhage and is dead. I did not know, the

Seventh Army Command did not know, Supreme Headquarters and General Eisenhower did not know, Prime Minister Churchill did not know, the Press, the Enemy, the Congress were unaware, that FDR had been downed by a serious cerebral hemorrhage March 30 upon his arrival at Warm Springs, Georgia, for a rest. One of the greatest decisions of the War had to be made without his effective participation: the decision to withdraw from the race for Berlin.

Captain Hans Wallenberg and several of the soldiers are positively sick at the news of the President's death. Most of the troop are downcast. Some are indifferent, not a bad sign for a government struggling to live according to republican non-monarchic principles. Wallenberg cannot eat breakfast. I do, though seriously concerned; I always eat. Roos has never liked Roosevelt and is mainly indignant that "that pipsqueak Truman" has to be now sworn in to replace the dead President. The republican character of the government is what inflates me and I take it upon myself to reassure the others that what makes the Constitution great, among other things, is that it provides for the ready succession to the Office of the Chief Executive in such cases as this. The others are not theorists of government, or rather, like most people, including the political science professionals, are as sad and anxious as the Democratic ideologues in general.

Even some Germans are affected, I write, on the day of the news:

> *There is an ancient German man whom we have tolerated to live on these premises while we are camped here. He is silent, grim and formidably entrenched in the world that follows this one. This afternoon he straightened his old hulk and spoke to us: "I have learned that Roosevelt is dead. That is terrible, terrible. He should have lived." I believe he gave the eternal judgement, from an awful depth of experience, despair and wisdom. It was an eerie wind of unexplainable origin blowing across a forlorn prairie. No one was cheerful today. The President, with his fine sense of humor, would probably have chuckled over the consternation in the ranks of his foes as well as his friends. But now he is gone and the responsibility for the future rests very heavily upon his critics, a turn of fate they will feel*

> *more and more. There is no more Roosevelt to pass the buck to, to accuse and to denounce. They have their own chance to be great now - the whole motley assortment and may the best men win. I know little about Truman save that he will not win the peace by himself. He will need a working plurality of politicians to succeed. He will be able to use personally only a fraction of the power Roosevelt wielded. If he defines his own scope properly, I think he may be actually much better than generally estimated. I'm sure his past machine activities won't enter into the incomparably larger situation in which he now finds himself.*

I speak of the new President next a few days later:

> *Our radio monitors had Truman's speech to the armed forces written down this morning and I thought it was about equal to the task, neither more nor less. The Lincoln quotation was a good one, even because everyone knows it. Truman seems to be proceeding, as well he might, cautiously and conservatively. There will be time enough to express his originality, if he wishes ever to do so, after the country has gotten used to him. He is not a fairy tale's answer to calamity, a knight in shining armor, and I believe that he knows it.*

The effect of Roosevelt's death and of Truman's accession is quite out of mind in a few days. The immediate concerns deal with how a great War comes to an end. The U.S. Army is so well organized, "untouched by war" relatively, if ironically, and well-supplied, that it is turning into a thousand islands of self-containment and peace within an ocean of *Sturm und Drang,* practically a chaos. A letter shows this, even though it deals with guilt and punishment, one of many, and of the DP's:

> *Today was an easy one; yesterday was tiring; tomorrow promises to be the same. What the hell, huh? The war here seems to be on its last legs. I have a physical repulsion against moving. I have the same against staying still. I loathe the Germans who have no consciousness of their crimes. But I am equally repelled by the necessity for treating men as scum, even if they are scum. It speaks too much for*

> the devil within us. I feel that I might trust myself with any excess but know that as a social policy it might well be bad. Perhaps it is only an apology for my severity that I say I don't hate the German people, but I really believe it. I am surprised at the passivity of so many of the released PWs and workers. They behave better than they ought in respect to the civilian population. I would prefer our having to restrain them somewhat more. The Russians, particularly, seem in many cases to be deprived of all spirit; so long have they been abused and suppressed, that they are demoralized and inert. No wonder Uncle Joe promises a period of relief and rehabilitation for all his returned Pws and workers. They need it. There are some of the most amazing sights in the roads and in the cities. I have seen sights from Fantastic Stories' most lurid days. The corpses of cities, ghastly rubble piles, alone, still, with figures of men darting in and out every so often, a drunken Russian careening amid the chaos, waving a long sword at the moon.

The theme of the DP's runs through other letters. My troop has liberated a thousand Russians who have suddenly therefore become our responsibility; these are the countless faces of the gloomy factory of whom something will be said later.

On April 28 Benito Mussolini, Godfather of Fascism, Falangism, and Nazism, is lynched by Italian communist partisans, along with his lover, Clara Petacci. The Americans feel that justice has been rendered, though the sight of Petacci hanging upside down with her skirts blowing to the breeze is disgusting to me.

On May 1, near midnight, the German radio station begins to play long stretches of Wagnerian *Götterdamerung* music. Soon enough, the monitoring truck has alerted Captain Wallenberg and the others. They understand that *Der Führer* has died by his own hand, with Eva Braun, and in his Berlin bunker, leaving to Admiral Doenitz the Keys to the Kingdom.

There is to be no Redoubt around Berchtesgarten, no more, no more. Roos has been transferred on "temporary duty" (TD) to Denmark. I has become Commanding Officer in name as well as in fact; I will have only brief occasion to put into effect my ideals about the governance of a military company..

On May 2, two days before the German Nineteenth Army facing the Seventh Army, the German Armies in Italy surrender. I take Lt. Albert Constantine with me in a jeep and drive South. I head straight for the Brenner Pass; I am emboldened from remembering passing through it as a student tourist before the War. Near Innsbruck we come upon an airfield with the first jet airplanes we, or practically any Allied soldiers, have seen. The air force personnel has fled. Here would be the Redoubt's doughty "air fleet." After traversing Innsbruck without incident, I turn into the Brennero.

Hardly a soul is to be seen. No fusillade pouring from the elite troops of the Redoubt above. Half-way through the Pass something like a command car comes rushing towards us. It roars by as I whirl in a double take. It was filled with German officers in full regalia. Too bad, I curse; but there had been no time to react. There hadn't been even a road block that might have stopped them from turning off and burying themselves in an Austrian village.

The next thing the American jeep strike upon is an Army that is dressed for an Operetta by Franz Lehar. These are Czechoslovak troops, allies of the Germans, which could not be trusted for combat in Italy.

Ultimately we slow down as the road nears Bolzano, for there is a bad traffic jam of German infantry and artillery, managed by German MP's, who guide us American officers as if we belonged to the Wehrmacht. Not an Allied vehicle to be seen. Circling through the city, we eventually encounter several Americans leaning against their jeeps, spooning food from C-ration cans into their mouths. "How ya'doin?" "Ya really made it here from Germany? Damn! That's sompin." There isn't much more to say, it seems. Watch the scene a while longer; it gives you an absurd feeling, all these enemy soldiers with their burp-guns and artillery pieces marching hither and yon. Probably looking for places to bivouac. They can't seize Italian homes and buildings just like that any more, can they?

Now we turn our car back toward Germany. It is so silly: this German horde; they would give anything to be heading up the Brenner Pass. Yet all I need to do is to turn the head of my jeep and step on the gas. No one dares to interfere with us. We would have been blown away had we been here a couple of days earlier.

This may have been the first juncture of the Allied forces North and South: the Seventh and Fifth Armies; the otherwise uncontested claim of the Chronologist of the U.S. Army Historical Center is that on May 4, soldiers of an "Intelligence and Reconnaissance Platoon of the 349th Infantry, 88th Division" of the Fifth Army of the 15th Army Group (you remember them!), "establishes contact with the U.S. Seventh Army at Vipiteno, South of Brennero, on Austro-Italian frontier." The Seventh Army contact is said to be of the 411th Infantry Regiment of the 103rd Infantry Division. I had no intention of making the record books, but I did talk about the strange encounters at mess when I got back home. Anyhow the main point was not in the chronology: Churchill's so-called soft underbelly of Europe took as much time to conquer as the bristling backbone of the Nazi swine.

A couple of days later C.D. Jackson shows up from SHAEF with Major Roos and asks me to take them to Dachau. We proceed in the outfit's command car along the *Autobahn*. On the way we come upon a bad truck accident, two huge cargo trucks entangled and tipped over, a couple of black guys prone maybe dying, their comrades around them wondering what to do. I pull over, stop a vehicle with hospital markings and nurses and officers. They seem reluctant to help. I insist they do something. They promise to send help from nearby and scoot off. I delay, talking to the men; it's a matter of internal injuries and concussions; their eyes roll out of control. Roos and Jackson want to get away from the scene. C.D. is irritated; their fault, of course. A third truck has promised to get help, the men tell him. We cannot move them, I say, and they agree. It would make matters worse. Best wait for the ambulance. Back on the road, I sit severely, disliking Jackson: these men have been driving their trucks like crazy ever since the landings in Provence.

At Dachau, as you enter by way of the wide-open wire gates, you are confronted on the left by an enormous mound of corpses disintegrating in lime. Crowds of emaciates shamble around not knowing what to make of it all, smoking American cigarettes. They cannot eat much, just soup like before; but the soup is thicker and better now, says one man, contentedly. When I throw a butt down and move to crush it out of habit, I almost step on a man's hand bending to snatch it. I apologize and gives him a full cigarette. As I had promised a French officer in Augsburg, I leave gifts of tobacco and soap for two French political prisoners, Vincent Badie, a former Socialist Deputy, and François Michelet; they were out somewhere, scrounging around the town, helping themselves to such food and drink and clothing as they might come upon. A large fat SS guard has been uncovered hiding and is dragged past, being bludgeoned, rather feebly think I, by the inmates. "Should I interfere?" I ask myself. I do not.

From Heidelberg

To Mom with Love Bob

Chapter Seventeen

SCHLOSS DE GRAZIA

IT WASN'T my idea to call it "Schloss de Grazia," it was theirs - some of the men - and no one called it that to my face, because I would have been embarrassed. Yet I earned it in a way, because I had discovered it, and we lived very well in it for as happy a three months as the Army ever afforded us, one and all. It was there that I sat down with several of the most disgruntled men and penned a stern and demanding letter to the public columns of *Stars and Stripes,* describing the homesickness and physical and mental infirmities of all the men who had been away from the U.S.A. for over two years and urging the High Command to Do Something about getting them back. I signed my John Hancock to it and it was sent in but never printed. Nor was I arrested for conspiracy and radical agitation. The men were glad that I penned the missive, because nobody could think of anything better to do, and this was a show of solidarity that was not to be found in the manual of arms.

I had not snatched the castle from the enemy. It was more like taking candy from a baby. Literally. I was jeeping about, applying the *savoir-faire* of six campaigns toward seizing just the right kind of billet in view of the battles damping down, and had seen from afar this sturdy Schloss. It had been built not by some Ludwig the Mad, King of Bavaria, but by a Sigmund the Modest. Grey. Unornamented. With a plain courtyard. It fronted for a tiny village. It might have been a private school. As a matter of fact, when I entered I was met by women who seemed to be teachers, and they explained that it was being used to house children safe from the

Allied bombings. The children were anxious, they said, to leave for their homes, now that the bombings had stopped over Western Germany. Very good, said I, I will provide you with the trucks to bring the *kinder* home. Then they opened a door for me to view a classroom, and the tots cried as one voice: *"Heil Hitler!"*, leaping up stiffly to attention from their tiny stools. "Remarkable," I said. "At ease." I murmured to the Matron: "I hope that you will stop all that." "Oh, yes, *Herr Hauptmann,*" she exclaimed. And you can bet that it was their last *"Heil."*

I moved on Southeastward toward Munich, detouring to dip in the Ammersee en route, while my recce team captured the City's radio transmitter intact and the *Völkischer Beobachter,* the kingpin Nazi newspaper. On our way through the city streets, officials of the Central Police and Post Office called to us, waving, that they were surrendering here and now. Actually they should have been waving surrender leaflets, because General Patch had asked for such a leaflet just for them; this was quickly turned out by Tom Crowell and given to the Air Corps; but the aviation armorers mis-converted the incendiary shells to be employed and they failed to explode in air.

I returned to Schloss Strassberg and, just before driving South to Italy, wrote to Jill on the letterhead of the *Völkischer Beobachter:*

VÖLKISCHER BEOBACHTER
SCHRIFTLEITUNG FERNRUF
MÜNCHEN

Meine liebe Frau,

And why not this letterhead for the fitting end to German propaganda? Johnny Anspacher got a copy of the last book they published too, and that ironically enough was Rosenberg's Myth of the Twentieth Century, *back where their propaganda started. And as the hundreds of books lay there, thousands of freed prisoners and slaves stormed over the country hooting its prostrate form and sneering at those who remained in it. The Reality of the Twentieth Century, perhaps, one might name it.*

It's all about over now. With the surrender of the Southern forces and the practically complete occupation of Germany, we might as well change to that V-E mood, if we can manage it. Personally, I don't see much to be excited about. The end is duller than the gigantic battles that occurred in the middle of it. It is almost difficult to get into a discussion on Hitler's death, so uninterested is everyone. I have an intimation that the surrender of Japan will be a much more surprising affair and more deserving of thanksgiving. Truman's hint to the Japs on the occasion of the surrender in the South, the Japanese collapse in Burma, our approach to the main islands, the heavy raids, the condolences of the Japanese premier on the death of Roosevelt, and the Russian pressure in canceling the treaty and in the statements of Stalin point to a jockeying for position in the Far East for a quick conclusion of the war.

  At the moment, my visual perception here sees only rain. We are housed on a hilltop which sweeps a large plain with woods, towns and a couple of factories. We have a tower that is very high and we fly the flag there at half mast. It can be seen for miles and must serve as a constant reminder to the Germans of the location of power. Our billets are very good. I found enough beds for every man, and we have central heating and even hot showers, not to mention electric lights. I have fixed up my room in a creditable manner. Next to my bed is your picture, atop a small table, and next to it is my trumpet. On the wall above the bed are three other beautiful women in small frames, Nefertiti, Veneziano's Maiden, and Kathy, with her pants showing. Below the bed is an ammunition case which I use as a foot locker and a barracks bag. There are drapes on the two big windows which look out over the countryside, there is this writing table, there are sheets on the bed, and there is the radio I am going to fix soon.

  The weather here in Germany lately has been bitter. We have even had snow and sleet storms in the past few days and driving hasn't been much fun. It should pass soon, though, according to the latest local intelligence and be followed by a beautiful spell. The sun comes out, but it may disappear in a second, to be followed by cold winds, dark clouds and cold rain.

  ...I wanted to ask you when you think Kathy is going to be properly trained anally and otherwise. Isn't she rather elderly to be going about revealing her contempt of society in such a forthright manner?

> *This room would do very nicely for the two of us, I think. It is very light and we could practically look out of bed into the valley afterwards. It is clean and very large and it even has a couple of copies of the* New Yorker *and a book on public opinion scattered around to make it look like our customary environment. I don't think these years have made much difference. I still want pretty much what I want before and it all begins with You. I cannot visualize any ambition of mine, no matter how petty it be, without you fitting into the frame somewhere, in the center or in the corner, like Hitchcock doesn't release a picture he directs without being personally in some shot. You are in every shot I take of a future preference, your tossing about, your long legs, your ideas, your habits, and you are always photogenic.*
> *With many a kiss to you and Kathy, I'm always*
> *Yours,   Al*

A month later, sitting at the same window, overlooking the plain that runs from Augsburg to Munich, I read my Brother Edward's letter of chagrin. Eddie was now an Air Force Private, who had hoped by then to be a fly-boy. He was griping:

> *Today I received a shock via the mails, which, though I can't pretend it knocked me off my pins did kinda' stun me. It was to the effect that I, poor misguided wing-happy lad, am absolutely "Shit Out of Luck" (I write it out for emphasis) as far as any aspirations for cloud-chasing are concerned. Due to the epochal collapse of Germany, there will be absolutely no more training of members for Air Combat crew. The Air Corps, with its stupendous surplus, has enough men in training now and in the air now to "keep 'em flying" for the duration. In other words, I, and thousands of other guys, will, because of our deficiency in age...*

"Deficiency in Age!" He was eighteen, how deficient! I, it is understandable, could hardly break into tears at someone, even my brother, missing the glamorous war. But maybe he would have an occasion to help occupy the Reich. (He did.)

Meanwhile Eddie's big brother is taking matters into his own hands. Germany is jumping with Deplaced Persons, and just about every American unit is dealing with some of them. They are on the verge of starvation, and the Army is pouring out rations among them as fast as they can be brought in. There is the official and the informal effort, both of them large. It is no wonder, and indeed justifiable, that the million and more German prisoners coming into Allied hands from one month to the next, would not be eating regularly. There is not enough to go around, unless one were to cut back on American rations, which go against the ancient adage that "to the victor belong the spoils;" the troops would feel badly. What commonly happened was that the individual units would dish out a portion of their rations to those in want and near at hand, beginning with the half-starved Russians, Poles, French and other large groups - we speak of hundreds of thousands of these others.

Our propaganda company did more than its share, if only because we were better at it. One of the groups we adopted was found cooped up in a practically destroyed factory. My letter to Jill tells a story about it:

> *After a concerted attack on the mess sergeant today we finally had a decent meal tonight and as you can guess I suffered slightly from the consequences. So I took a walk with Lt. Constantine in the vicinity of our present bivouac, a term really too primitive to describe the houses we have taken over, and have now returned to it after having had an instructive and friendly talk with some Russian DPs (displaced personnel) we ran into. They are about all that is left of a thoroughly bombed out little factory and are waiting for something to be done about them. Tonight a group of them were whiling away time playing a game of cards - Russian bank I imagine, and I got into a limited sort of communication with a few of the others. They looked like a set of characters out of the* Dance of the Red Poppy, *and as might be expected, one of their number was actually formerly a ballet dancer, proof of which was soon forthcoming in the way of a pirouette and a couple of classic poses of the Ballet Russe. I gave them the latest lowdown on Shostakovich and they gave me a big mug of red wine, not very red, come to think of it, more of a vin rosette. There wasn't enough of it, however, to draw out my talents in the dance field*

and I gave no more than a passing thought to executing my three kicks in midair, a thing which, like that little runner of Saroyan, I am always convinced I can do until I try. The conversation then turned to the Germans and the usual maledictions were said over them. The ballet dancer and all of his troupe, musicians, dancers and director, were captured by the Germans and put to work as laborers on the usual level of brutality and starvation.

However, the main character of our DP scene became Lena of Odessa:

Darling Jill,

It started out to be a dull evening. Extrinsically, it perhaps still has been, but sensually I think it has been quite something. I must confess ab initio that I am full of Vodka like a Cossack in midwinter, and am just about ready to pour myself a cup of coffee that the unique Lena has just carried into my room.

And that is a good beginning to a story which certainly begins with Lena. It began on a bright day near here - tonight it is raining steadily and outside my room the trees bend and the mists push steadily over the valley. I had a scouting party out to find a billet for the troops who were moving into newly liberated territory. We moved into a German house late at night, told the occupants to get out in the morning, ate a good supper with some mediocre but welcome wine, and went to bed, after letting some wandering Russians in out of the cold. In the morning, I was in a hurry to leave, placing two men to guard the place. Just before I left, I noticed one of the Russians talking to a woman in Russian who was in the top floor of a house nearby. But I hadn't time to liberate every individual we met, and departed. The sergeant I left behind, it seems, then urged the Russians to kill a chicken in the yard of the nearby house, since they were famished. It took him [Sgt. Charley Wagner] some while to stir up some of their revolutionary spirit but they finally mustered up the courage and energy -- they were ridiculously weak -- to attack the coop. A square meal followed and the wine flowed freely. Suffused with the new blood, the Russians proposed more food and said that the Russian maid had indicated the cellar as an egg repository. This time the man appeared and protested, in a manner which so enraged the sergeant that he gave chase, ending up unfortunately in the arms of the MPs. But when he got back he was determined to liberate the maid, and out she came, happy and smiling. When we arrived back, she fell right in with the company and since has been most useful. She would be making a fortune in America today but here she doesn't take a cent. She isn't interested in money, she says. She comes from Odessa, is 42 years old, strong as an ox and very intelligent, although she has a block as far as learning German goes. She went to a mining school for three years and was some sort of a technical foreman until the Germans moved into Stalino one day and moved everything and everybody to Germany the next. She is a great favorite with all the men and officers and rolls right along with us wherever we go. And whenever there is civilian labor to handle, she looks as if she were addressing Cell no. 974 of the Krasnograd Soviet on a topic dear to the Party. Vigorous and emphatic are the best words for it.

    Last day or so she has been unusually colorful and active, because it has been the Russian Christmas [Easter] *holiday. This evening, she came in and asked me to go to a nearby DP camp for an hour or so -- she had told them she would bring me. So I donned my raincoat and we went. We had a reasonably communicable political discussion, considering the fluency of our respective German and the vodka, and then came back to where I am writing this. The Russian method of drinking vodka is completely mad. Tumblers full, and then bottoms down in one flash. The consequences can be horrible in a short time. Luckily, there was only one two-thirds liter bottle amongst the three of us drinking, and as a result I can be here to tell the tale. And more so, since I had eaten an hour before and had no appetite for the food placed before me which is counted on to absorb some of the shock. I have found, incidentally, that mirabelle, schnapps, and vodka are alike in that respect, that they go well with hearty eating, whereas whiskey stands alone for me.*

This group was squatting and standing all the while near the entrance of a huge cavernous barn so crowded that it looked like the stage of the Metropolitan Opera in the triumphal scene from *Aida*. They were vastly curious about me, but did not dare to press in close, so well-disciplined were they, or habitually intimidated. The discipline would have come from the young man whom Lena introduced. He was thin, below medium height, but self-possessed and prompt to deal with me in businesslike terms. He had around him several men and women who appeared to be a sort of staff. I figured that communist party rule had been reestablished in the barnyard.

When, several days later, my men came upon a warehouse filled with shoes, I remembered the mass of refugees, who would have to return to Russia and Poland unshod or in worn footgear and sent for the commissar. "These are yours to distribute among your people!" I said, and sent truckload upon truckload to the barn. There must have been a thousand well-shod ex-slaves the next day. A nice aspect of the project was its unsentimentality. I and my men conducted ourselves unaffectedly. So did the tough kids in charge of the mob. There is nothing like a war to make acts of charity global and infinite. As if to match its brutality and destruction.

One day, a protest delegation from several Polish slave workers provoked something close to brutality, or lynch justice. They had just been liberated, but the German owner of their small factory would not feed them unless they continued to work. Indignant soldiers brought the delegation before me. I called First Sergeant Jack Taubert and a couple of other men to accompany me to thefactory. We came upon the owner, a tall man in his fifties, sitting in his office. When the Polish delegates accused him of starving them, he answered them back angrily. At this, Sergeant Taubert seized him and dragged him out of his chair. The man's wife came running in, having heard the commotion, exclaiming in distress: "What is the matter?! What are they doing to you?!" And the man said: "Nothing, nothing, don't worry, leave us alone, go away." So she left. And there was I, with a fine excuse to proceed with the manslaughter. Yet when Taubert, death in his scowling black face, raised his fist again, I said - and I had to repeat myself, for passions were high - "Lay off, Sergeant. Lay off!" It was the woman who did it to me. Her concern, which made her burst in upon us. And then the man's courage in ordering her to get out of the room - knowing he would be in for worse, now, but wanting to spare her the sight.

(He couldn't be so stupid as to ignore this.) "Look," I said to the man, *"gibt them zu essen,* or else," or words to that effect. We left. After that, the Poles ate *besser, viel besser.*

I couldn't help but wonder from time to time who was suffering worst in this hellish world at war. I had an orderly mind that liked to make lists and classify things, the more qualitative and defiant of ordinary statistics the better. Like, who was suffering then most, of all the world's people? The answers available to me at the time were almost the same as a vastly knowledgeable historian would give today after half a century - if the historian were bold enough to speak up. The answers are not easy. Still the questions had been asked and argued on all sides from the first days of the war and were eternal subjects of discussion - angry discussion, heated discussion, occasionally calm, almost never logical.

To give you an example: You are picked up, in the middle of the night, and shoved roughly by uniformed thugs into a truck, hearing them say: "Get in, you dirty Jew. *Mach schnell!"* You have been suffering fear of this moment for five months, ever since the Germans came close to your frontier. You and the rest are driven to a rail siding, forced into a crowded boxcar, ridden for two days without food or water, dumped out, driven on foot into a camp, given some soup, and after a couple of days of freezing, given soap and a towel, told to take a shower with the rest of your barrack, gassed to death, and then the rest doesn't matter to you, but merely tortures your relatives and sympathizers for years and decades to come.

Then there is this American soldier who used to be a Broadway cowboy and is caught up one morning in an Army roll-call and in six months of lacerating drill and discomfort is qualified for a ship where conditions are so bad he is reminded of the slave ships and is thankful to be dumped in a camp on the edge of a New Guinea jungle into which he enters, with others, and sets up an ammunition dump, which is missed by Japanese bombers on several harrowing occasions, but he goes on rotting there, only to move on to another rotten place and finally is carried home in an even worse boat than before.

Then there is the Company Clerk in a Welsh artillery regiment which has one of those resounding names that are amusing until to bear it is a death warrant. Now all this man does after ending his miserable brief career as a miner is to train doggedly and bitterly on an English swamp, then push and pull a gun piece twice across the Libyan desert, usually with a good chance of escaping or being hit, but thirsty and worn out, and then following his piece into Italy, thence to France and Germany for more of the same, finally getting into a channel steamer and getting back to his mine shaft in good time for the next strike.

And there is the Soviet officer who could speak Chinese and spent the war choosing among the dishes on a Chinese menu in his favorite restaurant in Peiping until he was imprisoned for a week from August 8 to 15. I should go on profiling a few thousands to get a sample of the whole world at war, but the job here is to set forth a list of groups, arranged in order as their modal number of members suffered the war, realizing that in each group, believe it or not, you would find some of the gayest and saddest people in the world, whatever the rating of their group: Dame Psyche and Dame Fortune can together conceive of all possible mad scenarios. So:

1. German concentration camp victims
2. Russian and German infantry and German allied troops on Eastern Front
3. Russian prisoners of Germans
4. Russian Front civilians
5. Prisoners of Japanese
6. War prisoners of Russians
7. Japanese soldiers committed to combat
8. Hiroshima and Nagasaki victims
9. Russian Front tanks and artillery
10. Luftwaffe air crews and German submarine crews
11. U.S. troops in Pacific Islands and Philippines
12. Italian troops in North Africa
13. Allied infantry, Western Front
14. Displaced persons and workers from East
15. Japanese Navy and Air Force
16. Western Front German Regimental and Divisional

       troops
17. Allied Western Front Tanks (and some Artillery)
18. German civilians
19. Dutch, Belgian, French, Greek, Italian civilians
20. English civilians
21. South and Southeast Asian civilians
22. American civilians
23. South Americans
24. Swedes and Swiss

A monumental research would be required in order to establish acceptable parameters for all of the above groups and the many groups that have been left out! The irregular intervals between one and the next "level of suffering," for example, constitute one of the many problems that would need to be resolved. But it would all go by the board, anyhow, because as soon as you get to discussing the definitions of the groups and the sufferings they underwent (with all the subdivisions within the groups that confuse their histories), you will commence a dialectic that is infinitely abstruse and morally relative until you will finally collapse in exhaustion - and uncertainty. Except this: having started this all by virtue of my over-educated sensitivity to indirect consequences and relative ethical stances, I would conclude: if victory were acceptably defined, no one has ever won a war. If morals were acceptably defined and shared by all humans, all groups would suffer equally, when they were not suffering from others, for all the suffering that they were causing to be done to the others.

The moral questions of the German nation were immense and complicated. Instances came up before us. There was Hermann Goering, the fat Marshal of the German Nazi Reich. He was caught up with finally by the American Seventh Army, was now a refugee in Austria, after having given up on Hitler in Berlin and having ordered the last of the Luftwaffe to fight on the ground against the Russians who were attacking the Capital in a final assault. I was informed: Goering has been taken. Do you want to see him? "No." (I would admit to no morbid curiosity about this disgusting slob.) "Go ahead without me." I got two pictures, so fitting to the case:

Goering trying to squeeze his large ass into the small rear door of a sub-compact car; the second picture: Goering standing amidst his interrogators, who were as "Jewish-looking" as the worst anti-semite would deserve; Hans Wallenberg was standing alongside Goering, scowling as only he could scowl.

"What did he have to say?" I asked of Hans. "He said that the big mistake of the Nazis was the persecution of the Jews." We laughed sardonically. Was Goering trying to please his interrogators? Or was he really expressing an opinion about antisemitism as a tactic, never mind its morality? I had given thought to this point, years before; my conclusion: if the Nazis had embraced the Jews, they never would have achieved the totalitarian state, for most Jews would have held them back; besides, the idea was an impossible contradiction: antisemitism was of the essence of Nazism, inseparable nourishment of its cancer.

Then came a message from Dr. Robert Ley, the head of the Nazi party, NSDAP, himself and head of the "one-union" of Nazi workers and employers. A more villainous character would be hard to find. It was unclear for whom he meant his note: to whoever was commanding his interrogators, it would appear. I was the C.O. of the combat propaganda team, but the better line of command would be via Colonel Quinn. General Patch!

No. The men knew it. It was a joke for everyone. In translation it reads:

MESSAGE

To the Commander:
Sir:
I beg you most urgently to supply me with socks, underwear, shirt, handkerchief, trousers and a jacket. I have been arrested out of bed. I have not run away. I have arrived here almost naked.
With highest considerations,
Dr. R. Ley

Ley was a Jew-hater whose job included facilitating the holocaust in more ways than one. He was also a Russian-hater, believed they should be exterminated, had been overheard to order: "Get rid of those Russian prisoners." He identified himself with the program of the mass murderer, Gauleiter Koch. He was a General of the SS, SA, and as the top leader of several Nazi organizations, often implicated in the in-fighting for Hitler's favor among the Nazis elite. Hitler was known to be fond of his first wife, usually carrying flowers on visits to their cozy family circle. His mistress, a ballet dancer thirty-seven years his junior, stuck by him until the end, but also gave copious information to her interrogators about him. (All American interrogators agreed: Germans, male or female, sang like canaries under questioning.)

She, Madeleine Wanderer, and his Private Secretary, Paula Mueller, described a scheme of Dr. Ley that could have helped inspire rumors of the Redoubt. His last assignment by *Der Führer* was to carry on with his own scheme, the *Freicorps,* which he would organize and command. The *Freicorps* was to fight ahead of and behind the Front; it was to be composed of *Schwaerme* or "swarms" of nine men and one woman (a cook, a medic, and a fighter), armed with pistols and *Panzerfaust,* and riding bicycles. They did not get under way before the big show collapsed. The bizarre scheme tickled my imagination. It must have aroused in me memories of childhood games of war. It was a neat German version of partisans, guerrillas, "terrorists," as the Wehrmacht would call them.

Another project of Robert Ley had to do with a secret weapon that "a professor" was developing and that no one knew much about, save that it would work by remote control. When asked about experiments involving the weapon at Waldenburg, an adjutant of Ley said that it failed: that "it would not even have hurt a rabbit."

A more attractive prisoner was the movie-maker, Leni Riefenstahl, whose great film of the 1936 Olympic games was regarded, by the highest aesthetic standards, as a triumph of Nazi propaganda. Wallenberg and Langendorf interrogated her, and, it must be said, she won them over. All the bad that happened to her later, because her career survived the war, will have been in spite of their report:

> *Her statements give one the impression of honesty, and the dread which she expresses about the Regime and its leaders seems sincere. It is possible that she actually was not aware of what went on. That was her sin of omission, which appears all the more serious due to the fact that she, more than any other person, had the opportunity to get to the truth. She is a product of the moral corruption which characterizes the regime. But it would be false to picture her as an ambitious female who wanted to attain fame and wealth on the NSDAP bandwagon.*

What really happened, thought her interrogators, is that her admiration for Hitler closed her eyes, while his authoritative hand allowed her to pass unscathed through the nasty struggles and backstabbing politics inside the Regime. She could dream and live in her art. She could afford to help Jews from time to time. She could deny, because she was en route to America, the November 1938 Crystal Night pogroms about which she was asked when she arrived by boat; when she returned to Germany, she was told that they were true, that the American newspapers had not lied, but that the perpetrators of the pogroms were being punished. She believed that the concentration camps, of which she had heard, were places of detention and punishment of criminals. And so on.

It was not at all astonishing, I thought, given what the science of public opinion had discovered time after time, that the most "obvious" of occurrences were sincerely denied by people both because they did not want to believe them and because the controls over free flow of information were always serious and, in a totalitarian state, practically total in effectiveness. Did not the American public, even the Roman Catholics, still believe that the Germans had illegally and fully occupied the Abbey of Montecassino? Did not the powerful on-the-spot correspondent of the *New York Times,* later its chief, give it the headline that hundreds of German soldiers went scurrying from its premises following the Allied bombardment?

The big Nazi fish came flopping over the gunwales fleeing the Russians or were hooked aboard. Only when all was ended did the German generals surrender their troops. One exception had occurred long before, the surrender of Von Paulus of the forces in Stalingrad; they would have been shortly annihilated; still Hitler wanted to be able to say that they fought to the last man. Von Paulus denied him this political and erotic pleasure. Another case occurred in Tunis, May 12, 1943, when Jürgen von Arnim surrendered a second large army, this time to the Western Allies. A partial exception came at the end of the War in Italy, where contacts had been made with Allen Dulles, an American representative in Switzerland; it appeared that the German Army there would give up days before Hitler committed suicide, but when the Russians were already in the outskirts of Berlin; that is, it was practically not a separate surrender.

Why did the Generals order their troops to fight to the end? They could have saved the lives of a quarter of a million men and an equal number of civilians and foreigners; they might have mollified even if slightly their conquerors. Their country, and other lands, would be less destroyed. I am speaking only of the period from January 1, 1945, even though to any rational man, even only half-informed, the game was up upon the loss of Stalingrad and North Africa.

1. They were not dying personally and would increase their chances of dying upon surrender ("unconditional surrender" sounded ominous in this regard). They were also "freaks," to be blunt. They saw the world as made for war Prussian-style.

2. They would be killed by the SS immediately upon giving any intimation of dealing in surrender, under orders from Hitler, and their own troops and staffs would not fight to protect them.

3. If they fought on the Eastern Front, then they hoped to resist until the Western Allies broke through and conquered the remaining portions of the Reich.

4. They were tightly controlled by Hitler's Headquarters, by the Führer himself, who "called all the shots."

5. The doctrine of unconditional surrender was taken to mean the giving over of Germany to total rapine and likely total destruction.

6. They were not contacted or subjected to psychological and propaganda pressures by their Allied counterparts in the West.

American and British generals behaved like automatons; they supported psychological warfare of our kind in combat operations, but no general acquired a reputation for being cognizant of and sympathetic to the aspirations of any irresolute or resolute German general. It was against the rules for the American generals to do so; they must "stay out of politics," and fishing for a surrender would have been impossible. Just as Hitler wiped out any countervailing attitude in his generals, the Western Allies discouraged any personalism in their generals (except on silly levels of public images - pistol-toting, Bible-spouting, etc.). Eisenhower, at SHAEF, might have effected negotiations, reporting to Churchill and Roosevelt carefully, but he was bureaucratized, a reliable foe of any extraordinary maneuvers. Alexander was a dilettante, who might have been prepared to do more except for his famed hesitancy.

7. The July 1944 attempt at Hitler's assassination by a group of highly placed and respected German officers brought the massacre of all who were suspected to have been even remotely involved. The lack of appreciation of this heroism, on the part of Allied leaders and Allied propaganda, whether East or West, discouraged all further attempts at violating the will of the Führer, even unto his last crazed hours in his Berlin bunker.

8. Death diminishes to a small matter relative to the ignominy of surrender when one has been in charge of a great army in a great cause and has ordered the death of hundreds of thousands of men; what else is left to be achieved in life?

Over two months pass, a blissful, easy time at Strassberg. In May I arrange a final trip to Paris. I am not there this time for dissipation and sex; I behave like a proper citizen, *viz.:*

> *Jill, my Darling,*
> *I flew in here yesterday afternoon. The day was bright and calm, and the trip was likewise. I met Martin last night after supper which I had at Pittman's hotel. Martin is in the middle of changing assignments, as who isn't. We talked with Dick Crossman & several other people for a while. C. is running for parliament in quasi-absentia. He'll probably make it, and be a damned good MP.*

Afterwards, Martin and I walked up to Montmartre and came back, went to his room, had a drink, and adjourned around one. Chief social event was several games on a pinball machine, but Martin didn't afford me nearly the competition you used to be. The ones at the UT [the University Tavern, 55th St. and University Ave., Chicago] *were much better than these though. These paid off in slugs which of course went right back into the machine. The night clubs are closing around eleven these days. There aren't as many soldiers in town as before.*

Paris is gayer than usual, since the Victory flush hasn't worn off, and many flags are still flying. I had the finest Martini with Pittman since our days together, at an outdoor café which was very peaceful, sheltered on the Faubourg St. Honoré. This morning I spent talking to people regarding our outfit and this afternoon I hope to get over to the other side of the river to see the Rodin gallery. There's a good French movie running which I hope to see also, perhaps this evening. It's called Les Enfants du Paradis, *and the French claim it's the best produced in a generation. It was put out since the Liberation.*

I write a second letter the next day:

If I haven't done much in Paris, at least I can write to tell you as much. My day here has consisted until now, supper time, mainly of a luncheon with Bob Merriam and a lot of walking. After I wrote you yesterday, I visited the Rodin museum where practically all of Rodin's sculpture is housed. Don't you think that is cheating humanity? Here you come for an hour to be dazzled and stupefied by a man's genius & the rest of the time live in poverty of him. His works, or any artist's works, should be scattered over the world to be seen by everyone and at odd times. Wouldn't it be bad if all the great mountains were in only one spot. All the waterfalls spilling over each other only in Cook County, Ill., & all the palms waving in Florida? It is silly, too, to think that I enjoyed Rodin more because there was more of him there.

About his work itself, I feel that he is a painter gone wrong. His efforts to create realism of a most violent sort from marble and scenes of passionate transience ought better to have been done on canvas. There is something too eternal about rock to make it portray a moment well. "The Thinker", yes; "Balzac", yes, but many of the other groups, no, "Porte d'Enfer" no. Dostoevsky's temperament in stone. Il ne va pas [sic].

Perhaps my attitude here is a general one. I see that I have been growing increasingly critical of the realists and romanticists, mainly in painting and decoration. Some day I must stop and reconsider this change & try to account for it if it seems to be consistent.

My pen went dry and I have to write with the very useful pencil you sent me. Besides Bob Merriam, I've met several other U of C people here this time, Al Lepawsky, Major still, was at the mess last evening. (Bob says he's looking forward to getting to the states again & out of the army), a Col. [Charles "Chuck"] *Thompson whom you don't know & I know from Washington, a man named Borgen, brother of Frank Borgen whom I knew quite well, good old Major Waples* [Professor Douglas Waples] *who is very much interested in forthcoming book publications in Germany, and Bob told me Hugh Cole, former history prof. is his boss in the Historical Section of headquarters here. Bob has been over here a year now, mostly with the Shaef Historical Section. He said Hart Perry is in Italy with OSS and leading the usual life of OSS there. Hart got his commission at Davis too. Deadman has been released from his PW camp near Munich. Hart's wife Beattie is a Red Cross morale builder in a hospital back home. Bob's wife, Jane Fosmer, is a WAC in an Army Separation Center from where she writes that she is getting combat fatigue second hand. That's all the gossip I can remember.*

I'm going down to the bar now to have a drink before supper. I told a guy I'd meet him there.

It is early June. With Jacques Pregre, I check in on Army HQ now at Augsburg. Pregre takes me to a house to meet a French Red Cross group handling French workers and prisoners in Germany, three men, two women, one dark, sultry, beautiful, the other ruddy, cheerful, intelligent. I am impressed by the improvement in the landscape and envious of the Frenchmen. I have them to a dinner party at the Schloss. The French Red Cross Chef is quite jealous of the dark woman, who is the sexier but not so nice or bright as the redhead.

The day following, I managed to appear at the Red Cross house without Lt. Pregre. I found the red-head there and asked for the other woman, Odette, the first one being called Simone Thomas. "She is not here. *Je regrette*. But she is not your type anyway." " Really?" " No, I am more your type." "I'll have to take your word for it," I say, "will you be my guest for lunch" - because I can get a free lunch at the HQ 7A Officers' Mess and they have a bar. I can describe her by means of a letter, lacking some important detail, such as her more than ample bosom and generally fine figure. It is, as I have said, early April; Spring has begun.

> *Lt. Lankford, Sgt. Taubert and I went for a swim yesterday with four French officers and two French girls who work on the repatriation of Frenchmen. The place was a small lake alongside the Autobahn near Augsburg. One of the girls is the mistress of the French captain. I told you about her a couple of days ago. The other girl is called Simone Thomas and is a very nice, lively girl who shares your penchant for climbing under and over things and cracking very good witticisms. She was in Germany for the last year and a half working for the French Red Cross, and graduated in literature from the Sorbonne. Her home is in Paris. She doesn't speak* [much] *English but speaks excellent German. The first girl, Odette, is a real minx, the kind that drunken beachcombers beat, lazy, sharp, and sexy. After the swim, Lankford went with them to their place for supper and I came back here. We had a good dinner of pork chops, potatoes, FRESH lettuce salad, and ice cream. One couldn't ask for more. At eight-thirty we showed the film* To Have and To Have Not *during which all the men panted lustfully at Lauren Bacall and "thrilled to the torrid romance and high adventure of the French West Indies" just as they were supposed to do. I liked especially the dialogue in the parts where it was as flat and dry as a Martini, the piano player and all the music and songs.*

More detail comes in later letters, five that mention Simone over a period of two months, representing a total of twelve rendezvous. The letters of Jill in reply do not mention Simone. I believe, probably correctly, that Jill is secure enough to feel very little jealousy; she knows I will return. As for me, from time to time I wonder, but there is nothing like a pregnant woman and infant's mother to stem the flow of male suspicion.

I, accent on the *'frrehd,'* and Simone got together whenever it was discreet and convenient. She stayed a couple of nights at the Schloss when the party ended late and I had drunk too much to gad about, but the place was large enough so that, in the course of gossiping about her, she might have been said to have slept in another room, not that she would have cared. She was affectionate, willing, a luxuriant armful, not great at love-making but lovable nonetheless, always considerate, always ready to go and uncomplaining, fluent in German and pushing out a kind of English, and capable of holding her own in professional discussions of the complex state of the war and the alliances and the hereafter, of music, films and food. Were I not so hopefully and determinedly in love with Jill, and all that she represented in my past, present, and future, I would probably have moulded an enduring relationship. But that's what was so good about my friendship with Simone. She made not the slightest gesture to capture me, let out no hint of jealousy, asked nothing of me.

The Army was redistributing its forces around Germany. Sixth Army Headquarters, our superior command, was up North now, and I went to see how my friends were doing there and to seek a few favors for my Company.

> *Darling Jill,*
>
> *I have about three-quarters of an hour in which to write you a letter now, before I go about finding a car to take me to an airport for the return trip to Augsburg. I had meant to leave yesterday afternoon, but there were a couple of things yet to do this morning and I stayed over. It was good that I did, for Tom* [Crowell], *Shields and I had a fine time with two quarts of Scotch at Shields' home. Tom got in a swell mood in the afternoon and by the time we went over for supper he was irrepressible. He got up in the mess hall in front of all*

the staid people and let out a yell that startled them out of their wits. Then he cleared away the chairs and did a tap dance with his famous bumps. It was all in honor of his return to the old country. We continued at a more sober pace after eating a good meal and ended up at one o'clock. This morning we didn't feel badly at all considering everything, which goes to prove how good Johnny Walker is. I was sad to see him go though. He's one of the few good friends I've made overseas. I know lots of people passably well but Tom I know extremely well. Because of a jam in air transport he'll most likely ride a boat back.

Now that I'm here in the center of things, I don't know much more than if I had stayed in bed. I guess I'll be bringing the outfit up here one of these days for its final disposition. I don't like it here. Too many offices and administrative people. Life is something like YMCA life back home. I hope I won't have to stay here long when I do arrive. There is no news on going home in the immediate future. It seems from the little information in the newspapers that redeployment is proceeding more rapidly than it was originally and pessimistically scheduled. However, these troops that are going to the Pacific afterwards have first priority on transport and then the flood of 85ers will follow. I do hope to see you before September, but, if anything happens and I can't, could you wait for me until October? I am very unhappy now with this waiting, so please don't accuse me of not exhausting all possibilities of returning.

I've seen Martin Herz several times while here. In fact this letter is being written on his typewriter. He just got his orders to go to Austria, for which he has been waiting. He'll be stationed there for some time in an as yet uncertain capacity. Last evening I saw Hans Habe for a few minutes. I hadn't seen him since Italy, and he has grown a lot heavier. He was rather thin originally, you may remember. He's stationed farther north and heads up the German press section.

Constantine is around too in an administrative job. Right now he is rationing out some newly arrived liquor to the officers.

I hope I can get back in time for the big ball game tonight. We are playing the FA outfit we licked a week ago, this time on our home grounds. I ought to make it, since the plane leaves here at four-thirty and only takes an hour to get to Augsburg. That's very fast, two hundred and seventy miles, but the plane is a B-25 converted bomber and doesn't fool around much. I wish it would head West and not stop. I would be home tomorrow sometime. The company sends a car to pick me up at the airfield and that's how I get home to Strassberg. I hope there'll be some mail from you waiting for me there. It's almost three days so there should be something.

The last payday of the company arrived. I sat by the winch of the half-track watching as the Pay Officer handed out the Marks of the Allied Occupation Forces. I knew every face and figure, every man, so well. I was winding down the company now. What would be their future? It was hard to picture them as individuals, out of uniform, walking down the street alone, standing in some shop or factory or service station. It was strange how little the men talked of their future, nor did the officers say much: it must have been because they were afraid of their future, or had forgotten what life was like at home, or were enchanted with their routines.

Every morning I got them up and marched them up the lane to and through the village and into the woods, startling the folk and deer with our "sound-off's" and smacking of gun-butts. They had become a threat at softball to the much larger battalions of infantry and ordnance and artillery. They gobbled and guzzled like Robin Hood's Merry Men. They had even staked out, a few of them, the Russian DP camp below, the camp of the shoes, for many a trim ankle pointed a foot well-clad for dancing now, and sometimes they came straggling back late at night or not at all.

"Captain, the men are complaining of crabs." "Crabs! You don't say! From the camp below, I suppose." The C.O. is angry, orders the mattresses turned out, the philanderers and their clothing purged, DDT sprinkled like talcum powder, and quarantines the DP camp. The Puritans among the troop were pleased. The guards were alerted to interrogate men going and coming. Blackie was among them; like Cook, who killed a man and another time grabbed a truck on an escapade, Blackie, who almost killed me, went after the girls and violated the curfew. This was too much.

The next day, by coincidence, the French squad was at last to depart for the French First Army. Their happy time with the

Americans was over. Lt. Pregre would lead them off. Blackie was pleased with his last illicit night. Not so I, who ordered a showdown inspection of the departing men. They stood by their packs and showed what they had. This was done but rarely, and for various purposes: to recover lost or stolen objects, to discover excess gear and forbidden articles, to determine that every man's equipment was complete and in order, and so on. In the present instance, the point was at first uncertain. Lined up in the courtyard, the soldiers, at my command, dropped their bags and opened them for examination. I passed swiftly along the line, and halted at Blackie's pack. "This Belgian automatic and that Italian Beretta are forbidden to an enlisted man. Sergeant, put them aside. These spoons and forks are loot, forbidden. This sweater is extra, Army property, retrieve it. O.K. Close it up!" Blackie is red under his brown skin. One can only hope that he had great fun the night before. I like Blackie, a cheerful type, he'll forget it all soon.

Sadder than this morning was the day that trucks arrived at the camp below and the DP's climbed into them to begin the long journey back to the Soviet Union. Promised a return to a welcoming homeland, they had learned by rumor and some reliable reporting that bad things were happening to the returnees. The American officers and men knew this even better. Here they were: prisoners of war, forced workers driven back into the Reich, and voluntary workers. Who among them had surrendered too readily, let themselves be enslaved too freely, offered their services to the Nazis, even helped to enslave and beat and starve their own people and people of other countries?

I would have forgiven of them, because they had been so severely dealt with by the Germans and by fate. It would have been practically impossible and a dear waste of energies to distinguish the shades of patriotism and desertion. But then, I was not of the mind of Stalin; I was not of the OGPU. I was not even of the mentality of those who had managed to stay on the right side of the Front in spite of everything. For these were vengeful, too. And my own people had suffered infinitely less.

Two million DP's were returned to the Soviet Union in the end, and a great many of these died in the camps of the Soviet Union, were sent to Siberian settlements, and some were denounced and killed outright, probably a few even by the young tough communist organizers with whom I treated. And perhaps those whom they fingered were really traitors who deserved no better.

One thing the soldiers agreed upon: the sadness of parting with Lena of Odessa. I got her address, "should I ever get to Odessa." Pfc. George Glade, to whom she had become a mother, was in tears. Lena was in tears. They loaded her down with gifts. They brought her in the command car down to the camp when the trucks were loading. This was what the Allied leaders had promised. Carried out to the last wave of hands as the truck drove off.

Col. Quinn of G-2 gave a party at a villa he'd taken over. He was leaving for the States and the Pacific Theater. Hardly anyone was left whom I knew; my friends were being fed into other jobs. I commited excesses from malaise. The morning after, I had a hangover, as I explain to "Dear Love":

> *With two aspirins, much fruit juice and lots of coffee, I should be able to stave off the jitters long enough to think this letter through. For once, I think I can say that summer is here to stay. For two days, it hasn't rained and the sky has been cloudless. I drove back home from Col. Quinn's party last night about two AM and all the stars were out, the road was clear and the air was cool and sweet. It was a good party, attended mostly by intelligence officers, the latest and best in the series of social events high officers give to celebrate the victory and the associations the war made. There were more American women than I've seen in a long time there, several ARC girls, one or two DP's, and four girls from a USO show that's playing in Augsburg. They all worked very hard at dancing and being amusing. A band from an engineer outfit played and an EM did magical tricks which were astounding. I sat in for several numbers with the band and enjoyed that more than anything else, although the drums were too loud and I couldn't hear the piano chords or get in any subtleties in consequence. There was lots of cognac and some vodka and vermouth to drink. I tried a vodka martini and it wasn't very good. Col. Quinn at the beginning had declared that there would be no high diving into*

the fish pond before midnight but even afterwards I couldn't find anyone to jump in. I was willing but I needed someone with your intrepid character and where can one find that save where you are, standing alone in a world of fuddy-duddys. I didn't miss you only then. I did also whenever a silly girl said something in character. All of them seemed nice enough but so uneducated. One would think I would have lost my discrimination by this time, but it's sharpened, if anything -- starvation not only makes a man create ideal images of food, but when he finally sees the food again he gives it a much more realistic appraisal, sees all the details he didn't see in the period of gluttony. And when finally I turned to, back here, I felt that I needed your arms to rest my face against. I could have gone to sleep beautifully, kissing them. Instead, I read a few pages of C. S. Forester's Beat to Quarters.

Simone disappeared, and reappeared in a couple of weeks, Lieutenant Thomas, in a chic French Army uniform. Soon enough, her uniform became rumpled. She was not the dressy type. She brought me a copy of *Madame Bovary* but the French was too difficult to hold my interest. Besides, I had read it in English translation. We went on a deer hunt. We fanned out. A nice but jealous French lieutenant was next to me; he was just the type who would be good for Simone, upper class, well-educated, sensitive, he even looked like her brother, husky, blonde, and smiling; still, I kept well to the right and two paces behind the man: accidents can happen. No deer.

Right near Schloss de Grazia were deer, they practically eat out of your hand. On a solitary walk one day I decided to hunt them with just my .45 automatic, and after several futile shots concluded that the famous Colt 45 cal. Automatic was as inaccurate a weapon as was ever strapped to a man's body and impressively pulled and fired. It's a weapon that lives in myth. War was governed largely by myth, costly blunders, and unreliable history, or am I repeating myself?

At the beginning of 1945 I prepared a calculation of the cost effectiveness of my outfit. The results were highly favorable. I showed it to Roos and a couple of other men and thought of giving it to G-2, our boss, but held off. If I could recalculate now, I would have a complete account up to the end of the War. I might even calculate it for myself alone; I did toy with the theory behind the system of points that was used in some part to select men for redeployment to the States, a system which was devised by my acquaintance, Sam Stouffer, Professor of the University of Chicago and his Army research staff. Most soldiers thought it fair. I certainly did for various reasons, not the least being that I had more points signaling me homewards than anybody in the company.

I could commence by listing what I cost the Army overseas, assuming I would have been overseas for twenty-nine months before reaching a home port again. Then I should add an estimate (almost impossible) of what my operations cost the Army. Then I could discover the total of what it had cost the Allies to win the war in Africa and Europe, adding into this the total value of all that was shipped to the Allies from outside their theater of operations. Adding to it also the destruction and casualties visited upon the Allies by the enemy. This huge total would then be divided by the total personnel of the Armies in order to find out how much per soldier the war there cost.

Afterwards, an ideal but impossible computation would give an estimate of the damage done to the enemy in human flesh and property. Since we "won" the war, subtracting all our costs from the enemy costs results in some exceedingly rough positive sum which I shall not mention else I would have to defend it. The same goes for me personally. I can figure my costs to a fairly accurate degree and also that of the total Allied armies (but the calculation would break down at the need to put charges against wounds, deaths, homesickness, etc.)

Thereupon we should ask ourselves what was the profit or value of my activity and of the whole armed forces. I could set forth the value of my services and compare it with the average of the Army in the Mediterranean and European Theaters. If I could divide the total value by the number of men and women it had taken to achieve it, I would have some probably silly figure to represent the gain of warfare per involved person. But I do not dare to go so far without a generous study grant

All I can say is this. I can give a figure for all that the army experience of 29 months cost me and the army, and all the internal value to the army of my services, which is actually a cost to the army, and then concoct some partly-believable figure for all the damage that I inflicted on the enemy. Now if I take my personal costs and the internal value that I gave to the army, I obtain a total that can be compared with the value of the damage that I inflicted on the enemy, with my leaflets, loudspeakers, interrogations, information of value to our side, and casualties; then I will have a madcap figure representing my net contribution to the war effort. If something similar were done for the other millions of American and Allied soldiers, my contribution could be compared with the average and we would be able to judge how praiseworthy were my efforts. But, please note, that in order to get my personal and my army's winnings, we would have to know the extent and value of the damages to the enemy.

Here is what I could figure in my own case

Cost Item	Cost (est.)
Wages & allowances	9,000
Food	2,000
Clothing (including 2 helmets)	200
Mail	80
Medical and dental care	100
Gasoline consumed for pleasure	20
Total	$ 11,400

Operating costs	
Ammunition (20,000 shells)	100,000
Maintenance	20,000
Crews of cannon and command system -part-time	8,000
Personal crew rendering official services: jeep driving, etc.	7,000
Loud-speaker ops, crew, radio, vehicles, ammo conversion	15,000

Printing	100,000
Overhead of War (roughly equals my unit overhead and personal costs)	20,000
TOTAL OF ALL COSTS	$ 281,400

One may proceed now to the *"benefits"* side of the cost-benefit ratio. My functions, to review them, are listed, with an estimate of my performance:

1. To discover useful facts for others to use in winning the war politically, psychologically and militarily. Worth $55,000 on basis of what is paid consultants and professors.
2. To take custody of and operate media in freed territory. Worth $150,000 in fees customarily charged for such operations.
3. To order the minds of liberated and occupied populations. Worth $35,000 as social welfare work.
4. To increase enemy desertions and surrendering. My outfits may have caused to desert or surrender "beforetimes" 1000 men. This is worth an unbelievable figure so I won't venture it. To give a hint, we could figure the value by multiplying the figure of 1000 men by the total cost of the Western European and Mediterranean operations divided by the number of the enemy who were killed, disabled or captured by the First of May.
5. Lessened resistance by average of 1% of 200,000 troops of enemy would have a large value to add as well. The total is quite unbelievable.
6. To help my own friendly units understand and do their job better. Instructed many units on how to deal with enemy psychologically and increase captures or kills, and how to deal with enemy and friendly populations. Professorial fees: $25,000.
7. Indirectly and involuntarily I may have set up some 50 enemy to be killed by using propaganda as a ruse or giving friendly troops occasion to shoot enemy trying to give up, despite my instructions to the contrary. This would be a large individual contribution to winning the war, as such awful perspectives would indicate. I led the capture of several enemy. My shooting probably killed noone.

I don't dare say.

8. In doing the above, to take care of the men, to take care of myself, to care for the equipment in my charge, to maintain liaison all around, to command troops. Attending to managerial functions: $60,000.

    Total cost-benefits balancing requires the quantifying of the qualitative, something done perforce, yet intuitively and badly most often. Morality needs strictly to be avoided.

I would not defend my figures here but do feel that this form of calculation should be perfected and applied. I would be the first to challenge in this case my share of the benefits, even after subtracting what I cost, with all my "business expenses" of some $280,800. For the necessarily absurd computation ends up with a "positive benefit" of unspeakable size. Not a poky contribution to the War Effort, Megabucks! Adjusted to today's dollar-value, that would rise to ten times as much.

One could not win the War with me and my kind doing more of the same jobs. Still, up to ten units, such as the Seventh Army Team, might well have been fielded in the Seventh Army alone, but then no more. The Seventh Army single team could actually have done better work.

    One might hazard a dollar value for these benefits:
APPROXIMATE TOTAL VALUE OF BENEFITS PROVIDED = $1.4 BILLIONS.

This figure may be reduced 95%, by postulating that I was operating in all my tasks with nineteen other hypothetical unit-persons of considerable ability and achievements, and that each such unit, just like me, warranted an equivalent costs-benefit assignment. (Actually we have already charged off these costs and contributions, but still, one must be scrupulous in these matters. There will be those who would calculate costs-benefits solely and materially, in pairs of shoes and times worn, and shells and number fired, in ratio to presumed damage done, etc., whereas total cost-benefits balancing requires the quantification of much that is qualitative, as attempted here, something done perforce, yet intuitively and badly most often.) In this case, my share of the benefits, because I must still pay up my costs, is greatly lowered, so that the total net value of my 2,5 years of warring came to $71,076,250.00. Not a poky contribution to the War Effort, Seventy-one Big Megabucks! Adjusted to today's dollar-value, that would rise to 700 Megabucks! I am sure that my accounting principles are faulty, at the very least, ridiculous probably, misinformed and undemonstrable.

They certainly miss a major truth: that war is not about killing or disarming enemy soldiers, but about reaping benefits for one's country, such as conquest of resources, increasing our own national security, opening up markets to our products, imposing behavior onto the conquered enemy according to the principles of our own advantages and not to his, installing durably our own power and control over his territory, increasing our ability to act in other parts of the world, enlisting his resources to fight our own wars and his politicians to implement our own politics, etc.

In this regard, America's victory in World War II might well have been the greatest in any war ever fought. More than six decades later, the USA still occupies dozens of military bases in Germany and Italy, over a hundred in the European Union. American commercial and financial interests reign supreme everywhere. McDonald's and Coca Cola signs are ubiquitous; so are American cultural products. Germans, French and Italians fight in America's wars in Afghanistan, Italians fight in Iraq. As do Dutch, Belgians, Norwegians, Greeks and others. If we consider *these* benefits, the ridiculous amount stated above turns out to be ridiculously low - in fact, one cannot even begin to give an estimation.

Moreover, this victory was actually achieved at a relatively low human cost, as the Soviets suffered most of the losses and effected most of the killing, which makes the cost/benefit ratio even more staggeringly positive for the United States. The benefits of almost seven decades of American supremacy are simply beyond estimation. Yet, every American soldier, dead or alive, carries his share.

One could not win the War with me and my kind doing more of the same jobs, although I will say that up to ten larger units, such as the Seventh Army Team, might well have been fielded in the

Seventh Army alone, one per division with a central team, but no more. My Seventh Army single team could also have done better work with less personnel.

Warfare is much discussed but little understood. I permit myself another case. Many more soldiers are needed who have a different kind of job assignment than the propaganda warrior, but a very special job; strangely, the number of these has been improperly estimated or not at all, for they are regarded as rare exceptions, to be given medals instead of being regarded as a self-selecting elite type who literally fight and win the crucial enemy engagements that form a vital part of a War. Or they are crowded into a "crack unit," called "Marines" or "parachute brigades" or "Special Forces," or "airborne divisions."

I refer to killer-soldiers or super-soldiers, Rambo, the one in thirty or forty in an infantry or tank regiment who has the opportunity, the will and the ability to close with the enemy and despatch one or more. Usually these men become casualties themselves before long, but meanwhile they seal breaks in their lines, open breaks in the enemy lines, kill their opposite numbers like Achilles does Hector and many other Trojans, create despair and fear in enemy hearts, and encourage and enable their own troops to win in the name of all.

Reducing their performance to pecuniary value gives net benefit figures on the order of $8,000,000 per super-soldier or Rambo. The location, training, and deployment among the mass army-in-action of such men should be the grand focus of theory and application in all other aspects of warfare. The bringing-out and effective employment of such men should be the greatest test of the value of an officer, not only the immediate officer of the man, but all officers, logistical, artillery, aviation, naval, and the rest.

Alongside these Rambos should be stressed the unlucky tenth in the infantry battalions who notably endure the insensate grinding boredom of training and waiting, but have also to undergo their few hours of heavy risk and terror, of danger and death, of disablement, of rotten memories that are like wounds without Purple Hearts. And all the while firing their pieces. And alongside these are to be counted the air crews, the submarine crews, and the men in the bowels of ships, who have the most similar experiences, of seemingly eternal waits and brief episodes of fight and fright.

However, back to the "crack units," these are questionable as independent forces, and should be infiltrated to each division or task force or kept in readiness for such assignment. They should not be used as the U.S.Marines were employed, as divisions in their own right. The Germans misemployed the early SS combat divisions in the same way. A crack division that loses half of its effectives is still highly effective; a regular division that incurs a 50% loss of fire-personnel becomes largely ineffective, because its Rambos now become only 3% (instead of 8% of the total assigned the job of inflicting casualties by small-arms).

An overall solution would be to place more Rambos in the regular divisions, with a special rating as, say, "Arms Specialist," and educate command and staff to ask for or respond to reinforcement or procurement needs, not simply with hardware or indiscriminate warm body requisitions, but with requests for specific numbers - 2, 5, 8, 20, etc. - in measure with the difficulty of the task facing the unit.

In some cases, the specialized "snipers" became such distinctive warriors.

Hardly an Allied commander appeared to appreciate this basic human conditioning of the battle, World War II style. The Soviets seemed to recognize the wisdom of restraining the formation of large elite formations in favor of a more even distribution of aggressive soldiery throughout its multitudinous divisions. I thought of the basic flaw in the understanding of the elements of direct combat operations first on a visit to Quantico to see Bill Evers and heard of the training afforded the Marines there, and next upon hearing of the heavy German paratrooper casualties in Crete, and of course in Sicily. (I believe that a certain envy of the "gung-ho" of the Marines also made me think: "Why not us, too?" meaning the Army.)

Now let us perform a mental gymnastic that I could not have boasted about fifty years ago. It would have brought down ridicule upon me. After all, was not the "bottom line" of warfare the killing of the enemy? I mean that I could have reversed the idea of "benefits," or, rather, doubled roughly the net profit of my operations. That is, I could count benefits from the "German" side, or from the "pacifist" position: then I would be granted the value of the hundreds of German life-equivalencies and thousands of hours of enemy suffering that I saved. No question about it, a considerable number of Germans ended World War II alive because I extricated them from it, not to mention the suffering I saved all the others who gave up a little earlier than would have been the case without me. Considering that many of these young Germans became fathers, I might as well claim to be the Godfather of quite a number of elderly and third generation Germans living today. Another 60 Megabucks should be toted on my account. I should at least be pensioned by the German government! And, please to recall the messages I was sending: unlike the enemy's messages, mine were words I - and you - could live with for the rest of my life. Nothing to be ashamed about.

What I've been saying is an accrual of fifty years of casual amateur cogitation. The Age of Computerized Missiles has brought such a qualitative revolution, that there have become four kinds of war: the old conventional warfare of World War II, between armies whose ground battles determine victory at war, which may not occur again for a while; nuclear missile war, which would introduce, if at all, an anarchic chaotic struggle among any survivors; the punitive expedition of the Panamanian, Grenadian or Iraqi kind; and the political war, as in Vietnam and Afghanistan, with one or both armed forces working under constraints, and without sharp distinctions of friend-foe, or front-rear. No-War would be the best war, of course, but let us leave it at that.

But shouldn't I be permitted to exclaim that large-scale organized violence - warfare, that is, is so crazy, that every effort ought always to be made to keep peoples from becoming diseased with hostility; we should strip down to our bare essentials of material goods and ethical principles in order to expend the economic and cultural resources needed to resolve conflicts between peoples.

Now to finish with World War II. July arrives at Schloss Strassberg and I received the expected formal orders to merge my troop with higher headquarters. The Information Control Command was located a few miles south of Bad Homburg and not far from Wiesbaden, at Schloss Hohenbuchau, a spa reported to be a marvel of luxury. I had not been there, but had maps and knew that its signs would be picked up as my column approached.

With a certain sadness - although every move was advertised as leading to home - we readied ourselves for the trek. This was our last day as a free outfit and the last move together. The courtyard echoed to a great roar as all the vehicles started up their motors. Inside, the rooms were impersonally bare, the kitchen ammoniacally clean. The American flag had been lowered and packed away. All windows and doors were closed. Schloss Strassberg belonged now to nobody and anybody; the gnomish villagers were probably crouched to spring upon it. My command car this once was last to leave. I overtook the front of the column as it began to make its sharp right turn. I twisted my head and watched as the noses of the vehicles appeared one by one, until finally the full convoy stretched out on the long descent to the plain below.

> *Eingabe*
>
> An den Herrn Kommandanten
>
> Sir!
>   Ich bitte inständigst
> um Strümpfe, Unterwäsche,
> Hemd, Taschentuch, Hose und
> Jacke. Ich bin aus dem Bett
> verhaftet worden, bin nicht
> geflohen u. bin fast nackt hier
> hergekommen.
>   Hochachtungsvoll
>   Dr. R. Ley.

Robert Ley's note to me following his arrest. A rabid Jew-hater, he was the head of the political section of the Nazi Party (NSDAP), as well as of the sole workers' union, the DAF. He committed suicide before standing trial in Nürnberg by strangulating himself with his underwear.
(Translation to be found in the text of the chapter above.)

Arrest of Goering by the Seventh Army Interrogation Team
(Wallenberg is 2nd from the right, above)

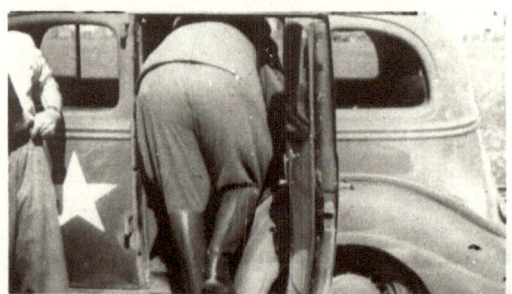

The author at Dachau

Chapter Eighteen

AT THE VICTORS' TABLE

Arriving midday, we drove all dusty and noisy into the compound of the Information Command. A few yards to the left is a magnificent lodge. A glance told me that the officers have crowded around the windows from their lunch table to watch our old team dismount. "Damn," I think, "we're not ready to go on show! They'll get a bad first impression, these fucking voyeurs!" I beckoned to First Sgt. Taubert, who never moved fast but like a dreadnought, and said in urgent tones: "Sergeant, let's get them out of the vehicles, all of them, and lined up, for instructions and dismissal, full attention." "Let's go, men, snap shit," snarls Taubert, *sotto voce,* surprising the nonchalant soldiers. They hastened into a fairly neat row, straightened up and rendered fair semblance of well-drilled soldiers at attention. I pretended to take a report from the Sergeant, order "Dismiss the Company," and Taubert, who managed an about-face without stumbling, dismissed them properly.

That was fine for them, they just hung around now; but their Captain had to find out what to do with them and that meant, since no one was coming out to help me, finding the entrance to the dining room, walking stiffly up to the head of the table, having spotted there a Colonel whom I presumed to be the Commander, throwing a freshly cut salute at him and reporting the company's arrival in proper army style, third person and all. It was appreciated. The quite unmilitary and inexperienced group at the table felt good about having this weatherbeaten crowd bring in a breath of the real War that had eluded them, the War that was already becoming a memory even before they could take part in it.

The High Life began in the castle above Georgenborn. Full dress at all times except during outdoor recreation. Shiny vehicles. A private room and bath. A string-quartet playing the quintessential repertoire at cocktails and dinner. Meals served by white-jacketed German waiters. A menu as it once had been, with venison, wild boar, Black Forest tort, strong coffee, fine wines, cordials. Bad Homburg, a sumptuous spa, was nearby. My snobbish British friends should have been here to appreciate it; Robbie by now had repossessed his tuna fishery on Elba; he would have called all of this, like the "Corny Beef" *Hotel Corneille* in Algiers, "Bad Hamburger" or "Bah, Humbug!"

Lt. Simone Thomas came up to visit from Seventh Army Headquarters and charmed the officers, especially the quaint South Carolinian, Lt. Col. Hardin, who was typical of some of my closer acquaintances, not highly educated or intellectual, good-humored, interested in and not hostile to the world about, with a quaint, ethnic stamp about himself. Col. Hardin had a Lt. Horsey as sidekick, a little large-spectacled guy - both of them were ugly - who, when in the cups, would delight me by chanting a poem from the nethermost recesses of the unreconstructed Confederacy, beginning "Ah hates the Constitution..." (Col. Hardin smiled apologetically over his unconscious ventriloquist's puppet.)

Col. J.B. Stanley was in charge, a sweet character. He had a bosom companion, a stage beauty named Maggie Hammerstein. The only other pretty woman around was an Icelander, faithful to a husband who had disappeared into the British navy somewhere, and with whom I became friend and demi-lover as the days and cocktail hours passed. I had a lot of time to read, for I was still carried as Commanding Officer of the Seventh Army Team, largely inoperative. I had stated firmly to all and sundry that I would escape to the Big PX upon my first opportunity.

I dropped in upon the men of my company from time to time. The distance between us was growing within the larger framework of the Information Command. We were well fixed and awaiting the call to go home. Jill had written with some concern as to whether I had achieved the 85 points - five for this and five for that campaign, and for a medal, and a landing, and a wife and a child and a wound and a couple of other merits and hardships, like being over a long time - that were supposed magically to transport a soldier home; I had 122 points and could have claimed even more; there were only a few thousands like me in the European Theater; practically all of my men had the 85 points. I was beginning to send the worst cases home, holding my own worst case back a bit. The several who wished to stay had already been well assigned.

The G.I. Bill was hardly exciting to the men, nor even to me, strange to say, who had approached within hailing distance of a doctor's degree. It came rather late, and was not fully appreciated: its offer of a college education with full tuition and allowances for living and books, a perfectly generous act of the Congress that did more than anything else to smoothen out, lengthen, and make profitable the otherwise dismal period of refitting socially the veteran. But the men long overseas felt themselves beyond the exciting promises of veteranship. Finding a job and a girl and knocking around: these seemed all of the good life that most men would admit to. They were already mooning about the good old days at Schloss de Grazia.

When Simone Thomas paid them a visit all cheery with a thoroughbred dachshund in tow, they gave her big brotherly smiles; and when I was left with the dachshund, and the massively muscled, low-slung beast tripped me and dashed off into the woods, they did not laugh and jest but joined in seriously combing the woods in search of the animal. It was, alas! not to be found. I told Simone that I would send her a real American dog after I got back home. I did not; but we did meet again.

On August 6, as the Plane carrying the Atom Bomb to Japan is being armed, I write Jill of such other matters,

> *Darling,*
>
> *I got up bright and early this morning to get rid of a pile of work that had piled up over the week-end in order to get started on a letter to you. I can now report with pride that the task has been accomplished in one hour and I can enter the second phase. You ought to see me apply myself to work. I can't stand it and therefore get rid of it as soon as possible in what is sometimes an almost revulsive frenzy.*

I would be more concerned over my attitude if it weren't so constructive in its effects. When it's over and I'm left with so much free time, I wonder why I was so energetic about it.

I must go over to Frankfurt sometime today to see if they've received a quota for home yet. It's quite a job to keep one's burning interest in the issue concealed. I know that if a clerk should turn his back while cutting the orders I've cut my own name into them before you could wink an eyelash.

I heard a concert Thursday night by the newly revived Wiesbaden Symphony Orchestra that I don't think I mentioned to you yet. It was a programme of Brahms, Mendelssohn, and Tchaikovsky mostly, standard stuff and played without much inspiration. The hall was too small for the sixty-piece orchestra and the acoustics were very bad but the audience of some five hundred Germans ate it up. There were a few Americans in uniform present. I thought that this being the first concert since the occupation the Germans couldn't help but be impressed by the new color of the uniforms and the absence of all their old traditional insignia, songs, flags, etc. but I don't think they are very imaginative except on the subject of Cossack cavalry, and flying fortresses.

After the concert I was standing outside the building, preparatory to driving off, and talking with Curtis, the Red Cross representative in this zone, and noticed out of the corner of my eye a tall officer who had come up to us. I thought it was our Lt. Keller and paid no attention to him until I finished with Curtis. Then I was amazed to see Tom Stauffer there. (He might well be: he last saw Tom as a KP, busy among a lot of pots, upon his first day in the Army, at Camp Grant.) We exchanged greetings. Naturally Tom would seek out a cultural event if it were in Darkest Africa. He said he was going to work with the Group Control Council in Berlin and seemed for some reason to be embarrassed by the fact. He's a first Lt. and I don't believe he's been over for long. As weird as ever, though. I wonder what havoc he'll wreak in Berlin. Wally's [Wallenberg's] *newspaper goes off the presses in a day or so there incidentally. It's the most important press job in Germany now certainly; it will be in direct competition with the Russian papers on the newsstands.*

Saturday night Simone Thomas drove up with Col.

Landstrom who is our representative at Seventh Army Headquarters for dinner and the Sat. Night concert we have here. She is a fine party girl, buzzes all over the place, is very lively and always smiling, she is uninhibited and without illusions of any sort which does credit to her family. Her attitudes in politics are in correspondence. She is not sensitive or jealous towards Americans as so many French are, especially from the middle classes. We had a lot of champagne and things for dinner and afterward while the musicians rested, Bass on the piano and I on the violin accompanied bad singers in drinking songs. Then I played "Love in Bloom" by popular request just as well as Jack Benny.

Sunday morning I went with Kvam who controls theaters to Wiesbaden to look in on a revue which was cheap and bad, a violin player that made me feel cocky even.

Last evening was very quiet. I read Bret Harte's Story of a Mine *and took a long walk with Col. Hardin and Lt. Horsey.*

On August 7, I write briefly that we have heard of a great bomb, and, seemingly indifferent, talk of other matters. But, next day, I write at length about the Bomb:

Jill Darling,

As our very clever little Morning Bulletin *put it this morning, today is AB + 3. So far most of the news programs have given us superlatives in fact and expression more than anything else about the bomb. It is very difficult to conceive but everyone is awed and although hopeful of its bringing to an early end the Japanese war a little dismayed by the future prospects of life on this earth. It certainly should make any future war impossible. Perhaps it can accomplish what peace conferences cannot accomplish, and once more, remind man that he is incapable of willing and planning any of the big things of his life, but must wait for a catastrophe to direct him. I understand that the* New York Times *was ready with forty pages on the bomb, not only a good piece of journalism but giving the devil his due. The consequences are being analyzed by people with more time and research materials than I and I suppose I will get to read about some of them in due time. Meanwhile this morning it occurred to me that just as the British*

Labor Party gets into power to take over the coal industries, the coal industries may be soon replaced by this new source of power. Another first consequence of the application of the new power will be the hastening of socialism, because the power is so enormous and important as to tie people together almost inextricably.

A local by-product of the news was that Lt. Rosette of the 6871 was more depressed than ever last night. He is a medievalist of the Hutchins, T. S. Eliot ilk, convinced of the malignity of material progress and of the greater happiness of other peoples in other times. He says he can't find life in America compatible with his way of living and plans to live in London, Paris or somewhere on the continent after the war. He was with Newsweek *before going into the army and was with OSS just before going into Inf Control. I can't find much sympathy for him. It is such an absurd escapism and of course it is completely selfish. I would feel for him more if he didn't think he was basing it on a true philosophy.*

The soldiers talked a lot about the Bomb. They were awed, perhaps all the more because they saw all about them the effects of thousands of bombs and high explosive projectiles. At the same time, they were not inclined to see in it anything especially immoral, because they measured its murderousness against the otherwise loss of a million American lives estimated to be necessary to take Japan. Since they believed that this anyhow was the last war that they would see, they were not preoccupied with the handling of the Bomb in the future or whether more of them should be made. They assumed there would be a halt to their manufacture; there would be no more bombs made after the annihilation of Nagasaki. After all, against whom would the nuclear bomb be employed? No aggressive power remained to threaten a peaceful world. The idea of a Cold War hardly occurred to anyone.

I walked about the castle gardens, pondering a formula for Europe. No one spoke of the United Nations as the organization that was to settle a New Europe into a New One World. This was the way I would have liked it and I perked up when I read that the United Nations might even set up its headquarters in San Francisco, where it started up life, for I would have seen combined there two dear wishes, to live in San Francisco and to work for world federalism.

I had given up the idea of becoming a Professor. I thought of going into publishing on the West Coast or in Chicago, rather than New York where, though I did not know it, "everybody who was anybody" in the industry worked. I thought that the center of world politics would now shift to the United Nations and to Washington, and to the free media of communications, in publishing, in the press, where I pictured myself, rather prematurely, as qualified.

The Colonel asked me in an informal way if I would like to join him and his party at Berlin, to join the Allied Control Mission there, having been promoted to Major to begin with. It would have been a ball. I was gratified. I could be integral to whatever the Allies would be doing with the prostrate monster Reich. I could justify staying or returning so far as my little household was concerned: Jill and Baby Kathy could be brought over soon enough. At this point especially, but, in general, too, as ought to be quite clear by now, I did like Army life and felt more at home in the Army than anywhere else in the world except - and this was in my imagination - the University of Chicago neighborhood - an increasingly vague dreamland.

Still, it would have committed me to more years in the Army, perhaps forever, even though just now it was the kind of Army that every gold brick dreamt about. There might not be anything afterwards, and soon my role would shrink, and become less and less political, indeed therefore dangerous, for I was a political animal. I would be voicing opinions in ever higher councils and, while flexible on most matters, would be obdurate in giving credit to the Soviets for the major role they had played in breaking the back of the Third Reich. (I counted every other American soldier as a saved casualty by virtue of the Soviet Army.)

This was soon to become an uncomfortable reminder for the Western Allies. More and more of the occupying force would not have felt poignantly the effects of the War in the East. The ever-increasing influence of the Germans would be felt against the Russians, even though the Germans would know the true history. The Germans then were still good mythographers; they could tell historical lies with a straight face or placidly permit others to do so. They were not yet so sincerely democratic as they would later become (most of them is meant, of course, not all).

Bitter talk against the Soviets was beginning. The savagery and rapine by the victorious Soviet troops in conquered territories was widely publicized, though mostly by eye-witnesses and word of mouth. My personal informant had been Larry Walker, who had driven straight through the lines into Prague and there encountered the Russian troops, and who had returned shocked with tales of rape, looting, and murder. I told him to make allowances - what allowances, how many? Well, Walker, whatever allowances you might grant yourself if you had your country torn apart by these arrogant murderous aggressors, had been forced to live like a pig, eat like a convict, submit to merciless discipline and fight fearfully for years and seen half your comrades killed, had your home blown apart and your family scattered into misery or captivity. With all this and the promise of extermination, it is a wonder that the Soviets were not even more harsh.

The word out of Berlin was not so good. The Western and Eastern Allies were infrequently talking to each other, hardly even at the top level. They were drawing lines, on the ground and in their minds. The Russians were too suspicious. Still, while berating the Russians, the men around me were not yet dealing in the unspeakable, the need to make numbers of A-Bombs in order to keep the Communists at bay.

I brooded about the fate of the good people, the democrats of Europe, and the death and destruction everywhere. I saw few signs of the great roundup of the confirmed Nazis who had survived. The SS, the murderers, the slave-drivers. Under certain circumstances - if the Allied Command were fierce down to the junior officer level, for instance - I would have taken up the hue and cry; I believed still in summary execution of the worst enemy types (I figured that there were a quarter of a million of them), and a scolding and exhortation for the general population; I wanted, too, to go after all of the non-German Nazis and collaborators around Europe: Russian, Latvian, Lithuanian, Finnish, Polish, Ukrainian, Byelorussians, Bessarabians, Cossacks, Tatars, Arabs, Hindustani, Baluchistani, Spanish,

Argentinans, French, Irish, Norwegian, Swedish, Dutch, Flemings, Croats, Hungarians, Montenegrins, Greeks, Slovaks, Bohemians, and, of course, Italians and Austrians.

Most of the experienced officers and men would go home as soon as possible. Men who had never felt an enemy presence nor the deprivations of campaign life were to be in charge of reconstructing Germany and assisting the victims of other countries. Would not they be too lenient, because the enemy had not hurt them? Some would. Would they be too harsh out of guilt? Some would. Would the conquered enemy respond better to rule by men who had not destroyed them? Yes. If the conquering troops were forced to stay as rulers, would they not be falsely persuaded that they knew "how to handle the Germans?" Many of them would be so deluded.

Actually only a tiny proportion of the conquering soldiery knew anything useful about Germany or civil affairs; for that matter only a small proportion of them had ever seen a German soldier under hostile circumstances, mostly a half-million surviving riflemen, not the artillery, not even the airmen, who had had occasion to kill enemy troops, and also had been ordered to kill enemy civilians en masse (whereas the ground forces had been forbidden to commit crimes against the same civilians).

The old officers and soldiers had dealt with themselves; no more than one-twentieth of the time during the most violent campaign was spent even by a front-line combat officer in dealing with the enemy; the rest went to his own troop and his auxiliary services and higher command. Hardly anyone saw the enemy face to face and a third of those who did didn't live to tell the tale. So what could they know about rebuilding and controlling the German nation?

Considering everything, it was better to get rid of the old soldiers and let in the new bunch to do the job. The new ones were much more reasonable and constructive. No one planned it that way: as I said, practically every old soldier, I myself included (I was 25 years old by then) would have been welcome to stay on for the occupation and given preference over the newcomers.

I would have liked, then and there - so I imagined as I walked the twilight gardens in July whipping - I remember it that well! - at limp stalks with my riding crop - to take part in a general round of proclamations, punishment, restitution, recovery, and utopian social reconstruction, binding upon all of Europe, not Germany alone.

Enough of this! It was time to turn my back on Europe. The orders arrived, directing me to go where I so had wanted to go for years, home to Chicago. When Jill learned about it, she could not help but write to me, even though I was supposed to be leaving the next day - a final spasm of her incredible epistolary musculature:

August 22, 1945

Darling -

I don't know if there's any sense in writing you - I got your letter this morning that you were leaving the 23rd & I don't know what to do, I am so dizzy. With difficulty I gave Kathy lunch but am unable to eat myself - much less sleep, read or do anything but (at first) cry with joy & call Mom & talk, rather babble, endlessly.

I don't know whether to write any more. I might better devote the time to cleaning the house & fixing my clothes.

Darling I don't know what else to say except that I'm the happiest woman alive.

OOOXXX
Jill

The last pay day

Chapter Nineteen

THE SLOW BOAT HOME

THE rage to return might have made smart travelers out of the men. Why organize a complex and universally disgusting system for conveying them home? The Army Command and Paymaster should simply have given the first hundred thousand men with the highest number of points an extra thousand dollars with their June pay and a permission, valid for three months, to go home if they wished - and then let them get home however they could manage; double the number for July; and so on, raising the number to a half-million per month in October. Everyone who deserved to go home and wanted to go home would have been home by Christmas.

Here is what could well have happened in most cases, and might have happened to the five men and me from the Seventh Army Combat Propaganda Team. One hour after being paid off, we would have departed in the command car with a driver who would return the car. Stopping only to eat from our enormous picnic basket, we would have driven to Calais in a single day. We would sleep comfortably on the ground because of the crowd (unless local boys had set up cots and tents at a price), found a boat driven by an Englishman to take us to Dover (the crush of boats coming and going would be greater and much more joyful than Dunkirk), crossed over to Ireland, drunk Guinness and found there a ship bound for the Caribbean islands; we would have landed in Cuba, played a few rounds of roulette while waiting for the regular launch to Miami, and, once landed in the U.S. of A., taken a bus, train, share-a-ride car or airplane for home. Elapsed time, fifteen days.

Misery of 15 days at a level of 2 on a ten-point Misery-Scale. Average fun level 7 on a ten-point Fun-Experience-Learning Scale. A hundred variants of this scenario would have brought the hundred thousand men home on the average in a month's time, a most interesting time, one should add, that they would forever remember favorably.

Within weeks, the free enterprise system would have brought in a dozen travel agencies and a host of carriers, especially if the Army and Navy had begun to release its contractors. The families of the troops would begin to buy their boys tickets, put pressure on the commercial carriers, and even call for their soldiers in cars and buses and planes at incoming places like Halifax and Montreal and New York and Hampton Roads. The Texas State Legislature would vote a free ticket to Any Soldier, Sailor or Marine from Texas. The Pacific situation would be much the same. (Incidentally, I note my failure to mention the Japanese Surrender; it was a foregone conclusion when it came and barely raised a drinking arm at the Hohenhaufen bar.)

Instead of this happy mad Victory send-off Party for millions of men, the Army found the worst solution. Recall the jeering paraphrase: "There's the right way and there's the Army way." Score on the Misery Scale = 9.5; score on the FEL Scale = 1.2.

The high-point men returned in bands of several soldiers that became larger groups at each stage of their journey. Though physically never more crowded, they were lonely in the sense that they usually left units to which they had been closely bound for a long time. Our six set out from Bad Homburg on August 22 in a weapons carrier. We had a morose party the night before in the Team's villa, and were given a send-off in the morning by Colonel Stanley, who had called out all of the officers and presented the travelers with a bottle of Cognac. Our orders read "Return by Air." We drove as far as Luxembourg the first evening, figuring upon a pleasant evening there among friends and a quick journey to our destination, the 14th Reinforcement Depot near Thionville, in the morning. Sgt. Joe Green, who had operated a loud-speaker truck for us down South, had become Manager of the *Hotel Continental*. We ate, drank and slept splendidly. Two officers, out for the night from the Depot, disquieted us by speaking of poor conditions and delays.

In the heavy rain the road to Thionville was as ugly as Europe could afford, showing dirty and lifeless villages, grim rows of factory buildings making one think uneasily of East Chicago. Dead fortifications obtruded: it was the Maginot Line, with its holes, pill-boxes, blind roads, dragon teeth, and wasteland. The Depot itself turned out to be a cluster of jaundiced and cracked pink stuccoed buildings.

The men were despatched to a so-called squadron in one direction. I waited until several other officers were collected. We were led to bungalows, and told to help ourselves to a room and bed. I found in one of them its last empty room, up a narrow staircase, and plunked myself on its only cot. Three officers came in together, a Lieutenant Colonel, a Major, and a Lieutenant, looked in, swore, went down and came back carrying cots. So there were four roommates and they might all curse together.

The sharpest irritation came with news that air flights from Thionville to America had been canceled and the usual stay here was now eight to ten days. Almost immediately the officers began talking of a subject that became increasingly emotional and tiresome with the passage of the days, of how well they had lived in Germany and how disgusted they were with France. It became more and more of a tirade, moving from the depreciation of privileges to absurdities. It became hard to say on whose side they had fought. Cast the accounts for this to a couple of million men and it is fair to say that there was almost no good will left among the American expeditionary forces in Europe toward France and the French. I found myself on one occasion in a stark mad eyeball-to-eyeball confrontation with an officer after I had finally reminded the man that "the French did not start this war; the Germans did."

In the dilapidated dining halls, the worst of Army rations were served, the oldest type of C-rations, a canned fruit compote and a weak bad coffee. The implements were banged up. The tables were cleared and coffee poured by slovenly French girls. Aside from the meals there was little to do. The enlisted men were restricted to camp; the officers could escape only if they had kept their vehicle.

We were alerted to a speech by the Camp Commandant the next morning and looked forward to it. It went like this, almost to the word:

> "I know things are tough here, but they're tough for us too. I wouldn't ask you to do anything that I wouldn't do. I wash out of a helmet just like everyone else. We're understaffed; we have a lot of limited-service people; our personnel is constantly being lost through re-deployment, and we have a much larger number of men than we ever expected to handle.
>
> However, I know that you can take anything for a few days. We expect to get you out of here just as soon as possible. But we have no control over that. You'll probably be here eight to ten days. We can't get labor to fix up your quarters. Don't think the men in this outfit don't realize your situation. A lot of them are old combat men themselves. We were supplying reinforcements to the infantry before we took over the job of redeploying troops home. I hope you enjoy your stay here, and if there is anything you have to complain about, you can see me at any time."

Unfortunately the next day he left for Paris, where he was inaccessible. Said a Lieutenant: "If that old bastard is dumb enough to wash himself in his helmet, that's no reason for making the rest of us do it." No one could figure out a good reason for the camp, since the men could have stayed with their units until called to a departure point on twenty-four hours' notice. The real reason was that the total operation was mismanaged, SNAFU (One is permitted to use the hoary phrase this once in 500 pages: *Situation Normal: All Fucked Up.*)

In the morning the enlisted men were formed into a long straggling column that wandered out of the *"Konzentrationslager"* and down the road a while. We rested and smoked. No one deserted;

this was the only route home. Then we walked back. Bad old movies were shown in a small crowded room full of smoke. Here and there card and crap games went on. The ugly indigestive boredom continued, spiced by rumors that we were to fly and not to fly. We were placed into "Project Green" to go by air; genuine orders were cut to this effect. Clothing that had been issued for boat was exchanged for clothing for passage by air, and baggage was stripped down to 35 pounds. This allowed almost nothing besides a man's souvenirs for the folks back home.

The Green Plan promised an air trip at the end of a train trip to Marseilles. The same day a message came through to fly us quickly to Marseilles, where planes had suddenly become available to fly us to America. But the planes were not to be had locally. Two more days at Thionville followed, and the whole lot of us were told to assemble to ride the train to Marseille and to fly from there. Off we trucked to the railhead, on the evening of September 3.

The long train was composed mainly of wooden-benched third-class carriages. They were full and the men took turns sleeping on the floor night and day. The toilets malfunctioned and the right of way served instead, during stops. Officers had a second-class carriage. All places were occupied and we slept in place. A Major who was permanent train commander lived in a comfortably furnished boxcar with his several men. He was a former regular Army sergeant, lean, hard-faced, impassive at unpleasantries. Once the train had chugged off, he sat down to poker with several officers and played out the trip, emerging comfortably ahead of the game. There were two old boxcars stocked with rations and holding kitchen ranges, with two mess crews in residence.

The 1800 men lined up at each meal stop, which took three hours. The train spent almost the full second night in the Lyons railyards, shifting about from time to time. At one point the train stopped where there was water to wash oneself. South of this, shortly, the train locked into a long tunnel where the troops almost suffocated and panic began to take hold; after forty minutes, the voyage resumed, with a panicky scrambling to jump aboard. Midway into the third night the train arrived fifteen miles from a camp at Calas and we detrained into trucks for the ride there. We were shown to showers and told we would have to wait several days for airplanes. Food, in case we were hungry after fifteen hours of fasting, would come in the morning. The camp turned out to be excellent; German prisoners did all the dirty work.

 I and my lot were given a time of departure by plane, but shortly beforehand were notified that our departure would be delayed for an emergency flight; a call had been sent out for railroaders, we discovered, men who had been over no matter how short a time provided they had once worked for a railroad. They were being sent back to rescue the railroad system from chaos at home. It would appear that all the civilians who had postponed their vacations were now moving about, and that all the businessmen who had been under restraints for the sake of all-out warfare, were now making up for lost time. Moreover, the railroaders had been assured that upon their return they would be given leave before getting up steam for the great railroad rescue. These were all paranoiac suppositions, of course.

 Now my consignment was alerted. Two days later it was driven down to the docks and loaded aboard ship. Some 2800 men passed into the recesses of the *Hawaiian Shipper,* a medium-sized, fast, diesel-powered cargo ship, constructed with a subsidy from the Maritime Commission, now converted into a troop carrier and operated by the Matson Steamship Company. It was a sweet deal for the Company, also a tolerable well-paid arrangement for the civilian Merchant Marine crew, a nonsensical assignment for forty Naval personnel, and a misery for the passenger troops.

 The civilian crew hogged far too much of the ship, with perhaps ten times the space of a soldier; their attitude stank; several were selling T-shirts at twice their cost in the ship's store (and were forced to return the money and had their wages docked). The crew and Navy lived in a super-structure that covered over what had been deck space. They had their own deck above, that they hardly used. The Navy merely loafed; they said their camp for armed guards back home was crowded and they had to live on the sea, like the Flying Dutchman. No one had thought to give them indefinite home leave.

 The troops were ordered into four holds, forward port and starboard, aft port and starboard. In the holds hammocks stood and swayed in stacks of four, that marched to far dark corners. There were too few by two hundred but, more than that, many men refused to climb into one under any conditions, and many more men were seasick most of the time and gasping for breath on deck. Barracks bags swung dizzying off the hook of each man's hammock. Here and there a dim bulb shined. They could not unpack, they could not sit. Very little ventilation entered, this from the open bulkheads. All were ordered to wear unspeakably filthy life jackets at all times (they did not, could not). The few passageways below decks, up and down and above decks, were filled at all hours with restless exhausted men. A good part of their time was taken up with waiting in line for a toilet or waiting in line for food. Only salt water was available except for an occasional cup of fresh water.

Crap games went on throughout the voyage: lucky the ones who could manage to observe it from above or alongside! The main crap game, aft of the superstructures, was unending. Players hated to give up their place. The stakes were as high as soldiers could afford. Many dropped out broke. By the time the voyage ended, one man had won fifteen thousand dollars in small bills and change, and paid two sidekicks to help him carry it all ashore safely.

A system of book distribution had been worked out. A branching of assistants was arranged so that a man could get his vague expression of interest handed up two levels to the Ship's Library and might get a book on the downturn that would interest him. The Library was open one hour a day to the representatives. A Special Service Officer, a Lieutenant, labored heroically to sponsor a Ship's Newspaper, organize a Ship's Band, manage the Library, and distribute games. Volunteers assisted him in typing, cutting, pasting, mimeographing the daily afternoon bulletin, sitting pasty-faced from the rocking ship and insufferable air of the Lieutenant's tiny cabin.

The same Officer found other officers to organize and put on a daily music recital and variety show. Battered instruments were brought out and instrumentalists persuaded that they might make music on them; they did not, but played anyway: what can you do with a tenor sax missing three keys? An accordionist, Corporal Bizek from Cleveland, appeared from the dark of a hold and performed an extensive repertoire of Slovak polkas and mazurkas. A Corporal

Schmidt from Nebraska became Master of Ceremonies by virtue of a corn-fed country humor; he saved the show occasionally, when the performers or their instruments collapsed. On Sunday, he could hardly preside, because his religion forbade him to swear on the Sabbath. Motion pictures were shown, too; the screen was set according to the wind, where, if they could resist choking to death from the oily smoke of the funnel, some men might view them. The passenger-officers had in their cabins a little more room than the men below decks, and had a small mess hall that was cleared an hour each evening so that they might write or play cards.

The Chaplain, preacher to three thousand men, tried nobly. The men no longer feared death and mutilation in combat and were disgusted with the Army, especially now, with gripes that God would certainly find too petty for intercession. The Chaplain found a volunteer to play the portable organ he had brought up on deck and each morning at ten-thirty would preach a sermon. Then he would lift his voice atonally in song, and beat the air in hopes of arousing some of the soldiers to sacred song. He looked into the faces of perhaps a dozen men at some degree of attention. The rest of the crowd had their eyes shut in exhaustion or their backs turned, while as many as could were watching the crap game. On Sunday, for his sake, gambling was forbidden; nevertheless the huge game, mentioned earlier, kept on going flagrantly, throughout Sunday, and even through the religious services and all.

At four-thirty in the morning, biting roughly into one's bunk, blared the ship's loudspeaker with the call, "All mess tickets Number One form in the mess line." Each hour the call would be repeated until nine shifts had gone through the line. The food was sufficient and good at breakfast and dinner, but there was no reward for those who sweated out the lunch line except an orange and a baloney sandwich. Three days out to sea, cans of fruit, cookies and cigarettes were sold, in a one-time sale. For their part, the officers ate in four shifts, beginning at six-thirty in the morning.

On September 29, the thirty-ninth day after leaving the Table of the Victors at Bad Homburg, feeding began at two A.M. The ship was approaching Hampton Roads and heading toward Newport News, Virginia. Orders were out to change from fatigues into woolen uniforms, whatever the heat outdoors, and to shave. It was a time to reflect upon the miseries of war, or at least a time for us to reflect, since I was but a numb scarecrow from the effects of the tedious voyage.

I would soon have been gone for 850 days from the United States. That is 20,400 hours. How much of this experience had been *pleasant,* how much *agreeable,* how much *tolerable,* how much *unpleasant,* and how much *distressing?* Please look again and see that I have a five-point scale here, ranging from best to worst. If I could get into my far-stored memories deeply, and could fit them to these five words, then add them up and figure what percentage they made up of the 20,400 hours, I might well comprehend my own taste of war.

The biggest problem in becoming a statistician of one's feelings over time is that no experience - mine, yours - is likely to be encompassed under one emotion, and, worse than that, under one category of behavior.

For instance, I am riding in a jeep from my bivouac to a hospital near Naples, and enjoy the beautiful, terrible eruption of Mt. Vesuvius (do you recall it?). My primary feeling is distress, but I am also feeling exaltation, a pleasant feeling. Or, to exemplify the second problem, I am talking sociably to others at dinner under the volcano of Mt. Etna; there are two tolerable if not agreeable activities going on here; yet should the activity and time spent upon it be accredited to eating or to sociability? This and other problems could be solved in a volume or two of applied sociological analysis; here, I may have gone too far already, and therefore I shall not construct the multiple ratings and the many graphs needed to cut in microscopically: *Sufficient unto the day is the evil (and good) thereof.*

We end up therefore with a table of my principal activities overseas, the time in hours spent on each one, and the average feelings I had about each kind of activity.

The Slow Boat Home

Pains & Pleasures

Activity	#	%	Feelings				
			Dis.	Unp.	Tol.	Agr.	Pl.
1.Reading letters	200	0.98					x
2.Writing letters	500	2.45			x		
3.Sleep, comfortable	2200	10.78					x
4.Sleep, disturbed	4000	19.78		x			
5.Finding food, eating	2000	9.8			x		
6.Sick or hurt	250	1.23	x				
7.Personal hygiene	680	3.33			x		
8.Tending equipment	1000	4.9			x		
9.Reading manuals	170	0.83		x			
10.Reading reports	250	1.22			x		
11.Reading chosen works	900	4.41					x
12.Pure sociability	800	3.29					x
13.Administering troops	800	3.29			x		
14.Conducting operations	1700	8.33				x	
15.Necessary travel	1600	7.84			x		
16.Pleasure travel	500	2.45					x
17.Games&sports	50	0.25					x
18.Think,look,fantasy	1750	8.58				x	
19.Manual work	600	2.94			x		
20.Sexualizing	200	0.98					x
21.Anguish -misc.& extracted from above	250	1.23	x				

Total Hours: 20400

I have not allowed myself the sardonic victory of placing in the column a category for "Homesickness/Lovesickness," gnawing ailments that cast a melancholy haze over the total picture. Not that these are not tormenting and even deadly illnesses. I justify myself by saying that this dimension of suffering is reflected in the ratings of everything else I did, lowering them somewhat in agreeability.

However, more important, I have not included a category for "Pride of Cause and Nation." Now, I was no German who could wet his pants with pride at the salute and sacrifice to *Der Führer und Das Reich*. I suppressed all such extravagant expression and feeling. But I did obtain a continuous positive charge from fighting for the "good ol' U.S.A." and the "Four Freedoms." My war morale was never less than high. And that is why I am not letting myself insert "Homesickness/Lovesickness" into the list. These positive and negative ions mixed in a fine ideological fog that overhung my thousands of hours.

Note also that "distressing" periods must have been brief and scattered throughout the hours and months and activities. They could and did crop up at any time. Where they were intense and prolonged I put them in a special category of "anguish." Any such anguish or distress was rapidly diminishing now. Yet, do not count it out!

Five hours later the *Hawaiian Shipper* docked, a military band struck up a tune, and Red Cross girls appeared to show what American beauty must be like. Any further reception would seem out of place. The dream of the glorious homecoming proved to be one of the more prominent illusions of the war. Perhaps the meanness of the return was better than parades and lavish honors that would delude the veteran into over-estimating his achievements, his worth, and his place to come in the strange new society.

The arrivals were segregated into officers, white soldiers, and black soldiers - yes - and each troop marched off in a column to the trains that brought them to Camp Patrick Henry. There they were treated gravely and wonderfully, served steaks by German P.O.W.'s, and let loose upon a battery of telephones. Bands played all night for contingents going out.

Shipment #2097, bound for Fort Sheridan, Illinois, got going the next day. It contained me, now a Car Commander, and several-score men on one of a train of twenty cars, that could afford an upper bunk to one man, a lower bunk to every two enlisted men, and a bunk to the officer in charge.

The trip should have taken eighteen hours; it took fifty. There had occurred an avalanche along the Chesapeake-and-Ohio right-of-way. But that was only incidental. The main delay was the large number of halts on sidings to let freight trains and passenger trains pass us. The food gave out on the second evening and the train paused in Cincinnati to pick up C-rations and coffee for next morning's breakfast. This was the last of food until the end of the trip near midnight.

When the train entered the great switching yards of the South Side of Chicago, it was halted, while countless commuter and passenger trains zoomed by. None of the railroad personnel admitted to understanding the delay, much less to any responsibility for it. One said that, after all, the men did have bunks, another that he could appreciate their restlessness. The philosophical discussion of the treatment provided by the railroads to the returning soldiers found expression in a few expletives, clear, precise, but to no avail.

Some of the men were in a frenzy. Their homes were only a few blocks away. I myself was only a couple of miles from home. Several just took off across the tracks. I urged the men to hold on for a few more hours so that they could get their discharge papers and money. When, after several hours of waiting, the train moved on and shortly pulled into Fort Sheridan, I reported that the missing men, half-starved, had run off to buy hot dogs, and were left behind. So everybody colluded and sadly affirmed.

By midnight, I had been signed out of Fort Sheridan. There were few people out and around. I caught a bus, then an electric train, then an elevated train, then a cab, and by three o'clock am cautiously reconnoitering a tan brick apartment building, numbered 5436 S. Ridgewood Court. Then I carefully rang the doorbell where it was written that I lived.

She wakes up. She lets me in, with a polite hug and kiss. Then you stand back, and test reality: yes, she is there and I am here. Now see in the light of the hallway what has happened over the past 845 days.

In her cotton nightgown she looks just as she did then, pink-faced, with twinkling eyes of Baltic blue, thick tousled reddish light hair, high-pitched voice, a good body smell, embraceable, nothing to worry about at first sight. A drink of whiskey is called for. A shower. Chit-chat.

Time for bed. Laughing at her big Murphy bed that springs out from the wall helps us feel close again. Time to make love. I have prefigured well this first night. My beribboned Captain's jacket hangs flagrant upon a chair.

From the baby's room comes a call. "Shh!" An impatient call. "Don't answer." A loud cry, then, really loud, an imperative shriek, unending. She won't stop, dammit. "Oh, honestly!" Jill exclaims, "What a nuisance!" And she gets out of bed. "Kathy!.. What is it Darling?.. Daddy has come home!..You know Daddy!.. Wouldn't you like to see Daddy?"

"No!"

With Kathy, the day after...

Army of the United States
CERTIFICATE OF SERVICE

This is to certify that

ALFRED J DEGRAZIA O1 043 313 Capt
6622nd PM Det Seventh Army

honorably served in active Federal Service in the Army of the United States from 4 September 1942 to 18 January 1946

Given at SEPARATION CENTER, Fort Sheridan, Illinois

on the 18th day of January 1946

MILITARY RECORD AND REPORT OF SEPARATION
CERTIFICATE OF SERVICE

- Last Name – First Name – Middle Initial: DEGRAZIA ALFRED J
- Army Serial Number: O1 043 313
- Grade: Capt
- Arm or Service: CAC
- Component: AUS
- Organization: 6822 PM Det 7th Army
- Date of relief from active duty: 18 Jan 46
- Place of separation: Separation Center, Ft Sheridan Ill
- Permanent address for mailing purposes: 5436 Ridgewood Ct Chicago 15 Ill
- Date of birth: 29 Dec 1919
- Place of birth: Chicago Ill
- Address from which employment will be sought: See No 9
- Color eyes: Brown
- Color hair: Brown
- Height: 5'10"
- Weight: 155
- No. of dependents: 1
- Civilian occupation and no.: College Teacher

MILITARY HISTORY

- County and State: Cook Illinois
- Home address at time of entry on active duty: See No 9
- Date of entry on active duty: 4 September 1942
- Military occupational specialty and no.: Propaganda Analysis Officer 9305
- Battles and campaigns: Central Europe Sicilian Naples-Foggia Rome-Arno No Appennines Southern France Rhineland
- Decorations and citations: Bronze Star Medal GO 361 HQ 7th Army 3 Aug 45 Croix De Guerre 1stArmy 16 July 45 EAME Thea Rib W/Sil Battle Star W/2 Bronze Battle Stars Bronze Service Arrowhead 4 Overseas Service Bars
- Wounds received in action: None
- Service schools attended: CAC OCS CAC Barrage Balloon
- Reason and authority for separation: Reld fr AD HD TNX SPCAP 26 Sep 45 PSO 20 7S WDPC
- Current tour of active duty: Ft Sheridan Ill 2 Oct 45

Service Outside Continental U.S. and Return			
Date of departure	Destination	Date of arrival
9 May 43	EAME	20 May 43
19 Sep 45	USA	28 Sep 45

Continental Service		Foreign Service		Education (years)		
Years	Months	Days	Years	Months	Days	Grammar School	High School	College
0	11	25	2	4	19	8	4	6

INSURANCE NOTICE

X	X	X	31 Jan 46	28 Feb 46	6.60

Remarks: AGS Score (2 Sep 45) 122
Lapel Button Issued

Signature of officer being separated: Alfred J. De Grazia
Personnel officer: GILBERT HOWELL Capt Inf 1612 SCU

ARMY SEPARATION QUALIFICATION RECORD

LAST NAME	FIRST NAME	MIDDLE INITIAL	ARMY SERIAL No.	GRADE	DATE OF ENTRY INTO ACTIVE SERVICE	SEX	DATE OF BIRTH
DEGRAZIA	ALFRED	J	01 043 313	Capt	4 Sep 42	M	29 Dec 19

PERMANENT ADDRESS FOR MAILING PURPOSES: 5436 Ridgewood Crt, Chicago, Illinois

CIVILIAN EDUCATION

HIGHEST GRADE COMPLETED	LAST YEAR OF ATTENDANCE	HIGHEST DEGREE RECEIVED	MAJOR COURSE OF STUDY	NAME AND ADDRESS OF LAST SCHOOL ATTENDED
16 + 2½	1939	AB	Political	Univ Chicago, Chicago, Illinois

OTHER TRAINING OR SCHOOLING

COURSE	NO. YRS.	PLACE
Pol. Sci.	2 yrs.	U. of Chicago
Law	½ yr.	Columbia Univ.

SERVICE EDUCATION

SERVICE SCHOOL	COURSE	WKS OR HRS	RATING
CAC	OCS	12	comp
CAC	Barrage Balloon	4	comp

CIVILIAN OCCUPATIONS

MAIN OCCUPATION TITLE: College Teacher

JOB SUMMARY: Taught classes in American Govt.; conducted research and writing on comparative government, American politics and propaganda.

NO. OF YEARS	LAST DATE OF EMPLOYMENT	NAME AND ADDRESS OF EMPLOYER	NO. OF YEARS	LAST DATE OF EMPLOYMENT	NAME AND ADDRESS OF EMPLOYER
2	1942	Univ of Indiana, South Chicago, Ill.			

MILITARY SPECIALTIES

YEARS	MONTHS	GRADE	PRINCIPAL DUTY	ARMY CODE NO.
2	5	Capt.	Propaganda Analysis Off	9305

SUMMARY OF MILITARY OCCUPATION AND CIVILIAN CONVERSIONS:
Executive Officer and then commanding officer of a psychological warfare detachment of 120 men, engaged in propaganda operations against the enemy in Italy, France and Germany. Special political intelligence missions in Africa, Sicily, Sadinia and Italy. Controlled operation of press, and information service in occupied territories. Directed and supervised analysis and preparation of propaganda material for use by radio, press and loud speaker, trucks. Analyzed customs, habits, morale and psychology of Italians, French,

Germans, and other European inhabitants. Evaluated press, radio, pictorial and other releases, collaborated with counter intelligence, prisoner interrogation, and Allied agencies. Also previously platoon commander and battery executive officer in automatic weapons battalion.

DATE OF SEPARATION: 16 Jan 46
SIGNATURE OF SOLDIER: Alfred DeGrazia
SIGNATURE OF SEPARATION CLASSIFICATION OFFICER: Harold K. Quinn, Major, AGD
Separation Center, Ft. Sheridan, Ill.

WD AGO Form 100

ABOUT THE AUTHOR

Alfred de Grazia was born in Chicago on December 29, 1919, the second of four sons of a musician and conductor born in Sicily. He became a political scientist (M.A., PhD University Chicago) and taught at U. of Minnesota, Brown U., Stanford U. and NYU, a. o. , publishing some twenty books in the field, among them seminal works such as *Public and Republic,* and *The Elements of Political Science.* He became interested in the ideas of Immanuel Velikovsky and, after having left academia, wrote the ten volumes of *The Quantavolution Series.* He also wrote plays and poetry, as well as autobiographical works. Most of his works are available on his website: http://www.grazian-archive.com. There, can also be found, under the title *Letters of Love and War,* the very large correspondance exchanged between him and his wife Jill Oppenheim during the period of their separation during World War II.* Jill died in 1996. Alfred de Grazia, now in his nineties, lives in France with his wife, Anne-Marie, who edited this version of *A Taste of War..*

* http://www.grazian-archive.com/love_letters_NEW/intro/intro.pdf

BOOKS BY ALFRED DE GRAZIA

Public and republic: political representation in America. New York: Knopf, 1951.
The elements of political science. Series: Borzoi Books in Political Science. New York: Knopf, 1952.
The Western Public: 1952 and beyond. [A study of political behaviour in the western United States.]. Stanford: Stanford University Press, [1954.]
The American way of government. National edition. New York : Wiley, [1957].
American welfare. New York: New York University Press, 1961 (with Ted Gurr).
World politics: a study in international relations. Series: College Outline Series. New York: Barnes & Noble, 1962.
Apportionment and representative government. Series: Books that matter. New York : Praeger, c1963
Revolution in teaching: new theory, technology, and curricula. With an introduction by Jerome Bruner. New York: Bantam Books, [1964] (Editor, with David A. Sohn).
Republic in crisis: Congress against the executive force. New York: Federal Legal Publications, [1965].
Congress, The First Branch of Government, editor, Doubleday – Anchor Books, 1967
Congress and the Presidency: Their Roles in Modern Times, with Arthur M. Schlesinger, American Enterprise Institute for Public Policy Research, Washington, 1967.
Politics for Better or Worse, Scott, Foresman, Glenview, Ill., 1973.
Eight Branches of Government: American Government Today, w. Eric Weise, Collegiate Pub., 1975.
Eight Bads – Eight Goods: The American Contradictions, Doubleday – Anchor Books, 1975.
Supporting Art and Culture: 1001 Questions on Policy, Lieber-Atherton, New York, 1979.

The Quantavolution Series (Metron Publications, Princeton, N.J. 1981-1984):

Chaos and Creation
God's Fire - Moses and the Management of Exodus
The Lately Tortured Earth
Homo Schizo I.
Home Schizo II.
The Divine Succession
The Disastrous Love Affair of Moon and Mars
Solaria Binaria (with Earl R. Milton)
The Burning of Troy
Cosmic Heretics

Also:

Passage of the Year, Poetry, Quiddity Press, Metron publications, Princeton, N.J., 1967.
A Cloud Over Bhopal: Causes, Consequences, and Constructive Solutions, Kalos Foundation for the India-America Committee for the Bhopal Victims: Popular Prakashan, Bombay, 1985.
The Babe, Child of Boom and Bust in Old Chicago, umbilicus mundi, Quiddity Press, Metron Publications, Princeton, N.J., 1992.
The Student: at Chicago in Hutchin's Hey-day, Quiddity Press, Metron Publications, Princeton N.J., 1991.
Twentieth Century Fire-Sale, Poetry, Quiddity Press, Metron Publications, Princeton, N.J., 1996.
The Iron Age of Mars (Metron Publications, Princeton, 2009)
The American State of Canaan – the peaceful, prosperous juncture of Israel and Palestine as the 51st State of the United States of America, Metron Publications, Princeton, NJ, 2009

www.ingramcontent.com/pod-product-compliance
Lightning Source LLC
Chambersburg PA
CBHW032012230426
43671CB00005B/61